The Development of the Self

DEVELOPMENTAL PSYCHOLOGY SERIES

SERIES EDITOR
Harry Beilin

Developmental Psychology Program
City University of New York Graduate School
New York, New York

The list of titles in this series continues on the last page of this volume.

The Development of the Self

EDITED BY

Robert L. Leahy

Department of Psychology
Hofstra University
Hempstead, New York

1985

ACADEMIC PRESS, INC.

(Harcourt Brace Jovanovich, Publishers)

Orlando   San Diego   New York   London
Toronto   Montreal   Sydney   Tokyo

ACADEMIC PRESS, INC.
Orlando, Florida 32887

United Kingdom Edition published by
ACADEMIC PRESS INC. (LONDON) LTD.
24–28 Oval Road, London NW1 7DX

Library of Congress Cataloging in Publication Data

Main entry under title:

The Development of the self.

Includes bibliographies and index.
1. Self-perception in children. 2. Cognition in
children. 3. Child psychology. 1. Leahy, Robert L.
[DNLM: 1. Self Concept BF 697 D4885]
BF723.S28D42   1985   155.4'18   84-24253
ISBN 0-12-439870-7 (alk. paper)

PRINTED IN THE UNITED STATES OF AMERICA

85 86 87 88   9 8 7 6 5 4 3 2 1

To my students

Contents

7 Adolescent Self-Concept Development

Jacqueline Smollar and James Youniss

8 The Costs of Development: Clinical Implications

Robert L. Leahy

9 The Development of the Self: Conclusions

Robert L. Leahy

Contributors

Numbers in parentheses indicate the pages on which the authors' contributions begin.

William Damon (151), Department of Psychology, Clark University, Worcester, Massachusetts 01610

Marion Glick (1), Department of Psychology, Southern Connecticut State University, New Haven, Connecticut 06515

Daniel Hart (151), Department of Psychology, Rutgers University, Camden, New Jersey 08102

Susan Harter (55), Department of Psychology, University of Denver, University Park, Denver, Colorado 80208

Robert Kegan (179), Graduate School of Education, Harvard University, Cambridge, Massachusetts 02138, Massachusetts School of Professional Psychology, Newton, Massachusetts 02159, and The Clinical-Developmental Institute, Belmont, Massachusetts 02178

Robert L. Leahy (123, 267, 295), Department of Psychology, Hofstra University, Hempstead, New York 11550

Morris Rosenberg (205), Department of Sociology, University of Maryland, College Park, Maryland 20742

Stephen R. Shirk (123), Department of Psychology, Judge Baker Guidance Center, Children's Hospital-Boston, Boston, Massachusetts 02115

Jacqueline Smollar (247), Center for the Study of Youth Development, The Catholic University of America, Washington, D.C. 20064

James Youniss (247), Center for the Study of Youth Development, The Catholic University of America, Washington, D.C. 20064

Edward Zigler (1), Department of Psychology, Yale University, New Haven, Connecticut 06520

Preface

From the time of William James and Wilhelm Wundt interest in the self has shown periodic rises and declines. Although the strict behaviorist may still argue that the *self* is an ephemeral fiction better left ignored, interest in the self is now in the ascendence. Indeed, behavior therapists now acknowledge the importance of self-statements in the understanding and treatment of affective disorders and have entered into a hyphenated detente known as cognitive-behaviorism.

Developmental psychologists have recognized that to understand the child we need to know more than how stimuli, responses, and rewards are linked through contingencies: We need to know how the child or adolescent links together experiences to form a self-concept or a set of values. This volume is an attempt to bring together a variety of perspectives on the development of the self in which the cognitive level and interpersonal experiences of the child or adolescent produce qualitative changes in how the self is constructed.

In the first chapter Glick and Zigler review the considerable contribution of Zigler and his colleagues in articulating a cognitive-developmental approach to self-concept development. Contrary to the "conventional wisdom" of Carl Rogers, Zigler's cognitive-developmental model argues that increased development is characterized by an increasing capacity for guilt. Further, Zigler's work indicates that the effects of "experience" (for example, retardation status or race) may result in differences in both real self-image (self-esteem) and ideal self-image. The practical implications of Zigler's research are that symptomatology, for example, internalized versus externalized symptoms, may need to be understood as a consequence of developmental level and experience.

xiii

In my chapters, including one written with Stephen Shirk, I have attempted to extend Zigler's and Kohlberg's ideas in some new directions. One direction is to ask which social cognitive abilities affect self-image. Of specific interest to me have been role-taking and moral judgment levels. This choice is largely dictated by belief that the self is a social construction, that is, a recognition that the self exists with others and apart from others. In contrast to the evolutionary bias of many developmentalists, I have attempted to describe some negative consequences of development—specifically, increased uncertainty about the self and capacity for self-critical depression. One might label this new bias as the "dark side" of development. In developing this theme I have drawn on my fortunate experience in working with Aaron Beck, the founder of cognitive therapy, to describe how depressive self-schemas may develop and how they may be altered through a developmental approach to cognitive therapy.

Susan Harter's chapter provides an important contribution to the history of the study of the self and, in particular, the study of competence. The historian of developmental psychology will note that it was 25 years ago that Robert White raised the dilemma for learning theory by proposing an *intrinsic* motivation to be effective. Harter demonstrates how this intrinsic motivation is differentiated and developed— that there is no single competence but a variety of competencies that characterize children.

Hart and Damon also show how the self has a variety of domains (e.g., physical, active, social, and psychological selves) which develop in a manner not entirely similar to the understanding of others. Thus, Hart and Damon argue that self-cognition is not simply another form of social-cognition. The ambitious reader will attempt to find those points of commonality in this model with Harter's description of domains of competence.

Kegan, whose *The Evolving Self* has provoked so much interest in this topic, writes with elan and grace of how Piaget and Freud may be viewed on common ground. His developmental model is, in some ways, one of the tragedy of the self, that is, the loss of earlier selves as new self-conception emerges. The emphasis here is on the "emotional" selves (for example, the impulsive self) which surrenders to new controls and new possibilities.

Rosenberg provides a valuable overview of his research on the development of self-concept during adolescence. In his study of a variety of self-concepts, such as self-esteem, mattering, certitude, and locus of control, Rosenberg provides support for the view that *early* adolescence is an age of turmoil that is often overcome later. Further,

Rosenberg indicates that the female adolescent is more likely than the male to experience self-concept disturbance—certainly consistent with the demographics of adult depression, which show that women are twice as likely as men to experience severe depression.

Smollar and Youniss attempt to integrate Sullivan's social interactionist theory with Piaget's theory of intellectual development. In their chapter they propose that the self-concept is a relational construct that develops in different ways in different relationships. A major finding is that adolescents show more of this differentiation of self across relationships than do preadolescents.

In the conclusion I attempt to integrate the developmental trends in self-concept development that are described in this volume. In my review I have examined both the theoretical and applied implications of a developmental approach with specific attention to the importance of this work in diagnosis and psychotherapy of child, adolescent, and adult patients.

This volume should be of interest to developmental, social, personality, and clinical psychologists as well as to sociologists interested in the interpersonal nature of the self and the relevance of cognitive level in the emergence of personality. Readers interested in education of children may find these contributions helpful in understanding how the child's values and social interactions change with age and how the child's ideas of competence may not correspond to the adult's views.

In editing a volume one learns that the Muses that inspire one's writing and that of others are not always on schedule. I should like to thank Academic Press and the contributors for their patience in seeing this project to fruition. I thank Karen Richardson for her diligence in constructing the index. It is a special pleasure for me to wax nostalgic and thank the many students at the Graduate Faculty of the New School for Social Research who have worked with me over the years: Jo Ann Posner, Steve Shirk, Teresa Hunt, Pam Lenon, Jim Breismeister, Tom Moran, and Jill Bresler stand out fondly in my mind. I have also been most fortunate in mentors and faculty colleagues over the years and I wish to thank Ed Zigler, Aaron Beck, Irv Child, Jeff Young, Jim Youniss and Hans Furth who have had a lasting effect on how I see the self.

1

Self-Image:
A Cognitive-Developmental Approach*

Marion Glick
Edward Zigler

INTRODUCTION

The importance of the self-image as a major determinant of human behavior has long been recognized (Allport, 1937; James, 1890; Maslow, 1954; Mead, 1934). Since the seminal work of Rogers and his colleagues (C. R. Rogers & Dymond, 1954), much research in this area has focused on *self-image disparity*, that is the disparity between the individual's current view of self (*real self*) and the ideal person that he or she would like to be (*ideal self*). Within the Rogerian framework (C. R. Rogers, 1951; C. R. Rogers & Dymond, 1954), congruence between real and ideal self-images is interpreted as indicating positive self-regard and assumed to be linearly related to personal and social adjustment. As such, a sizeable self-image disparity, is viewed as being ominous in nature and a sign of maladjustment (Scott, 1958). Based on this interpretation, the reduction of discrepancies between real and ideal self-perceptions has been commonly employed as a measure of improvement in psychotherapy (Raimy, 1948; C. R. Rogers & Dymond, 1954; Sheerer, 1949; Stock, 1949).

*Preparation of the manuscript was supported by Research Grant HD-03008-12 from the National Institutes of Health.

The cognitive-developmental formulation stands in contrast to the nondevelopmental approach of Rogers and his colleagues. First formulated by Achenbach and Zigler (1963), the cognitive-developmental position interprets an increasing self-image disparity as the natural concomitant of normal growth and development. The twofold rationale for this formulation is as follows:

1. In accord with the developmental principles of Werner (1948, 1957) and Piaget (1951, 1960), higher levels of development imply greater degrees of cognitive differentiation. In any cognition, therefore, the more highly developed person should tend to employ more categories and finer distinctions within each category than should a person of lower development. This greater differentiation should result in a greater likelihood for disparity between an individual's conceptualization of the real self and the ideal self. It is important here to recognize that the self-images are symbolic conceptual constructions and as such are particularly amenable to cognitive analysis.

2. An individual's capacity to experience guilt increases over the course of development with the individual's growing ability for incorporating social demands, mores, and values (L. Phillips, 1968; Zigler & Child, 1969; Zigler & Phillips, 1960). The high- as compared to the low-developmental individual must measure up to many more internalized demands, and these greater self-demands and the guilt that accompanies them should be reflected in a greater disparity between real and ideal self-images than that found for individuals at lower developmental levels.

Research efforts over almost two decades have provided considerable empirical support for this developmental interpretation of self-image disparity and have led as well to the broadening and to some modifications of the original formulation. This chapter chronicles this work.

At the outset, however, certain aspects of the general developmental approach underlying this work must be clarified as they pertain to a central aspect of the research strategy, namely the use of child and adult samples and of pathological as well as nonpathological groups as means of advancing the developmental line of inquiry. Zigler's developmental approach is based upon an organismic model wherein development is conceptualized as an orderly sequence of structural changes or internal reorganizations in response systems. In viewing development as a series of structural or formal changes, the organismic position relegates to temporal sequence and chronology a minor and nonessential role. As Zigler (1963, 1969) has emphasized, time is not a psychological variable. The developmentalist is interested in change, not as a function of time but rather as a group of organismic processes which take place over time. Thus developmental psychology is not seen as limited to the study of childhood.

Moreover, developmental level is viewed as a very broad construct indeed. The characteristics of an individual's developmental level are assumed to pervasively influence behavior and to pertain equally to pathological and nonpathological forms of functioning. In contrast to formulations that sharply distinguish between adaptive and maladaptive functioning, Zigler's position has always been that there is an underlying relation between these two forms of functioning. In becoming symptomatic, the individual does not appear to change habitual modes of responding. Rather for every maturity level, there are presumed to exist effective patterns of coping as well as maladaptive deviations from these patterns. In contrast to positions that view regression as fundamental in the shift from adaptive to maladaptive functioning (Goldman, 1962), the developmental position takes as its given the level of maturity attained and views the defenses employed, particular symptom clusters, and other specific aspects of personality organization as outgrowths of this level.

The developmental investigations reported here are not confined to children but encompass adult individuals including those with psychopathological disorders. Despite the disparate populations, the underlying developmental issues remain constant. For example, some of the research with children concerns developmental differences in symptom expression, and the issue of experiential determinants in self-image formation, while more prominently featured in the research with children, pertains also to the interpretation of findings with adult pathological groups. Thus, although two populations are considered, the theoretical formulation proceeds along a single line.

SELF-IMAGE DISPARITY AS A COGNITIVE-DEVELOPMENTAL PHENOMENON: THE ORIGINAL STUDY

The cognitive-developmental interpretation of self-image disparity was first formulated and tested by Achenbach and Zigler (1963) in a study employing 20 (10 male and 10 female) psychiatric patients and 20 (10 male and 10 female) nonpsychiatric (medical) patients as subjects. On the basis of the Zigler–Phillips Social Competence Index, high- and low-social-competence subgroups consisting of equal numbers of males and females were formed within each (psychiatric and nonpsychiatric) sample. Conceptualized as a benchmark of personal and social maturity (Zigler & Phillips, 1960; Zigler & Levine, 1981), social competence has been related to Rorschach developmental level (Lerner, 1968) and developmental differences in moral reasoning as assessed by Kohlberg's test (Quinlan, Rogers, & Kegan, 1980). A full description of this measure and its underlying rationale along with the evidence for its validity has been recently presented by Zigler and Levine (1981).

Two types of self-image disparity were examined: (1) the disparity between the individual's real and ideal self-image, and (2) the disparity between the real and the *social self-image,* that is, the self as one believes others see it (Brownfain, 1952). For each (real, ideal, and social) self-image, two instruments differing in the amount of possible response differentiation were employed. One instrument was a questionnaire made up of 30 self-referent statements to which the individual could respond by selecting one of six alternatives for each statement ranging from *very true* to *very untrue.* The second instrument was a list of 40 personal traits for which the subject merely circled "yes" or "no" to indicate correspondence to the various (real, ideal, and social) self-images.

The major hypothesis was that within both psychiatric and nonpsychiatric samples, the patients of high-social competence would show more disparity between their real and ideal self-images than would patients of low-social competence, due to the greater differentiation and the greater internalization of societal standards associated with higher maturity levels.

In order to further examine the roles of cognitive differentiation and the internalization of standards as contributors to self-image disparity, two subsidiary hypotheses were formulated. In regard to the disparity between the real and the social self-image, it was again expected that high-competence individuals would evidence more disparity than low-competence individuals, but that these group differences would be less than for real–ideal disparity. Inasmuch as social guilt should contribute little to real–social-self disparity, it would be only the tendency of the high group to differentiate more finely that would increase the amount of disparity manifested. The final prediction concerned differences due to the instrument (questionnaire versus trait list) employed to gauge the individual's self-concepts. While both instruments would be expected to show greater real–ideal disparity among high- as compared with low-competence people due to the greater influence of social guilt, the trait list, which permits little response differentiation, was expected to produce smaller differences between the groups, since

TABLE 1.1
Mean Scores for Each Group

Group[a]	Real–ideal self-disparity		Real–social self-disparity		Extreme responses on questionnaire			
	Question-naire	Checklist	Question-naire	Checklist	Real self	Ideal self	Social self	Total
High competence								
Psychiatric	21.3	15.0	17.0	5.7	4.1	9.5	3.8	17.4
Nonpsychiatric	21.4	10.9	16.0	6.3	5.3	15.4	5.2	25.9
Low competence								
Psychiatric	12.8	10.3	13.4	7.7	20.3	22.1	20.3	62.7
Nonpsychiatric	17.3	8.8	14.0	7.3	10.5	12.6	8.5	31.6

[a]$N = 10$ for each group.

differences due to finer differentiation in response tendencies would be minimized. Furthermore, the trait list, because it allows little response differentiation, was expected to produce no differences related to social competence on real–social-self disparity inasmuch as this type of disparity in conjunction with the trait list format would remove both the factors of social guilt and cognitive differentiation. The tendencies of patients to give extreme responses (*very true* and *very untrue*) on the questionnaire measures were also noted inasmuch as such extreme response tendencies should constitute a further indication of the undifferentiated cognitive style presumed to be associated with developmentally lower forms of functioning. Finally because differences between psychiatric and nonpsychiatric patients would bear centrally upon the Rogerian formulation which interprets real–ideal self-image disparity as a sign of maladjustment, differences between these two patient groups were examined, although no hypothesis was generated.

All hypotheses were confirmed. The pertinent measures of the four groups' performance are presented in Table 1.1.

High-social-competence patients were found to display greater real–ideal self-image disparity than low-competence individuals on the questionnaire ($p < .001$). The findings also supported the view that both the greater social guilt assumed to be associated with higher social competence and the tendency towards greater cognitive differentiation in high-competence subjects contributed to the differences discovered in real–ideal self-image disparity. Where social guilt and response differentiation could both become manifest, as in the real–ideal questionnaire disparity score, the differences between high- and low-social-competence patients were greatest (p < .001). Where only response differentiation but not social guilt was involved (i.e., real–social-self disparity as assessed by questionnaire), differences between high- and low-social-competence individuals, while they remained significant were smaller (p < .05). Similarly where only social guilt but not response differentiation was involved (i.e., real–ideal disparity assessed by trait list), the effects of social competence while significant were again smaller (p < .03). Finally, where both social guilt and the opportunity for response differentiation were minimal (i.e., real–social-self disparity as measured by trait list), no significant differences in disparity appeared between high- and low-competence groups. In contrast to these predicted relationships obtained between social competence and self-image disparity, psychiatric versus nonpsychiatric status was not found to be related to any of the measures of self-image disparity employed in this study.

Further evidence of the greater cognitive differentiation and finer discimination of high- as compared with low-competence subjects was found in the tendency of low-competence subjects to use extreme response categories (i.e., *very true* and *very untrue*) on the questionnaire far more frequently than did high-competence individuals (p < .001). While the high-competence individuals appeared to make finer discriminations introducing a number of shades of grey into their judgmental processes, low-competence subjects appeared more likely to merely bifurcate their perceptions into extreme categories. While no main effects due to psychiatric status appeared, a significant interaction was obtained between social competence and psychiatric status in the number of extreme responses made. This interaction reflected both the tendency for high-competence nonpsychiatric patients to use more extreme responses (M = 25.9) than high-competence psychiatric patients (M = 17.4), but even more strongly the tendency of low-competence psychiatric patients to give many more extreme responses (M = 62.7) than low-competence nonpsychiatric patients (M = 31.6). The nature of this interaction suggests that in high-competence people who become mentally ill, the tendency to discriminate finely is either not affected or is strengthened, while low-competence people who become mentally ill tend to discriminate even less finely than prior to their illness. Such a view is consistent with both clinical observation and empirical evidence (L. Phillips & Zigler, 1964; Zigler, Glick, & Marsh, 1979; Zigler & Phillips, 1960, 1961b) that high-competence patients continue to think about and attempt to cope with the problems that have befallen them and thus evidence a better prognosis than low-competence patients who often lapse into chronicity evidencing inattention, avoidance, and apathy.

A significant relationship also appeared between subjects' self-image disparity scores obtained on the questionnaire instrument and those on the trait list. In conjunction with Hilden's (1958) similar finding, this represents some evidence of the construct validity of the self-image disparity construct.

The consistency of the findings of Achenbach and Zigler (1963) thus provided a strong initial corroboration of the developmental view. Contrary to the Rogerian position, self-image disparity did not appear as a simple function of maladjustment. Indeed it was those individuals who demonstrated the capacity to achieve in areas most valued in our society (high-social competence) who displayed the greatest self-image disparity. Rather than being ominous in nature, therefore, greater self-image disparity may be a necessary concomitant of higher maturity levels.

These developmental findings furthermore point to an alternative explanation of other self-image disparity results that previously had been interpreted through a modification of the basic Rogerian position. The findings that neurotic individuals manifest greater real–ideal disparity than either schizophrenics or normals (Hillson & Worchel, 1957) and that "sensitizers" display greater disparity than "repressors" (Altrocchi, Parsons, & Dickoff, 1960) led these investigators to advance the position that, although invariably ominous, a large self-image disparity would be found only among individuals employing particular psychological defenses, that is, sensitizers and neurotics. Neurotic patients have consistently been found to obtain high-social-competence scores (Lewine, Watt, Prentky, & Fryer, 1980; Zigler et al., 1979; Zigler & Phillips, 1961a). Moreover the defining characteristics of *repressors* as those who use avoidance, denial, and repression as the primary mode of adaptation (Altrocchi et al., 1960) are quite similar to descriptions of individuals who show "turning against others" or "turning away from others" role orientations (Phillips & Rabinovitch, 1958) which have both been consistently found to be associated with low-social competence in psychiatric patients (e.g., Raskin & Golob, 1966; Zigler & Phillips, 1960). Conversely the description of *sensitizers* as those who use intellectual and obsessive defenses is similar to the symptomatic picture of individuals manifesting the "turning against the self" orientation found in high-competence patients. In light of these developmental findings, Achenbach and Zigler suggested that the greater self-image disparities of neurotic and sensitizing patients can be subsumed within the developmental framework. That is, different defensive styles are presumed to reflect different levels of underlying maturity, and as such the disparity scores of sensitizing patients would be seen as yet another expression of their maturity.

SELF-IMAGE DISPARITY IN CHILDREN

Although the findings of Achenbach and Zigler (1963) represented a convincing beginning demonstration of the efficacy of developmental thinking in the area of self-image disparity, developmental research employing adult subjects is inevitably hampered by problems in gauging developmental level in adulthood (see Loevinger, 1976, for a cogent discussion of this issue as well as her own efforts in this regard). While considerable evidence supports the use of the social competence measure as an indicator of maturity level in adulthood, research with children provides more traditional and direct means for assessing developmental differences, both through the observation of ontogenetic changes and more importantly through the use of indexes reflecting developmental differences in cognitive structuring.

Beginning with the work of Katz and Zigler (1967), a series of studies were performed with children (Katz, Zigler, & Zalk, 1975; D. Phillips & Zigler, 1980, 1982; Zigler, Balla, & Watson, 1972) in which chronological age, mental age, and other developmental variables were employed as indicators of maturity level. In addition to the consideration of disparity scores, this research has focused on developmental changes within both the real and ideal self-images. As Wylie (1974) indicated in her comprehensive evaluation of self-image research, a disparity or difference score per se conveys relatively little information. If disparity increases with maturity level, one must also inquire into the qualitative nature of this disparity. Does it reflect a more positive ideal self-image, a more negative real self-image, or both?

Finally, the work with children has been instrumental in broadening the original developmental formulation to include the examination of nondevelopmental experiential factors in self-image disparity and their interaction with developmental determinants.

Self-Image Disparity and the Real and Ideal Self-Images of Children

Katz and Zigler (1967) investigated self-image disparity in children at three age levels dichotomized into high- and low-intelligence groups. The major intent of this study was to examine Achenbach and Zigler's (1963) formulation as it applies in ontogenesis. The specific prediction, therefore, was that younger children would manifest less disparity between the perceived and the ideal self than would older children.

Although chronological age is perhaps the most frequently used indicator of development, there is little question that chronological age is not the most sensitive reflector of those changes in cognitive structuring that are presumed to be defining characteristics of the developmental sequence (Zigler, 1963). A better indicator of a child's cognitive structure and thus developmental level is his or her mental age. Thus the second prediction in this study was that high- as compared with low-IQ children would display greater self-image disparity at each age level. Although IQ scores represent a psychometric gauge of the rate of mental growth rather than a qualitative assessment of the level of cognitive organization attained, there is ample reason to believe that these two aspects of mental development are largely indistinguishable in childhood. High IQs within any chronological age (CA) level are higher mental age (MA) levels (Zigler, 1969). Substantial correlations have consistently appeared between IQ scores and more qualitative Piagetian measures of cognitive organization. Moreover, the succession of items on IQ tests do in fact reflect qualitative differences in level of cognitive organization. Elkind (1969) has presented a particularly cogent analysis of the commonalities, despite differences, between psychometric and Piagetian approaches to cognitive assessment.

Finally, an ambiguity in the Achenbach and Zigler study was the failure to delineate the qualitative nature of the larger self-image disparity found in the more mature subjects. Is such greater disparity due to higher ideal self-expectations, lower real self-perceptions, or both? Thus the actual scores obtained on real-, ideal-, and social-self ratings were examined by Katz and Zigler.

One hundred and twenty children at three grade levels (the fifth, eighth, and eleventh grades) served as subjects. All the children were randomly selected from public school classes in a homogeneous middle class community. Within each grade level, the children were dichotomized into high- and low-intelligence groups on the basis of Otis Quick-Scoring Mental Ability Test scores. Whereas the mean IQs of the three low groups ranged from 91 to 94, those of the high groups ranged from 124 to 127. Equal numbers of male and female subjects were employed within each age and intelligence classification.

The measures employed were designed to be as similar as possible to the ones used by Achenbach and Zigler and still be relevant for children. As in the Achenbach and Zigler study, six measures were collected on every subject—three self-image measures (real, ideal, and social), each in two formats (a six-alternative questionnaire, and an adjective checklist permitting only two response alternatives, "yes" or "no"). The instruments were administered to entire classroom groups.

In regard to the various measures of self-image disparity, the expectation, following Achenbach and Zigler's (1963) formulation, was that disparity would be highest where both guilt and cognitive differentiation were reflected, that is, real–ideal-self disparity on the questionnaire, and lowest where the effects of both these factors were minimized, that is real–social-self disparity on the adjective checklist. Furthermore, the developmental position generated the prediction that differences between developmental groups would be greatest on measures sensitive to both factors, less on measures sensitive to a single factor, and least on measures relatively insensitive to both factors.

All predictions in this study were confirmed. Older children exhibited greater real–ideal self-image disparity on both the questionnaire ($p < .001$) and the adjective checklist ($p < .01$) as well as greater real–social self-image disparity on both measures ($p < .05$ on the questionnaire and $p < .01$ on the checklist). Similarly the brighter children displayed greater real–ideal disparity on the questionnaire ($p < .01$) and tended to do the same on the adjective checklist ($p < .10$). Unlike the real–ideal discrepancy, however, the real–social self-image discrepancy was not significantly influenced by IQ. These age and IQ differences obtained with the various measures are presented in Table 1.2. Moreover, as was the case in the Achenbach and Zigler study, a highly significant correlation between real–ideal disparity scores on the questionnaire and the checklist measure ($r = .69$, $p < .001$) provided further evidence for the construct validity of the self-image disparity concept.

Paralleling Achenbach and Zigler's findings, the greater real–ideal disparity of the more mature (chronologically and conceptually) children appeared to be a function of two underlying factors related to maturity level: cognitive differentiation and capacity for social guilt. Comparisons of the various measures employed indicated a general trend whereby the real–ideal-self questionnaire (assumed to reflect both cognitive differentiation and social guilt) was maximally sensitive to developmental trends, the real–social-self questionnaire (cognitive differentiation only) and the real–ideal adjective checklist (social guilt only) were moderately sensitive to developmental differences, and the real–social-self adjective checklist (reflecting neither factor) was least sensitive to age and intelligence effects. Finally and again paralleling the analyses and findings of Achenbach and Zigler (1963), the tendency to give extreme responses (*very true*, *very untrue*) on the questionnaire diminished with increasing age and in higher IQ groups. This additional evidence of the importance of the cognitive differentiation factor is also consistent with results reported by Light, Zax, and Gardener (1965). These investigators, employing the same

TABLE 1.2
Mean Self-Image Scores for Each Group

Group[a]	Questionnaire					Checklist				
	Absolute scores[b]			Disparity		Absolute scores[b]			Disparity	
	Real	Ideal	Social	Real–ideal	Real–social	Real	Ideal	Social	Real–ideal	Real–social
Fifth grade										
Low IQ	57.4	46.4	55.6	11.0	2.2	4.2	1.9	4.8	2.3	−.6
High IQ	51.2	40.0	49.0	11.2	2.2	3.2	.9	3.0	2.3	.2
Eighth grade										
Low IQ	61.6	46.2	54.2	15.4	7.4	5.5	1.0	4.3	4.5	1.2
High IQ	60.4	31.6	57.1	28.8	3.3	6.6	1.0	5.4	5.6	.8
Eleventh grade										
Low IQ	57.4	38.4	51.4	19.0	6.0	4.6	.5	4.4	4.1	.2
High IQ	60.8	33.9	54.7	26.9	6.1	6.5	.6	5.4	5.9	1.1

[a]N = 20 for each group.
[b]On both the questionnaire and checklist measures, lower absolute scores reflect more positive self-concepts.

developmental rationale concerning cognitive differentiation found that older and brighter children made fewer extreme responses in rating Rorschach inkblots on semantic differential scales.

Extending beyond Achenbach and Zigler's analyses, Katz and Zigler's examination of developmental changes within the real, ideal, and social self-images yielded consistent differences due to age in both the real and the ideal self-image. On both the questionnaire and the checklist measure, older children displayed higher (more positive) ideal self-images than did younger groups. Conversely on both measures, the real self-images of the older children were more negative than those of younger children. In regard to the effects of IQ, more positive ideal self-images were displayed by the brighter children on the questionnaire but not on the checklist. No significant age or IQ differences were noted regarding the social self-image.

As regards the choice between the Rogerian psychodynamic view that interprets increased real–ideal self-image disparity as an ominous sign reflecting maladjustment, and the developmental position that regards increased disparity as a necessary concomitant of growth, Katz and Zigler's findings clearly support the latter view. Not only were all developmental predictions concerning self-image disparity confirmed, but exploratory findings suggested that with age the ideal self-image becomes more positive, whereas the real self-image becomes more negative. However as Katz and Zigler noted, their study was designed to highlight developmental differences and did not inquire into the effects of psychodynamic variables. Thus they suggested that future investigators, while they should be cognizant of developmental factors when interpreting self-image disparity findings, should also expend energy in determining exactly how the various psychodynamic factors emphasized by many workers interact with developmental determinants.

A concern with both developmental and psychodynamic determinants in self-image disparity is addressed in the next study in the series.

Developmental and Experiential Determinants of Children's Self-Image Disparity

Based on the assumptions that self-image disparity is influenced by general developmental-cognitive factors and by particular psychodynamic factors that are outgrowths of an individual's unique experiences, Zigler, Balla, and Watson (1972) investigated self-image disparity in groups of children differing in regard to cognitive development and life history experiences. The study included institutionalized and noninstitutionalized children of retarded and normal intellect, matched on mental age. From a purely formal developmental-cognitive point of view, no differences would be expected in self-image disparities among these four groups. From the psychodynamic formulation, differences in self-image disparity would be expected as a function of both intellectual retardation and institutionalization, inasmuch as both variables are associated with unique experiential histories that give rise to atypical motivational structures (Zigler, 1966a, 1966b, 1971). Two groups of older children of normal intellect (one institutionalized and the other not) were also examined in an attempt to replicate the developmental findings of Katz and Zigler (1967).

The subjects were 118 boys subdivided into three groups each of institutionalized (retarded $N = 18$; younger normal, $N = 20$; and older normal, $N = 20$) and noninstitutionalized (retarded, younger normal, and older normal; all Ns = 20) youngsters. The institutionalized retarded children were obtained from the Southbury, Connecticut, Training School; the noninstitutionalized retarded children from the Meriden, Connecticut public school system; the institutionalized normal children from Boys Town, Nebraska; and the noninstitutionalized

TABLE 1.3
Mean Self-Image Scores for Each Group

Group	N	Questionnaire			Checklist		
		Real self-image	Ideal self-image	Real–ideal disparity	Real self-image	Ideal self-image	Real–ideal disparity
Institutionalized							
Retarded	18	58.6	74.5	10.2	15.2	17.0	3.4
Younger normal	20	53.3	77.1	12.1	15.0	18.9	4.0
Older normal	20	55.6	85.1	14.8	13.6	19.2	5.6
Noninstitutionalized							
Retarded	20	66.7	78.7	8.0	15.8	17.1	1.9
Younger normal	20	65.9	86.9	11.7	18.3	19.5	1.3
Older normal	20	64.7	88.3	14.5	15.3	19.1	3.8

normal children from summer camps in the New Haven, Connecticut, area. The retarded subjects were exclusively of familial etiology and had no gross motor or sensory disorders. The mean chronological age (mental ages in parentheses) for the institutionalized retarded, younger normal, and older normal boys were 16.24 (10.51), 10.86 (10.64), and 16.12 (15.36) respectively. The mean chronological ages (with mental ages in parentheses) for the noninstitutionalized retarded, younger normal, and older normal groups were 14.51 (9.96), 9.83 (10.56), and 16.10 (16.00) respectively.

The real and ideal self-image measures employed by Katz and Zigler (1967) were used in this study again employing the two formats: (1) a six-alternative questionnaire and (2) an adjective checklist which allowed only two response alternatives, "yes" or "no." Because the samples included retarded individuals, the measures were individually administered.

The findings in this study supported an interpretation of self-image disparity that incorporates the influence of both developmental and experiential–psychodynamic factors. Table 1.3 presents the mean real self-image, ideal self-image, and disparity scores obtained on both measures for each subject group.

Consistent with the developmental formulation and in keeping with the earlier findings of Katz and Zigler, the children at the higher mental age level (older normal children, both institutionalized and - noninstitutionalized) displayed greater self-image disparity than children (retarded and younger children both institutionalized and noninstitutionalized) at a lower mental age ($p < .001$). A correlation of .40 between disparity scores on the questionnaire and on the checklist

provided some evidence of the construct validity of self-image disparity. Furthermore, and consistent with earlier findings (Achenbach &
Zigler, 1963; Katz & Zigler, 1967), the number of extreme responses
was found to decline with increasing cognitive development. The retarded children gave the greatest number of extreme responses, the
older normal children gave the fewest, and the younger normal children fell in between ($p < .05$ for all comparisons). Again in keeping
with the findings of Katz and Zigler, the children at the higher mental
age level (the older normal children) displayed both a lower real self-
image (as measured by the adjective checklist) and a higher ideal self-
image (as measured by the questionnaire) than did the children (retarded, and younger normal) at the lower mental age level (both ps
$< .01$). Once again it would appear that with increasing development,
children think less of themselves while at the same time incorporating
higher standards of conduct.

The remaining results of the study pointed to psychodynamic features of the self-concept that appeared to be outgrowths of the subjects'
unique life histories. Independent of developmental level, institutionalized children were found to have greater self-image disparities
than noninstitutionalized children ($p < .01$). This greater disparity was
found in spite of the fact that the institutionalized children had significantly lower ideal self-image scores (on the questionnaire) than did
noninstitutionalized children ($p < .05$). The greater disparity of the
institutionalized children was apparently due to the significantly
lower real self-image scores exhibited on both instruments by these
children compared to their noninstitutionalized counterparts (both ps
$< .001$). The children living in institutions, whether retarded or not,
thus appeared to set lower standards for themselves in addition to
having very low senses of self-esteem.

Two alternative but not mutually exclusive explanations can be
offered for the lowered aspirations and self-images of the institutionalized children. They could reflect the effects of institutionalization per se, or they may stem from the fact that children who are
institutionalized have often encountered an inordinate number of negative experiences (Zigler, 1971). However, inasmuch as no relationships
were discovered between the length of institutionalization and any self-
image measures in this study, the self-concepts of the institutionalized
children would not appear to have been a simple function of length of
institutionalization.

Although the two groups did not differ in mental age, the retarded
children displayed smaller self-image disparities than did the younger
normal group ($p < .05$), an effect that was independent of institu-

tionalization. Primarily the lowered disparity scores of the retarded children appeared to reflect the lower ideal self-image of this group in comparison with the normal subjects of similar mental age ($p < .05$ on the questionnaire, and $p < .001$ on the adjective checklist). This finding is consistent with the frequent assertion that retarded children have lower aspiration levels and orient themselves to failure avoiding rather than striving for success (Cromwell, 1963; Zigler, 1971).

The findings that both institutionalization and retardation were associated with low ideal self-images takes on particular importance when the adaptive dimensions of the self-concept are considered. The ideal self-image, embodying as it does the individual's aspirations and goals, provides motivation in development and a focal point for the integration of experience (Allport, 1955; Baldwin, 1911; Van den Daele, 1968). If this image becomes sufficiently attenuated in response to stress or failure, it is possible that an important determinant of optimal adaptation and development has been impaired. Given the finding that systematic programming of success experiences can alter some maladaptive problem solving in institutionalized retarded children (Ollendick, Balla, & Zigler, 1971), it might be possible that some variation of such programming could be employed to modify the low self-images found for both retarded and institutionalized children.

This study thus supports both developmental and experiential–dynamic formulations of self-image disparity and indicates that any comprehensive understanding of the self-concept requires a synthesis of both formulations. The data regarding changes in the self-image as a function of normal maturation have been remarkably consistent, both in regard to disparity measures and in concerning the direction of change in both the ideal and real self-images. Equally important, however, appear to be a variety of nondevelopmental experiential factors.

The Effects of Age, Maladjustment, and Symptom Style on Children's Self-Image Disparity

The self-images of children at two age levels (corresponding to the fifth and eighth grades) classified as maladjusted or nonmaladjusted were examined by Katz, Zigler, and Zalk (1975). In addition, however, styles of symptom expression displayed by the maladjusted children were classified developmentally along an action–thought continuum and related to their self-images. This investigation thus provides a direct test of both the Rogerian and the developmental formulations which were described previously. Particularly important, however, is the issue of symptom style. In addition to the Rogerian and the cognitive-developmental viewpoints, a third position has been advanced, suggesting that a large self-image disparity, although invariably ominous, would be found only among individuals employing particular psychological defenses, that is sensitizers and psychoneurotics (Altrocchi et al., 1960; Hillson & Worchel, 1957). Those committed to the emphasis upon experiential and/or psychodynamic factors would view this third position as a variant of the basic Rogerian thesis. However, as was indicated previously, Achenbach and Zigler (1963) proposed that this third position can be totally subsumed within the developmental formulation since the psychological defense patterns found to be associated with greater self-image disparities are ones most commonly found among individuals who have attained higher maturity levels. The developmental position takes as its given the level of maturity attained and views both the defenses employed and the amount of self-image disparity manifested as outgrowths of this level.

Developmental theorists (e.g., Freud, 1952; Piaget, 1951; Werner, 1948) have suggested that primitive, developmentally early behavior is marked by immediate, direct, and unmodulated responses to both external and internal stimuli. In contrast, higher levels of maturation are characterized by the appearance of indirect, ideational, conceptual, and symbolic or verbal behavior patterns. Thus the shift in emphasis from action to thought is viewed as a fundamental characteristic of developmental change. In addition to the importance of this dimension in normal development, considerable evidence has been presented to indicate that in psychologically disturbed individuals, action as compared to thought symptoms are associated with lower developmental status as assessed by chronological age and ability to delay gratification in children (Prugh, Staub, Sands, Kirschbaum, & Lenihan, 1953; Santostefano, 1970; Weintraub, 1973) and by social competence and Rorschach developmental level scores in adults (Kruger, 1954; Misch, 1954; L. Phillips & Zigler, 1961).

A major purpose of the Katz et al. (1975) study was to examine whether maladjusted children's positions in regard to the action–thought continuum in symptom expression were related to the magnitude of their self-image disparity. Given the presumably developmentally lower status of action symptoms, the prediction was that children exhibiting these symptoms would display less self-image disparity than children exhibiting a thought orientation in symptomatology. In keeping with earlier findings (Katz & Zigler, 1967; Zigler et al., 1972), the expectation in regard to age differences was that older children would display greater self-image disparities than would younger children. Finally the maladjusted–nonmaladjusted dimension provided an opportunity to test the Rogerian thesis that greater disparity would be associated with maladjusted status per se.

The children in this study were 80 boys ranging in age from 9 years 6 months to 14 years 6 months selected from a middle-class school system whose special classes for children designated emotionally disturbed were organized according to chronological age. Placement in these classes constituted the operational definition of psychological maladjustment for the study. Each class contained children with both action and thought types of symptomatology. However, in the entire group there were only two girls. For this reason, it was decided to eliminate them from the sample and focus attention only on males.

Classification along the action–thought continuum was based upon a categorization of symptoms as either *externalizing* (i.e., action) or *internalizing* (i.e., thought). This categorization was derived from a factor analytic study of children's symptoms conducted by Achenbach (1966). A finding in this study was that the major proportion of variability in children's symptom expression was accounted for by a bipolar internalizer–externalizer factor. Externalizing symptoms included antisocial, aggressive, and hyperactive behavior, whereas internalizing symptoms included anxiety, depression, withdrawal, and somatic concerns. This factor thus corresponds closely to the action–thought dimension utilized by L. Phillips and Zigler (1961, 1964) for the classification of adult symptom expression. The classification of children as internalizers or externalizers by Katz et al. (1975) was based upon the total configuration of the symptoms described in the student's record. When the preponderance of symptoms were externalizing, the child was classified as an externalizer. Alternatively, children displaying a preponderance of internalizing symptoms were classified as internalizers. Interrater agreement for this classification was 85%, and only children who could be unambiguously classified and who also displayed no signs of organic impairment were included in the study. This yielded a sample of 40 emotionally disturbed boys. The normal sample of 40 boys was then selected from the same school system and matched as closely as possible with the emotionally disturbed group in age, IQ and racial composition. Thus 20 nonmaladjusted fifth-grade boys were matched with 20 maladjusted (10 internalizers and 10 externalizers) boys of equivalent ages and IQs. Similarly the eighth-grade sample was comprised of 20 nonmaladjusted boys matched with 20 maladjusted (10 internalizers and 10 externalizers) boys. This study employed the same six-alternative questionnaire for measuring real and ideal self-images as was used in the Katz and Zigler (1967) and the

TABLE 1.4
Mean Self-Image Scores for Each Group

Group	N	Questionnaire score		
		Real[a]	Ideal[a]	Real–ideal disparity
Fifth grade				
Normal subjects	20	54.25	43.25	11.00
Internalizers	10	66.60	53.60	13.00
Externalizers	10	67.70	62.80	4.90
Eighth grade				
Normal subjects	20	58.65	42.05	16.60
Internalizers	10	57.20	36.20	21.00
Externalizers	10	61.50	52.50	9.00

[a]On both the real- and ideal-self measures, lower scores reflect a more positive self-concept.

Zigler *et al.* (1972) studies. The questionnaire was administered to classroom groups.

The self-image and self-image disparity scores of all groups are presented in Table 1.4. No support was obtained in this study for the Rogerian position that maladjustment per se is related to self-image disparity. Consistent with the adult findings of Achenbach and Zigler (1963), emotional maladjustment was found to be unrelated to self-image disparity, whereas both age and symptom style were found to be predictive of the magnitude of self-image disparity.

Regardless of adjustment status, self-image disparity was significantly greater in older children. Moreover, children with externalizing symptoms were found to have smaller self-image disparities than either internalizing or normal children. The disparity scores of the normal and the internalizing children did not differ significantly from each other, although the highest disparity scores were in fact obtained by the internalizing children. The mean disparity scores of the internalizing, normal, and externalizing children were 17.00, 13.80, and 6.95 respectively.

Analyses of the ideal self-image scores once again pointed to the influence of developmental variables (age and symptom orientation) but not to the effects of adjustment status per se. Consistent with the results of Katz and Zigler (1967) and Zigler *et al.* (1972), older children were found to have higher ideal self-image scores than younger children ($p = .01$). Similarly the internalizing and the normal children were found to be quite similar with regard to ideal self-aspirations (M

= 44.90 and 42.65 respectively), whereas the externalizers had much more negative ideal-self scores (M = 57.65).

In contrast to the findings of Katz and Zigler (1967) and Zigler et al. (1972), the older children in this study were not found to have less favorable real self-images than the younger groups. However, adjustment status was found to influence this aspect of self-perception. Both externalizers and internalizers displayed less favorable real self-images than normal children, although this difference was significant only for the externalizer–normal comparison. Consistent with previous findings (Zigler et al., 1972), there is again the strong suggestion that, independent of cognitive-developmental variables, the child's life history qualitatively influences self-image disparity, particularly as regards the real self-image. In the Zigler et al. (1972) study, institutionalized children as a group displayed particularly low real self-images. Just as the life history experiences associated with being placed in an institution may well result in lowered self-regard, it is reasonable to expect that children stigmatized with the label *maladjusted*, removed from the mainstream of their school's activities, and placed in classes for the emotionally disturbed, develop an attenuated sense of self-worth. Moreover, the finding that the sense of self-worth was particularly depressed in children with externalizing symptoms is understandable if one remembers that it is just such acting-out children who seem to be least countenanced by peers (Kohlberg, Lacrosse, & Ricks, 1972), family, school personnel, and community members.

Although the low ideal self-images of the externalizing children may primarily reflect the influence of cognitive-developmental variables (less internalization of societal expectations, and possibly also less ability to think abstractly), the lowered aspirations coupled with the depressed self-regard of this group would seem to raise concern about adaptive consequences. However, rather than being reflected in self-image disparity scores (which were particularly small in this group), the potential source of difficulty would seem to be that these children both think poorly of themselves and show little aspiration for change. As Wylie (1974) has suggested, self-image disparity represents an unanchored difference score. At least as important are the qualitative aspects of the real and the ideal self-images. The same self-image disparity score may have a very different meaning depending upon where, along a positive-to-negative continuum, the self-images are located. The person with a positive view of self, high aspirations, and a consequently small disparity score would seem to be very different from the individual whose small disparity score reflects an unfavorable view of the self with few aspirations.

The Effects of Age, Socioeconomic Status, Ethnicity, and Gender on Children's Self-Image Disparity

   The evolving position of Zigler and his colleagues may now be stated as follows. Cognitive-developmental factors have a fundamental causal influence on self-image disparity and its components; nevertheless, pervasive experiential factors constitute a second major source of influence that may moderate the unfolding of the developmental sequence which has been consistently noted in the studies already described. A critical theoretical issue is how great must the variation in everyday experiences be to override the developmental determinants.

   Factors related to how others respond to the individual in everyday social–psychological interactions have been found to be especially influential. Such factors, for example, appear to include experiences leading up to and associated with living in an institution or being labeled maladjusted and assigned to special classes for the emotionally disturbed at school (Katz et al., 1975; Zigler et al., 1972). A child's socioeconomic status (SES), ethnicity, and gender are obvious examples of additional characteristics that may have pervasive effects on social–psychological interactions and might, therefore, be related to differences in the self-image.

   Both popular and scholarly interest in the importance of SES, ethnicity, and gender differences for self-image development have until recently converged on the assumption that the deleterious life experiences of minority group and disadvantaged children will inhibit the acquisition of positive self-image (see Proshansky & Newton, 1968). However the validity of this seemingly self-evident assumption has been called into question by recent evidence that demonstrates that the self-images of these children are at least as positive as those of their wealthier white peers (see Rosenberg, 1979). The role that gender plays in self-image development has similarly been obfuscated by unexamined assumptions and contradictory evidence (Maccoby & Jacklin, 1974). A potentially important oversight in this literature concerns different developmental patterns that may be found in the ideal self-images and real–ideal disparities of children who are exposed to disparate social–psychological experiences. The contribution of these three variables, in interaction with developmental status, to the real and ideal self-images of children was examined by D. Phillips and Zigler (1980).

   Eighty children (40 second graders and 40 fifth graders) served as subjects in this investigation. Within each grade level, there were four groups ($N = 10$) defined by SES (middle or lower class as assessed by parents' scores on the Hollingshead Index of Social Position; see Hollingshead, 1967), and ethnicity (black or white as designated by the identification accorded to them by the school community) with 5 boys and 5 girls included in each group. The public schools these children attended were predominantly white, although participating classrooms each contained a small number of black students.

Given the young ages of the children in this study, three self-image disparity measures were employed: a six-alternative questionnaire; an adjective checklist allowing only two response alternatives, "true, like me" and "false, *not* like me"; and a picture instrument. The questionnaire and the checklist were designed to be as similar as possible to the instruments employed by Katz and Zigler (1967) and still be appropriate for second and fifth graders. On both measures, the response alternatives were represented pictorially as colored boxes to help the children conceptualize the choices to be made. The picture instrument consisted of 10 series of four-frame pictures, each depicting a child (a boy or a girl, depending upon the gender of the subject) described in terms of an assessment of self-image. A statement was made about the child in each of the four frames; for example, Frame 1: "This girl (boy) is very smart; she has just gotten all A's on her report card." Frame 2: "This girl (boy) is pretty smart; she has just gotten all B's on her report card." Frame 3: "This girl (boy) is not too smart; she has just gotten all C's on her report card." Frame 4: "This girl (boy) is not smart at all; she has just gotten all D's on her report card." The real self-image was assessed by asking the child, "Which girl (boy) is most like you?" while the ideal self-image was assessed by asking, "Which girl (boy) would you most like to be?" The vocabulary utilized in all statements and response choices on all instruments was at or below the second-grade level (Thorndike & Lorge, 1972). All measures were individually administered. In a later session, the children's IQs were assessed by the Peabody Picture Vocabulary Test, Form B. Inasmuch as modest correlations appeared between IQ and both real- and ideal-self scores on both the questionnaire and the checklist measures, and because significant differences in IQ appeared as a function of both social class and ethnicity, IQ scores were covaried in all analyses of group differences on the various self-image measures.

The mean self-image scores for groups are presented in Table 1.5. The developmental trends consistently obtained in previous studies (Katz & Zigler, 1967; Katz et al., 1975; Zigler et al., 1972) were once again found. The older children evidenced greater self-image disparity than the younger group on both the questionnaire ($p < .01$) and the

TABLE 1.5
Mean Self-Image Scores for Each Group on Three Instruments

Group[a]	Questionnaire			Checklist			Picture		
	Real	Ideal	Real–ideal disparity	Real	Ideal	Real–ideal disparity	Real	Ideal	Real–ideal disparity
Second-grade boys									
Black									
Low SES	86.8	103.0	16.2	13.0	15.6	2.6	32.8	35.2	2.4
Middle SES	90.0	107.2	17.2	16.0	18.8	2.8	35.0	38.2	3.2
White									
Low SES	88.0	110.4	22.4	16.0	19.0	3.0	37.4	38.0	.6
Middle SES	91.2	102.8	11.6	15.2	19.6	4.4	34.4	36.4	2.0
Fifth-grade boys									
Black									
Low SES	100.4	109.4	9.0	15.8	19.2	3.4	34.4	38.8	4.4
Middle SES	85.4	102.4	17.0	15.8	18.4	2.6	32.4	36.8	4.4
White									
Low SES	92.2	110.4	18.2	15.4	19.6	4.2	34.4	38.2	3.8
Middle SES	94.4	111.6	17.2	16.6	19.6	3.0	32.8	37.0	4.2
Second-grade girls									
Black									
Low SES	95.8	93.6	−2.2	16.6	18.2	1.6	37.0	34.2	−2.8
Middle SES	91.8	98.2	6.4	15.2	18.6	3.4	36.2	36.4	.2
White									
Low SES	97.4	105.8	8.4	15.0	18.4	3.4	36.6	39.0	2.4
Middle SES	96.0	109.0	13.0	17.2	19.2	2.0	34.0	37.6	3.6
Fifth-grade girls									
Black									
Low SES	86.6	110.0	23.4	14.6	18.0	3.4	34.2	36.6	2.4
Middle SES	93.6	108.6	15.0	15.8	18.8	3.0	34.8	36.6	1.8
White									
Low SES	91.4	111.0	19.6	17.4	19.2	1.8	35.4	38.8	3.4
Middle SES	92.8	113.6	20.8	17.0	19.4	2.4	35.0	37.8	2.8

[a]$N = 5$ for each group; SES = socioeconomic status.

picture ($p < .001$) instruments. However, one interaction effect was noteworthy; this difference in self-image disparity between second- and fifth-grade children did not appear for low-SES boys. The developmental formulation that cognitive differentiation increases with maturity was also confirmed by findings that fewer extreme responses were given on both the questionnaire ($p < .001$) and the picture ($p < .002$) instruments by the older children. This finding again replicates earlier work (Achenbach & Zigler, 1963; Katz & Zigler, 1967; Zigler et al., 1972).

As in the earlier studies the larger self-image disparities of the older children were again found to reflect both lowered real self-images ($p < .05$ on the picture instrument) and higher ideal self-images ($p < .01$ on the questionnaire and $p < .05$ on the checklist). Such consistent evidence that differences in both real and ideal scores influence the magnitude of self-image disparity calls into question McCandless's (1967) view that the disparity score can be replaced by the real-self measure alone without loss of information.

In addition to these developmental changes, the findings of Phillips and Zigler also make it clear that developmental factors alone cannot explain all of the variation encountered in children's self-image disparity scores. Experiential determinants of self-image disparity associated with gender, ethnicity, and SES were also indicated. Although these variables had a differential and sometimes complex influence, their relationship to the components of self-image was sufficiently substantiated to suggest that they cannot be ignored in future work.

Independent of developmental level, boys were found to exhibit greater self-image disparities than girls on the picture instrument ($p < .01$), but not on the other measures. This finding is consistent with that of Stoodt and Balla (1974), but inconsistent with a large number of self-image studies reporting no gender differences (see Maccoby & Jacklin, 1974). Thus additional work is required to determine whether the two genders differ on this psychologically important measure. At the same time, however, it should be recognized that certain aspects of the D. Phillips and Zigler (1980) study may have contributed to the gender difference noted. First, the self-image measures were administered by a female examiner, and thus cross-gender effects in social reinforcement (Stevenson, 1965) may have been operant. Second, the study was conducted in the children's schools, and school settings, particularly in the elementary grades, may represent a feminized environment (Kagan, 1964). Finally the gender difference was noted only on the picture instrument, a format which has been less frequently utilized in self-image disparity research. Given the gender differences that have been noted in young children's verbal abilities (see Maccoby & Jacklin, 1974), it is possible that the picture instrument was more comfortable or appealing for the boys than for the girls. As such, it may have been a more sensitive measure of variations in the boys' self-images.

Black compared with white children were found to have smaller real–ideal disparities on the questionnaire ($p < .05$). Consistent with the findings of McDonald and Gynther (1965), black girls were found to have particularly small disparity scores. Some evidence (on the checklist) suggested that the lower disparity scores of the black children were due to an attenuation of their ideal scores in comparison with those of the white children ($p < .05$). This finding runs counter to that of a number of studies in which black children's aspirations have been found to be as high as those of white children (see Rosenberg & Simmons, 1971). However, Rosenberg and Simmons did find that black children exhibited a decline in their aspirations as they grew older and entered integrated high schools. Moreover several researchers have observed that one of the repercussions of racial integration may be a decline in the aspirations of black children (Coleman et al., 1966; Powell & Fuller, 1970; Yando, Seitz, & Zigler, 1979). This phenomenon may have been pertinent even for the young sample examined by Phillips and Zigler, inasmuch as all of the children studied were in integrated, predominantly white schools.

The smaller disparity scores of the black children might also be understood in terms of a distinction drawn between desired and expected attainments (Proshansky & Newton, 1968). It is very possible that young children confuse these two meanings in their response to ideal-self items. If this was the case, the lower ideal self-images of the black children may have reflected a realistic assessment of their expected future success in a society in which widespread prejudice and discrimination persist.

More reassuring was the observation that the black and white children's ideal-self scores did not differ significantly on either the questionnaire or the picture measure. Moreover the real self-images of the black children were commensurate with those of the white children on all of the instruments. This finding challenges the pervasive assumption that the deleterious environments of low-SES black children inhibit the development of positive self-images (Carpenter & Busse, 1969; Deutsch, Katz, & Jensen, 1968; Proshansky & Newton, 1968) and lends further support to the view that black children acquire positive evaluations of their self-worth (Porter, 1971; Rosenberg & Simmons, 1971; Wylie, 1979). These children apparently do not directly internalize the negative racial stereotypes promulgated by the majority culture. A number of mechanisms whereby the deleterious effects of widespread prejudice may be counteracted have been suggested, including the supportive nature of the black communities that constitute these children's immediate social environments, the greater value and credibility that black children place on the messages they receive from their own parents and other blacks compared with those communicated by white peers and adults, and these children's capacity to selectively emphasize their good qualities rather than their weak points in forming their overall self-estimations (Rosenberg, 1979; Silverstein & Krate, 1975).

Socioeconomic status (SES) was found to affect the children's self-image scores, with this effect being interactive and complex. The SES effects varied with gender and age and also as a function of the particular self-image instrument employed. The major interaction effects were (1) that the ideal self-images of low-SES second graders, as measured by the checklist, were less positive than those of their middle class peers ($p < .05$) and (2) that on the questionnaire, and in contrast to all other groups assessed with this instrument, self-image disparity was not found to increase with age for the low-SES boys.

As with the black children, the low-SES children did not exhibit depressed real self-images relative to middle-SES children of the same age. Thus, they may also have developed a positive self-protective orientation such that the rejection accorded their economic status by the society's majority is not directly internalized (see Rosenberg, 1979; Trowbridge, 1972). Nevertheless some evidence pointed to lower ideal self-images in low-SES as compared with middle class children. A possible confusion between desired and expected aspirations, coupled with the low-SES children's incipient understanding of their families' dependent position in society and low societal evaluation (see Tudor, 1971) could conceivably affect their future aspirations as reflected in some lowering of their ideal self-images. Particularly perplexing was the finding on the questionnaire that low-SES boys represented an exception to the frequently discovered developmental finding of an increase in real–ideal disparity with increasing age.

The most significant theoretical implication of D. Phillips and Zigler's (1980) work lies in its demonstration that the development of self-image in a diverse group of children exhibits both similar age trends and differences derived from their diversity. These findings provoke questions concerning the specific ways in which developmental and experiential factors interact and modify each other's influence. Gender, social class, and racial group membership may affect the size of a child's self-image disparity indirectly by influencing the developmental level achieved. Alternatively, the self-images of children who differ along these dimensions may develop within substantially different social contexts such that what constitutes the healthiest developmental trend may vary for different children. For example, the lower ideal self-images of black and lower-class children may, as was suggested, be most appropriately understood as a reflection of increasingly realistic appraisals of what constitutes a reasonable set of aspirations rather than as an indication of these groups' deviation from a natural developmental trend.

In relation to the debate concerning the self-image development of disadvantaged and minority group children, the results of D. Phillips and Zigler provide additional compelling support for the position that children who are reared under conditions of relative economic privation and social prejudice are capable of developing positive self-images commensurate with those of their white and middle-class peers. However, the discovered attenuation of these children's ideal-self scores and the concomitant decrease in real–ideal self-image disparity underscore the importance of directing our concerns to these children's adoption of personal goals and optimism concerning their achievement rather than exclusively focusing on their extant self-images.

The Reliability, Validity, and Factorial Structure of Children's Self-Images

As part of the study just described (D. Phillips & Zigler, 1980), D. Phillips and Zigler (1982) also examined the reliability and construct validity of the three self-image measures (questionnaire, checklist, and picture instrument) employed and the factorial structure of the questionnaire for both second- and fifth-grade students.

The appropriate evaluation of large-scale childhood intervention efforts (for example, Head Start and Follow Through) remains a perplexing and controversial issue (Horowitz & Paden, 1973; Lazar, Hubbell, Murray, Rosche, & Royce, 1977; Rhine, 1981; Zigler & Trickett, 1978). Due to their ready availability, evaluation efforts have generally relied heavily on standard IQ and school achievement tests—measures that are themselves highly intercorrelated. However considerable evidence has been presented to indicate that the attenuated functioning of economically disadvantaged children is due to a variety of motivational factors rather than being due solely to formal cognitive shortcomings (Zigler & Butterfield, 1968; Zigler, Abelson, & Seitz, 1973; Zigler, Abelson, Trickett, & Seitz, 1982). Thus the consensus has developed that the ultimate criterion for the success or failure of early childhood intervention programs should be the enhanced general social competence of the children who participate in the programs (Anderson & Messick, 1974; Mediax Associates, Inc., 1980; Zigler & Trickett, 1978) and that however the social competence construct is ultimately defined, its assessment must include motivational and emotional variables. The self-image has been prominently featured as an important characteristic to be assessed in the broad evaluation of competence (Anderson & Messick, 1974; Garmezy, Masten, Nordstrom, & Ferrarese, 1979; Sundberg, Snowden, & Reynolds, 1978; Zigler & Trickett, 1978). Given the dearth of measures with satisfactory psychometric characteristics for assessing motivational and emotional facets of young children's (preschool and early elementary school age) functioning (Walker, 1973), information about the reliability and construct validity of self-image measures for such children seems particularly timely.

It has become increasingly clear that children's self-assessments vary across several relatively independent domains (Harter, 1983; Kokenes, 1974) such that positive judgments of one's academic abilities can, for example, stand alongside negative assessments of one's popularity with peers (Harter, 1978; Rosenberg, 1979). The factorial structures of the children's self-images and changes in this structure between the second the fifth grades were, therefore, examined. In keeping with standard developmental thought, the expectation was that the structure of the self-image would be more differentiated at the older age. Evidence that the self-image of children undergoes just such differentiation with increasing age has been presented by Mullener and Laird (1971).

The second- and fifth-grade samples examined and the measures employed were described previously. Test–retest reliability was assessed with a random subsample of 10 second and 10 fifth graders who were retested on the three self-image measures approximately 10 days after their initial testing. The internal consistency of the instruments was assessed for all subjects ($N = 80$) using the split-half method. The test–retest and split-half findings indicated adequate internal consistency and stability for both the real and the ideal self-images, on each of the three instruments even for children as young as second graders. Both test–retest and split-half reliabilities were typically in the .50 to .85 range.

The intercorrelations of real and ideal self-image scores across the three measures provided some evidence that the child's self-image is a stable conceptualization which manifests itself in a related fashion across different types of measures. Not too surprisingly, this evidence for construct validity was more marked for fifth than for second graders. For the real-self measures, two of the three correlations (questionnaire with picture instrument, $p < .01$; checklist with picture instrument, $p < .05$) were significant. For fifth graders all three intercorrelations were highly significant (questionnaire with picture, p

< .001; questionnaire with checklist, and checklist with picture, both $ps < .01$). For the ideal self-image, one of the three correlations was significant for the second graders (questionnaire with picture, $p < .001$), whereas two of the three correlations (questionnaire with picture $p < .001$, and questionnaire with checklist $p < .01$) were significant for the fifth graders. Inasmuch as the reliability scores of the children at the two age levels were comparable, the smaller correlations across instruments obtained by the second graders did not appear to reflect the failure of these children to adequately comprehend the items or the task. (If the children were responding randomly, this would be reflected in attenuated reliability coefficients.) A more likely interpretation for the greater construct validity at the fifth grade is that the child's self-image does become a more stable conceptualization with increasing age and thus has a greater likelihood of manifesting itself in comparable fashion over a rather broad array of instruments.

In relation to the debate concerning the appropriate evaluation of early intervention efforts, it appears that valid assessments of children's self-image can be accomplished as early as the second grade. The next step, of course, involves extending the method employed in this study to preschool children. The use of picture measures would appear to be particularly well suited to such young children.

An unexpected finding was that real and ideal self-image scores within the same instrument were highly correlated. For second graders, these correlation coefficients ranged from .48 to .55, whereas for fifth graders the range was .54 to .65. The fact that responses to the ideal measure were always obtained immediately after presentation of the real measure generates the interpretation that the child's desire for consistency underlies the positive correlations discovered between real and ideal measures. Another interpretation of this positive relationship between real and ideal self-images should be entertained, however. These two facets of the child's self-image may be inherently related, such that a child with a high real self-image also has a high ideal self-image. A corollary of such an interpretation would be that children with relatively low real self-images would defend themselves against the psychological implications of this disparaging self-assessment by lowering their ideal self-images. Some evidence supporting this view has recently been presented by D. Phillips (1981).

Principle component factor analyses, followed by varimax rotations were run on the 20 real-self questionnaire items separately for the two age groups. Five factors were extracted at each age level, based on the magnitude of the eigenvalues. These factors are summarized in Table 1.6. Since the number of factors was the same for both ages, the view

TABLE 1.6
Factors Extracted for the Questionnaire Real-Self Items

Factor labels	Percentage of variance accounted for
Second graders	
Basic Outlook and Effectiveness	
(e.g., "When I try, I do a good job.")	18.1
Intellectual Competence	
(e.g., "I'm as smart as the other kids.")	13.5
Self-Protectiveness	
(e.g., "I'm glad to be the way I am," coupled with a negative loading on, "It's easy for me to make friends.")	10.9
Social Relations	
(e.g., "I am nice to other kids.")	8.3
Attractiveness to Peers	
(e.g., "Friends are easy to find.")	7.1
Fifth graders	
Social Relations	22.5
Basic Outlook and Effectiveness	12.9
Friendship	
(e.g., "Other kids want to play with me.")	10.7
Self-Acceptance	
(e.g., "I do not wish to be someone else.")	8.7
Following	
(e.g., "I don't have to have things my way.")	7.5

that the child's self-image would become more differentiated with age was not supported. However the requirement that the items be kept simple so as to be easily understood by second graders, may have restricted the range of behaviors tapped by the items and thus limited the possibility that increased differentiation could be shown. When a broader range of behaviors have been included in self-image assessments, increased differentiation has been found with increased age (Mullener & Laird, 1971).

However, changes in the nature of the factors between the two age levels indicated that the self-image undergoes a marked evolution between second and fifth grades. The principle distinction that was apparent was that between a young child whose concerns reflect a large degree of egocentrism and an older child who exhibits a capacity to view himself or herself as an object. The second graders placed considerable emphasis on identifying themselves in terms of what they could do and how others reacted to them. By contrast, the fifth graders evidenced a concern with self-acceptance—a perspective that requires a self-reflective stance. A second difference in the content of the self-images between the younger and older group was the more central role assigned to peer relations by the older children. The Social Relations factor was the first to be extracted in the fifth grade solution, whereas concerns with Basic Outlook and Effectiveness, Intellectual Competence, and Self-Protectiveness took precedence over interpersonal concerns for the second graders. The shift in emphasis discovered here is consistent with other findings that indicate that children as they grow older undergo a major shift in the relative importance of the peer as opposed to the adult culture (Bowerman & Kinch, 1959).

Other Corroborating Work: Role-Taking Ability and Self-Image Disparity

The work of Leahy (Leahy, 1981; Leahy, Balla, & Zigler, 1982; Leahy & Huard, 1976) converges closely with the efforts already discussed in this chapter. Leahy too ascribes to a cognitive-developmental formulation (Leahy, 1981) within which experiential variables have important moderating influences (Leahy *et al.*, 1982). However Leahy's formulation differs from the model of Zigler and his colleagues in that Leahy posits role taking as the fundamental process whereby the self becomes known as an object and is internalized. This position derives from the social interactionist formulations of Kohlberg (1969) and Mead (1934). For Leahy then, the differentiation of real and ideal self-images and the greater internalization of societal values that occur with development are seen as outgrowths of social interaction and role-taking opportunities.

Central in Zigler's position is Werner's orthogenetic principle that "wherever development occurs it proceeds from a state of relative globality and lack of differentiation to a state of increasing differentiation, articulation, and hierarchic integration" (1957, p. 126). Thus for Zigler, differentiation and integration are seen as the essence of development, as *the* fundamental processes, and role-taking ability along with increased reciprocity in social interactions constitute exemplars of the orthogenetic principle with respect to self–world relationships. At immature levels, subjective experience and external events tend to be fused, and neither the boundaries nor the point of view of the self can be adequately distinguished from the boundaries or the point of view of the other. By contrast, at more mature levels, not only are self and other distinguished, they are also reintegrated in complex and relatively stable ways. Thus a sense of personal identity can be achieved. The individual can perceive the separateness and the distinct needs and point of view of the other, and self and other can be reintegrated so that the individual perceives himself or herself as a member and participant in social interactions. For Zigler, therefore, differentiation is axiomatic and underived. While development can be facilitated by a supportive environment and opportunities for social interaction, these circumstances are not needed to account for the basic nature of the development process which they, nonetheless, may help to unfold. In this regard, Leahy's and Zigler's views diverge. Apart from this, however, their work is complementary.

The relationship between role taking and self-image disparity was examined by Leahy and Huard (1976) in a sample of 68 children in the fourth ($N = 20$), fifth ($N = 16$), and sixth ($N = 32$) grades. The self-image disparity instrument was the six-alternative questionnaire utilized by Katz and Zigler (1967). Role-taking ability was assessed using Chandler's (1973) cartoon sequence role-taking task. A referential communication measure was also employed. However, no significant effects were obtained with this second measure; neither was it found to be significantly related to scores on the Chandler (1973) task. The children displaying nonegocentric role-taking performance were found to have greater self-image disparity and higher ideal self-images than egocentric children.

In a later study (Leahy, 1981) the relationship between self-image disparity and level of moral judgment was examined in adolescents (37 male and 67 female tenth graders) in conjunction with the child rearing attitudes of their parents. Again the six-alternative questionnaire of Katz and Zigler was employed as the self-image measure, and level of moral judgment as defined by Kohlberg (1969, 1976) was assessed using Rest's (1975) Defining Issues Test.

Most pertinent to the cognitive-developmental formulation under discussion in this chapter were the findings that greater self-image disparity, more positive ideal self-images, and less positive real self-images were all associated with higher (postconventional) levels of moral judgment. In addition a number of factor scores derived from a parental assessment of child rearing practices were found to be related to higher ideal self-images and higher levels of moral judgment in the adolescents, although gender (of both the adolescent and the parent) was found to be a strong moderating variable. Although Leahy ascribes a more causative role to social interaction and role-taking experience in the development of self-image disparity than does Zigler, Leahy's findings, as he himself indicates, also support Zigler's view. Leahy's work provides two additional widely accepted measures of cognitive maturity to which self-image disparity has been found to be related. Moreover, inasmuch as measures of nonegocentric thought and moral reasoning reflect a qualitative Piagetian approach to cognitive assessment, findings with these two measures nicely supplement the work of Katz and Zigler (1967) and Zigler et al. (1972) in which greater self-image disparity was found to be associated with psychometric indexes of cognifive maturity (IQ and MA).

Self-image disparity, role-taking ability, and imitation in retarded and intellectually average children were examined by Leahy et al. (1982). A group of retarded children ($n = 24$) was compared with two groups of intellectually average children. One nonretarded group was similar in chronological age to the retarded children; the other was similar in mental age to the retarded children. Each group was equally divided by gender. The mean chronological ages (mental ages in parentheses) for the retarded, younger nonretarded, and older nonretarded groups were 11.9 (6.9), 6.9 (7.7), and 11.6 (13.9) respectively. Given the younger mental ages of two of the groups of children, self-image disparity was assessed using the picture and checklist instruments employed by D. Phillips and Zigler (1980). Chandler's (1973) task was again employed to gauge role-taking ability, and the imitation task was adapted from Achenbach and Zigler's (1968) measure of imitation (Experiment III).

The findings of this study pointed to the importance of both cognitive-developmental and experiential determinants of self-image in retarded children. Consistent with the cognitive-developmental interpretation, higher IQ and mental age (MA) were significantly associated with more positive ideal self-images as assessed by both the checklist (both $ps < .001$) and the picture (IQ: $p < .001$; MA: $p < .01$) instrument. A marginal relationship appeared between nonegocentric role-taking performance and higher ideal self-images on the checklist ($p < .07$). Consonant with developmental expectations both egocentricity and greater imitation were associated with younger chronological age and lower mental age. In contrast to previous work (Katz & Zigler, 1967; Katz et al., 1975; Leahy, 1981; Leahy & Huard, 1976; D. Phillips & Zigler, 1980; Zigler et al., 1972), self-image disparity was not found to be related to any of the variables examined (chronological age, mental age, IQ, role taking, or imitation). However, the real self-images of the retarded children were found to be significantly lower than those of either intellectually average group (both $ps < .01$). Thus although the disparity scores did not differ, the pattern of the retarded children's self-images was substantially different from that of nonretarded groups. The retarded children evidenced both lower ideal self-images and lower real self-images than intellectually average groups.

The lower real self-images of the retarded children and findings that retardation status moderated the relationship between role-taking ability and the ideal self-image appear to underscore the importance of experiential determinants in self-image formation. Whereas previous findings with intellectually average children (Leahy & Huard, 1976) bore out the developmental expectation that nonegocentric thought would be positively related to higher ideal self-aspirations, an opposite relationship was discovered with the retarded children in this study. For the retarded sample, nonegocentric thought tended to be associated with less positive ideal self-images ($p < .10$). As was the case with institutionalization (Zigler et al., 1972) and with being labeled emotionally disturbed and placed in special classes (Katz et al., 1975), being labeled mentally retarded may result in both a less positive view of the self and in lowered aspirations, particularly for the more intellectually able and socially aware retarded children.

Children's Self-Image Disparity: Summary

The research with children has substantially advanced the cognitive-developmental interpretation of self-image disparity. First, it has provided greatly expanded evidence that cognitive-developmental variables influence not only self-image disparity but the nature of the real and ideal self-images. Equally importantly, this work indicates that nondevelopmental experiential variables, particularly those factors that influence how others respond to the individual in everyday social–psychological interactions, may have pervasive moderating influences on the unfolding of the developmental sequence. Before moving on to the further consideration of research efforts in the area of adult psychopathology, these findings are reviewed and certain theoretical implications noted.

Developmental Changes in Self-Image Disparity

Considerable evidence has now been presented to indicate that increased self-image disparity may be a natural concomitant of development. In the work with children, greater disparity has been associated with a broad array of measures of cognitive maturity, including chronological age (Katz & Zigler, 1967; Katz et al., 1975; D. Phillips & Zigler, 1980; Zigler et al., 1972), mental age (Katz & Zigler, 1967; Zigler et al., 1972), the presence of thought rather than action symptoms (Katz et al., 1975), evidence of nonegocentric thought in a role-taking task (Leahy, 1981; Leahy & Huard, 1976) and developmental level in moral reasoning (Leahy, 1981).

The developmental differences in self-image disparity appear to reflect changes in both the real and the ideal self-images. The findings have been particularly consistent in regard to the ideal self-image. More positive ideal self-images have been found to be associated with higher maturity levels as assessed by all of the measures employed in the various studies, that is, chronological age (Katz & Zigler, 1967; Katz et al., 1975; D. Phillips & Zigler, 1980; Zigler et al., 1972), mental age (Katz & Zigler, 1967; Zigler et al., 1972; Leahy et al., 1982), the presence of thought rather than action symptoms (Katz et al., 1975), nonegocentric role-taking ability (Leahy, 1981; Leahy et al., 1982), and more mature levels of moral reasoning (Leahy, 1981).

A lowered real self-image at older age levels has also been frequently observed (Katz & Zigler, 1967; D. Phillips & Zigler, 1980; Zigler et al., 1972), and Leahy (1981) found that less positive self-images were associated with higher (postconventional) levels of moral judgment in adolescents. Consistent with these findings obtained with children, Rabinowitz (1966) found that more negative qualities were incorporated into the self-image by 25-year-old subjects in comparison to 18-year-olds. Moreover, Rorschach scores which have been associated with higher maturity levels (i.e., greater M, higher $F + \%$, and a predominance of FC over CF) have been related to lower self-acceptance in college students (Bills, 1953).

Evidence for the reliability and construct validity of self-image disparity for even very young children has been presented by D. Phillips and Zigler (1980) who moreover discovered that different emphases in the real self-image were reflected by different factor structures obtained for younger and older children. In contrast to second graders, fifth graders evidenced a more self-reflective stance. Comparable developmental changes in the content of children's self-images have also been reported by Montemayor and Eisen (1977), Rosenberg (1979), and Harter (1983).

In regard to the idealized self-image, Van den Daele (1968) has reported parallel changes with increasing age in the direction of increased differentiation and hierarchic integration, greater abstraction, and an increased internalization of societal values. Young children's descriptions of the person they would like to be were found to be hedonistic and conflict avoidant, predicated upon parental actions and admonitions. At intermediate levels, the children's responses reflected cultural and group expectations, while at the highest levels that characterized older adolescents, rigid conformity to social proscription appeared to be replaced by an integrating structure of individualized goals involving personal–social and transcendent values. This developmental trend is obviously reminiscent of the developmental progressions described by Kohlberg (1969) and Loevinger (Loevinger, 1966; Loevinger & Wessler, 1970).

The more positive ideal self-images associated with higher maturity levels can most plausibly be interpreted as a reflection of two developmental processes: (1) the greater incorporation of societal demands and values at higher developmental levels and the consequent increase in social guilt (Achenbach & Zigler, 1963) and (2) the capacity for abstract hypothetical thinking that emerges at higher developmental levels. The ideal self-image, if conceptualized as distinct from the real self, does after all represent an abstraction.

The lowered real self-images which have frequently been found to accompany development may also reflect two aspects of developmental change. In the first place, they may reflect the higher standards incorporated in the ideal self-images. When these standards are applied to the real self-image, this may result in a more negative self-evaluation (Leahy, 1981). In addition, structural changes in the self-concept over the course of development may give different meanings to negative attribution at different developmental levels. At lower developmental levels, the various aspects of the self-concept would be expected to be fused with each other and with the quality of the whole. Thus self-perception would be expected to have an all-or-none quality such that any perception of negative attributes would negatively color the view of the whole. The admission of negative attribution would, thus, be particularly damaging at this level. At more advanced levels, characterized by greater differentiation and hierarchic integration, negative and positive characteristics of the self should be able to be considered simultaneously, and a sense of positive self-regard would not be expected to depend upon a positive evaluation of all aspects of the self or even upon an additive conceptualization, whereby the sum of positive qualities exceeds the total number of negative characteristics. (An additive conceptualization presupposes a juxtaposed organization of parts wherein equal value is ascribed to each part.) With increased maturity, the valence of self-regard would be expected to depend upon a more complex organization wherein certain characteristics would assume central importance while other attributes would be of peripheral significance.

Experiential Determinants in Self-Image Disparity

A variety of experiential variables that affect how others respond to the individual in everyday social–psychological interactions have been found to have important moderating influences on children's self-images. In comparison to their noninstitutionalized counterparts, institutionalized children have been found to display lower ideal self-images and lower real self-images (Zigler *et al.*, 1972). Retarded children have been found to have lower aspirations, as indicated by the ideal self-image (Zigler *et al.*, 1972), and lower real self-images (Leahy *et al.*, 1982) than nonretarded children of similar mental age. Moreover, the findings of Leahy *et al.* point to the moderating influence of retardation status on other developmental measures and suggest that these influences may at times be particularly damaging to the more able retarded children. Similarly the findings of Katz *et al.* (1975) suggest that social stigmatization resulting from being labeled emotionally disturbed and placed in special classes negatively affects children's real self-images. Ethnicity and low SES were found by D. Phillips and Zigler (1980) particularly to affect children's ideal self-images. In addition, a variety of other complex and interacting effects of gender, ethnicity, and SES were noted (D. Phillips & Zigler, 1980). Thus these findings suggest that children's daily social contexts and interpersonal exchanges may lie at the source of different developmental patterns in self-image disparity. Such evidence attests to the potential usefulness of adopting an individual differences orientation to the study of self-image. In addition to facilitating sensitive investigations of oftentimes subtle influences on children's self-images, this approach may be most appropriate for those efforts aimed at clarifying the phenomenological significance of the real–ideal disparity. As suggested by Gough's work with adults (Gough, Lazzari, & Fioravanti, 1978), although the self-image disparity cannot be considered an unequivocal indicator of psychological adjustment, differing degrees of real–ideal self-image discrepancy may promote personal striving for improvement, resourcefulness, and social effectiveness in different individuals. It would not be surprising to discover both group (e.g., children versus adults) and individual differences in the magnitude of self-image disparity that promotes self-improvement.

SELF-IMAGE DISPARITY IN ADULT PSYCHOPATHOLOGY: FURTHER RESEARCH

Self-Image Disparity, Social Competence, and Defensive Style

Although much of the subsequent research was with children, the cognitive-developmental interpretation of self-image disparity was first formulated and tested by Achenbach and Zigler (1963) with adult patient samples. Moreover, given the predominant concern of Rogers and his colleagues (C. R. Rogers & Dymond, 1954) with adult clinical populations (clients in psychotherapy) and the widespread use in the field of self-image disparity measures as indexes of adjustment and favorable outcome in psychotherapy, the issue of the relationship of self-image disparity to developmental level and adjustment status in adult patient groups continues to be of central importance. Achenbach and Zigler found that self-image disparity was significantly related to social competence as an indicator of maturity level, but not to adjustment status (psychiatric versus medical patients). Moreover they suggested that the developmental formulation could encompass the repression–sensitization findings in the self-image disparity literature (Altrocchi et al., 1960; Hillson & Worchel, 1957) inasmuch as sensitizing defenses can be interpreted as reflecting developmentally higher forms of functioning than repressive defenses.

A direct examination of the relationships between self-image disparity, adjustment status, defensive style, and social competence was undertaken by Feder (1968). The only significant relationship uncovered in this study was between self-image disparity and defensive style, with sensitizers showing larger disparity scores than repressors. Neither adjustment–maladjustment (medical versus psychiatric patients) nor social competence was related to magnitude of self-image disparity. Neither was defensive style found to be associated with maturity level as gauged by the social competence measure. These results, therefore, contradict the developmental thesis on two important points. First, Feder did not replicate Achenbach and Zigler's finding of a positive relation between degree of disparity and developmental level. Secondly, Feder's results did not yield a significant relationship between social competence and defensive style.

A number of procedural aspects of Feder's study may have contributed both to the discrepancy between her results and those of Achenbach and Zigler and to the failure to find any relationship between social competence and the repression–sensitization dimension. The design of Feder's investigation readily suggests one reason why she failed to confirm a relation between defensive style and social competence. Her design required an equal number of repressors and sensitizers at each competence level, thus creating a forced independence between the two variables. Furthermore, in contrast to Achenbach and Zigler's method of scoring social competence on the basis of patients' case history records, Feder classified subjects into high or low social-competence groups on the basis of an information sheet which they completed. Yet if low competence individuals are also repressors (who tend to use denial and repression in response to threatening situations), they might tend to falsify information regarding education, occupation, and employment history for an unknown researcher. This, of course, would result in erroneous placement of these subjects into competence groups.

Differences in the self-image measures employed across the two studies may likewise have contributed to the inconsistent findings. Feder's measure was in a Q-sort format which could be considerably more difficult to complete than the questionnaire and checklist instruments used by Achenbach and Zigler. It is also possible that low competence subjects may have had difficulty rating themselves on some of the Q-sort items, such as "ardent," "candid," or "intuitive." The forced rectilinear distribution of responses on Feder's instrument would also minimize the effects of cognitive differentiation on the task. This might be expected to limit potential differences between subject groups.

Mylet, Styfco, and Zigler (1979) looked into these procedural issues in an attempt to reconcile and/or clarify the conflicting results obtained by Achenbach and Zigler (1963) and Feder (1968). The primary focus of Mylet et al. was on interrelationships between social competence, self-image disparity, and defensive style, although adjustment status was also considered. In addition, the work of Achenbach and Zigler was extended through the examination of the components of self-image disparity (i.e., the real and the ideal self) as well as disparity scores.

Eighty hospitalized male psychiatric and nonpsychiatric patients served as subjects. Based on scores on the Zigler–Phillips social competence index, the groups of 40 psychiatric and 40 medical or surgical patients were subdivided into equal groups ($N = 20$) of high and low competence individuals. All psychiatric subjects were first admission patients with primary diagnoses of schizophrenia, psychoneurosis, or personality disorder. The medical and surgical patients had no history of psychiatric hospitalization and no illnesses judged to have a major psychiatric component or to be terminal.

Three instruments were employed to measure self-image disparity: the six-alternative questionnaire and the checklist instruments employed by Achenbach and Zigler and the Q-sort measure used by Feder. The repression–sensitization scale used by Altrocchi et al. (1960) as modified by Byrne (1964) was employed to gauge defensive style. To test the possibility that subjects might not have been able to respond knowledgeably to the items in Feder's Q-sort, a multiple-choice vocab-

TABLE 1.7
Mean Disparity Scores for Each Group

Group[a]	Questionnaire	Trait list	Q-sort
High competence			
Psychiatric	22.90	12.85	38.70
Nonpsychiatric	22.00	8.60	36.30
Low competence			
Psychiatric	16.00	8.40	29.20
Nonpsychiatric	9.45	7.05	32.25

[a]$N = 20$ for each group.

ulary test containing items from the Q-sort and from the other two self-image measures was devised. To test the hypothesis that defensive style is related to social competence, a correlational procedure was employed in which the repression–sensitization scores of the total sample (differing widely in social competence) were related to competence ratings. A check on biographical information provided by subjects was obtained when possible.

The mean self-image disparity scores on all three measures are presented in Table 1.7. In clear confirmation of developmental expectations, the high competence patients displayed greater real–ideal disparity on the questionnaire ($p < .001$), the trait list ($p < .05$), and the Q-sort measure ($p < .001$).

The tendency of low developmental individuals to give more extreme responses than high developmental groups ($p < .001$) was strongly evident in this study as it has been in the previous work surveyed (Achenbach & Zigler, 1963; Katz & Zigler, 1967; D. Phillips & Zigler, 1980; Zigler et al., 1972). However, an interesting interaction effect was also noted. A greater difference in extreme responding appeared between the two low competence groups (psychiatric and nonpsychiatric) than between the two high competence groups. This finding lends some support to the suggestion of Achenbach and Zigler that in high competence individuals who become mentally ill the tendency to discriminate finely is little affected, but that low competence people who become mentally ill tend to discriminate even less finely than they did prior to their illness. This phenomenon may underlie the commonly observed and reported pattern in which high competence patients continue to think about and attempt to cope with the problems that have befallen them, and thus evidence a better prognosis than low competence patients (Marsh, Glick, & Zigler, 1981; Zigler et al., 1979; Zigler & Phillips, 1961b).

Contrary to the findings of Achenbach and Zigler, the psychiatric patients were found to have higher self-image disparities than the non-psychiatric group on the questionnaire ($p < .001$) and trait list ($p < .05$) measures. This finding is consistent with the Rogerian position that maladjusted individuals will have higher self-image disparities than psychologically adjusted individuals. However, in the analysis of the questionnaire measure, the difference in disparity between psychiatric and nonpsychiatric patients was found to hold only for the low competence patients. It thus appears that the high competence individual, even when judged maladjusted, continues to resemble equally high competence individuals considered to be psychologically adjusted.

The differences between the patient groups (high versus low social competence and psychologically adjusted versus maladjusted) in self-image disparity appeared to reflect differences in the manner in which these groups assessed both their real and ideal selves. On both the questionnaire and the checklist instruments, the high competence patients (in both the psychiatric and nonpsychiatric samples) evidenced lower real self-images than low competence patients ($p < .025$). In addition, however, the psychiatric patients' assessments of their real selves were lower than those of the nonpsychiatric group ($p < .001$). The finding that high competence individuals think less well of themselves than low competence individuals, although counterintuitive, is consistent with the developmental theorizing advanced by Zigler and his colleagues. The finding that psychiatric patients have a poorer self-image than nonpsychiatric patients presents a problem of interpretation.

Within the Rogerian framework, a causal chain is suggested whereby the maladjusted individual thinks poorly of himself or herself and as a result experiences dissatisfaction and/or anxiety which leads to the individual receiving psychological assistance (i.e., going into outpatient treatment or being hospitalized). A quite different interpretation of the low self-image of psychiatric patients can be advanced. Rather than a low self-image resulting in psychiatric status, psychiatric status may result in a low self-image. This latter interpretation is consistent with the view that in addition to developmental influences, the real and ideal self-images are influenced by gross differences in life histories, especially those differences related to how others react to the individual in everyday social–psychological interactions (Katz et al., 1975; Leahy et al., 1982; D. Phillips & Zigler, 1980; Zigler et al., 1972). As was the case with institutionalized children and children assigned to special classes for the emotionally disturbed and mentally retarded, it would not be surprising to discover that the stigma associated with being a psychiatric patient, particularly a hospitalized one, would result in a lowered self-image.

However, contrary to the developmental trend observed with children (Katz & Zigler, 1967; Katz et al., 1975; D. Phillips & Zigler, 1980; Zigler et al., 1972), the low competence patients were found to have higher ideal self-image scores ($p < .05$) on the questionnaire, but not the checklist measure. This finding may have been due to the very strong tendency of the low competence patients to make more extreme responses. Extreme response tendencies have been found to be more marked on ideal self-image ratings (Katz & Zigler, 1967; D. Phillips & Zigler, 1980) and selecting extreme positive responses would result in higher ideal-self scores.

Significant relationships were obtained between the repression–sensitization measure and both social competence and self-image disparity. Consistent with the developmental position, high competence patients, both psychiatric and nonpsychiatric, were found to have higher sensitization scores than low competence patients ($p < .001$). Consistent with the findings of Feder, significant correlations were obtained between repression–sensitization scores and each of the three self-image disparity measures ($p < .001$ for the questionnaire and trait list, $p < .01$ for the Q-sort). Psychiatric patients were found to have higher sensitization scores than nonpsychiatric patients, a finding which is not surprising inasmuch as the repression–sensitization measure was based upon Minnesota Multiphasic Personality Inventory (MMPI) scales which were developed to be sensitive to maladjustment of various types.

Further evidence for the construct validity of self-image disparity (see especially D. Phillips & Zigler, 1982) was provided by the finding that all three measures (questionnaire, checklist, and Q-sort) were significantly intercorrelated (all p's $< .001$). This does not mean, however, that every measure of self-image disparity is as good as every other measure. Findings involving the number of patients who refused to complete the Q-sort and the greater number of vocabulary test errors made by low competence patients ($p < .001$) and on Q-sort words in comparison to words derived from the other two self-image instruments ($p < .001$) suggest that the Q-sort instrument may be a poor measure of self-image disparity especially for low competence individuals. Thus the inconsistency between the findings of Achenbach and Zigler and Feder appeared in part to be due to the different measures employed in the two studies. In addition the different procedures employed by Achenbach and Zigler and Feder to assess social competence may have contributed to the divergent results obtained in the two studies. When the information provided by the self-report biographical form from which Feder obtained social competence information was checked against case history records within the psychiatric sample, almost half of the low competence patients were found to have provided inaccurate or misleading information. By contrast no conflicting information was found for the high competence group.

Self-Image and Psychopathological Disturbance: Other Research Findings

With the exception of work comparing individuals who enter outpatient counseling with those who do not and the self-images of clients at earlier and later points in the course of counseling, there is a relative paucity of information concerning self-image disparity in psychiatric patient groups, particularly inpatients. Nevertheless certain other findings bear on issues raised by the work of Achenbach and Zigler, Feder, and Mylet *et al.* In the first place, the relationship between defensive style and self-image disparity noted by Altrocchi *et al.* (1960), Feder (1968), and Mylet *et al.* (1979) receives further confirmation from other studies in which lower real–ideal disparity has been found to be associated with denial and repression in normal samples and psychiatric patients (Bauer & Achenbach, 1976; Berger, 1955; Block & Thomas, 1955; Byrne, 1961; Cowen, Heilizer, Axelrod, & Alexander, 1957; Zuckerman & Monashkin, 1957). Furthermore the postulation suggested by Achenbach and Zigler (1963) and tested in children by Katz *et al.* (1975) that greater self-image disparity would be associated with symptom patterns reflecting more mature forms of functioning is also supported by findings that greater real–ideal disparity and lower real self-images are associated with depression and self-blame and with anxiety in adolescent and adult (psychiatric and nonpsychiatric) subjects (Bill, 1954; Bills, Vance, & McLean, 1951; Cowen *et al.*, 1957; Engel, 1959; Flippo & Lewinsohn, 1971; Guerney & Burton, 1963; Kaplan & Pokorney, 1969; Ohnmacht & Muro, 1967; Rosenberg, 1965; Winkler & Myers, 1963; Zuckerman & Monashkin, 1957). By contrast, paranoid schizophrenics have been found to exhibit less real–ideal disparity than either nonparanoid patients or normal subjects (Havener & Izard, 1962; A. H. Rogers, 1958), a finding assumed to reflect characteristic paranoid defenses of denial and projection. As indicated previously, considerable work on the developmental approach to psychopathology has pointed to the developmentally higher status of depression, self-blame, anxiety and sensitizing defenses (e.g., Zigler & Phillips, 1960, 1962).

Mirroring the contradiction between the findings of Mylet *et al.*

(1979) and those of Achenbach and Zigler (1963), Feder (1968), and Katz *et al.* (1975) in regard to the relationship between self-image disparity and adjustment status, other research has yielded similarly inconsistent findings. Chase (1957) observed greater disparity in psychiatric rather than medical inpatients. In comparison with nonhospitalized normal controls, Zuckerman, Baer, and Monashkin (1956) found greater disparity in psychiatric inpatients. However, no relationship (Zuckerman & Monashkin, 1957) or a relationship opposite to expectation (Zuckerman *et al.*, 1956) was observed between degree of disparity and ratings of patients' adjustment based on the examination of case history summaries. In the Zuckerman *et al.* study, female patients who were rated as most poorly adjusted displayed less real–ideal disparity. Although their results are not directly comparable to other findings since they employed a nonverbal measure of self-esteem, Ziller and his colleagues (Long, Ziller, & Bankes, 1970; Ziller & Grossman, 1967; Ziller, Megas, & DeCencio, 1964) have repeatedly observed more negative self-evaluations in hospitalized neuropsychiatric patients and in children institutionalized for behavioral problems as compared with noninstitutionalized normal controls. Whether this attenuated self-esteem should be construed as reflecting psychological disturbance or interpreted as resulting from institutionalization, social stigmatization, and other negative experiences associated with psychiatric status is unclear. Certainly the latter interpretation can account for Zuckerman *et al.*'s (1956) finding that greater real–ideal disparity was associated with psychiatric status but not with degree of disturbance within an inpatient group. At a more general level, it becomes apparent that the effects of institutionalization and other stigmatizing circumstances must be taken into account in research concerned with the relation between psychiatric–nonpsychiatric status and the self-concept. At present, it does not appear possible to determine whether a low self-image results in psychiatric status or conversely whether psychiatric status eventuates in a low self-image (Mylet *et al.*, 1979).

INTERRELATIONSHIPS AMONG FACETS OF SELF-REGARD: A POSSIBLE RECONCILIATION OF DEVELOPMENTAL AND ROGERIAN POSITIONS

The cognitive-developmental formulation stands in contrast to the nondevelopmental approach of Rogers and his colleagues. Within the Rogerian framework (C. R. Rogers, 1951; C. R. Rogers & Dymond,

1954), congruence between real and ideal self-images is interpreted as indicating positive self-regard and assumed to be linearly related to personal and social adjustment. Conceptualized developmentally, such congruence becomes inadequate to gauge feelings of self-worth across maturity levels. While relationships may be obtained between a sense of self-worth and adaptation, the developmental formulation requires a more precise definition of the multifaceted and changing nature of self-regard and a more complex conceptualization of relations between this construct and adjustment.

As facets of self-regard, self-esteem, self-acceptance, the real self-image, and real–ideal-self disparity are not equivalent and may reflect different self-evaluating processes. Although these constructs have been distinguished at a theoretical level, they have frequently been treated as overlapping in self-concept research (Harter, 1983; Wylie, 1974). The cognitive-developmental interpretation requires that the various aspects of self-regard be clearly differentiated since relationships between them would be assumed to change over the course of development. Allport (1955, 1961) has differentiated attributive concepts of the real and ideal self (the self-image) from globally organized feelings of self-esteem and self-satisfaction (ego-enhancement), presumed to be rooted in earlier experience. If on the basis of structure and origin, the self-image is construed as developmentally more advanced, one may question the degree to which the real self-image and disparity between real and ideal self-images reflect or influence self-esteem or self-satisfaction. Is the individual who describes real and ideal self-images differently affectively bothered by the discrepancy, or might the descriptions, particularly at higher maturity levels, be undertaken primarily as cognitive tasks bearing limited relationship to persistent subjective feelings of self-doubt? Extremely negative responses in rating the real self-image and very large real–ideal disparities might conceivably reflect this aspect of self-experience more closely than moderate ratings and discrepancies. It is possible that like basic trust, a global sense of self-esteem derives from early nonverbal experiences and remains somewhat immune to conceptual modification. Like self-esteem, self-acceptance unquestionably implies an emotional component. However, self-acceptance would seem to depend upon developmentally more advanced functioning since it involves an articulated awareness of the self with the ability to recognize and accept negative qualities. A moderately positive rating of the real self and a moderately but not extremely small real–ideal-self disparity might most plausibly reflect self-acceptance.

In regard to the capacity of ratings of the real self and of subtractive measures of self-image disparity to indicate subjective feelings of self-worth, developmental research findings point to the need for a more complex categorization that can reflect patterns of organization. If magnitude of disparity indicates differentiation and is, therefore, not necessarily an ominous sign, might there be a point beyond which disparity becomes too great and must be interpreted as potentially debilitating? Given the more positive ideal self-image characteristic of higher maturity levels, a real–ideal disparity occasioned by a high ideal self-image and occurring at the positive end of the scale must be distinguished from a disparity reflecting a low ideal self-image and an even more negative conceptualization of the real self. Attention must be paid to absolute values of real and ideal self-ratings. However, merely shifting the focus of inquiry from discrepancy scores to absolute values of self-ratings would be insufficient. The real self-image cannot be accepted as an adequate gauge of self-regard, since negative attribution may have different meanings at different developmental levels. Moreover, as Wylie (1974) has suggested, an image of the ideal self may be implied in the rating of the real self-images. Categorization in terms of qualitative change must supplant the measurement of quantitative difference.

The developmental changes that have been observed in the organization of the self-images necessitate a more complex conceptualization of the relationship between the self-images and adjustment. The influence of the ideal self-image on adaptive functioning seems especially to merit wider investigation. Since the ideal self-image has been conceptualized as providing motivation and goal direction, and as facilitating development and enabling the organization and integration of experience (Allport, 1955; Baldwin, 1911; Van den Daele, 1968), a generally positive relationship between a high ideal self-image and adaptation would be expected, but with notable exceptions. Extremely high and unrealistic aspirations could paralyze rather than facilitate adaptive functioning. Such aspirations could also represent denial and the substitution of fantasy solutions for realistic striving. Characteristic in these exceptions is the absence of a perceived relationship between the ideal and the real self-images.

Applying the orthogenetic principle to these considerations, three levels can be distinguished in the organization of relations between real and ideal self-images. At the earliest level, characterized by global organization, the ideal self-image, being inseparable from the real self-image, could provide no motivation or direction for change. An intermediate level of organization can be conceptualized as involving differentiation with insufficient reintegration of real and ideal self-images.

Aware of the discrepancy between the ideal and the actual, an individual at this stage of development might be motivated for change but lack a sense of appropriate directions and means for its accomplishment. Feelings of self-dissatisfaction and helplessness might be especially evident at this stage. At the highest level of organization, the ideal self-image would be expected to be conceptualized in relation to an articulated image of the real self, incorporating personal as well as social values. Rather than desiring to be utterly different or aspiring to unyielding social stereotypes of the ideal person, individuals at this stage might be more likely to envision change as the development and modification of qualities they already perceive in themselves. Thus the reintegration of real and ideal self-images should not only provide motivation for change, it should enable conceptualization of appropriate directions and subgoals, thereby facilitating adaptation.

The positions of Kohlberg (1964), Loevinger (1966, 1976), and Van den Daele (1968) are compatible with this formulation in that they posit a curvilinear relationship between developmental level and conformity to external values with the integration of personal and social values characterizing advanced levels. Erikson (1968) has stressed both the cognitive complexity required for an integration of various images of the self and the central importance of this integration in facilitating adult development and adaptation.

Conceptualizing relations between real and ideal self-images on the basis of three levels of organization allows for a reconciliation of findings which have been presented in support of the Rogerian position with developmental research evidence and with findings indicating no relation between real–ideal disparity and psychiatric status and/or adjustment. Supportive of the Rogerian position is evidence indicating greater real–ideal disparity in therapy clients than control subjects and a decrease in disparity over the course of successful therapy (Raimy, 1948; C. R. Rogers, 1951; C. R. Rogers & Dymond, 1954; Sheerer, 1949; Stock, 1949). An intermediate level in the organization of relations between real and ideal self-images may be most characteristic in outpatient therapy clients since their entrance into therapy is frequently self-motivated and accompanied by expressions of self-disparagement, depression, and anxiety. For such individuals improvement might well entail reintegration of real and ideal self-images with a resulting decrease in real–ideal disparity. In contrast to these clients, a developmentally earlier global level of organization might be more characteristic in certain psychiatric inpatients and in children with action symptoms. For these groups, diminished real–ideal-self disparity would not be construed as a favorable sign, and effective treatment might well entail increased disparity.

REFERENCES

Achenbach, T. (1966). The classification of children's psychiatric symptoms: A factor-analytic study. *Psychological Monographs, 80* (6, Whole No. 615).

Achenbach, T., & Zigler, E. (1963). Social competence and self-image disparity in psychiatric and nonpsychiatric patients. *Journal of Abnormal and Social Psychology, 67*, 197–205.

Achenbach, T., & Zigler, E. (1968). Cue-learning and problem-learning strategies in normal and retarded children. *Child Development, 3*, 827–848.

Allport, G. W. (1937). *Personality: A psychological interpretation.* New York: Holt, Rinehart & Winston.

Allport, G. W. (1955). *Becoming: Basic considerations for a psychology of personality.* New Haven, CT: Yale University Press.

Allport, G. W. (1961). *Pattern and growth in personality.* New York: Holt, Rinehart & Winston.

Altrocchi, J., Parsons, O. A., & Dickoff, H. (1960). Changes in self-ideal discrepancy in repressors and sensitizers. *Journal of Abnormal and Social Psychology, 61*, 67–72.

Anderson, S., & Messick, S. (1974). Social competency in young children. *Developmental Psychology, 10*, 282–293.

Baldwin, J. M. (1911). *Genetic epistomology: Vol. 3. Thought and things.* New York: Macmillan.

Bauer, S. R., & Achenbach, T. (1976). Self-image disparity, repression-sensitization, and extraversion-introversion. A unitary dimension? *Journal of Personality Assessment, 40*, 46–51.

Berger, E. M. (1955). Relationships among acceptance of self, acceptance of others, and MMPI scores. *Journal of Counseling Psychology, 2*, 279–284.

Bills, R. E. (1953). Rorschach characteristics of persons scoring high and low in acceptance of self. *Journal of Consulting Psychology, 17*, 36–38.

Bills, R. E. (1954). Self-concepts and Rorschach signs of depression. *Journal of Consulting Psychology, 18*, 135–137.

Bills, R. E., Vance, E. L., & McLean, O. S. (1951). An index of adjustment and values. *Journal of Consulting Psychology, 15*, 257–261.

Block, J., & Thomas, H. (1955). Is satisfaction with self a measure of adjustment? *Journal of Abnormal and Social Psychology, 51*, 254–259.

Bowerman, C. E., & Kinch, J. W. (1959). Changes in family and peer orientation of children between the fourth and tenth grades. *Social Forces, 27*, 206–211.

Brownfain, J. J. (1952). Stability of the self-concept as a dimension of personality. *Journal of Abnormal and Social Psychology, 47*, 597–606.

Byrne, D. (1961). The Repression-Sensitization scale: Rationale, reliability, and validity. *Journal of Personality, 29*, 334–349.

Byrne, D. (1964). Repression-sensitization as a dimension of personality. In B. A. Maher (Ed.), *Progress in experimental personality research.* New York: Academic Press.

Carpenter, T., & Busse, T. (1969). The development of self-concept in Negro and white welfare children. *Child Development, 40*, 935–939.

Chandler, M. J. (1973). Egocentrism and antisocial behavior: The assessment and training of social perspective-taking skills. *Developmental Psychology, 9*, 326–332.

Chase, P. H. (1957). Self concepts in adjusted and maladjusted hospital patients. *Journal of Consulting Psychology, 21*, 495–497.

Coleman, J. S., Campbell, E. Q., Hobson, C. J., McPartland, J., Mood, A. M., Weinfeld, F. D., & York, R. L. (1966). *Equality of educational opportunity.* Report prepared for

U.S. Department of Health, Education, and Welfare. Washington, DC: U.S. Government Printing Office.

Cowen, E. L., Heilizer, F., Axelrod, H. S., & Alexander, S. (1957). The correlates of manifest anxiety in perceptual reactivity, rigidity, and self-concept. *Journal of Consulting Psychology, 21,* 405–411.

Cromwell, R. L. (1963). A social learning approach to mental retardation. In N. R. Ellis (Ed.), *Handbook of mental deficiency.* New York: McGraw-Hill.

Deutsch, M., Katz, I., & Jensen, A. (Eds.). (1968). *Social class, race, and psychological development.* New York: Holt, Rinehart, & Winston.

Elkind, D. (1969). Piagetian and psychometric conceptions of intelligence. *Harvard Educational Review, 39,* 319–337.

Engel, N. (1959). The stability of the self-concept in adolescence. *Journal of Abnormal and Social Psychology, 58,* 211–215.

Erikson, E. H. (1968). *Identity: Youth and crisis.* New York: Norton.

Feder, C. (1968). Relationship between self-acceptance and adjustment, repression sensitization and social competence. *Journal of Abnormal Psychology, 73,* 317–322.

Flippo, J. R., & Lewinsohn, P. M. (1971). Effects of failure on the self-esteem of depressed and nondepressed subjects. *Journal of Consulting and Clinical Psychology, 36,* 151.

Freud, A. (1952). The mutual influences in the development of ego and id: Introduction to the discussion. *Psychoanalytic Study of the Child, 7,* 42–50.

Garmezy, N., Masten, A., Nordstrom, L., & Ferrarese, M. (1979). The nature of competence in normal and deviant children. In M. W. Kent & J. E. Rolf (Eds.), *The primary prevention of psychopathology: Promoting social competence and coping in children* (Vol. 3). Hanover, NH: University Press of New England.

Goldman, A. (1962). A comparative-developmental approach to schizophrenia. *Psychological Bulletin, 59,* 57–69.

Gough, H. G., Lazzari, R., & Fioravanti, M. (1978). Self versus ideal self: A comparison of five adjective check list indices. *Journal of Consulting and Clinical Psychology, 46,* 1085–1091.

Guerney, B. Jr., & Burton, J. L. (1963). Relationships among anxiety and self, typical peer, and ideal percepts in college women. *Journal of Social Psychology, 61,* 335–344.

Harter, S. (1978). Effectance motivation reconsidered: Toward a developmental model. *Human Development, 21,* 34–64.

Harter, S. (1983). Developmental perspectives on the self-system. In P. H. Mussen (Ed.), *Handbook of child psychology* (4th ed.). Vol. 4. *Socialization, personality, and social development* (Ed. E. M. Hetherington). New York: Wiley.

Havener, P. H., & Izard, C. E. (1962). Unrealistic self-enhancement in paranoid schizophrenics. *Journal of Consulting Psychology, 26,* 65–68.

Hilden, A. H. (1958). Q-sort correlation: Stability and random choice of statements. *Journal of Consulting Psychology, 22,* 45–50.

Hillson, J. S., & Worchel, P. (1957). Self concept and defensive behavior in the maladjusted. *Journal of Consulting Psychology, 21,* 83–88.

Hollingshead, A. B. (1957). *Two-factor index of social position.* Unpublished manuscript, Yale University, New Haven, CT.

Horowitz, F. D., & Paden, L. Y. (1973). The effectiveness of environmental intervention programs. In B. M. Caldwell & H. N. Ricciuti (Eds.), *Review of child development research* (Vol. 3). Chicago: University of Chicago Press.

James, W. (1890). *Principles of psychology.* New York: Holt.

Kagan, J. (1964). Acquisition and significance of sex-typing and sex role identity. In M. L. Hoffman & L. W. Hoffman (Eds.), *Review of child development research* (Vol. 1.). New York: Russell Sage Foundation.

Kaplan, H. B., & Pokorny, A. D. (1969). Self-derogation and psychosocial adjustment. *Journal of Nervous and Mental Disease, 149,* 421–434.

Katz, P., & Zigler, E. (1967). Self-image disparity: A developmental approach. *Journal of Personality and Social Psychology, 5,* 186–195.

Katz, P., Zigler, E., & Zalk, S. (1975). Children's self-image disparity: The effects of age, maladjustment, and action-thought orientation. *Developmental Psychology, 11,* 546–550.

Kohlberg, L. (1964). Development of moral character and moral ideology. In M. L. Hoffman & L. W. Hoffman (Eds.), *Review of child development and research* New York: Russell Sage Foundation.

Kohlberg, L. (1969). Stage and sequence: The cognitive-developmental approach to socialization. In D. Goslin (Ed.), *Handbook of socialization: Theory and research.* New York: Rand McNally.

Kohlberg, L. (1976). Moral stages and moralization: The cognitive-developmental approach. In T. Lickona (Ed.), *Moral development and behavior: Theory, research, and social issues.* New York: Holt, Rinehart & Winston.

Kohlberg, L., Lacrosse, J., & Ricks, D. (1972). The predictability of adult mental health from childhood behavior. In B. Wolman (Ed.), *Manual of child psychopathology.* New York: McGraw-Hill.

Kokenes, B. (1974). Grade level differences in factors of self-esteem. *Developmental Psychology, 10,* 954–958.

Kruger, A. K. (1954). Direct and substitute modes of tension reduction in terms of developmental level: An experimental analysis by means of the Rorschach test (Doctoral dissertation, Clark University, 1954). *Dissertation Abstracts International, 14,* 1806. (University Microfilms No. 00-09,013)

Lazar, I., Hubbell, V. R., Murray, H., Rosche, M., & Royce, J. (1977, September). *The persistence of preschool effects.* Final Report to the Administration on Children, Youth and Families. Washington, D.C.: U.S. Government Printing Office.

Leahy, R. L. (1981). Parental practices and the development of moral judgment and self-image disparity during adolescence. *Developmental Psychology, 17,* 580–594.

Leahy, R., Balla, D., & Zigler, E. (1982). Role-taking, self-image, and imitation in retarded and nonretarded individuals. *American Journal of Mental Deficiency, 86,* 372–379.

Leahy, R. L., & Huard, C. (1976). Role taking and self-image disparity in children. *Developmental Psychology, 12,* 501–508.

Lerner, P. (1968). Correlations of social competence and level of cognitive-perceptual functioning in male schizophrenics. *Journal of Nervous and Mental Disease, 146,* 412–416.

Lewine, R. R., Watt, N. F., Prentky, R. A., & Fryer, J. H. (1980). Childhood social competence in functionally disordered psychiatric patients and in normals. *Journal of Abnormal Psychology, 89,* 132–138.

Light, C. S., Zax, M., & Gardener, D. H. (1965). Relationships of age, sex, and intelligence level to extreme response style. *Journal of Personality and Social Psychology, 2,* 907–909.

Loevinger, J. (1966). The meaning and measurement of ego development. *American Psychologist, 21,* 195–206.

Loevinger, J. (1976). *Ego development: Conceptions and theories.* San Francisco: Jossey-Bass.

Loevinger, J., & Wessler, R. (1970). *Measuring ego development* (Vol. 1). San Francisco: Jossey-Bass.

Long, B. H., Ziller, R. C., & Bankes, J. (1970). Self-other orientations of institutionalized behavior-problem adolescents. *Journal of Counseling and Clinical Psychology, 34*, 43–47.

Maccoby, E. E., & Jacklin, C. N. (1974). *The psychology of sex differences.* Stanford, CA: Stanford University Press.

Marsh, A., Glick, M., & Zigler, E. (1981). Premorbid social competence and the "revolving door" phenomenon in psychiatric hospitalization. *Journal of Nervous and Mental Disease, 169*, 315–319.

Maslow, A. H. (1954). *Motivation and personality.* New York: Harper & Row.

McCandless, B. R. (1967). *Children: Behavior and development* (2nd ed.). New York: Holt, Rinehart & Winston.

McDonald, R. L., & Gynther, M. D. (1965). Relationship of self and ideal-self descriptions with sex, race, and class in southern adolescents. *Journal of Personality and Social Psychology, 1*, 85–88.

Mead, G. (1934). *Mind, self and society.* Chicago: University of Chicago Press.

Mediax Associates, Inc. (1980). *Accept my profile: Perspectives for Head Start profiles of program effects on children.* Prepared for the Administration for Children, Youth, and Families, Office of Human Development Services, Department of Health, Education, & Welfare. Westport, CT.

Misch, R. (1954). The relationship of motoric inhibition to developmental level and ideational functioning: An analysis by means of the Rorschach test (Doctoral dissertation, Clark University, 1954). *Dissertation Abstracts International, 14*, 1810. (University Microfilms No. 00-09-016)

Montemayor, R., & Eisen, M. (1977). The development of self-conceptions from childhood to adolescence. *Developmental Psychology, 13*, 314–319.

Mullener, N., & Laird, J. D. (1971). Some developmental changes in the organization of self-evaluations. *Developmental Psychology, 5*, 233–236.

Mylet, M., Styfco, S., & Zigler, E. (1979). The interrelationship between self-image disparity and social competence, defensive style, and adjustment status. *Journal of Nervous and Mental Disease, 167*, 553–560.

Ohnmacht, F. W., & Muro, J. J. (1967). Self-acceptance: Some anxiety and cognitive style relationships. *Journal of Psychology, 67*, 235–239.

Ollendick, T., Balla, D., & Zigler, E. (1971). Expectancy of success and the probability learning of retarded children. *Journal of Abnormal Psychology, 77*, 275–281.

Phillips, D. (1981). *High-achieving students with low academic self-concepts: Achievements motives and orientations.* Unpublished doctoral dissertation, Yale University, New Haven, CT.

Phillips, D., & Zigler, E. (1980). Children's self-image disparity: Effects of age, socioeconomic status, ethnicity, and gender. *Journal of Personality and Social Psychology, 39*, 689–700.

Phillips, D., & Zigler, E. (1982). *Real and ideal self-images in second and fifth grade children: Reliability, validity, and factorial structure.* Unpublished manuscript, Yale University, New Haven, CT.

Phillips, L. (1968). *Human adaptation and its failures.* New York: Academic Press.

Phillips, L., & Rabinovitch, M. S. (1958). Social role and patterns of symptomatic behavior. *Journal of Abnormal and Social Psychology, 57*, 181–186.

Phillips, L., & Zigler, E. (1961). Social competence: The action-thought parameter and vicariousness in normal and pathological behavior. *Journal of Abnormal and Social Psychology, 63*, 137–146.

Phillips, L., & Zigler, E. (1964). Role orientation, the action-thought dimension and outcome in psychiatric disorder. *Journal of Abnormal and Social Psychology, 68*, 381–389.

Piaget, J. (1951). Principle factors in determining evolution from childhood to adult life. In D. Rapaport (Ed.), *Organization and pathology of thought.* New York: Columbia University Press.

Piaget, J. (1960). *The psychology of intelligence.* Paterson, NJ: Littlefield, Adams.

Porter, J. (1971). *Black child, white child: The development of racial attitudes.* Cambridge, MA: Harvard University Press.

Powell, G. J., & Fuller, M. (1970). Self-concept and school desegregation. *American Journal of Orthopsychiatry, 40,* 303–304.

Proshansky, H., & Newton, P. (1968). The nature and meaning of Negro self-identity. In M. Deutsch, I. Katz, & J. Jensen (Eds.), *Social class, race, and psychological development.* New York: Holt, Rinehart & Winston.

Prugh, D. G., Staub, E. M., Sands, H. H., Kirschbaum, R., & Lenihan, E. (1953). A study of the emotional reactions of children and families to hospitalization and illness. *American Journal of Orthopsychiatry, 23,* 41–79.

Quinlan, D. M., Rogers, L. R., & Kegan, R. G. (1980, April). *Developmental dimensions of psychopathology.* Paper presented at the meeting of the Eastern Psychological Association Convention. Hartford, CT.

Rabinowitz, M. (1966). The relationship of self regard to the effectiveness of life experiences. *Journal of Counseling Psychology, 13,* 139–143.

Raimy, V. C. (1948). Self-reference in counselling interviews. *Journal of Consulting Psychology, 12,* 153–163.

Raskin, A., & Golob, R. (1966). Occurrence of sex, and social class differences in premorbid competence, symptom and outcome measures in acute schizophrenics. *Psychological Reports, 18,* 11–22.

Rest, J. (1975). Longitudinal study of the defining issues test of moral judgment: A strategy for analyzing developmental change. *Developmental Psychology, 11,* 738–748.

Rhine, R. W. (Ed.). (1981). *Making schools more effective: New directions from follow through.* New York: Academic Press.

Rogers, A. H. (1958). The self concept in paranoid schizophrenia. *Journal of Clinical Psychology, 14,* 365–366.

Rogers, C. R. (1951). *Client-centered therapy.* Boston: Houghton Mifflin.

Rogers, C. R., & Dymond, R. F. (Eds.). (1954). *Psychotherapy and personality change.* Chicago: University of Chicago Press.

Rosenberg, M. (1965). *Society and the adolescent self image.* Princeton, NJ: Princeton University Press.

Rosenberg, M. (1979). *Concerning the self.* New York: Basic Books.

Rosenberg, M., & Simmons, R. (1971). *Black and white self-esteem: The urban school child* (Monograph: Arnold and Caroline Rose Series in Ecology). Washington, DC: American Sociological Association.

Santostefano, S. (1970). The assessment of motives in childhood. *Psychological Reports, 26,* 639–649.

Scott, W. (1958). Research definitions of mental health and mental illness. *Psychological Bulletin, 55,* 1–45.

Sheerer, E. T. (1949). An analysis of the relationship between acceptance of and respect for others in ten counseling cases. *Journal of Consulting Psychology, 13,* 169–175.

Silverstein, B., & Krate, R. (1975). *Children of the dark ghetto—A developmental psychology.* New York: Praeger.

Stevenson, H. W. (1965). Social reinforcement of children's behavior. In L. P. Lipsitt & C. C. Spiker (Eds.), *Advances in child development and behavior* (Vol. 2). New York: Academic Press.

Stock, D. (1949). An investigation into the interrelations between the self concept and feelings directed towards other persons and groups. *Journal of Consulting Psychology, 13,* 176–180.

Stoodt, J., & Balla, D. (1974). *Developmental and experiential determinants of the self-concept of younger children.* Unpublished manuscript, Yale University, New Haven, CT.

Sundberg, N. D., Snowden, L. R., & Reynolds, W. M. (1978). Toward assessment of personal competence and incompetence in life situations. In M. R. Rosenzweig & L. W. Porter (Eds.), *Annual review of psychology* (Vol. 29). Palo Alto, CA: Annual Reviews.

Thorndike, E. L., & Lorge, I. (1972). *The teacher's word book of 30,000 words.* New York: Columbia University Press.

Trowbridge, N. (1972). Self-concept and socio-economic status in elementary school children. *American Educational Research Journal, 4,* 525–537.

Tudor, J. F. (1971). The development of class awareness in children. *Social Forces, 49,* 470–476.

Van den Daele, L. (1968). A developmental study of ego ideals. *Genetic Psychology Monographs, 78,* 191–256.

Walker, D. K. (1973). *Socioemotional measures for preschool and kindergarten children.* San Francisco: Jossey-Bass.

Weintraub, S. A. (1973). Self-control as a correlate of an internalizing–externalizing symptom dimension. *Journal of Abnormal Child Psychology, 1,* 292–307.

Werner, H. (1948). *Comparative psychology of mental development.* New York: Follett.

Werner, H. (1957). The concept of development from a comparative and organismic point of view. In D. B. Harris (Ed.), *The concept of development.* Minneapolis: University of Minnesota Press.

Winkler, R. C., & Myers, R. A. (1963). Some concomitants of self-ideal discrepancy measures of self-acceptance. *Journal of Counseling Psychology, 10,* 83–86.

Wylie, R. C. (1974). *The self-concept: Vol. 1. A review of methodological considerations and measuring instruments* (rev. ed.). Lincoln, NE: University of Nebraska Press.

Wylie, R. C. (1979). *The self-concept: Vol. 2. Theory and research on selected topics.* Lincoln, NE: University of Nebraska Press.

Yando, R. M., Seitz, V., & Zigler, E. (1979). *Intellectual and personality characteristics of children: Social class and ethnic group differences.* Hillsdale, NJ: Erlbaum.

Zigler, E. (1963). Metatheoretical issues in developmental psychology. In M. Marx (Ed.), *Psychological theory* (2nd ed.). New York: Macmillan.

Zigler, E. (1966a). Mental retardation: Current issues and approaches. In L. W. Hoffman & M. L. Hoffman (Eds.), *Review of child development research* (Vol. 2). New York: Russell Sage Foundation.

Zigler, E. (1966b). Research on personality structure in the retardate. In N. Ellis (Ed.), *International review of research in mental retardation* (Vol. 1). New York: Academic Press.

Zigler, E. (1969). Developmental versus difference theories of mental retardation and the problem of motivation. *American Journal of Mental Deficiency, 73,* 536–556.

Zigler, E. (1971). The retarded child as a whole person. In H. E. Adams & W. K. Boardman III (Eds.), *Advances in experimental clinical psychology* (Vol. 1). New York: Pergamon Press.

Zigler, E., Abelson, W., & Seitz, V. (1973). Motivational factors in the performance of economically disadvantaged children on the Peabody Picture Vocabulary Test. *Child Development, 44,* 294–303.

Zigler, E., Abelson, W., Trickett, P., & Seitz, V. (1982). Is an intervention program necessary in order to improve economically-disadvantaged children's IQ scores? *Child Development. 53*, 340–348.

Zigler, E., Balla, D., & Watson, N. (1972). Developmental and experiential determinants of self-image disparity in institutionalized and non-institutionalized retarded and normal children. *Journal of Personality and Social Psychology, 23*, 81–87.

Zigler, E., & Butterfield, E. C. (1968). Motivational aspects of changes in IQ test performance of culturally deprived nursery school children. *Child Development, 39*, 1–14.

Zigler, E., & Child, I. (1969). Socialization. In G. Lindzey & E. Aronson (Eds.), *The handbook of social psychology* (2nd ed.). Reading, MA: Addison-Wesley.

Zigler, E., Glick, M., & Marsh, A. (1979). Premorbid social competence and outcome among schizophrenic and nonschizophrenic patients. *Journal of Nervous and Mental Disease, 167*, 478–483.

Zigler, E., & Levine, J. (1981). Premorbid competence in schizophrenia: What is being measured? *Journal of Consulting and Clinical Psychology, 49*, 96–105.

Zigler, E., & Phillips, L. (1960). Social effectiveness and symptomatic behaviors. *Journal of Abnormal and Social Psychology, 61*, 231–238.

Zigler, E., & Phillips, L. (1961a). Case history data and psychiatric diagnosis. *Journal of Consulting Psychology, 25*, 458.

Zigler, E., & Phillips, L. (1961b). Social competence and outcome in psychiatric disorder. *Journal of Abnormal and Social Psychology, 63*, 264–271.

Zigler, E., & Phillips, L. (1962). Social competence and the process-reactive distinction in psychopathology. *Journal of Abnormal and Social Psychology, 65*, 215–222.

Zigler, E., & Trickett, P. (1978). IQ, social competence and evaluation of early childhood intervention programs. *American Psychologist, 33*, 789–798.

Ziller, R. C., & Grossman, S. A. (1967). A developmental study of the self-social constructs of normals and the neurotic personality. *Journal of Clinical Psychology, 23*, 15–21.

Ziller, R. C., Megas, J., & DeCencio, D. (1964). Self-social constructs of normal and acute neuropsychiatric patients. *Journal of Consulting Psychology, 28*, 59–63.

Zuckerman, M., Baer, M., & Monashkin, I. (1956). Acceptance of self, parents, and people in patients and normals. *Journal of Clinical Psychology, 12*, 327–332.

Zuckerman, M., & Monashkin, I. (1957). Self-acceptance and psychopathology. *Journal of Consulting Psychology, 21*, 145–148.

2

Competence as a Dimension of Self-Evaluation: Toward a Comprehensive Model of Self-Worth*

Susan Harter

INTRODUCTION

The dimension of *competence,* either implicitly or explicitly, has found its way into most formulations concerning the self-concept. Our intellectual heir, James (1892/1963) was one of the first to highlight the general importance of one's accomplishments in his definition of self-esteem. He considered *self-esteem* to be the ratio of one's "successes" to one's "pretensions," and in so doing implied that the relationship between our competence and our aspirations was a critical determinant of how we evaluate the self. White (1959, 1960, 1963) has also underscored the importance of competence, suggesting that in infancy self-esteem is closely linked to feelings of efficacy and, with development, to the more general cumulative sense of competence.

More recently, the dimension of competence has explicitly been identified in a variety of multidimensional models of the self (e.g., Coopersmith, 1967; Epstein, 1973; Gordon, 1968; Hales, 1979; Harter, 1983; L'Ecuyer, 1981, Mullener & Laird, 1971; Shavelson, Hubner, &

*Preparation of this chapter was facilitated by N.I.C.H.D. Grant # HD 09613.

Stanton, 1976). Moreover, in those psychometric instruments designed to assess self-concept, items and subscales tapping a range of competencies have typically been included (e.g., Coopersmith, 1967; Harter, 1982b; Piers & Harris, 1969). Academic skills, athletic skills, and social skills are among the most common.

In this chapter we first briefly review the role that competence plays in the various models of the self. Competence is viewed as one of several dimensions that feed into our sense of self-worth. Although competence is a focus, the major purpose of this chapter is to identify issues that we should consider in developing a comprehensive theory of self-worth. Within this context we deal with the issue of whether constructs such as self-worth or self-esteem are best viewed as global self-appraisals, or as an aggregate of differentiated self-perceptions across domains such as competence. Following James's lead, we explore the possibility that the relationship between one's ability estimates in a given domain and the importance of that domain to the individual is a critical determinant of one's sense of worth. We also deal with the issue of the *accuracy* of one's perceptions of competence, and how this may impact one's general sense of self.

In general, our models of the self-concept have been devoid of any serious developmental considerations; the more primary focus has been the demonstration of individual differences in how children or adults view the self. In this chapter there is an attempt to provide a theoretical framework for how the dimension of competence might undergo developmental change, particularly with regard to the *structure* of the self-concept. Implications of these developmental changes for general self-worth also are explored.

A major portion of this chapter is devoted to another theme that has received insufficient attention, namely the role of self-related *affect*, particularly with regard to one's competence judgments. We not only examine the specific affects aroused by the evaluation of one's competencies in different domains, but discuss the role of self-related affects as mediators of behavior. We also deal with those affects that uniquely refer to actions or attributes of the self, for example, pride and shame. We then explore how the issue of affect can be integrated into our emerging model of general self-worth.

The implications of another construct, *perceptions of control*, are also examined. For example, to what degree does a sense of responsibility for one's competencies influence one's evaluation of self? Moreover, what evidence is there that children will tend to take more responsibility for their successes than their failures, as a mechanism through which to protect the self? Greenwald (1980) has recently introduced the concept of *beneffectance* which refers to the tendency for the human organism to take credit for successes while denying the responsibility for one's failures. Through such an attitudinal orientation, wherein the self is viewed as selectively responsible for desired, but not undesired, outcomes, one can maintain or enhance one's sense of competence and self-worth. While Greenwald musters strong evidence for this tendency in adults, there has been virtually no data bearing upon the operation of beneffectance in children. Findings from our own recent research on the existence of this tendency in children, as well as its developmental course, are presented.

Finally, there is an attempt to provide a synthesis of these themes, in suggesting that our models of the self should contain more than the self-evaluations or self-judgments we typically obtain. It is argued that a richer picture of the self is gleaned if we not only take into account one's evaluation of dimensions such as competence, but also consider the accuracy of such judgments, the relative importance of success in the given domains, the affects attached to these judgments, and the person's sense of control in bringing about the desired outcome.

COMPETENCE WITHIN A MULTIDIMENSIONAL MODEL OF THE SELF-CONCEPT

At the outset, we acknowledged that competence represents an important self-evaluative judgment within many models of the self. One type of model involves the specification of a number of differentiated domains within the self-concept. Mullener and Laird (1971), for example, have identified five such domains, and in so doing place heavy emphasis on a number of different competencies. Their domains include intellectual skills, achievement traits, physical skills, interpersonal skills, and a sense of social responsibility. Thus, four of the five domains directly address issues involving competence or skillfulness.

The dimension of competence can also be discovered within those psychometric attempts to assess the self-concept or self-esteem of children. For example, intellectual competence emerges as one of the more stable factors on the Piers–Harris (Piers & Harris, 1969) self-concept scale. On the Coopersmith Self-Esteem Inventory (1967) *competence* (defined as one's success in meeting achievement demands) was initially designated as one of the major components of self-esteem, and approximately one-fifth of the items on this scale pertain to scholastic competence. Unfortunately, however, neither of these instruments can tell us much about the specific role that competence plays as a dimension of the self. With both instruments, an overall self-concept or self-esteem score is obtained by summing across all items, ignoring the specific content domains tapped.

In one sense this strategy seems defensible since psychometrically neither of these scales provides compelling evidence for the existence of scholastic competence as a distinct dimension. The findings are more suggestive in the case of the Piers–Harris instrument, where what is termed "intellectual and school status" does emerge as a factor. However, to date, these investigators have not sought to dimensionalize their instrument. In their initial model, the self-concept was viewed as relatively unidimensional. As a result, their scale construction strategy was not designed to demonstrate the possible underlying dimensions of the self-concept. Thus, while factors have appeared in their analyses, the magnitude of factor loadings, taken together with the large number of cross-loadings, do not point to a clear picture of differentiated dimensions that define the self.

In contrast to the unidimensional model underlying the initial construction of the Piers–Harris instrument, Coopersmith explicitly identified four dimensions of self-esteem that guided the construction of his measure. In addition to the dimension of competence, he also included peer interactions, family, and general references to the self. However, his cluster analysis, performed on an insufficiently small sample of children, did not reveal the systematic differentiation among these domains. Thus, Coopersmith concluded that children do not make distinctions among these domains; as a result, his instrument is scored by simply summing up responses to items across all domains to yield a global measure of self-esteem.

Unfortunately, as has been discussed elsewhere (see Harter, 1982b, 1983), Coopersmith's conclusion is unwarranted for a number of reasons: inadequacies in the model underlying the construction of this instrument, problems with domain and item selection, inappropriate data-analytic strategies, as well as a question format that pulls for socially desirable responses. Thus, while both the Piers–Harris and the Coopersmith measures include self-evaluative judgments concerning the child's competence, these items are indiscriminantly combined with items from other domains, such that there is relatively little we can learn about the specific contribution of competence judgments to the self-concept.

In contrast to the models and methods underlying the construction of the instruments just discussed, our own efforts to understand the role of competence have been domain specific from the outset, and this approach guided the construction of our Perceived Competence Scale for Children (Harter, 1982b). This scale was explicitly designed to tap three salient competence domains in the elementary school child's life, cognitive or scholastic competence, physical or athletic competence, and social competence with regard to one's peer relationships. The findings repeatedly reveal a very stable factor structure, indicating that children make clear distinctions among these competence domains, although the factors also correlate moderately with one another. Thus, we feel that there is compelling evidence for a differentiated model of the self that dictates the separate assessment of each possible dimension.

However, a number of critical questions remain to be addressed. For example, while the identification of several competence domains has been adequately demonstrated, if we are to develop a more all-encompassing model of the self, do we not need to include additional domains, and further demonstrate that these can also be meaningfully differentiated? We may well need to consider such dimensions as appearance, conduct and morality, and personality characteristics in addition to one's competence. Moreover, is a multidimensional approach sufficient, or do we need to consider a more hierarchical model in which lower-order postulates of the self-system are organized under higher-order personal constructs? If our preference is for a more hierarchical organization of dimensions, can we be content to structure the specific domains we have identified, or do we need to postulate some superordinate category of self-worth or self-esteem under which the more specific dimensions are organized? And if we feel the need for such a superordinate construct of self, how is it to be measured? Do we weigh the specific components in the aggregate to determine one's overall sense of self, or do we assess one's overall sense of self independently? We turn to these issues next.

HIERARCHICAL MODELS OF THE SELF

Generally, those who have favored a hierarchical approach to the self have begun with the assumption that the *self* is best viewed as a self-theory, a cognitive construction concerning one's attributes and characteristics (see Brim, 1976; Epstein, 1973; Kelly, 1955; Sarbin, 1962). For Kelly, one of the earliest such proponents, the self-theory was hierarchically organized into *core personal constructs*—those by which a person maintains his identity and existence—and *peripheral constructs* which can be altered without serious modifications of the core structure.

More recently, Epstein (1973) has suggested a hierarchical model in which *self-esteem* represents the superordinate category under which other subcategories of the self are organized. Four second-order postulates are identified: competence, moral self-approval, power, and love worthiness. Under the dimension of competence, Epstein suggests that there may be further subdivisions in terms of mental and physical competence; the lowest order postulates would involve the assessment of one's specific abilities. Epstein notes that as one moves from lower-order to higher-order postulates, the postulates become increasingly important to the maintenance of the individual's self-theory.

It is of interest to note the convergence between Epstein's second-order postulates and the four general dimensions of self-evaluation that have been isolated by Coopersmith (1967). Corresponding to Epstein's dimensions of competence, moral self-approval, power, and love worthiness are the following four dimensions for Coopersmith: (1) competence, (2) moral virtue, (3) power, and (4) significance (the acceptance, attention, and affection of others). To date, Epstein has not sought to demonstrate the empirical validity of his model, however. Coopersmith, on the other hand, has directed his attention toward the examination of two of these components, competence, and significance in the eyes of others (peer and family). However, his findings have not revealed the dimensionality of these domains, in large part due to methodological inadequacies in his approach.

There are others who have put forth more complicated hierarchical models of the self. For example, Shavelson *et al.* (1976) have proposed a model in which *general self-concept* (analogous to Spearman's g) is at the apex of the hierarchy. Two broad components of the general self-concept are identified, the academic and nonacademic self-concepts. The further subdivisions of the academic self-concept involve specific school subjects, for example, English, history, math, and science. The substructure of the nonacademic self-concept is somewhat more complex. Three dimensions are proposed, social self-concept, emotional self-concept, and physical self-concept. These are then further subdivided or defined. Social self-concept subsumes both peers and significant others. Emotional self-concept is viewed in terms of particular emotional states. Physical self-concept is subdivided into physical ability and physical appearance. Thus, in this hierarchical model, academic competence plays a major role, whereas other competencies, for example, physical ability and perhaps social skills, are viewed as lower-order constructs.

An even more differentiated picture of the constituents of the self-concept has been proposed by L'Ecuyer (1981). He first distinguishes between five self "structures" which he labels the material self, the personal self, the adaptive self, the social self, and self–nonself. Each of these has two substructures, as well as lower-order categories below each substructure. Thus, the *material* self is divided into the somatic self and the possessive self. The somatic self is further subdivided into physical traits and physical condition, whereas the possessive self is divided in the possession of objects and the possession of persons.

For L'Ecuyer, the *personal* self is divided into what he terms self-image and self-identity. Self-image is further divided into six categories, including aspirations, interests, emotions, and capacities or aptitudes; whereas self-identity is broken down into such categories as role and status, ideology, and abstract identity. The *adaptive* self is subdivided into self-esteem and self-activity, where self-esteem refers to competence and personal worth; and self-activity is divided into such subcategories as autonomy, ambivalence, dependency, and actualization. It is interesting to note that in L'Ecuyer's hierarchy, both competence and self-esteem are viewed as lower-order constructs, whereas in other models these are viewed as either first- or second-order postulates in the self-system.

L'Ecuyer's fourth major dimension, the *social* self, is subdivided into "preoccupations and social activities" as well as "reference to sex," each of which undergo further subcategorization. Finally, the *self–nonself* dimension is subdivided into reference to others and others' opinion of self. To date, L'Ecuyer has devoted major attention to charting developmental change in the lowest-order catgories, across the life span. Thus, while his theoretical model involves an elaborate hierarchy of self-constructs, at best his empirical work has revealed the existence of a number of dimensions, rather than the organization of these constructs into a hierarchical self-system.

At first glance, these hierarchical models have considerable appeal over those formulations that merely deal with the self-concept in general, or those which specify dimensions or components, but do not speak to their organizational structure. However, upon closer examination, two major questions become apparent: (1) What does it mean to identify *general self-concept* or *self-esteem* as a superordinate construct, as in the Epstein and Shavelson *et al.* models, and (2) what is it, exactly, that we are hierarchizing? Each of these questions needs to be addressed, before we can return to the more specific question of the role which competence plays in the self-system.

The Self as a Superordinate Construct

The following question seems to have haunted the self literature for many years: Is the self best characterized as a global self-evaluation or is it more fruitfully viewed as an aggregate of specific self-evaluative judgments across a variety of dimensions or domains? Both James and Cooley wrestled with this issue at the turn of the century, concluding that somehow we need to capture both. While James (1892/1963) acknowledged that we make evaluative judgments about our specific successes and failures, he contended that over and above these judgments "there is a certain average tone of self-feeling which each one of us carries about with him, and which is independent of the objective reasons we may have for satisfaction or discontent" (p. 171).

Cooley (1902) voiced a similar belief, claiming that one could possess a sense of "balanced self-respect" in which there was a stable image of self that could not be upset by passing phases of praise or blame. Thus, for both James and Cooley, some global sense of self-worth was seen to exist, over and above the more discrete evaluations of one's attributes at any given point in time.

More recently, Rosenberg (1979) has followed in the intellectual footsteps of James and Cooley, urging that we retain the notion of global self-esteem while at the same time focusing on the constituent parts of this whole, since the two are not identical. That is, Rosenberg argues that we acknowledge the phenomenological experience of general self worth over and above the evaluations attached to more discrete characteristics of the self. He claims that "both exist within the individual's phenomenal field as separate and distinguishable entities, and each can and should be studied in its own right" (p. 20).

Precisely how these entities are to be studied, however, is a matter of some debate. Rosenberg's primary focus has been on the assessment of one's global sense of self, rather than the construction of a model that deals with both global self-worth and the specific evaluative components of the self. Toward his goal, he has constructed a unidimensional measure which taps one's global perception of self-worth. His 10-item scale taps the degree to which one is generally satisfied with one's life, feels one has a number of good qualities, has a positive attitude toward oneself, feels useless, desires more self-respect, or thinks one is a failure.

Rosenberg's approach should be contrasted to those in which general self-esteem or self-worth is simply viewed as the sum of evaluative judgments across items of heterogeneous content that presumably reflect the specific relevant dimensions of self-evaluation (see Coopersmith, 1967, as well as Piers & Harris, 1969). Shavelson *et al.* (1976) have also favored a combinatorial approach to the general self-concept analogous to certain hierarchical models of intellectual abilities. Thus, general self-concept is likened to Spearman's *g*, which in turn dictates a data-analytic strategy in which commonalities among the specific components of the self are extracted as an index of the general self-concept.

In our own theorizing and research we have grappled with such questions as whether to focus primarily on evaluations in discrete domains, whether to include a construct such as global self-worth and define it as some combination of these discrete judgments, or whether to assess self-worth separately, as something over and above, or different from, the combination of specific self-evaluations. Our preference, to date, has been to isolate specific domains or dimensions, each of which is tapped by its own set of items, and to assess general self-worth independent of these specific judgments (Harter, 1982b). Our strategy for assessing general self-worth is very similar to Rosenberg's in that we ask the child very general questions concerning the degree to which one wants to stay the same, is happy with the way one is, likes the way one is leading one's life, likes the kind of person one is, thinks the way one does things is fine, and so forth. This approach has the advantage of treating self-worth as a psychological commodity over and above some combination of one's specific self-evaluation judgments, in keeping with the gestalt notion that the whole is greater than the sum of its parts. Yet it also has a potential disadvantage in that this approach may yield little insight into the processes by which children or adults make such global judgments.

Rosenberg (1979) has been an articulate commentator on this dilemma. In criticizing those procedures that merely combine specific judgments in an additive fashion to arrive at a global self-esteem score, he has argued that this procedure

> overlooks the extent to which the self-concept is a structure whose elements are arranged in a complex hierarchical order. Hence, simply to add up the parts in order to assess the whole is to ignore the fact that the global attitude is the product of an enormously complex synthesis of elements which goes on in the individual's phenomenal field. It is not simply the elements per se but their relationship, weighting, and combination that is responsible for the final outcome. (p. 21)

Upon reflection, it might seem that Rosenberg's approach is not inconsistent with those who have argued for hierarchical models of the self. Thus, our strategy should involve the empirical determination of the relationship, weighting, and combination of elements responsible for the final outcome, namely one's global sense of self-worth. For Rosenberg, however, one would encounter serious empirical roadblocks since in all likelihood the individual is not aware of the beta weights in this delicate equation.

> The subject himself may be as ignorant as the investigator about how this complex synthesis of elements has been achieved, but he is in a unique position to recognize, as a matter of immediate experience, the final result. He alone can experience whether he has a generally favorable or unfavorable, positive or negative, pro or con feeling toward himself as a whole. (Rosenberg, 1979, p. 21)

Given his belief that the individual cannot reconstruct the hierarchy leading to one's feelings of self-worth, Rosenberg has been content to assess the global phenomenological appraisal itself, ignoring the complexities of the hierarchy that may underlie such an appraisal. There are those of us who are a bit more sanguine about the possibility of reconstructing such a hierarchy. Yet in so doing, we must pay careful attention to what it is we are hierarchizing and why, toward what end.

What Are We Hierarchizing and Why?

In the discussion thus far, the terms *self-theory, sense of self, self-concept, self-esteem,* and *self-worth* have seemingly been used interchangeably. However, in our construction of networks which supposedly underlie these superordinate concepts of self, we need to address the following distinction: Are we constructing a hierarchy of the *salience* or *importance* of the elements or components in one's self-theory, or are we concerned with a network of positive or negative *self-evaluations* which may somehow combine to produce an overall evaluation of self-worth? We have been less than clear on this point, in our theorizing, as well as our methodological approaches to the study of the self.

There are those who have attempted to make this distinction; for example, McGuire (McGuire, 1982; McGuire & McGuire, 1980; McGuire & Padawer-Singer, 1976) has urged that we separate the issue of *"what* I am" from the evaluation of "how *good* I am." Moreover, McGuire has urged that we place more emphasis on the *spontaneous* self, examining self-descriptors that are generated by the subject, rather than merely being content to examine the *reactive* self, employing procedures in which subjects respond to descriptions preselected by the investigator. McGuire's empirical focus has been on the spontaneous self, recording subjects' responses to the question of who or what am I. In so doing he has employed an elaborate content coding system devised by Gordon (1968) which classifies the responses to the open-ended question, "Who am I?" Gordon's classification system taps such dimensions as ascribed characteristics, roles and membership, abstract identifications, interests and activities, personality characteristics, sense of moral worth, of self-determination, of competence, and sense of unity.

Gordon, with adult samples, and McGuire, as well as Montemayor and Eisen (1977), with child samples, have analyzed the frequencies with which these categories are spontaneously mentioned, thereby providing a picture of dimensions most relevant to one's self-representation. Thus, these approaches focus on the issue of the salience or importance of the components in the self-system. While this empirical strategy does yield a hierarchy in terms of an ordering of the relative importance of each possible component, these investigators have not yet sought to develop more complicated models that speak to the question of levels of organization within the self-system.

L'Ecuyer, in constructing his hierarchical organization of the dimensions of the self, has also utilized the "Who Am I?" technique, and thus his model (outlined in a previous section) pertains to the *salience* of the various dimensions generated by the subjects. In contrast, the hierarchical model presented by Shavelson *et al.* (1976) appears to focus more on the *evaluative* parameters of the self, given the methodological procedures selected to partially validate the model. These investigators have examined existing findings from five major self-concept instruments (including the Coopersmith instrument and the Piers–Harris measure), each of which are self-evaluative in nature. That is, these measures tap how well the child thinks of the self, not what salient dimensions the child generates, as in the L'Ecuyer model. Drawing upon factor-analytic studies of each of these scales, as well as a multitrait, multimethod approach to the identification of meaningful clusters of items and subscales, Shavelson *et al.* find some support for portions of the multidimensional, hierarchical model they have hypothesized.

However, it would seem that we need to question whether hierarchies based on the salience or importance of the dimensions in the self-system (see L'Ecuyer, 1981) are comparable to those hierarchies developed on the basis of the degree to which self-evaluative judgments cluster together (Shavelson *et al.*, 1976). Might not these two types of hierarchies take on a very different look? If the answer is yes, this is not necessarily a distressing conclusion, since different types of hierarchies may serve different purposes. However, as theoreticians we need to be much more precise about the purposes for which such hierarchies are being devised, as well as how our conceptual formulations dictate the particular methodological approaches we employ.

We have underscored the need to make a distinction between whether our hierarchies refer to the importance or salience of self-descriptions generated by the subject, as opposed to the valence and strength of the evaluative judgments made about dimensions which have been preselected by the investigator. However, there is another point on which we need to be clearer. Do we intend that these models actually describe the pattern of cognitive self-representations within the person, or are they merely heuristic devices to aid us in organizing our own thinking about the dimensions of the self-system? Such models are typically *introduced* as nomological networks that exist in the minds of individual subjects. However, the methodological procedures employed have not allowed for a test of this proposition. In support of his model depicting the salience of the dimensions of the self, L'Ecuyer, for example, has examined the number of subjects producing statements about the specific components of the self, and these frequencies form the basis for the hierarchy proposed. Similarly, in the work of Gordon (1968), McGuire (McGuire, 1982; McGuire & McGuire, 1980), and Montemayor and Eisen (1977), the frequencies with which groups of subjects mention the various component categories are examined, as the operational definition of salience. In the case of the Shavelson *et al.* (1976) model, factor structures and cluster analyses across groups of subjects form the basis for the network of self-constructs included in the hierarchy. At best, then, our current models merely provide interesting frameworks that allow us to test broad relationships among the constructs in the network. As such, they constitute theories in the minds of psychologists, not necessarily self-theories within the mind of the individual. These models may well simulate the organization of cognitive self-representations for a given individual. However, if our goal is to truly describe the phenomenological network of constructs within the self-system, then we must devise appropriate methodologies to demonstrate this unequivocally.

IMPORTANCE PLUS SELF-EVALUATION AS DETERMINANTS OF OVERALL SELF-WORTH

In the previous section it was pointed out that while certain models and approaches have concentrated on the importance or salience of the particular dimensions of the self, other models have focused more on the valence and strength of the self-evaluations made by the individual. In this section, it is suggested that if our goal is to understand the bases on which children and adults make judgments of overall self-worth, we may well need to consider both.

The studies by Rosenberg (1979), as well as our own efforts (Harter, 1982b; 1983), clearly demonstrate that one can reliably assess general self-worth in adults, as well as in children over the age of 8 years. Moreover, there are tremendous individual differences in the regard with which subjects hold themselves. Rosenberg has been content to identify both predictors as well as correlates of general self-esteem or self-worth, eschewing the more problematic task of identifying its component structure. In our own work, we have become fascinated with the issue of what determines the level of a child's self-worth, particularly since the child's perceived competence in the domains we have assessed does not appear to tell the entire story. While correlations between competence and self-worth are moderate, clearly there are other factors that contribute to the child's overall sense of worth as a person.

How does one determine the bases on which children make such global evaluations? One strategy involves the direct approach, just ask them! We have attempted to do so, through initial interview procedures that eventually led to the construction of a "reasonnaire" which allows children to check which reasons he or she used in making prior general self-worth judgments (Minton, 1979). Interestingly, while competence is one of the dimensions that children sometimes mention, the more frequent dimensions involve personality characteristics, such as being nice, friendly, or helpful, as well as issues involving conduct and morality, for example, obeying one's parents, controlling one's temper, and being good in school.

These findings are interesting, however in what sense do they illuminate the construct of general self-worth? Have we really uncovered the bases for these global judgments, or have we merely identified several other dimensions of self-evaluation that should be included in a more all-encompassing network of personal constructs? That is, our interview procedures and "reasonnaires" invite the child respondent to produce specific examples of why one likes (or does not like) oneself as a person. However, these procedures do not adequately pull for a description of the more complicated process through which global self-judgments may be made. For example, one's self-worth may well involve some weighting of the *adequacy* with which one is performing in each of the domains in one's network, relative to the *importance* of each of these dimensions.

In considering this type of personal equation, we must acknowledge that this was precisely the issue which James (1892/1963) addressed when he defined self-esteem as the ratio of one's successes to one's pretentions. More recently, Dickstein (1977) has also endorsed such an approach, suggesting that the importance of an activity to the individual will determine the degree to which success or failure affects one's overall self-evaluation. Rosenberg (1979) has also emphasized the role of the importance of a given attribute to the individual. In his terminology, the "psychological centrality" of the attribute in question must be determined since this will affect the degree to which an evaluation of this characteristic will affect one's global self-esteem.

Rosenberg has empirically demonstrated his point with regard to the characteristic of likeability. His findings reveal that the strength of the relationship between perceived likeability and global self-esteem on his measure depends upon how important or central the characteristic of likeability is to the individual. Rosenberg found that among those for whom likeability was central or important, the relationship between their self-estimates of likeability and global self-esteem was very strong; in contrast, among those to whom the quality of likeability mattered little, the relationship was much weaker.

Within our own competence framework we have also begun to look at the role that judgments of importance play as determinants of general self-worth. In our first empirical foray, we examined how the relationship between importance judgments and perceived competence affected self-worth, by comparing the following extreme groups: (1) those for whom the rank ordering of their competence across the three domains (cognitive, social, physical) was *identical* to their rank ordering of importance judgments and (2) those for whom the rank ordering of their competence was just the *opposite* of their rank ordering of the importance of these domains. We found that the general self-worth scores of the group whose rankings were congruent were considerably higher than those of the mismatched group (Harter & Engstrom, 1981).

The construction of these extreme groups, however, tells us little about how these relationships operate in the vast majority of the population. Thus, we are currently exploring a procedure in which children rank order the importance of each domain, as well as their adequacy, for five domains, cognitive, social, and athletic competence, in addition to appearance and conduct. Based on our interview data, we have included dimensions other than competence, since these clearly seem to be important in the self-evaluative process. For each subject, a rank order correlation is calculated between these two orderings; this score reflects the degree of congruence between one's judgments of importance and one's judgments of one's adequacy across these domains. To the extent that this relationship is a critical determinant of one's global sense of worth, we would expect this score to predict the child's general self-worth score. We are currently in the process of testing this hypothesis empirically (see Harter, 1985).

Upon closer reflection, it becomes apparent that this type of strategy has much in common with the approaches of those who have sought to make comparisons between subjects' *real* self and their *ideal* self. For Rogers (see Rogers & Dymond, 1954) the magnitude of this discrepancy was a primary index of maladjustment. Others, notable Zigler and his colleagues (Achenbach & Zigler, 1963; Katz & Zigler, 1967; Zigler, Balla, & Watson, 1972; Katz, Zigler, & Zalk, 1975), have challenged this assumption, suggesting an alternative developmental framework. They have argued that when developmental level is taken into account, the magnitude of the discrepancy between the real and ideal self increases with age, suggesting that such a discrepancy is an index of maturity. These positions need not be contradictory, however, in that while developmental differences may well exist, extreme discrepancy scores within a given developmental level may well be predictive of maladjustment or low self-esteem.

Both Wylie (1974) and Rosenberg (1979) have been critical of those studies that have employed self-image disparity scores. Wylie notes that one's reported ideal self may simply represent a cultural stereotype rather than the image to which one truly aspires. Rosenberg has also urged that we distinguish between one's idealized image, which may well be a pleasant fantasy, and one's "committed" image, the image we take seriously as an aspiration. Typically this distinction has been overlooked, making it unclear just what subjects take into consideration when they are asked to rate what they would "ideally" like to be. The framework proposed earlier, emphasizing the potential role of *importance* judgments, would appear to come closer to Rosenberg's notion of the committed self-image. That is, the focus is on the congruence or discrepancy between how *critical* it is to the individual to succeed in a given domain and one's level of success. It is this discrepancy that we feel will best predict the individual's feelings of general self-worth.

It should be pointed out that procedures designed to predict global self-worth, based on the congruence or discrepancy between domain-specific importance and self-adequacy judgments, will *not* yield a general hierarchical model that describes how self-representations are organized. Undoubtedly, there will be notable individual differences in the hierarchies that subjects generate, both with regard to the importance of dimensions or domains as well as one's perceived competence or adequacy in these domains. At best, if we adopt a developmental approach, we may be able to document certain differences in the salience of particular dimensions at different ages. For example, our own findings suggest that physical appearance becomes more important, as children move from the elementary school grades into junior high.

Such an approach would also yield information on the relative importance of various competencies at different ages.

The intent here, however, is not to devise an alternative hierarchical model of the underlying structure of the self-system, based on either importance judgments or judgments of one's adequacy. Rather, the goal is to devise a model for predicting one's general sense of self-worth, based on the congruence of one's importance and adequacy judgments, as a starting point. As we see, in subsequent sections of this chapter, we may well need to take additional considerations into account, in building a model of self-worth. We now address one such consideration, namely the accuracy of subjects' evaluations of the attributes in the self-system, focusing primarily on competence, since we have some empirical evidence in this domain.

ACCURACY OF ONE'S COMPETENCE JUDGMENTS

In the development of a model of self-worth, it may well be that we will also need to take the accuracy of one's self-evaluative judgments into account. Might it be, for example, that the relationship between importance and adequacy judgments will only predict general self-worth for those children who are relatively accurate in judging their competencies? That is, could errors in the estimation of one's abilities or characteristics lead to an unreliable score with regard to the correlation between importance and competence judgments? Alternatively, if it is one's *perception* of his or her attributes which is truly critical, then we would not expect the accuracy of these judgments to affect general self-worth.

What do we know about the issue of accuracy? Our data come from the cognitive domain where it is possible to compare children's evaluations of their scholastic competence with more objective indexes such as achievement scores and teachers' ratings. From a developmental perspective, we know that the magnitude of these relationships changes with age (Harter, 1982b). Across Grades 3 through 6 the magnitude of the correlation between perceived and actual cognitive competence steadily increases from about .30 in the third grade to about .60 in the sixth grade. However, for seventh-grade junior high school students, this correlation drops to .30 and then recovers over the eighth and ninth grades, to reach a high of .65 in the ninth grade. Our interpretation of these trends is that gradually, during the elementary school years, children become increasingly better at judging their scholastic competence. Undoubtedly, this results from their greater ability to understand how their competence is being evaluated by others, that is, they come to share a common set of criteria with teachers, peers, parents, and so forth. With the advent of the new school structure that they encounter in junior high, including different expectations and shifting standards of social comparison, seventh graders must relearn the criteria by which to evaluate their competence. Over the junior high school period of seventh through ninth grade, students appear to gradually master this new system, allowing them once again to make relatively accurate judgments about their competence.

In addition to these general developmental trends, however, we see striking individual differences in children's ability to judge their cognitive competence. These differences have recently become an empirical focus of interest and have led us to isolate three groups of children: (1) those who *overrate* their competence, relative to the teacher's judgment, (2) those who *underrate* their competence, relative to the teacher's judgment, and (3) those whose ratings are quite *congruent* with the teacher's judgment. Given the generally high correlation between a teacher's ratings of pupils' scholastic competence and achievement test scores, we have inferred that the pupils in this third group are relatively accurate in their judgments, whereas those in the first two groups are relatively inaccurate.

In one study, a dissertation by Bierer (1982), two sets of findings were revealing. The first sought to examine a network of achievement-related cognitions including perceived cognitive competence, anxiety over schoolwork, perceptions of control in the academic domain, as well as preference for challenge. The findings revealed that for the congruent or accurate raters, these personal constructs were meaningfully interrelated. Children who perceived their competence to be high also reported low anxiety, evidenced an understanding of the factors that controlled their successes, and rated themselves high in preference for challenge. In addition, a positive sense of control predicted preference for challenge and was inversely related to anxiety. This pattern of correlations was noticeably weaker for those pupils who underrated their competence, and for those designated as overraters these relationships were virtually negligible. These findings suggested that for the two incongruent groups, but especially the overraters, their self-related perceptions did not form an integrated network of constructs, at least with regard to the academic domain.

Our second set of findings bears on the actual *behavior* of these groups, when placed in a situation where their preference for cognitive challenge was assessed. A decoding task was constructed, along the lines of the Wechsler Intelligence Scale for Children (WISC) digit symbol subscale. Although on this task, letters were to be paired with symbols in order to decipher a series of words. Four difficulty levels were employed, operationally defined in terms of the word lengths to be decoded. We anticipated that the underraters would select relatively easy anagrams, consistent with their underestimation of their abilities. It was also hypothesized that the overraters would be likely to choose relatively easy anagrams, based on the assumption that they would attempt to avoid failure, in order to protect their inflated sense of competence. The findings revealed that as predicted, both groups of inaccurate raters, the overraters as well as underraters, selected easier tasks to perform than did the accurate raters.

In a recent follow-up study, we attempted to replicate these findings, employing better controls for the actual competence of the groups included. In this study, the preference-for-challenge task involved the choice of anagrams at five difficulty levels, 3-, 4-, 5-, 6-, and 7-letter anagrams. Subjects were given an initial opportunity to sample two anagrams from each difficulty level, prior to a choice phase during which they were permitted to select eight anagrams at whatever difficulty levels they preferred.

The design of the study, including the mean difficulty level choices for each group, is presented in Table 2.1. Note that there are two groups of accurate raters, a high accurate, and a medium accurate group. The *high* accurate group is matched on *perceived* competence with the overraters and on *actual* competence with the underraters (both groups are rated as high in competence by teachers). The *medium* accurate group is matched on *perceived* competence with the underraters, and on *actual* competence with the overraters. Through such a design, we can begin to untangle the relative importance of perceived and actual competence in predicting preference for challenge.

If one looks first at the two groups of *accurate* raters, along the upper-left–lower-right diagonal, it would appear that either perceived or actual competence ratings will predict their preference for challenge scores, since these ratings are highly congruent. The more competent group, using either criterion, select more difficult anagrams. However, if one examines the performance of the *overraters*, in comparison to the other group, it would appear that their *actual* competence is a better predictor of their preference behavior than their perceived competence. These overraters pick anagrams that are much easier than those selected by the high accurates, although the self-reported compe-

TABLE 2.1

Relationship between Actual Cognitive Competence and
Perceived Cognitive Competence in Defining Groups Based on
the Accuracy of Their Ratings[a]

Perceived cognitive competence	Actual cognitive competence (based on teacher ratings)	
	High	Medium
High	High accurates (4.5)	Overraters (3.2)
Medium	Underraters (4.0)	Medium accurates (3.8)

[a]Numbers in parentheses refer to mean number of letters per
anagram selected by each group.

tence of these two groups was initially the same. In fact, the overraters
select anagrams that are even easier than would be predicted on the
basis of their actual competence. That is, the overraters select anagrams that are significantly easier than those chosen by the medium
accurates, who are at the same level of actual competence. These findings suggest to us that, at some level, the overraters are aware that they
are not nearly as competent as their self-reported judgments imply.
Moreover, to protect what may be a fragile and distorted sense of scholastic ability, they were driven to select the easiest anagrams, in order
to avoid failure and its implications for the self.

When one examines the performance of the *underraters*, it would
appear that they are making their choices based on their *perceptions* of
their competence, not their actual ability. That is, their perceived abilities are within the midrange of the scale, and they are selecting anagrams that are similar in difficulty to those accurate raters whose
perceptions are also within the midrange. Thus, the underraters do not
appear to be selecting anagrams that are consistent with their high
level of actual competence, if one compares their performance to the
high accurate group. It is as if the underraters believe that they are of
only medium competence, and this belief mediates their behavioral
choices.

There is much that remains to be understood about the dynamics of
these various groups. For example, what criteria are the inaccurate
raters employing when they make their judgments of competence? It
would appear that they are evaluating their competence based on different standards than those employed by the teachers who rated the

children's actual competence. Or, could the inaccurate raters be utilizing the same criteria, but misreading the feedback they receive? Moreover, what does it mean to claim that "at some level" the overraters must be able to accurately judge their competence in order to have selected the easiest anagrams? Are we talking here about a conscious attempt to present oneself in a socially desirable light? Or do we wish to imply that perhaps these children have some level of unconscious awareness of their true abilities? In addition, do children who inaccurately perceive their competence in one domain exhibit a similar tendency in other domains? Is this a pervasive self-evaluative style, or are these inaccurate judgments confined to a specific domain? These are the types of questions we hope to address in pursuing the implications of the accuracy of children's competence judgments.

With regard to our attempt to devise a more comprehensive model of general self-worth, it will be interesting to determine how the accuracy of one's specific judgments affects this more global self-evaluation. The finding that the network of achievement-related cognitions was much less integrated for the inaccurate raters leads to the speculation that the correlation between importance judgments and perceived adequacy across a number of domains might not be as useful a predictor of general self-worth for these groups. Moreover, if there is a tendency to distort one's evaluations in specific domains, might not this tendency affect one's judgment of overall worth? It would seem, then, that the accuracy issue needs to be pursued on at least two conceptual and empirical fronts: there is much to be learned about the specific dynamics of these groups of accurate and inaccurate raters. Second, we need to determine whether accuracy is a construct to be included in our emerging model of the determinants of general self-worth. We return to this issue after a discussion of certain developmental factors that have implications for the accuracy of children's judgments of the self.

DEVELOPMENTAL CHANGES IN THE CONTENT AND STRUCTURE OF THE SELF-THEORY

In a previous section, several multidimensional hierarchic models of the self were reviewed. In large part, these models suggest how networks of self-evaluative content categories might be organized. However, two major problems with such efforts must be acknowledged. As pointed out earlier, these networks speak more to the theories that psychologists hold about the relationship among these categories, across groups of people, than they speak to the actual phenomenological network of self-representations that are cognitively constructed by the individual.

Second, to date, developmental differences in the content and structure of the self-theory have been virtually ignored. Where age-related differences have been examined (e.g., Montemayor & Eisen, 1977), often dimensions based on content have been conceptually confounded with those features that are more structural in nature (see Harter, 1983, for further discussion of this point). In this section predictable developmental changes in both the nature of the content, as well as the manner in which this content is structured, are proposed. Examples from the domain of competence are offered. After describing these possible shifts, the implications of such changes for a theory of self-worth are explored.

The framework to be described has been presented in detail elsewhere (Harter, 1983). An effort is made here to summarize the major points, hopefully without being either too sketchy or too redundant. For the more visually inclined, imagine a matrix in which content dimensions represent row headings on the left and the structural levels represent the column headings, across the top. By content dimensions, we are really referring to *types* of content rather than specific domains, per se. The five types of content, ordered to suggest one possible developmental trajectory, are as follows:

1. *Physical attributes,* for example, size, age, gender, race, appearance, possessions
2. *Behavioral descriptions,* including actions, skills, preferences
3. *Emotional descriptions,* for example, feeling states, affects, moods
4. *Motivational descriptions,* for example, perceived intentions and casual attributions
5. *Cognitions,* for example, descriptions of one's attitudes and the nature of one's thoughts, theories, and cognitive constructions

These types of content dimensions can be applied to any number of domains, where by *domain* we refer to such categories as one's scholastic performance, one's social relationships, one's athletic prowess, one's sense of moral worth, and so forth. Moreover, within a given domain, for example, one's cognitive competence, descriptions can potentially occur for each type of content dimension. Developmentally, the earliest descriptions will probably be couched in terms of *physical attributes,* for example, "I am smart because I am big or because I am a boy or because now I am five." At the next level of *behavioral* descriptions, the child would cite such specific skills as the ability to count or to say the alphabet as evidence for one's competence.

The subsequent level of *emotional* descriptions might expand on these dimensions to include references to the pleasure one derives from doing challenging schoolwork. Self-descriptions of cognitive competence might later shift to the level of *motivational* descriptions where one makes reference to one's personal effort as the cause of one's success. At the highest level, involving descriptions in terms of one's *cognitive* activity, one might focus on the ability to logically think through problems and deduce the answers.

With development, it is hypothesized that one will witness the ability to use higher levels of description. However, it is likely that the lower levels will continue to be employed. That is, these levels are hypothesized to represent an acquisition sequence (rather than an acquisition–deletion sequence in which earlier forms drop out). Whether a given developmental level shows a modal preference for one type of description is an empirical question, as is the issue of individual differences within developmental level.

Structural Changes

The *structural* dimensions refer to how these content categories are cognitively processed or conceptualized. These structural changes are cast into a developmental sequence of four "stages," each of which has two levels. During Stage I, self-descriptions are couched in terms of *specific single* attributes, behaviors, emotions, and so forth. At Stage II, these are integrated into *traits*. At Stage III, traits become integrated into *single abstractions*. At Stage IV, single abstractions are combined into *higher-order abstractions*. Thus, movement to a new stage involves *integration*. It should be noted that there are approximate correspondences between these stages and the Piagetian stages of cognitive development. The first structural stage roughly corresponds to preoperational thought, the second stage to concrete operational thought, and the third stage to early formal operational thought during adolescence. The fourth stage represents further development during adulthood.

The two levels *within* each stage represent distinctions not articulated in Piaget's theory. Movement from the first to the second level within each stage involves *differentiation*. At the first level of a given stage, the attributes, traits, or abstractions are typically global and often overgeneralized, for example, one is all smart or all dumb. Self-descriptions at the first level of any stage are not necessarily stable, however. One may vacillate from one extreme or pole to the other, for example, "while yesterday I felt all smart, today I feel all dumb." These descriptions become more differentiated and situation specific at the second level of each stage for example, one may feel smart in one situation but dumb in another. To illustrate these structural changes, we will take the content domain of *competence*, and trace it through the postulated stages and levels.

Stage I. In this stage, self-descriptions are couched in very specific labels, labels which designate specific skills. Thus, the young child will describe how he or she is good at puzzles, knows the alphabet, as well as numbers and colors, is good at climbing, running, singing, and so forth. At Level 1, the child will tend to view these skills in an all-or-none fashion, that is, one is very good at everything. Theoretically, the young child could also describe the self as "all bad" at these skills. However, our own findings (Harter & Pike, 1984), based on children's self-descriptions on our pictorial scale of competence and social acceptance for young children, reveal that the majority of children describe themselves as "all good." Our interpretation is that they are not yet able to differentiate between the wish to be all competent and their actual ability with regard to these skills, that is, they are unable to distinguish their real, from their ideal, self. At Level 2, these judgments become more differentiated. The child comes to acknowledge that he or she is good at certain skills, for example, drawing, puzzles, knowing one's colors, but not so good at other skills, for example, knowing one's alphabet or numbers. However, these self-descriptions exist in conceptual isolation from one another, that is, they have not yet become integrated or hierarchized.

Stage II. During this stage, the child's specific self-descriptions become integrated into trait labels, for example, *smart* or *dumb*. For example, one constructs the trait label of dumb by integrating the observations that one is poor at math, science, and social studies, or smart because one is good at writing, art, and music. However, at Level 1, particularly for trait labels like smart and dumb which can be viewed as polar opposites, the child is able to control only one trait label in the pair. Thus, the child will conclude that he or she is all dumb, or conversely, all smart. Alternatively, in constructing the uni-dimensional trait of dumb, the child ignores the fact that he or she is simultaneously doing well in art, music, and creative writing.

Our evidence for this comes from a task in which children are asked to make a circle puzzle of themselves where they may select six pieces in the form of "pie slices" to complete the circle. They may choose from a selection of yellow pieces labeled *smart* or brown pieces labeled *dumb*. Invariably, our young subjects, between the ages of 5 and 7 years will depict themselves as all smart. Clinical observations, with children in play therapy who have been referred for school learning problems, have revealed the other extreme in that such children tend to see themselves as "all dumb" (Harter, 1977). Consistent with this tendency toward all-or-none thinking, young children on our "pie puzzle" task will also depict their friends as all smart and their non-friends as all dumb. Similar findings come from Hand (1981) who has demonstrated that young children deny the possibility that they can simultaneously be nice and mean. Children's understanding of the co-occurrence of these trait labels develops gradually, through a predictable sequence, culminating with a stage in which the abstract concept of intention is invoked to account for the simultaneous occurrence of both nice and mean characteristics in the self.

At Level 2, trait labels become differentiated, in that the child comes to appreciate that he or she can simultaneously be both smart and dumb. Thus, to follow our hypothetical example, the child comes to appreciate that while one is dumb with regard to math, science, and social studies, one can simultaneously be smart at creative writing, art, and music. The advance at this second level, then, is greater differentiation in terms of the situation specificity of the trait labels. However, these trait descriptions exist side by side, as it were, each restricted to a separate skill domain. They are not yet integrated.

Evidence from our "pie puzzle" task supports this developmental shift. Beginning around the age of 8 years, children depict themselves as part smart and part dumb. Two kinds of explanations are typically offered. One focuses on different subject matter as in the example given above. Thus, children cite those school subjects in which they are smart and contrast them to those in which they are dumb. Another type of explanation, offered by somewhat older children, involves the distinction between two types of smartness or dumbness. One can be smart or dumb in school subjects. However, smart and dumb also refer to one's ability to make wise decisions in one's daily life, for example, doing your chores before you go out to play with friends, or getting enough sleep before a test or athletic event. Thus, one can simultaneously be smart and dumb if one is smart at school subjects but makes dumb decisions, or conversely if one makes smart or wise decisions, but does not do well academically.

Stage III. A more advanced type of integration is achieved during the third stage with the emergence of single abstractions (Fischer, 1980). The budding adolescent now attempts to integrate the existing trait labels that were formed in the previous stage. To continue with our competence example, the adolescent may conceptually wrestle with the traits of smart and dumb, in trying to construct the single abstraction of *intelligence.* However, during the Level 1 of this stage, one may overgeneralize, or demonstrate all-or-none thinking and conclude that one is of low intelligence since one is dumb at the more conventional indexes of intellect, namely performance at such school subjects as math and science. Thus, one's talents at writing, art, and music are not integrated into the single abstraction of intelligence. While one may be smart in those areas, this type of smartness is not part of one's definition of intelligence.

During Level 2, single abstractions become more differentiated. Thus, this same adolescent may combine the perception of self as a skilled writer of poetry and short stories with one's perceived talents at drawing and painting to form a separate single abstraction of himself or herself as an artistic, creative person. Although this second abstraction is now differentiated from the abstraction concerning his or her conventional intelligence, the adolescent may not yet be able to integrate these two abstractions. Initially, they are conceptually separate. However, at some point, the adolescent may become confused or perplexed about what seems to be a contradiction: how can one be of only low intelligence in conventional areas of knowledge but seemingly very bright or gifted in other spheres?

Reintegration at this level might involve the formation of higher-order abstractions such that there is no longer an apparent contradiction, and the self no longer seems fragmented. For example, in moving toward Stage IV, the young adult may come to define himself or herself as a Bohemian, one who rejects the conventional intellectual values of the society in favor of pursuing one's artistic endeavors.

Stage IV. Initially, at Level 1 of Stage IV, the higher-order abstraction of Bohemian may be overgenerlized, such that the young adult ignores a possible contradiction, for example, his or her avid interest in politics. Then, at Level 2, another higher-order abstraction may be differentiated, such as that of a political radical. Initially, however, this second abstraction will merely coexist with one's self concept of a Bohemian, remaining conceptually separate. At some point, a reintegration may take place with regard to these higher-order abstractions, such that one comes to view the self as an iconoclast.

When one considers each of these structural stages and levels in relation to the content categories postulated, one can create a matrix in which one can have all combinations of structural levels and content categories. Our illustrations have traced one type of content, skills or competence, through all structural levels. Earlier we gave an example of how one could have self-descriptions of competence that also involve all of the content dimensions. To further illustrate the interaction between structure and content, the structural level of abstractions can be applied to each content dimension. Abstractions can be based on physical characteristics (e.g., statuesque), skills (intelligent), emotions (iracible), motives (determined), and thought processes (introspective).

Developmentally, it is hypothesized that the level of structural usage and content category will be correlated, to some degree, in that one may tend to use higher structural stages in conjunction with more advanced content categories. However, it is not possible to specify a single developmental sequence incorporating both of these dimensions. It was suggested earlier that the emergence of new content categories might best be characterized as an acquisition sequence, rather than an acquisition–deletion sequence, in which earlier forms of self-description drop out of one's repertoire. The latter seems unlikely, given the types of self-descriptions that are generated on the "who am I?" types of tasks.

The developmental course of the structural stages and levels may be more difficult to predict. The cognitive-developmental nature of this progression might lead us to postulate that these structural dimensions define an acquisition–deletion sequence in which the earlier stages or levels gradually drop out. However, a more enlightened approach to stage theory would alert us to the possibility that there may be considerable unevenness or decalage in the development of our self-descriptions such that one may be at one stage and level with regard to one life domain, but not others. Thus, our best characterization of an individual, or a particular age group, may be in terms of some modal structural stage and level. Given these complexities, we can appreciate the difficulty of trying to construct a single multidimensional or hierarchical model of the self.

Static versus Dynamic Models of the Self

Our existing models of the self have not only been static with regard to the lack of attention to developmental change, but static in terms of our lack of concern for the dynamic interplay among the components of the self-system. We have treated the individual as a cognizer who tidily classifies and hierarchizes the personal constructs in his or her self-theory, performing much like a computer, analyzing the data of experience. In our recent models of the self, we have not seriously considered the degree to which these personal constructs may be in conflict or may clash in terms of the phenomenological experience of the individual. Nor have we considered the degree to which certain constructs may not be integrated, but are perceived as fragmented or isolated within the individual's self-system.

Historically, James alerted us to this issue in his treatment of the "conflict of the different Me's." His focus was on the incompatibility of the potential roles one might want to adopt, a conflict that necessitated a choice. These themes have also been addressed within the clinical literature, as well as in the literature on adolescence. The Freudian hydraulic model is founded on the assumption of psychological power struggles within the self. Moreover, a number of clinicians and personality theorists have placed major emphasis on the individual's efforts to construct a unified, integrated self (Allport, 1955, 1961; Horney, 1950; Jung, 1928; Lecky, 1945; Maslow, 1954, 1961, 1971; Rogers, 1950). These writers have highlighted the individual's strivings toward integration, in large part by pointing out the clinical consequences when such unity is threatened.

Allport (1955) viewed integration as the major concern of the self which he relabeled the "proprium". The *proprium* included all aspects of the personality that make "for a sense of inward unity," and Allport postulated a particular motive, "propriate striving" that seeks such a unification. Another personality theorist, Lecky (1945), fashioned an entire theory around the theme of self-consistency, emphasizing how the individual's behavior expresses the effort to maintain the integrity and unity of the self. Like later writers (Brim, 1976; Kelly, 1955; Epstein, 1973), Lecky observed that the individual organizes his or her ideas about the self into a personal theory, much like a scientist. Ideas that are inconsistent create disturbances in this system and therefore must be rejected or expelled.

Rogers (1950) echoes this theme in noting that negative feelings about the self arise when the organization of the self-structure is threatened by perceptions viewed as inconsistent with that structure. More recently, Epstein (1981) has formalized many of these observations under the rubric of the "unity principle," emphasizing that one of the most basic needs of the individual is to maintain the unity and coherence of the conceptual system that defines the self.

Within the literature on adolescence, Erikson (1950, 1959, 1968) and others have highlighted the importance of "sense of unity among one's self-conceptions" for the establishment of a stable ego identity. For the adolescent, role integration becomes the primary developmental task, for example, the integration of one's social, sexual, familial, ideological, and occupational roles. The potential hazards of this period involve what Erikson termed identity diffusion or role confusion, manifest by the adolescent's inability to select and integrate the roles he or she wishes to pursue. The conflictual nature of this period has been the topic of sound empirical research within the field of adolescence. Constantinople (1969), for example, has longitudinally examined identity diffusion and its resolution in college students. Marcia's work (Marcia, 1966; Marcia & Friedman, 1970; Toder & Marcia, 1973) is also intriguing in its isolation of four types of identity statuses in adolescents, one of which is identity diffusion. For the most part, however, neither the research on adolescents nor the clinical observations on the unified versus the nonintegrated self have found their way into current theories or models of the self.

One exception is Gordon's (1968) system for classifying the self-descriptions given in response to the "Who am I?" task. One of his 30 categories explicitly refers to "sense of unity," and was conceptually derived from Erikson's formulations of the ego-identity process. Gordon cites examples of the types of verbal self-descriptions that would be included under sense of unity: in harmony, mixed up, ambivalent, a whole person, and straightened out now. Developmentally, Montemayor and Eisen (1977) have found that this particular type of self-description is absent among children aged 10 and 12, whereas it rises to 15% at age 14, to 17% at age 16, and to 21% at age 18.

However, the mention of this issue as a personal concern, while interesting, tells us little about the nature of this construct and its phenomenological expression. Moreover, one is credited with a "sense of unity" score if one either describes the perception of *unity*, for example, in harmony, or *lack* of integration, for example, mixed up. Thus, this affords us little insight into the dynamics of either unity or its absence. Nor does it permit a determination of what particular contents of the self-system may be at odds with one another or, conversely, more harmoniously arranged.

The challenge is methodological as well as theoretical. Within our own group, Ann Monsour and I have constructed a task that may address some of these issues in adolescents. The focus is on potential clashes, or lack of integration, among multiple roles, for example, the self within the academic setting, the self within the family setting, and the self within the peer culture. Each of these selves is first described by the subject employing a variant of the "Who Am I?" task. Through this procedure we can determine the degree of commonality among roles. The subject then provides a self-description of the real self, the "real me whom I know best." Next, the subject literally creates a picture of his or her personality by taking all of these self-descriptions and arranging them spatially on a larger piece of paper. (These are first transferred to round gummed labels of several sizes where size designated importance or centrality.) Subjects may cluster these attributes however they wish, just as they may spatially isolate particular attributes.

They are also instructed to depict those pairs of attributes that appear to clash with each other (by drawing in clash lines between the two). In this manner, we can determine not only the magnitude of possible conflict between the attributes of the self (number of such clashes) but we can examine where these clashes occur. Do they occur between the various selves as identified in the roles they play, or do they exist between these roles and the real self? Through this procedure we hope to not only learn more about the content categories employed by adolescents and how they are structured or clustered, but to glean some insights into the dynamics of the role conflicts that they are experiencing (see Harter, 1985).

Implications for Self-Worth

The preceding discussion emphasized the importance of a developmental perspective, considering changes in the content and structure of the self-system, including a consideration of the dynamic interplay among the components of this system. However, what implications might such an approach have for our earlier discussion of self-worth or self-esteem, namely the global regard which one holds for the self?

Several hypotheses suggest themselves. With regard to potential conflict within the self-system, the clinical literature would suggest that the more conflict, and/or the less integration, experienced by the individual, the lower one's sense of self-regard. Rogers (1950), for example, is quite explicit in arguing that negative feelings toward the self arise when attributes are viewed as inconsistent with the basic organization of the self-structure. Horney (1950) has focused on a somewhat different barrier in the struggle toward an integrated sense of self, namely the person's alienation from his or her real self. These positions lead to the prediction that subjects expressing a great deal of conflict, particularly if this involves conflict between one's real self and the selves as perceived in the various roles one plays, will experience the lowest levels of self-esteem.

This prediction, however, may be limited to adolescents and adults. It may well be that children do not have the capacity to experience this type of conflict. If our previous developmental analysis has merit, the self-structure of the child may involve parallel sets of attributes that do not provoke the experience of conflict, even though certain attribute labels appear contradictory, for example, smart and dumb. In all likelihood, it is not until adolescence, when formal operational capacities allow one to construct a legitimate theory of one's personality and subject it to scrutiny and analysis, that one has the ability to perceive such attributes as inconsistent (see Harter, 1983). The appreciation of this inconsistency goes beyond the idenfification or cognitive recognition of contradiction in that intrapsychic conflict is actually experienced, with negative affective consequences. Thus, the adolescent is bothered by these contradictory self-perceptions, whereas the younger child is not. These various hypotheses, concerning both differences between preadolescent children and adolescents, as well as the implications of conflict for self-esteem during the period of adolescence, are currently under investigation (see Harter, 1985).

In an earlier portion of this chapter it was suggested that discrepancies between one's feelings of competence or *adequacy* across the domains in one's life and one's judgments of the *importance* of these domains would predict feelings of self-worth. However, this relationship may be more evident at some developmental levels than at others. It was suggested, in the preceding developmental analysis of structural changes in the self-system, that at each new stage, Level 1 is characterized by overgeneralization and all-or-none thinking. Thus, one is either all smart or all dumb, or one is either extremely attractive or hopelessly ugly. It was also suggested that the self-perceptions at Level 1 of a given stage may not be stable over time or situation.

To the extent that these features adequately characterize the pattern of self-perceptions, it might be hypothesized that the relationship between importance judgments and perceived adequacy would *not* be a good predictor of self-worth or self-esteem during Level 1 of a given stage. Both the exaggeration or polarization of one's characteristics, in combination with the potential instability of these self-perceptions, would mediate against such a relationship. The tendency toward polarization and vacillation would undoubtedly lead to inaccuracies in one's estimate of one's competencies.

Some support for this argument comes from our data on children's perceptions of their cognitive competence. The weakest relationships between one's perceived and one's actual competence occur during (1) the preschool years (corresponding to Level 1 of Stage I), (2) third grade (corresponding to Level 1 of Stage II), and (3) seventh grade (corresponding to Level 1 of Stage III). Perceived competence is more realistic (in terms of its correlation with objective indexes) during those ages or grades that would correspond to Level 2 of each stage, for example, first and second grade, then fifth and sixth grades, and then eighth and ninth grades. It would be during these latter grades, then, that one would expect the relationship between importance judgments and estimates of competence or adequacy to best predict self-worth. One can extend this logic to make predictions for individuals within these developmental levels, as suggested earlier. The more accurate the individual, the better the importance–adequacy relationship would predict self-worth.

It was pointed out in this section that our models of the self in recent years have been relatively static in that they have not reflected the dynamic interplay between the attributes of the self-system, they have not spoken to the phenomenological experience of the self. There is a related sense in which our models do not seem to mirror this experience in that they are virtually devoid of affect or emotion. That is, they do not adequately deal with one's affective reactions to one's self-perceptions. We turn to the topic of self-related affect in the next section.

SELF-RELATED AFFECTS

A major focus of this chapter involves the topic of self-worth or self-esteem that in the layperson's parlance typically refers to how one feels about one's worth. Yet in our recent models of the self little attention has been devoted to the specific role that affect plays in the self-system, despite the historical precedent in the works of James and Cooley. For James (1892/1963), the emotions that were aroused by one's self-definition, for example, pride and vanity, as well as shame and mortification, were an integral part of the self-system. In fact, James divided the various aspects of the self into three parts: (1) the constituents of the self, namely the domains of self-evaluation, for example, the material me, the social me, and the spiritual me; (2) the feelings and emotions they arouse, for example, specific forms of self-appreciation or self-dissatisfaction, as well as (3) the acts that they prompt. Thus, for James, affects were not only reactions to one's self-evaluation, but the impetus, the motivation as it were, for the behaviors that followed.

Cooley (1902) also placed considerable emphasis on affect. For Cooley, what becomes the self is what we imagine that others think of us, of our appearance, aims, deeds, character, and so forth. Thus, others in our social network play the role of a mirror, leading Cooley to the concept of the *looking-glass self*. Cooley addressed three components of the looking-glass self: (1) the imagination of the attributes that others ascribe to us, (2) the imagination of how others judge or *evaluate* those attributes, and (3) some sort of "self-feeling" such as pride or mortification. Moreover, he identified a wide range of potential emotions or self-affects. His treatment of this topic differentiates between such positive affects as pride, vanity, self-respect, reverence, confidence, and hope, and between such negative affects as shame, mortification, guilt, contrition, self-abnegation, and resentment. His discussion also includes the identification of the particular conditions under which these various self-feelings are aroused.

Within the clinical literature, certain affective components of the self have also been highlighted, particularly among neo-Freudians, although the focus has been largely on the negative emotions associated with low self-esteem (Adler, 1927; Horney, 1945, 1950; Sullivan, 1953). In Horney's theory of neurosis, self-demeaning feelings are at the root of one's basic anxiety. In order to successfully cope with this anxiety, the neurotic must construct an idealized image toward which one strives, in order to enhance one's self-esteem. Sullivan also emphasized the individual's need to ward off anxiety provoked by threats to one's self-esteem, threats that primarily caused the rejection or negative evaluation of others.

More recently, Epstein (1973) has been one of the few theorists to resurrect affect as an important component of the self-system. He contends that a major function played by the self-theory is to optimize the psychological pleasure–pain balance and to maintain self-esteem. Epstein notes that in childhood, we begin to observe how threats to the sense of self cause emotional "pain," although how such hurt or injury to the psychological self comes to be experienced is less than clear. However, Epstein points out that phenomenologically, the feeling is perceived as something in the body that appears to have an identity all its own. In bolstering his point about the importance of affect, he concludes that "it is not surprising that the self is conceptualized as a spiritual homunculus rather than as a hierarchical organization of concepts that assimilates experience and guides behavior" (p. 414).

In recent years, we have witnessed the emergence of affect within a related theoretical arena, namely the development of models of self-control. These models (e.g., Bandura, 1978; Kanfer, 1970, 1971, 1980; Duval & Wicklund, 1972; Wicklund, 1975; Wicklund & Frey, 1980) postulate the sequential operation of several components in the self-control process. The chain begins with self-observation or self-monitoring, followed by self-evaluation, which in turn ushers in self-reward or self-punishment. These self-rewards or punishments typically have affective correlates. In the theories of both Bandura and Wicklund, the affective reactions are more explicit. For Wicklund, the third component in the chain is identified as an affective reaction, either positive or negative, and it is this affective response that then mediates behavior. In Bandura's most recent model (1978) self-affects are produced as part of the self-evaluation process, and these affects also mediate subsequent behavior. For Bandura, "Much of human behavior is regulated through self-evaluative consequences in the form of self-satisfaction, self-pride, self-dissatisfaction, and self-criticism" (p. 350). To date, however, both Wicklund and Bandura have inferred such affectively laden reactions from either the positive or negative self-evaluative judgment made by subjects; they have not yet measured this affective component directly.

From a variety of theoretical perspectives, then, we see that affect has been introduced as an important consideration in the treatment of the self. However, these theoretical arguments have yet to provoke a compelling empirical attack on the role of self-related affect. A contrasting picture emerges when one examines those psychometric attempts to assess self-concept or self-esteem. From an empirical standpoint, we do encounter items that are couched in affective language, for example, "I worry about my schoolwork," "I am often afraid," "I get upset at home." However, the responses to these items are typically given no theoretical or conceptual status, but are merely averaged in with evaluative items that do not make reference to affect, for example, "I am good at my schoolwork," "I have alot of friends."

Recent work from our own laboratory suggests the fruitfulness of attending to the distinction between items that primarily tap the latter evaluative judgment and those that make reference to affect. In examining the items that comprised the cognitive subscale of our perceived competence scale, Connell and I observed that approximately half of the items seemed to tap the evaluation of one's competence based on relatively objective criteria such as the speed of doing one's work, the ease of remembering material, getting good grades. However, a separate subset of items were couched in more affective language, making reference to feeling good or badly about one's work, worrying about completing schoolwork, and so forth. In one study, therefore (Connell, 1981; Harter & Connell, 1984) we calculated two separate scores, one of which we labeled competence *evaluation* and one of which was designated as competence *affect.* Employing causal modeling procedures, we sought to investigate how each of these components was related to other constructs in our model, namely perceptions of control, achievement, and intrinsic mastery motivation, all within the cognitive domain.

Our findings revealed the following predictive chain: perceptions of control predicts actual scholastic achievement which in turn influences the evaluative component of one's perceived cognitive competence. This evaluation predicts the affective reaction, which in turn mediates the motivational–behavioral component, namely intrinsic mastery motivation. Of further interest was the finding that mediating the link between affect and mastery motivation was stronger for junior high school pupils than for elementary school children (see Harter & Connell, 1984).

One limitation of the study just described was the fact that the number of items comprising both the evaluative and the affective components was relatively small, which in turn attenuated the reliability of these indexes. Thus, in a related study Beigel (1982) sought to remedy this problem by devising a 15-item affect subscale. All items required that children make judgments about whether they felt either good or bad about various aspects of their scholastic performance. Beigel found that the affect score, reflecting the degree to which the child felt good or bad about school performance, bore strong relationships (between .52 and .63) to other self-perceptions in the academic achievement, and perceived *initiative* in attempting and completing schoolwork. (Initiative items focus on trying hard to do well, trying to understand and remember what one learns, doing homework assignments, paying attention to the teacher, and studying alot.)

Of further interest was the question of which variables in the network best predict the affective component. Beigel found that one can best account for competence affect with an additive model involving both perceived competence and initiative. Thus, the children who expressed the most positive affect over schoolwork were those with the highest level of perceived cognitive competence in combination with the highest level of perceived initiative in the scholastic domain. Those who felt the worst about their performance were those with low levels of perceived competence in conjunction with a low level of perceived initiative. Thus, it would appear that not only must one have a positive view of one's competence, but display some effort toward this end, in order to experience the most positive affect. We return to this issue in the subsequent section on perceptions of responsibility and control.

Individual and Domain Differences

We also have evidence that different emotions are evoked by success and failure at different competence levels. In one study, Kowalski and I asked fifth and sixth graders to select from a list of good and bad feelings those that they would experience in relation to both academic success and academic failure. Good feelings included happy, proud, relieved, and surprised, whereas bad feelings included mad, frustrated, worried, ashamed, guilty, sad, depressed, and jealous. With regard to academic success, proud was mentioned most frequently (43%) followed by happy (35%), and then the categories of relieved and surprised combined (22%).

However, the first two categories of happy and proud were employed somewhat differently for those whose cognitive competence was above the group mean compared to those below the mean. Proud was acknowledged by 51% of those above the mean compared to 34% below the mean, whereas the pattern was reversed for "happy" with 29% of those above the mean citing this emotion compared to 41% of those below the mean. Thus, for the cognitively competent child, pride is the emotional reaction more likely to accompany scholastic success whereas for the less competent child, happy is favored slightly over proud.

When one examines the negative emotions, in response to academic failure, reactions are relatively evenly divided across five emotion categories: frustration (24%), anger (23%), sadness plus depression (22%), shame plus guilt (21%), and worry (13%). Here, there was no pattern associated with competence level, however with regard to two emotional reactions, there were gender differences. There was more acknowledgment of anger among boys (36%) compared to girls (11%), whereas there was more admission of worry among girls (23%) compared to boys (4%).

In pursuing the affects associated with various self-evaluative judgments, we will also need to attend to the issue of domain. For example, in the study just described, we also asked children to give us their emotional reactions to success and failure within the social domain of peer relationships. There were some interesting departures from the patterns obtained in the cognitive domain. For example, the predominant emotional reaction to social success is happiness, in contrast to pride for the cognitive domain. For the social domain, 63% of the children cited happiness, 32% reported pride, and only 6% relief or surprise. Moreover, unlike the cognitive domain, there were no differences associated with perceived level of social acceptance or gender.

With regard to negative affective reactions, the pattern was also different when compared to the cognitive domain. The predominant negative emotion when one encounters social failure involves sadness and depression (46%), with anger as the second most frequent reaction (23%). Frustration, worry, shame and guilt, as well as jealousy were also relatively low in frequency (each between 5% and 10%). These findings indicate, therefore, that we not only need to take into account the specific affect experienced, but its relationship to domain.

We began this general section on affect with an intellectual tribute to James and Cooley whose particular interest was in *self*-related affect, namely emotions directed toward the self as the target. In the study just described, two specific self-affects were included: (1) proud, among the positive emotions and (2) ashamed, among the negative feelings. We saw that these two self-affects were more likely to be cited in the cognitive realm, where the focus was on competence, than in the social realm, where social acceptance was the concern. Thus, it may be that in domains where the specific skills of the self are involved, self-affects will be more prevalent than in domains where other factors are responsible for one's success or failure. Bolstering this relationship are our findings on the types of attributions children of this age make for their successes and failures in these two domains. Children are much more likely to take responsibility for both their successes and failures in the cognitive domain than in the social domain, where powerful others and/or unknown factors are cited. We return to these findings in the section on perceptions of responsibility and control.

Weiner's (Weiner, Kun, & Benesh-Weiner, 1980) work is also relevant here. Weiner has made a strong argument for the fact that emotions are more highly related to the nature of the attributions one makes than to success or failure outcomes per se. Thus, if one attributes one's successes to one's own ability, one will feel confident and competent, whereas if one attributes success to others, one will feel gratitude. To take another example, if one attributes failure to lack of effort, one will experience guilt or shame, whereas if one perceives others as the cause of one's failures, one will feel aggression. It is of interest that some of the affects in Weiner's model are affects directed toward the self, for example, guilt and shame, whereas the target for the other affects is external, for example, in the case of aggression. We explore this distinction further, in the following section on self-affects.

The Development of Self-Related Affects

In addressing the specific affects experienced by children, we must turn our attention to which emotions are truly affects directed toward the self and which are directed elsewhere, toward others or toward the situation. For example, when our older elementary school children acknowledge that they are mad or angry, we do not know whether they are angry at teachers, the scholastic situation, or at themselves. Nor do we know at what point in development children become capable of self-related affect, for example, anger toward the self.

We have some clues from our work on the development of children's understanding of two affects, pride and shame (Harter, 1982a). In one study children were asked to define these two feelings which were embedded in a list of several other emotions including happy, loving, sad, mad, scared, and worried. For both of the potential self-affects, pride and shame, a four-stage developmental sequence was suggested. Our youngest subjects (ages 3 and 4 years) were unable to define these terms, although they *could* give adequate definitions of emotions such as happy, mad, sad, and scared. At the next level (ages 4 to 5 years), children reported that proud is a "good" feeling and ashamed is a "bad" feeling, although they could not give examples of appropriate situations in which these would occur. The first adequate examples and/or definitions to emerge (ages 5 to 7 years) focused on how *others* could be proud or ashamed of the *self*. Sample responses were "Dad was proud of me when I took out the trash" or "Mom was proud of me when I brought home a good report card." For ashamed, examples were "My mom was ashamed of me for doing something I wasn't supposed to do" or "Mom said, 'shame on you' for making a mess in the basement."

It was not until the age of 8 years and older that children could give acceptable examples of how one could be proud or ashamed of oneself. These responses also implied that children experience these feelings in the absence of observation or surveillance from others, for example, "When you throw milk at someone, the next day you are ashamed of yourself"; "Like when you pass a test or do a good deed you feel proud of yourself"; "When I thought about how I hurt someone's feelings, I was ashamed of myself;" "I put up a bathroom shelf and I felt so proud of myself."

This four-stage sequence suggests that the acquisition of self-affects such as pride and shame undergo a developmental internalization process in which socialization plays an important role. Children first develop a very rudimentary awareness of the valence of these two feelings, realizing that proud is a good feeling and ashamed is a bad feeling, presumably from the contexts in which these terms are employed by parents or other socialization agents. However, it is not until about the age of 5 or 6 years that children use these terms more specifically; interestingly their first understanding at this level involves their realization that others are proud or ashamed of the self. Their descriptions at this level include references to the emotional reactions others have toward the self. In describing proud, others are happy with the self, whereas in shame, others are angry toward the self. At this stage, however, they cannot yet appreciate that the self can be proud or ashamed of itself. Gradually, however, children come to be able to adopt the outlook of the significant others in their life, they internalize this evaluative function as well as the accompanying emotional reaction. That is, they can perform the evaluative role of others, they can evaluate an action performed by the self, and then emotionally react by being either proud or ashamed of the self.

This analysis suggests that self-affects such as pride and shame undergo a complicated internalization process and that the final stage involves three components: (1) the self performs an action for which it claims responsibility; (2) the self evaluates that action either positively or negatively; and (3) the self experiences an emotional reaction of either pride (if the evaluation is positive) or shame (for negative evaluations) which can occur in the absence of surveillance or specific feedback from others.

One of the interesting questions that Cooley addressed with regard to adults involved the particular actions that lead one to feel self-affects such as pride or shame. We have been able to analyze children's responses in order to identify the specific actions that cause them to experience pride and shame. Often it appears that the layperson thinks of these two emotions as natural opposites, pride versus shame, as if somehow the actions leading to both bear some relationship to each other. Our content analyses suggest otherwise. For pride, the responses clearly indicate that one feels proud of oneself for accomplishments or achievements that involve competence. These accomplishments involve the display of cognitive competence (getting an A or 100 on a test, getting a good report card), physical competence (scoring a goal, hitting a home run, doing a gymnastics feat), or other achievements such as babysitting for the first time, making something like shelves, or general references to doing something the best. In certain instances children make specific references to winning an award, medal, or prize, whereas in other cases there is no mention of such public recognition.

In contrast to these content categories, those that emerge for the self-affect of shame largely make reference to actions that are anti-social or morally bad. That is, one engages in acts that one is "not supposed to" perform. Examples include stealing food or toys, throwing milk at someone, telling on somebody, hitting people, disobeying one's parents, and losing one's temper. Descriptions of shame in response to lack of competence are rare, although upon occasion we will have such a response (e.g., "I was ashamed when I got two Cs"). We should note that the children in our samples have been 12 years of age or younger. Thus we have no data on whether competence emerges at later ages as a domain in which shame is commonly experienced. Similarly, we do not have data on the issue of whether morally proper conduct leads to feelings of pride at older ages. However, for children between the ages of 8 and 12 years, the picture is quite clear: pride is an emotional response to an evaluation of one's competence, whereas shame is an affective reaction to antisocial conduct, behaviors that are not morally condoned.

Implications for a Model of General Self-Worth

In the preceding section, we have dealt with such issues as the affective reactions that accompany self-evaluations, affect as a mediator of behavior, the effects of perceived initiative and perceived competence on affect, individual differences in affective reactions, the need to consider the domain-specific nature of affective reactions, and the development of self-related affects such as pride and shame. However, we have yet to explore the implications of these issues for a comprehensive theory of self-worth. Two suggestions emerge from the discussion of these issues. The more general suggestion involves the need to consider domain-specific affects in our prediction and understanding of one's more global sense of esteem. The second involves our focus on self-related affects, as the major emotional reactions that will influence sense of self-worth. We first deal with the latter consideration.

If we are to introduce affect into the equation, it behooves us to determine whether we need to limit ourselves to those emotions that have direct bearing on the self. This would seem to be a logical constraint, at least as a first step. That is, those affects that directly implicate the self, emotions such as self-pride and self-blame, should have the major impact on our sense of global self-worth. Yet this task may be easier said than done. For example, when subjects indicate that they are angry or depressed, do these constitute self-affects or do they represent emotions directed toward someone or something outside of the self? Our procedures to date do not allow for this kind of determination. Therefore, we need to devise methods to determine the particular targets of such emotions, in order to identify the degree to which the self is both the experiencer of these feelings as well as the target toward which they are directed.

In this regard, the emotion of depression is particularly interesting. For example, what is the difference between depression and sadness among children? In presenting the findings in the section on individual and domain differences, we combined these two categories since there was no clear basis on which to distinguish them. Yet if one considers the adult literature on depression, we would anticipate that the negative emotional reaction involves anger toward the self, which is distinguishable from sadness due to loss or other unhappy events that are more external in origin. With children, therefore, we need to examine the meaning attached to their use of such terms as depression, in order to determine the extent to which this is truly a self-related affect. We hope to address this question within a larger project in which we are devising a new self-report instrument to tap a number of potential components of depression in children, affect, energy/interest, self-worth, and self-blame (Harter & Polesovsky, 1985).

Presumably, then, we will want to include those emotions that appear to be legitimate self-affects, as potential determinants of global self-worth. The strength of these self-affects would be predicted to impact this overall judgment such that high scores on such positive emotions as pride, coupled with low scores on such emotions as shame, would be indicative of high regard for the self. However, within what context do we assess or obtain such ratings? Do we merely examine the positivity or negativity of self-affects that are attached to the adequacy judgments for the particular domains in the model? This would be one strategy. For example, if these domains include cognitive competence, physical competence, social acceptance, conduct, and appearance, we would simply assess the level of one's affective reaction (from positive to negative) for each of the emotions that we have previously identified as self-affects. These values would be incorporated into our prediction equation.

However, might there not be other affective reactions in question? For example, an argument was presented earlier emphasizing the need to consider the relationship between one's self-estimates of ability or adequacy across the various domains in one's life and the importance of these domains. Thus, it was argued that the more one's abilities were in tune with one's values, the more one would feel a positive sense of self-worth. If this relationship is critical, might we not also want to obtain some measure of one's affective reaction to the congruence or disparity between one's aspirations and one's abilities? Might not *that* emotional response be the critical predictor of one's global sense of worth? Or does that affect reduce, somehow, to the sum of the affects attached to each of the specific domains deemed relevant? These are the types of issues we will need to pursue in determining which affective reactions are the most critical in leading to our overall feelings of self-worth. While ambiguities remain, the major point of this section is that both children and adults have strong affective reactions to the entities that comprise the self, and in order to appreciate the factors contributing to one's global sense of self-worth, we undoubtedly need to take these emotional reactions into account.

PERCEPTIONS OF CONTROL

An examination of both our current models of the self and those psychometric instruments designed to tap the self-concept reveals that we have focused primarily on relatively static characteristics or attributes of the self. That is, we assess the degree to which an individual judges the self to be athletic, smart, popular, attractive, morally good, and so forth. However, we have yet to include the more dynamic consideration of the extent to which the individual feels causally responsible for these attributes and/or the actions on which much judgments are based. There is a burgeoning literature, to be sure, on such constructs as locus of control (Rotter, 1975), learned helplessness (Seligman, 1975), self-efficacy (Bandura, 1977, 1981), self-determination (Deci, 1975; deCharms, 1968), effectance motivation (Harter, 1978; White, 1959, 1960, 1963), and beneffectance (Greenwald, 1980). However, we have yet to adequately incorporate these constructs into our specific models of the self, although certain theorists have pointed to the importance of these constructs at a more general level.

Cooley (1902) was one of the first to assert that one's "self-feeling" was intimately bound up in the exercise of power and one's sense of being a casual agent. He placed the origins of this relationship in infancy, citing the infant's earliest attempts to control his or her limbs, playthings, his bottle, as well as the later attempts to control the actions of the people in one's social environment. In a similar vein,

White (1963) has postulated that the roots of self-esteem lie in the developing infant's sense of efficacy.

More recent theorists have echoed this theme. For example, Bannister and Agnew (1977) have contended that the personal sense of cause is one of the defining features of the self. In their words: "The construing of ourselves as agent is clearly a superordinate contribution towards a total construction of the self" (p. 102). Brim (1976) has also argued that one's sense of personal control is central to one's self-theory. As noted earlier in this chapter, both Coopersmith (1967) and Epstein (1973) identified *power* as one of the major dimensions of self-evaluation, although in these formulations power seems to be more narrowly defined as the ability to control and influence other people.

Most recently, Bandura (1977, 1978, 1981) has introduced the concept of *self-efficacy*, noting that among the different facets of self-knowledge, perhaps none is more central to people's everyday lives than their sense of personal efficacy. More specifically, he has related this concept to the self-affects experienced by the individual. People, he writes, "take pride in their accomplishments when they ascribe their success to their own abilities and efforts. They do not derive much self-satisfaction, however, when they view their performances as heavily dependent upon external factors" (1978, p. 349).

Within the child literature there are some data to support the position that one's sense of control is somehow critical to one's evaluation of the self (see Harter, 1983). Studies (e.g., Prawat, Grissom, & Parish, 1979) examining the relationship between global measures of both self-esteem and locus of control report moderately high correlations. Others, for example, Piers (1977a), have found that self-concept was significantly related to responsibility for success, but not for failure. However, there are also findings (Felker & Thomas, 1971) suggesting that this relationship holds only for girls, but not for boys.

In our own research we have concentrated to date on domain-specific relationships between one's perceived competence and one's sense of control. Our control scale (Connell, 1980) allows for the independent assessment of three sources of control: Internal, Powerful Others, and Unknown. The history of the emergence of the Unknown subscale has been described in detail elsewhere (see Connell, 1980; Harter, 1980; Harter & Connell, 1984). Basically it taps the degree to which children acknowledge that they do not know who or what is in control. For all three sources of control, there are separate subscales for success and failure within each competence domain (cognitive, social, and physical).

Within both the cognitive domain (Harter & Connell, 1984) as well as the domain of athletics (Costomiris, 1984), we have found that it is the Unknown scale which is most highly correlated with perceptions of competence. The more children say they do not understand what controls their successes and failures, the lower their perceptions of competence. Conversely, children "in the know," as it were, have positive perceptions of their competence. In two studies, we have examined the relationship between perceived competence and perceptions of control for successes and failures, separately. Here we find the same pattern for both the cognitive (Bierer, 1982) and athletic (Costomiris, 1984) domains: it is the Unknown *success* score that correlates most highly with perceived competence. Thus, it is the understanding of who or what controls one's successes as opposed to failures, that best predicts one's sense of competence. Internal responsibility for success also predicts perceived competence, although the magnitude of this correlation is not as great, in part due to a somewhat attenuated range for the internal success score.

In a related study, Beigel (1982) found that personal initiative was also highly related to children's competence judgments in the cognitive domain: the more scholastic initiative children reported, the higher their perceived cognitive competence as well as the more positive their affect regarding their school performance. Thus, these findings point to a pattern in that one's understanding and sense of responsibility for one's successes, in particular, appears to be positively related to feelings of competence within that domain.

What is needed, however, is a broader picture of how feelings of control and responsibility relate to global self-worth. In so doing, we will undoubtedly need to build upon certain themes introduced earlier in this chapter. For example, we may well want to only consider one's sense of control over those domains that have been deemed important by the individual. That is, lack of control may be less critical in those domains identified as less less important. Whether we should restrict our consideration to one's sense of control over successes, or include failures as well, is a more complicated issue. We return to this question after we discuss a related topic, namely the tendency for individuals to take more responsibility for their successes than their failures.

Beneffectance among Children

In an interesting twist on the concept of locus of control, Greenwald (1980) recently introduced a new construct which he terms "beneffectance." Basically, *beneffectance* is the "tendency to take credit for success while denying responsibility for failure" (p. 605). This predisposition to be selectively responsible for desired, but not undesired outcomes, was viewed as a mechanism through which one's image of self is protected or enhanced. The particular term beneffectance was derived by Greenwald from a combination of benefficience (achieving desirable outcomes) and effectance (White, 1959), namely the motivation to act competently. Greenwald musters an array of evidence suggesting that this self-protective tendency is alive and well among adults. However, he did not address the question of whether one would also expect to find it among children.

Recently, Mari Jo Renick and I have sought to address this question empirically. As a first step, we attempted to define beneffectance operationally, based on scores that we could create from Connell's (1980) perceptions of control scale. Recall that this scale taps one's sense of responsibility for successes and failures separately. Moreover, independent control scores are available for internal control as well as for two sources of external control, powerful others or unknown.

The major contrast of interest was between internal control versus noninternal control for success and failure separately. Thus we could examine the pattern among four scores for an individual within a given domain: Internal Success, Internal Failure, External (powerful others or unknown) Success, and External Failure.

As can be seen in Table 2.2, we defined beneffectance in terms of three relationships (labeled as Component I, II, and III) among these four scores. Thus, the *strongest form of beneffectance,* in keeping with Greenwald's concept, was defined as follows: (I) Internal Success score greater than Internal Failure; (II) Internal Success greater than External Success; and (III) Internal Failure less than External Failure. Thus, the individual with this pattern of scores is, in effect, telling us that (I) I am more responsible for my successes than I am for may failures, (II) I am more responsible for my successes than are external factors, and (III) I am less responsible for my failures than are external factors.

We restricted our initial empirical inquiry to the *cognitive* domain, that is, control over one's academic successes and failures. In examining the scores of a group of approximately 300 third through sixth graders, we discovered that there were three additional patterns or types of children which could be identified, based on somewhat different relationships among these same four scores. We have labeled these as the weak form of beneffectance, high internality, and self-blame. The patterns defining these types are also presented in Table 2.2.

Children displaying the *weak form of beneffectance* exhibit Component I, taking more internal responsibility for success than failure, as

TABLE 2.2
Four Types of Children Based on Their Patterns of
Control Scores for the Cognitive Domain[a]

STRONG FORM OF BENEFFECTANCE

	II	
Internal Success	>	External Success
I ∨		
Internal Failure	III	External Failure
	<	

WEAK FORM OF BENEFFECTANCE

	II	
Internal Success	>	External Success
I ∨		
Internal Failure	III	External Failure
	>	

HIGH INTERNALITY

	II	
Internal Success	>	External Success
I ‖		
Internal Failure	III	External Failure
	>	

SELF-BLAME

	II	
Internal Success	≥	External Success
I ∧		
Internal Failure	III	External Failure
	>	

---

[a]Roman numerals I, II, III indicate three types of
relationships that define beneffectance.

well as Component II, taking more internal responsibility for success than they credit to external factors. However, the direction of Component III is reversed, such that these children take more internal responsibility for their failures than they give to external factors. To us, this appeared to be a diluted form of beneffectance, as Greenwald has described it, since these children are *not* denying responsibility for their failures. However, they do manifest elements of the beneffectance concept in that they take more responsibility for successes than failures and take more responsibility for their successes than they are willing to give to factors outside the self.

A third type of child exhibited the pattern we have labeled as *high internality*. As can be seen in Table 2.2, the hallmark of this pattern is found in Relationship I where these children take *equal* responsibility for their successes and failures, and these scores are at the extreme high end of the scale. Component II and Component III are similar to the weak form of beneffectance in that these children take more responsibility for their successes than they give to external forces, however they also take more responsibility for their failures, relative to factors external to the self.

Finally, a fourth type of child was identified, those who appear to manifest what we have termed *self-blame*. These children take more responsibility for their failures than their successes (Component I), take more responsibility for their failures than they give to external factors (Component III), and take either equal or slightly greater responsibility for their successes than they credit to external factors (Component II).

Having defined the groups in this manner, one might next ask what was the magnitude of the differences between the scores defining these four patterns or types of children. Figure 2.1 presents these data. As can be seen in this figure, those children exhibiting the *strong* form of beneffectance take substantially more responsibility for their successes, compared to their failures, and markedly more responsibility for their successes compared to the credit they give to external sources. They take less responsibility for failures compared to external sources, although the magnitude of this difference is not as great.

For those exhibiting the *weaker* form of beneffectance, there is more internal responsibility for successes than failures, however, this difference is not as marked as for those showing the extreme form. Similar to the strong form, these children take much more responsibility for their successes than they credit to external sources (Component II). However, there is a dramatic reversal in the third component, relative to those exhibiting the strong form, a reversal which represents the primary difference between these types: those manifesting the weak form take much more responsibility for their failures than they attribute to external factors.

When one examines the pattern for *high internality*, one finds that with regard to the first component, scores for both Internal Success and Internal Failure approach the ceiling for this scale, namely four points. Component II and Component III are consistent with this pattern in that these children take more responsibility for successes, as well as failures, than they attribute to external factors.

Finally, an examination of the pattern for those manifesting *self-blame* reveals that more responsibility is taken for failures than for successes, a reversal of the three previous patterns. With regard to the second component, Internal Success scores are only slightly higher

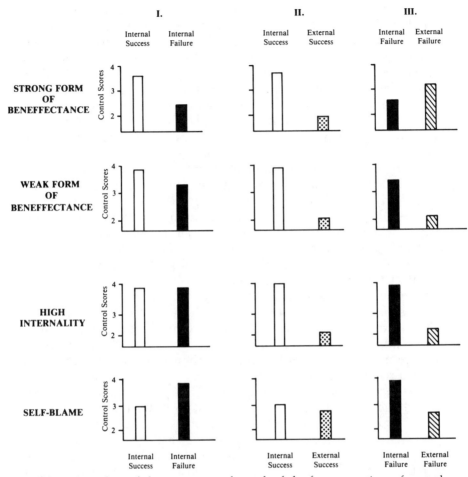

Figure 2.1 Values of the components for each of the four perceptions of control patterns in children.

than External Success scores, and finally, for the third component, more responsibility is taken for failurs than is given to external factors.

Frequency of Children Exhibiting Each Pattern

Our next question involved an examination of the frequency with which these patterns were exhibited among elementary school children. In particular, we were interested in whether beneffectance, which had been identified by Greenwald as a relatively pervasive self-protective strategy in adults, existed with such seeming universality among children. We first determined that 88% of the children in our sample could clearly be characterized as exhibiting one of the four patterns described. The remaining 12% either did not completely meet a given criterion or showed idiosyncratic patterns that were difficult to characterize or interpret. The 88%, which we could clearly type, broke down into the following percentages for each of the four patterns: only 7% exhibited the strong form of beneffectance, 24% manifested the weak form of beneffectance, 52% were classified as high internal, and only 5% met the criteria for self-blame.

The answer to the question of whether beneffectance is a pervasive tendency among children for the cognitive domain is a resounding *no*, particularly if one treats the strong form as most consistent with Greenwald's definition. Rather, the predominant pattern is high internality, where children take equally high responsibility for their academic successes and failures. Approximately one-fourth of the elementary school children in this sample exhibited the weak form of beneffectance. However, recall that children exhibiting this pattern take considerably more responsibility for their failures, relative to external sources. In fact this relationship characterized three of the four patterns, the exception being the strong form of beneffectance. Thus, among this group of third through sixth graders, only 7% saw others as more responsible for their failures than they were, namely those who showed the strong form of beneffectance.

We sought to pursue this interesting finding, by addressing three related questions. We first asked what other characteristics are manifested by these four types of children, by examining their perceived competence, their preference for academic challenge, as well as their scholastic anxiety. In looking at these profiles, we hoped to glean some insight into the network of self-related constructs for the four types of children. Secondly, we entertained the possibility that there may be some domain specificity with regard to the frequency of children in each pattern. Thus, while beneffectance may not be prevalent in the cognitive domain, might it be more likely to emerge in other domains, such as the responsibility that one takes for one's social successes and failures? Thirdly, we were interested in whether there might be developmental difference in the frequency with which children displayed these patterns. If beneffectance does indeed seem to represent a self-enhancement strategy employed by adults, might we find that while it is not common among elementary school children, it becomes more common as one moves into adolescence, and perhaps beyond?

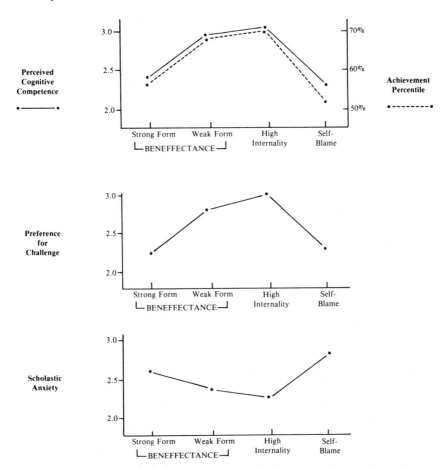

Figure 2.2 Perceived cognitive competence, achievement, preference for challenge, and scholastic anxiety for each of the four perceptions of control patterns in the cognitive domain.

Characteristics and Self-Perceptions of Each Type

For this same sample of children we had the following self-report scores available for the cognitive domain: (1) perceived cognitive competence, (2) actual scholastic competence in the form of standardized achievement test scores, (3) preference for scholastic challenge, and (4) anxiety in the scholastic domain. These findings are presented in Figure 2.2, for the fifth- and sixth-grade children only. While a similar pattern was observed for the third- and fourth-grade subjects, the magnitude of the differences among types of children was not nearly as striking.

As can be seen in Figure 2.2, when one examines both the perceived and actual competence of the four types, the picture is quite clear. Those children exhibiting high internality and the weaker form of beneffectance are the most cognitively competent, with regard to their perceptions as well as their actual achievement. The two extreme groups, those showing the strong form of beneffectance as well as those manifesting what we have labeled as self-blame, have considerably lower perceptions of their academic competence, perceptions that are consistent with their achievement levels.

When one examines the preference for challenge, as well as the scholastic anxiety scores, one finds patterns consistent with the perceived competence findings. It is the high internal group, followed closely by those manifesting the weak form of beneffectance, who report the highest preference for challenge. Both of the extreme groups, those characterized by the strong form of beneffectance and by self-blame, have substantially lower scores. The anxiety scores are consistent with this pattern in that the weak beneffectance and the high internal groups report the least anxiety, whereas the anxiety levels of the two extreme groups are higher.

These additional data allow us to begin to construct cameos, as it were, of the different groups. It is the high internal group that makes the strongest showing, *if* one views high competence, high preference for challenge, and low anxiety as positive, adaptive, characteristics. These children are achieving at a relatively high level, they perceive themselves to be relatively competent, they prefer challenge, and they are among the least anxious. Thus, their extremely high sense of responsibility for their academic failures does not appear to be psychologically detrimental. These are children who undoubtedly experience less *actual* failure, compared to the other groups, and their high preference for challenge suggests that they do not anticipate failure; that is, they do not appear to be avoiding difficult work that might lead to failure experiences. Their relatively low anxiety score is consistent with this interpretation. One could speculate that these children take responsibility for failure, if and when it should occur, but do not engage in self-blame. Such children may be better able to learn from failure experiences, rather than see these as a devastating commentary on the self. These interpretations are merely conjecture. However, they suggest that in pursuing the perceptions of control construct we might want to make a distinction between *responsibility* and *blame*. That is, attributions interpreted as responsibility may, for certain groups, have positive implications for the self, whereas attributions interpreted as blame, may lead to negative self-evaluations.

To pursue this reasoning, consider the pattern of attributions we have labeled as self-blame. If one compares the internal failure scores of this group to the internal flame scores of the group labeled as high internals, we find that they are virtually identical, that is, both groups have relatively high scores. However, for the self-blame group, we must consider that the responsibility for failure occurs within the context of relatively low perceived, as well as actual, competence. Thus, for this group such scores might be best interpreted as blame for poor performance. The finding that the group labeled as self-blame also exhibits the highest level of anxiety is consistent with such an interpretation. What we are suggesting here is that the meaning of the internal failure score may be different for the two groups in question, and thus have different implications for the self. However, this is merely an inference, given the overall constellation of scores for these groups. We need to pursue this possibility empirically, through methods which allow us to make clear distinctions between blame, responsibility, and their positive or negative implications.

How are the scores for those displaying the strong form of beneffectance to be interpreted? When one compares their perceived competence, actual competence, preference for challenge, as well as scholastic anxiety to the scores of those identified as manifesting self-blame, we find that the mean levels are virtually identical. Yet the pattern of causal attributions leading to the categorization of these two groups is extremely different. Children in the strong beneffectance category take more responsibility for their success than their failure, whereas children in the self-blame group do just the opposite, they take more responsibility for their failure than their success. Children in the strong beneffectance category see themselves as less responsible for their failures, relative to external factors, whereas those in the self-blame group do just the opposite, taking more responsibility for their failures than they attribute to external factors.

Thus, while both of these extreme groups have similar patterns on other dependent measures of interest, it would appear that we need to interpret these scores differently. Those exhibiting the strong form of beneffectance would appear to have a very different style which may be characterized as defensively self-protective. That is, these are children who are not doing well in school, seem to be aware that they are not, and are relatively anxious about their performance. In order to cope with this situation, perhaps they avoid challenge, lest it provide an arena for failure, and seem to project the blame for the failure they do

experience onto external factors. Of interest, in these interpretive speculations, is that the term *reponsibility* seems appropriate in some contexts, whereas the term *blame* seems to lead to a more accurate rendering in other contexts. In our further explorations into the dynamics of
these various types of children, therefore, we will need to be clearer in
terms of what we mean by responsibility versus blame.

Attributional Patterns within the Social Domain

One finding of interest within the typologies identified for the cognitive domain was that the majority of children fell within the category characterized by high internality for both success and failure. We
next sought to determine whether the picture differed if one examined
the domain of social acceptance by peers. For the same group of subjects, therefore, we first looked to see whether the same attributional
patterns even existed.

We found that the same four patterns did exist in the social domain,
the strong form of beneffectance, the weak form of beneffectance, high
internality, and self-blame. However, a fifth pattern emerged, one that
we could not ignore. For lack of a better term, at this point, we have
identified it as an intermediate form of beneffectance, intermediate in
the sense that it seems to fall between the strong and the weak form. It
meets the two criteria that both original forms have in common. That
is, with regard to the first component, these children take more responsibility for their social successes than they do their failures. With regard to the second component, they also take more responsibility for
their social successes than they credit to external sources. On the third
component, the relationship between Internal Failure and External
Failure, they share features in common with both the strong and the
weak form of beneffectance.

Recall that the control scale yielding scores for this typological analysis contained two potential external or noninternal attributions: children could indicate that either powerful others were in control or that
they did not know who or what was in control. Within the *cognitive*
domain, these two external control scores bore a consistent relationship to the internal score; for example, with regard to the third
component, the relationship between internal and external failure, the
internal responsibility score was consistently lower than both of these
external attributions for the strong beneffectance group, or consistently higher than both external attributions for the other three
groups. Thus, for the purposes of typing children, it made sense to
combine these two noninternal attributions and conceptualize them as
external.

TABLE 2.3
New Intermediate Form of Beneffectance to
Emerge for the Social Domain

Internal Success	II	External Success
	>	
I ∨		
	III	
	<	Unknown
Internal Failure		
	>	Powerful Others

In examining the empirical patterns represented by children in their ratings of the *social* domain, we found it necessary to treat the two external sources separately, with regard to the third component involving the relationship between one's internal and external attributions for failure. Herein emerged the intermediate form of beneffectance. This form resembled the strong form in that one external source of control over failure, the Unknown score, was *higher* than the internal score. That is, these children acknowledged that they simply did not know who or what was responsible for their social failures more often than they took personal responsibility for these failures. Thus, in one sense, they met the criterion for the strong form of beneffectance in that they were less responsible than was something external to them, in this case, something unknown (see Table 2.3).

However, these same children also acknowledged that they were *more* responsible for their failures than were Powerful Others, the alternative external source. In this latter sense, they resembled the pattern described as the weaker form of beneffectance. Thus, they were designated as an intermediate form of beneffectance. To summarize, these were children who shared both of the first two components of beneffectance, namely more responsibility for successes compared to failures, and more responsibility for successes relative to the credit given external factors. However, with regard to the third component, the relationship between internal and external failure, they were split: that is, they indicated that unknown factors were more responsible than they were for their social failures, although they, in turn, were more responsible for these failures than were other people.

Thus, in our analysis of the social domain, we found that while the initial four types identified for the cognitive domain emerged in the social domain, it was necessary to include an additional fifth attributional pattern, the one just described above. In particular, it was necessary because this fifth intermediate form of beneffectance contained the largest number of subjects. We found that in utilizing the five types

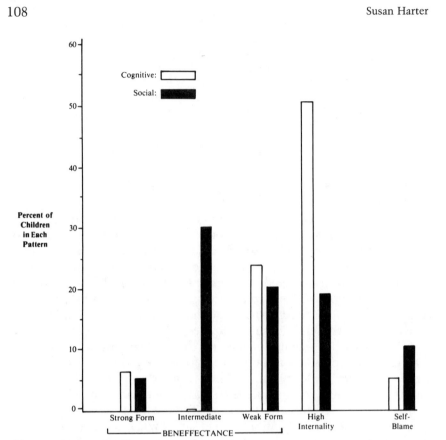

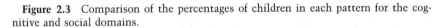

Figure 2.3 Comparison of the percentages of children in each pattern for the cognitive and social domains.

identified, we could account for 86% of the patterns within the social domain. Thirty percent of the children displayed the fifth intermediate pattern described. The weaker form of beneffectance followed, with 21%. High internality was displayed by only 19% of the children. Consistent with the overall pattern found in the cognitive domain, the smallest representation was in the group characterized by self-blame (10%) and the group defined as the strong form of beneffectance (6%). (See Figure 2.3).

When one compares the two domains, however, there are some striking differences in the distribution across types or patterns. Within the cognitive domain, 52% of the children fell into the pattern labeled as high internality. However, this percentage dropped to 19% when one looked at the distribution of these same children in the social domain. The more prevalent pattern within the social arena was our new intermediate form of beneffectance in which children's attributions for their failures were more complex than in the cognitive domain. For this pattern, the most salient feature was the finding that many children seem not to know who or what is responsible for their social failures.

One interpretation of these domain differences is that within the social realm, the criteria for success and failure are more ambiguous, compared to the cognitive domain. Scholastically, children receive considerable feedback concerning their successes and failures, in the form of grades, report cards, and explicit criteria designating when one is right or wrong. However, within the social realm, feedback and the criteria for success and/or failure may be more ambiguous. Thus, many children appear to simply not know why they may be failing socially, as reflected in the finding that this new intermediate form, where the unknown social failure score is high, describes almost one-third of the children.

Perceived Acceptance and Anxiety within the Social Domain

For the five types identified within the social domain, we had two additional self-report scores available, children's perceived peer social acceptance and their anxiety over peer relationships. These values are presented in Figure 2.4. Of particular interest is the finding that those manifesting the strong form of beneffectance perceived themselves to be the least accepted, and the most anxious. This pattern is consistent with the findings for the strong beneffectance group identified within the cognitive domain. Noteworthy, however, is the fact that those typed within the social self-blame category do not share these perceptions, in contrast to the pattern found in the cognitive domain where the self-blame children looked very similar to the strong form of beneffectance children on the additional self-report measures. Rather, within the social domain, the self-blame group looks very much like the other three groups, the weak form of beneffectance, the intermediate form of beneffectance, and the group characterized by high internality. The children exhibiting the other four social patterns share relatively positive perceptions of their social acceptance, and report only mild levels of anxiety.

The findings for the group labeled as self-blame alert us to the fact that perhaps blame may be somewhat of a misnomer here. As we indicated in the previous section, we might need to distinguish be-

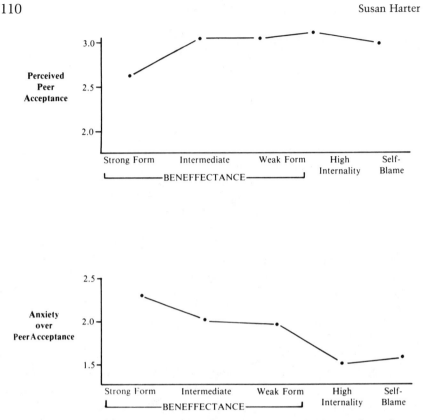

Figure 2.4 Perceived peer acceptance and anxiety over peer acceptance for each type within the social domain.

tween blame and responsibility. It could be hypothesized that these children take responsibility for unsuccessful social interactions, but do not blame themselves as such; that is, these attributions are not related to negative evaluations of the self, as evidenced by their perceived acceptance by others. When one compares the pattern of findings in the cognitive and social domains, therefore, it would appear that we need to make some differentiation between the self-blame pattern found for the academic domain and what we have also labeled as self-blame within the domain of social acceptance, since this may not be phenomenologically comparable.

Developmental Differences within the Cognitive Domain

A major purpose in examining these perceptions of control patterns was to determine whether beneffectance, as described by Greenwald for adults, could be identified in children. The most striking finding, within both the cognitive and social domain, was that in its strongest form, at least, beneffectance is relatively rare. Weaker and intermediate forms, as well as high internality, were more strongly represented. These findings raise an intriguing possibility, namely that there may be developmental differences in the frequency of these patterns of perceptions of control.

To date, we have only examined this possibility within the cognitive domain, across six grade levels. In addition to three elementary school grade levels, fourth, fifth, and sixth grades, data were available for three junior high school levels, seventh, eighth, and ninth grades. All children were within the same school system. Data were pooled from five different elementary schools, each of which fed into one large junior high school.

The findings are presented in Figure 2.5, where it can first be seen that for the two extreme forms, extreme in terms of their low frequencies, the number of children manifesting the strong form of beneffectance as well as self-blame remains relatively small throughout these six grades. While these data are cross-sectional in nature, one could conjecture that if longitudinal data were available, it would be the same group of children who consistently demonstrate these patterns over time. The main point to be underscored, however, is the fact that the strong form of beneffectance does not seem to undergo developmental change in that there is no evidence that this tendency becomes more pervasive with increasing grade level, at least in the academic domain.

The two more common patterns, however, the weak form of beneffectance and high internality, show major changes as a function of grade level. The weak form of beneffectance, which characterized 38% of the fourth graders in this sample gradually rises to a high of 65% by the ninth grade. Precisely the opposite age trend is found for high internality. While high internality is the largest category for the fourth grade pupils, namely 40%, this percentage steadily drops to a low of 19% by the ninth grade.

How are these developmental trends to be interpreted? From the standpoint of the pattern of scores that define each of these two groups, changes in the first component, the relationship between one's responsibility for one's successes and one's failures, are primarily responsible. With development, the tendency to take responsibility for one's academic failures decreases, while responsibility for successes remains high. Thus, children are much less likely to be typed as high internal as they become older, since their internal failure scores progressively decline. Another way to describe this developmental trend is that gradu-

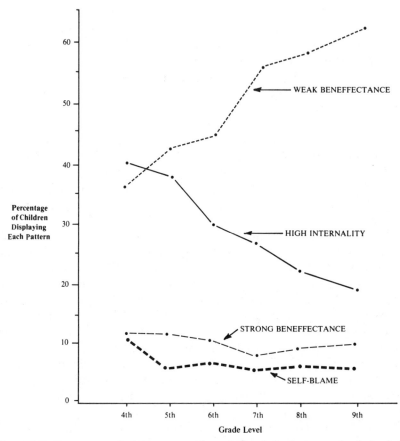

Figure 2.5 Percentage of children at each grade level displaying each of the four patterns in the cognitive domain.

ally, with increasing age level, children shift from the pattern described as high internality to the pattern described as the weak form of beneffectance.

We can interpret this pattern psychologically, perhaps, within the general beneffectance framework provided by Greenwald. Across the elementary and junior high years examined, it would seem that children gradually come to adopt a pattern that provides a certain degree of self-protection or enhancement. While in the earlier years they take a high degree of responsibility for their academic failures, gradually they come to take less responsibility for unsuccessful outcomes. However, they continue to affirm that they are responsible for their academic successes. This strategy may be particularly adaptive within the scholastic domain, in that many of the events that lead to the experience of academic failure may be beyond their control.

Two points are noteworthy, however. First, at least within the grade levels sampled, adolescents do *not* adopt the strong beneffectance pattern. That is, while responsibility for failure declines, they do *not* see others or external factors as *more* responsible than the self for failures. Thus, they are not blaming others, or denying responsibility for failures as Greenwald would have us believe in his characterization of how beneffectance operates in adults. This leads to the further question of whether in samples of older adolescents and adults, we might find the stronger form of beneffectance operative. Moreover, might it be more characteristic in other domains? These questions remain to be investigated.

A second point should be underscored. Typically, we make the value-laden assumption that internality is somehow "better" and should also increase with age. The findings question both of these assumptions in that internality for academic failure decreases with age in our sample, presumably as an adaptive mechanism to enhance or protect the self. This latter assumption is at the heart of Greenwald's argument, although it may have been a bit extreme. If, however, in its weak form, beneffectance does represent a strategy through which one can protect, maintain, or enhance the self, might not this tendency have implications for self-worth or self-esteem? Might we not expect that those who exhibit the weak form of beneffectance would report higher levels of global self-worth? We examine this issue in the final section in which we attempt to integrate the various themes which this chapter has pursued.

TOWARD A COMPREHENSIVE MODEL OF SELF-WORTH

The initial focus of this chapter was competence, and many of the empirical findings cited have pertained to competence-related issues. However, the major intent of this chapter was to go beyond the topic of competence in order to identify a number of themes we may need to consider if we wish to understand more global self-evaluative judgments. Thus, competence is only one of many domains that may be relevant to one's sense of global self-worth.

The major assumption underlying this conceptual exploration was that individuals do indeed make an overall evaluation of their worth as a person. Moreover, it was postulated that one's global sense of self-worth is more than the sum of the specific evaluative judgments from each domain. Empirically, from our own efforts, as well as the work of Rsenberg (1979), it would appear that we can assess this commodity in adults as well as children over the age of 8 years. General items that tap the degree to which one likes oneself, is happy with the way one is leading one's life, likes the kind of person one is, and so forth seem to provide an index of global self-worth or self-esteem. If one accepts the assumption that global self-worth is a meaningful construct, and that it can be measured in the fashion just described, we can then address the issue of how best to understand the factors that are responsible for such an overall self-evaluative judgment. In this chapter, we sought to identify a number of possible factors that may collaborate to produce a sense of global self-worth.

As a starting point, we built upon James' contention that one's self-esteem represents the ratio of one's successes to one's pretensions. We translated this formula into a consideration of the relationship between one's judgments of adequacy in specific domains and the importance of these domains to the individual. This congruence, or discrepancy, was hypothesized to be one factor that would influence or predict one's global sense of self-worth. The greater the congruence between estimates of adequacy and importance, the greater the person's sense of worth. The success of this predictive formula rests, however, on our prior identification of the relevant self-evaluative domains. Thus, while competence at various life tasks will undoubtedly be included, there will be other domains as well, for example, likeability, appearance, moral worth, personality.

It should be noted, however, that this type of approach places major emphasis on a very personal equation for each individual. That is, we examine the congruence or discrepancy between the particular adequacy and importance judgments for a given child or adult. We examine the individual or idiosyncratic hierarchies for each person. Such an approach may well preclude the specification of general hierarchical models of the self that seek to postulate a nomological network of content domains that supposedly represent the self-concept or self-theory of all or most individuals. We discussed some of the pitfalls encountered in those efforts that have sought to build such hierarchical models. The major problem would appear to involve the fact that, in reality, these content domains are weighted differently for different individuals. This does *not* imply, however, that we must abandon our efforts to devise a model of global self-worth. Rather, it suggests that we focus on the relationship between adequacy and importance judgments, for whichever domains are deemed important by a given individual. Thus, congruence or discrepancy becomes a major construct in the model, not the specific content domains, per se (see Harter, 1975).

In building upon this notion, it was also suggested that we may need to take the accuracy of one's adequacy judgments into account. It was hypothesized that the congruence factor may only predict global self-worth if adequacy judgments are relatively accurate. Two themes were pursued in this regard. It was noted that there may be particular developmental periods when accuracy is in question for the majority of those going through such a normative transition. Second, during those periods in which judgments do tend to be more accurate for the group as a whole, there will still be a minority of those who either overrate or underrate their adequacy in particular domains. To the extent that there are either developmental periods or individual differences characterized by inaccuracy, the congruence construct would not be expected to predict general self-worth with great precision for those periods or individuals.

The role of affect was also explored as a contributor to one's global sense of worth. Here, several possibilities were entertained. Findings clearly demonstrate that children have affective reactions to their adequacy in different domains. Thus, it may be that these emotional responses, namely their positive or negative affective valence, should be entered into the equation that predicts general self-worth. Two qualifications should be considered here. We may only want to consider the affective valence attached to judgments for those areas deemed important to the individual.

Second, we may wish to restrict our analysis to emotions that we have identified as *self-affects*, affects such as pride or shame in which the self is the target of the emotion. Consider, for example, two individuals who both judge their academic competence very highly, although one reacts affectively with pride whereas the other reports a feeling of happiness. Also consider two individuals both of whom report poor academic performance; one experiences shame whereas the other reports anger or frustration. It may well be that the self-affects of pride and shame add to our predictive equation, whereas the affects of happiness, anger, or frustration carry considerably less weight. That is, it is primarily affective reactions directed toward the self that have implications for judgments concerning self-worth.

This particular analysis has focused on the affects attached to one's specific judgments in those domains which are valued by the individual. However, we may also want to consider the more singular affective reaction to the congruence or discrepancy per se. That is, one's general emotional response to the degree to which one has succeeded in meeting one's aspirations may be a more critical determinant of self-worth than some combination of more domain-specific reactions.

In a final section, we explored the issue of how perceptions of control might influence one's sense of self-worth. A number of theoretical formulations, dating back to the turn of the century (e.g., Cooley, 1902), have emphasized how one's sense of the self as a causal agent is a critical component of one's general sense of self. This contention was examined more specifically, with regard to the findings on children's perceptions of control. It was suggested that we pay particular attention to the responsibility that children assume for their successes, relative to their failures. A strong sense of responsibility for one's successes in areas judged to be important to the individual, may well contribute to one's sense of self-worth or global esteem. However, the picture is undoubtedly more complex in that the findings suggest that the predictive constellation should *not* include denial of the responsibility for failure, at least in the extreme. It would appear that perhaps the most adaptive pattern involves a high degree of responsibility for success as well as the acceptance of responsibility for one's failures. Just what specific ratio best predicts overall self-worth, however, is an issue which awaits empirical examination.

We have explored, therefore, a number of possible factors that should be taken into account in predicting general self-worth. These have included the congruence between one's adequacy judgments and the importance of given domains, the accuracy of one's adequacy judgments, the affects attached to these judgments, and the degree of control which one experiences over successful and unsuccessful outcomes. In part, such a model attempts to simulate, perhaps, the complex process through which an individual weighs these various factors.

However, in exploring these parameters, there is much that we have neglected. For example, we have not dealt with issues involving the socialization history of the child. We have not begun to examine the possible antecedents of each of the components in the model. For example, what factors in the child-rearing experiences of an individual cause certain domains to be more important than others? And what types of experience lead to the affective experiences of pride and shame? Are there perhaps more parsimonious models of self-worth that focus on the child's internalization of parental regard, models that do not involve the more complex weighting of factors postulated to influence self-worth? There are additional developmental considerations, as well. For example, our own data suggest that children younger than 8 years of age do not make global evaluations of self-worth. Thus we will need to explore those factors responsible for the very emergence of this evaluative ability during childhood. These will all be intriguing pathways to pursue, not only from the standpoint of scientific inquiry but because, in the process, we might just learn how to like ourselves a little better.

REFERENCES

Achenbach, T., & Zigler, E. (1963). Social competence and self-image disparity in psychiatric and non-psychiatric patients. *Journal of Abnormal and Social Psychology, 67,* 197–205.

Adler, A. (1927). *The practice and theory of individual psychology.* New York: Harcourt.

Allport, G. W. (1955). *Becoming: Basic considerations for a psychology of personality.* New Haven, CT: Yale University Press.

Allport, G. W. (1961). *Pattern and growth in personality.* New York: Holt, Rinehart & Winston.

Bandura, A. (1977). Self-efficacy: Toward a unifying theory of behavioral change. *Psychological Review, 84,* 191–215.

Bandura, A. (1978). The self system in reciprocal determinism. *American Psychologist, 33,* 344–358.

Bandura, A. (1981). Self-referent thought: The development of self-efficacy. In J. H. Flavell & L. D. Ross (Eds.), *Development of social cognition.* New York: Cambridge University Press.

Bannister, D., & Agnew, J. (1977). The child's construing of self. In J. Cole (Ed.), *Nebraska Symposium on Motivation,* Lincoln: University of Nebraska Press.

Beigel, D. (1982). *Self-evaluations of competence and initiative in the academic domain.* Unpublished master's thesis, University of Denver.

Bierer, B. (1982). *Behavioral and motivational correlates of children's accuracy in judging their cognitive competence.* Unpublished doctoral dissertation, University of Denver.

Brim, O. G. (1976). Life span development of the theory of oneself: Implications for child development. In H. W. Reese (Ed.), *Advances in child development and behavior.* New York: Academic Press.

Connell, J. P. (1980). *A multidimensional measure of children's perceptions of control.* Unpublished master's thesis, University of Denver.

Connell, J. P. (1981). *A model of the relationships among children's self-related cognitions, affects and academic achievement.* Unpublished doctoral dissertation, University of Denver.

Constantinople, A. (1969). An Eriksonian measure of personality development in college students. *Developmental Psychology, 1,* 357–372.

Cooley, C. H. (1902). *Human nature and the social order.* New York: Charles Scribner's Sons.

Coopersmith, S. (1967). *The antecedents of self-esteem.* San Francisco: W. H. Freeman.

Costomiris, S. (1984). *The effects of parental attitudes toward little league performance on the self-perceptions of little-league baseball players.* Unpublished master's thesis, University of Denver.

deCharms, R. (1968). *Personal causation: The internal affective determinants of behavior.* New York: Academic Press.

Deci, E. L. (1975). *Intrinsic motivation.* New York: Plenum.

Dickstein, E. (1977). Self and self-esteem: Theoretical foundations and their implications for research. *Human Development, 20,* 129–140.

Duval, S., & Wicklund, R. A. (1972). *A theory of objective self-awareness.* New York: Academic Press.

Epstein, S. (1973). The self-concept revisited or a theory of a theory. *American Psychologist, 28,* 405–416.

Epstein, S. (1981). The unity principle versus the reality and pleasure principles, or the tale of the scorpion and the frog. In M. D. Lynch, A. A. Norem-Hebeisen, & K. Gergen (Eds.), *Self concept: Advances in theory and research.* Cambridge, MA: Ballinger.

Erikson, E. H. (1950). *Childhood and society.* New York: Norton.

Erikson, E. H. (1959). Identity and the life cycle. *Psychological Issues, 1,* 18–164.

Erikson, E. H. (1968). *Identity, youth and crisis.* New York: Norton.

Felker, D. W., & Thomas, S. B. (1971). Self-initiated verbal reinforcement and positive self-concept. *Child Development, 42,* 1285–1287.

Fischer, K. F. (1980). A theory of cognitive development: The control and construction of hierarchies of skills. *Psychological Review, 87,* 477–531.

Gordon, C. (1968). Self-conceptions: Configurations of content. In C. Gordon & K. J. Gergen (Eds.), *The self in social interaction.* New York: Wiley.

Greenwald, A. G. (1980). The totalitarian ego: Fabrication and revision of personal history. *American Psychologist, 7,* 603–618.

Guzman, M. E. (1983). *The effects of competence and anxiety levels on problem-solving performance and preference for challenge.* Unpublished master's thesis, University of Denver.

Hales, S. A. (1979, March). *A developmental theory of self-esteem based on competence and moral behavior.* Paper presented at the Society for Research in Child Development, San Francisco, CA.

Hand, H. (1981). *The development of concepts of social interaction: Children's understanding of nice and mean.* Unpublished doctoral dissertation, University of Denver.

Harter, S. (1977). A cognitive-developmental approach to children's expression of conflicting feelings and a technique to facilitate such expression in play therapy. *Journal of Consulting and Clinical Psychology, 45,* 417–432.

Harter, S. (1978). Effectance motivation reconsidered: Toward a developmental model. *Human Development, 1,* 34–64.

Harter, S. (1980). The development of competence motivation in the mastery of cognitive and physical skills: Is there still a place for joy? *Psychology of Motor Behavior and Sport,* 3–29.

Harter, S. (1982a). *Developmental differences in children's understanding of self-affect labels.* Unpublished manuscript, University of Denver.

Harter, S. (1982b). The perceived competence scale for children. *Child Development, 53,* 87–97.

Harter, S. (1983). The development of the self-system. In M. Hetherington (Ed.), *Handbook of child psychology: Social and personality development* (Vol. 4). New York: Wiley.

Harter, S. (1985). Processes in the formation, maintenance, and enhancement of the self-concept. In J. Suls and A. Greenwald (Eds.), *Psychological perspectives on the self* (Vol. 3). Hillsdale, NJ: Lawrence Erlbaum.

Harter, S., & Connell, J. P. (1984). A comparison of alternative models of the relationships between academic achievement and children's perceptions of competence, control, and motivational orientation. In J. Nicholls (Ed.), *The development of achievement-related cognitions and behaviors*. Greenwich, CT: J. A. I. Press.

Harter, S., & Engstrom, R. (1981). *The relationship between importance of success, perceived competence, and self-esteem*. Unpublished manuscript, University of Denver.

Harter, S., & Pike, R. (1984). The pictorial perceived competence scale for young children. *Child Development, 55*, 1969–1982.

Harter, S. & Polesovsky, M. (1985). Dimensions of depression in children: A new self-report scale. Unpublished manuscript, University of Denver.

Horney, K. (1945). *Our inner conflicts*. New York: Norton.

Horney, K. (1950). *Neurosis and human growth*. New York: Norton.

James. W. (1963). *Psychology*. New York: Fawcett. (Original work published 1892)

Jung, C. G. (1928). *Two essays on analytical psychology*. New York: Dodd, Mead.

Kanfer, F. H. (1970). Self regulation: Research, issues, and speculations. In C. Neuringer & J. L. Michael (Eds.), *Behavior modification in clinical psychology*. New York: Appleton-Century-Crofts.

Kanfer, F. H. (1971). Maintenance of behavior by self-generated stimuli and reinforcement. In A. Jacobs & L. B. Sacks (Eds.), *Psychology of private events*. New York: Academic Press.

Kanfer, F. H. (1980). Self-management methods. In F. H. Kanfer & A. P. Goldstein (Eds.), *Helping people change: A textbook of methods* (2nd ed.). New York: Pergamon Press.

Katz, P., & Zigler, E. (1967). Self-image disparity: A developmental approach. *Journal of Personality and Social Psychology, 5*, 186–195.

Katz, P. A., Zigler, E., & Zalk, S. R. (1975). Children's self-image disparity: The effects of age, maladjustment, and action-thought orientation. *Developmental Psychology, 11*, 546–550.

Kelly, G. A. (1955). *The psychology of personal constructs*. New York: Norton.

Kowalski, P. S. (1985). Affect as a dimension of the self-system in young adolescents. Docoral dissertation, University of Denver.

L'Ecuyer, R. (1981). The development of the self-concept through the life span. In M. D. Lynch, A. A. Norem-Hebeisen, & K. Gergen (Eds.), *Self concept: Advances in theory and research*. Cambridge, MA: Ballinger.

Lecky, P. *Self-consistency: A theory of personality*. New vork: Island Press.

Marcia, J. E. (1966). Development and validation of ego-identity status. *Journal of Personality and Social Psychology, 3*, 551–558.

Marcia, J. E., & Friedman, M. L. (1970). Ego identity status in college women. *Journal of Personality, 38*, 249–263.

Maslow, A. (1954). *Motivation and personality*. New York: Harper & Row.

Maslow, A. H. (1961). Peak-experiences as acute identity-experiences. *American Journal of Psychoanalysis, 21*, 254–260.

Maslow, A. H. (1971). *The farther reaches of human nature*. New York: Viking.

McGuire, W. (1982). The spontaneous self-concept as affected by personal distinctiveness. In A. A. Norem-Hebeisen & M. Lynch (Eds.), *Self-concept*. Cambridge, MA: Ballinger.

McGuire, W., & McGuire, C. V. (1980). Significant others in self-space: Sex differences and developmental trends in the social self. In J. Suls (Ed.), *Social psychological perspectives on the self*. Hillsdale, NJ: Erlbaum.

McGuire, W., & Padawer-Singer, A. (1976). Trait salience in the spontaneous self-concept. *Journal of Personality and Social Psychology, 33*, 743–754.

Minton, B. (1979). *Dimensions of information underlying children's judgments of their competence*. Unpublished master's thesis, University of Denver.

Montemayor, R., & Eisen, M. (1977). The development of self-conceptions from childhood to adolescence. *Developmental Psychology, 13*, 314–319.

Mullener, N., & Laird, J. D. (1971). Some developmental changes in the organization of self-evaluations. *Developmental Psychology, 5*, 233–236.

Piers, E. V. (1977a). Children's self-esteem, level of esteem certainty, and responsibility for success and failure. *Journal of Genetic Psychology, 130*, 295–304.

Piers, E. V. (1977b). *The Piers-Harris Children's Self-concept Scale. Research Monograph No. 1*. Nashville, TN: Counselor Recordings and Test.

Piers, E., & Harris, D. (1969). *The Piers-Harris Children's Self-concept Scale*. Nashville, TN: Counselor Recordings and Tests.

Prawat, R. S., Grissom, S., & Parish, T. (1979). Affective development in children, grades 3 through 12. *Journal of Genetic Psychology, 135*, 37–49.

Rogers, C. R. (1950). The significance of the self-regarding attitudes and perceptions. In M. L. Reymert, (Ed.), *Feelings and emotions: The Mooseheart Symposium*. New York: McGraw-Hill.

Rogers, C. R., & Dymond, R. (1954). *Psychotherapy and personality change*. Chicago: University of Chicago Press.

Rosenberg, M. (1979). *Conceiving the self*. New York: Basic Books.

Rotter, J. B. (1975). Some problems and misconceptions related to the construct of internal vs. external control of reinforcement. *Journal of Consulting and Clinical Psychology, 43*, 56–67.

Sarbin, T. R. (1962). A preface to a psychological analysis of the self. *Psychological Review, 59*, 11–22.

Seligman, M. E. P. (1975). *Helplessness: On depression, development, and death*. San Francisco: Freeman.

Shavelson, R. J., Hubner, J. J., & Stanton, G. C. (1976). Self-concept: Validation of construct interpretations. *Review of Educational Research, 46*, 407–441.

Sullivan, H. S. (1953). *The interpersonal theory of psychiatry*. New York: Norton.

Toder, N. L., & Marcia, J. E. (1973). Ego identity status and response to conformity pressure in college women. *Journal of Personality and Social Psychology, 26*, 287–294.

Weiner, B., Kun, A., & Benesh-Weiner, M. (1980). The development of mastery, emotions and morality from an attributional perspective. In W. A. Collins (Ed.), *Development of cognition, affect, and social relations. The Minnesota Symposium on Child Psychology* (Vol. 13). Hillsdale, NJ: Erlbaum.

White, R. W. (1959). Motivation reconsidered: The concept of competence. *Psychological Review, 66*, 297–333.

White, R. W. (1960). Competence and the psychosexual stages of development. *Nebraska Symposium on Motivation*. Lincoln: University of Nebraska Press.

White, R. W. (1963). Ego and reality in psychoanalytic theory. *Psychological Issues, Monograph 3*.

Wicklund, R. A. (1975). Objective self-awareness. In L. Berkowitz (Ed.), *Advances in experimental social psychology* (Vol. 8). New York: Academic Press.

Wicklund, R. A., & Frey, D. (1980). Self-awareness theory: When the self makes a difference. In D. M. Wegner & R. R. Vallacher (Eds.), *The self in social psychology*. New York: Oxford University Press.

Wylie, R. (1974). *The self-concept: A review of methodological considerations and measuring instruments* (Vol. 1, rev. ed.). Lincoln: University of Nebraska Press.

Zigler, E., Balla, D., & Watson, N. (1972). Developmental and experiential determinants of self-image disparity in institutionalized and noninstitutionalized retarded and normal children. *Journal of Personality and Social Psychology, 23,* 81–87.

3

Social Cognition and the Development of the Self

Robert L. Leahy
Stephen R. Shirk

INTRODUCTION

Since the time of Wundt, the validity of the self as a psychological construction has been periodically disputed. Nevertheless, the centrality of this construct in a variety of developmental theories (Baldwin, 1897; Kohlberg, 1969; Mead, 1934; Piaget, 1932; Sullivan, 1953; Winnicott, 1965) and the resurgence of empirical research on its vicissitudes suggest that the self has retained an important place in developmental psychology. However, as is often the case, concurrent explorations have proceeded relatively autonomously and have engendered a multitude of redefinitions of the object of inquiry. For example, a number of years ago Sarbin (1952) cited no less than twelve distinct definitions. More recently Dickstein (1977) classified conceptualizations of the self into five categories. Although there is a need for an eclectic resolution of this diversity, the compatibility of the diverse treatments of the self is rather questionable.

Given the growing heterogeneity of this field, an explication of some of the assumptions of a cognitive-developmental perspective on the self seems warranted. Consequently, the first task of this chapter is to bring into relief some of the often implicit conceptual distinctions within the cognitive-developmental approach to the self. The second task is to review the existing research on the relationships between social cognition and the concept of self and to indicate patterns of developmental change in the self-concept.

Research on social cognitive development has not been the province of any single theory. As Shantz (1975) has indicated, developmental social cognition can be seen as the offspring of cognitive-developmental theory and social psychological theory. Similarly, social cognitive investigations of the self have drawn upon a number of theoretical sources. The two perspectives that we shall consider are symbolic interactionism and structural developmentalism.

MEAD'S SYMBOLIC INTERACTIONISM

One source of theoretical direction for understanding the self and its development has been found in Mead's (1934) symbolic-interactionist theory. Mead posited the *self* as a phenomenal object distinct from all other objects in its reflexive character. Beginning with a phenomenological account, Mead distinguished between experiences in which the individual is "absolutely wound up in outside activity in which the self as an object does not enter, and an activity of memory and imagination in which the self is the principle object." This dichotomy led Mead to define the "essential psychological problem of selfhood" as the question of how it is possible for us to get outside the self experientially in order to become an object to the self. Mead's (1934) solution to the problem of self-reflection was through the cognitive activity of role taking. "The individual experiences himself as such, not directly but only indirectly, from the particular standpoints of other individual members of the same social group or from the generalized standpoints of the social group as a whole to which he belongs" (p. 202).

For Mead, self-reflection is a social construction, that is, it involves reflecting on the self from the perspective of other persons. We sweep ourselves into the experiential field by taking the attitudes of other individuals toward ourselves. Given the functional significance of role taking, it is not surprising that Mead maintained that the self is essentially "a cognitive rather than an emotional phenomenon".

According to Mead the individual's capacity for reflective understanding, and consequently, the character of the self as a reflective object, develops through a sequence of stages. Each stage is typified by a social activity that embodies a distinct form of self-reflection. The first stage is the *play stage* which is characterized by the child's play at reciprocal roles. For example, the child praises him- or herself as a teacher or arrests him- or herself as a police officer. In this type of sequential play, where the child passes from one role to another, Mead finds the simplest form of being another to oneself. At this stage the child views the self from the standpoint of *particular* others.

Following this phase is the *game stage* which is marked by the child's involvement in organized, rule-bound activities. As Mead (1934) contends, "The fundamental difference between the game and play is that in the former the child must have the attitudes of all the others involved in the game," (as opposed to just a single other person). For example, in a baseball game the baserunner must anticipate what the other players will do when the ball is hit in order to be able to carry out her own part. The structure of the game requires the child to coordinate the perspectives of those involved. From this organization of viewpoints emerges the perspective of the *generalized other*. At this stage the child reflects on the self not merely from individual perspectives but from the organized perspective of the social group. These distinct forms of self-reflection—viewing oneself from the standpoint of particular others and viewing oneself from the standpoint of the generalized other—bear directly on the character of the self.

In the play stage, where the child reflects on the self from a succession of individual perspectives, Mead contended that the self lacks organization and stability. As the child passes from one role to another in play, the self is viewed from a sequence of unrelated perspectives. Consequently, as a composite of these unrelated perspectives, the self lacks a definite organization. As Mead says, the child has "no definite character, no definite personality." The developmental task implied by Mead involves the evolution of a definite, organized self. The structure out of which such an organization evolves is found in the game. In games, multiple perspectives must be coordinated. Distinct perspectives on the self, unrelated in the play stage, are drawn into definite relationships in the game. By organizing and generalizing the attitudes of particular others, the standpoint of the generalized other, for example, the team perspective, is constructed. As Mead claimed, "the self reaches its full development by organizing these individual attitudes of others into the organized or social group attitudes" (p. 218). Self-reflection from the standpoint of the generalized other constitutes the organized self: that is, through a form of self-reflection that transcends the immediate perspectives of particular others a definite personality is constructed. In Mead's symbolic-interactionist theory, the character of the self as an object of reflection depends upon the nature of the reflective process.

Mead's theory has several empirical implications for the development of the self. First, according to Mead's model, the self becomes an object of experience by taking the role of others toward the self. Thus, aspects of the self are differentiated from one another from these "other" perspectives. Based on this rationale, Leahy and Huard (1976) proposed that increased role-taking ability would be associated with greater disparity between real and ideal self-image. The prediction that higher self-image disparity would be associated with higher developmental level is in contrast with Rogers' view that higher self-image disparity is indicative of psychopathology (Rogers & Dymond, 1954). A further implication of Mead's theory is that the development of internal standards of conduct is a consequence of anticipating the views of others and judging the self from the values of the generalized other. Thus, we also expected that referential communication ability and role-taking ability would be related to more positive ideal self-image. Children between 10 and 12 years of age were tested on real and ideal self-image using the Katz and Zigler (1967) self-image checklist. In addition, referential communication was evaluated using the Glucksberg and Krauss measure and role taking was measured by the Chandler (1973) cartoon stories. The findings offered general confirmation to Mead's theory: Higher self-image disparity and more positive ideal self-image were associated with greater role-taking ability. Referential communication, however, was unrelated to any measures.

Role-taking ability continues to develop throughout adolescence (Flavell, Botkin, Fry, Wright, & Jarvis, 1968; Selman, 1980; Selman and Byrne, 1974). Research on changes in role-taking performance demonstrate that the knowledge of the other's perspective becomes increasingly more abstract, flexible, and general. For example, Selman (1980) has identified a series of levels of perspective taking—egocentric, subjective, self-reflective, mutual, and conventional systems role-taking. Each level reflects a change in the understanding of how self and others differ and how the self is understood by others. At the level of the *egocentric* viewpoint the child fails to recognize differences between self and other in social perspective, whereas at the level of *subjective* or social-informational role-taking the child recognizes that there are different social perspectives, although he may focus on only one (e.g., authority). At the level of *self-reflective* thought the child understands that the self may be the object of cognition of the other, while at the level of *mutual* role-taking the adolescent or older child understands that self and other may be reconstrued from a third-person perspective. Finally, *conventional* system role-taking entails the recognition that conventions may help unify the understanding of participants in interaction, even when participants have different intentions, needs, or interests.

We may view each level as an example of decentering of self–other conceptions such that the child is seen as beginning with a general lack of distinction between self and other, to refocusing on these two perspectives in a sequential manner, to understanding how these perspectives (or individual differences) may be coordinated through either a mutual (third-party) perspective or through a generally accepted convention. Each level marks both an increasing recognition of the importance of the other's perspective in understanding the self and a recognition that the self and other differ from one another but attempt to mediate these differences through the adoption of social conventions. Moreover, the ability to engage in mutual role-taking (taking the third-person perspective) may facilitate more objective appraisals of the self, thereby serving the function of the "observing ego" in recognizing how the self may employ defense mechanisms to protect the self (Selman, 1980).

One process of self-evaluation that entails consideration of the other is found in social comparison whereby the individual compares her performance with that of others (Ruble, Feldman, & Boggiano, 1976). Ruble, Boggiano, Feldman, and Loebl (1980) investigated the effect of social comparison information on children's self-evaluations of their own performances. In their first study, 104 subjects, equally divided into first and second graders, were tested. Subjects worked on a task, similar to the Wechsler Picture Arrangement task, and received outcome feedback from the experimenter (pass/fail) and the performance of three other children who either all failed or all succeeded or about whom no information was given. After this social comparison information was supplied, children indicated how they felt about how they did on the task. In addition, subjects indicated their evaluations of their ability and effort as well as the difficulty of the task. Second graders made use of social comparison information for task difficulty and ability information, whereas first graders did not make use of social comparison information. These findings indicate that young children are not strongly affected by social comparison information in evaluating their own performance.

One possibility which Ruble et al. (1980) considered in accounting for the weak effects of the first study is that the subjects might not view the social comparison information as having utility for predicting their own future performance. Consequently, in their second study, children at three age levels (kindergarten, second, and fourth grade) were asked to predict whether they could "beat" the other children. The task was throwing a ball into a basketball hoop which was obscured by a curtain so that the experimenter could manipulate feedback. In addition, an added incentive was introduced: Successful performance could assure winning prizes. Similar feedback for all subjects was provided about how the self performed (i.e., two out of four baskets completed) and subjects were told of the success of eight other children. This social comparison feedback indicated the subject's relative success or failure compared to eight peers. Relative failure was indicated by seven of eight peers scoring four out of four baskets and relative success as seven of eight peers missing all four baskets. Control subjects were given no feedback about peers. Children were told that if they accurately predicted the number of peers they would beat, they would receive prizes. The prediction was about beating one, two, or no other children. The only children using social comparison information for predictions and ability ratings were the fourth graders, although affect ratings were not affected by experimental conditions. Open-ended questions as to why children rated their affect or ability indicated a much stronger tendency of fourth graders (40%) to refer to social comparison information compared to younger children (5% and 0%). These foregoing data are consistent with the developmental approach to Mead's theory in that they indicate that self-evaluations become increasingly dependent during later childhood on the subject's awareness of the performance of others.

Another line of research that has relevance to Mead's theory employs the "atypical" labeled population of retarded individuals. In this study (Leahy, Balla, & Zigler, 1982), it was hypothesized that self-image would be affected by membership in a category labeled as atypical—specifically, *retarded*. According to Mead, the self is constructed from the point of view of others. For the nonretarded child, the "other" might be presumed to convey reasonably positive feedback in the manner of evaluations of present behavior (relevant to the real self) and in the expectation of future performance (relevant to the ideal self). In contrast, as Goldfried's (1976) research demonstrates, nonretarded peers often have quite negative impressions of the retarded which are sometimes further exacerbated by mainstreaming.

Three groups of subjects—younger and older nonretarded and retarded matched with younger nonretarded on mental age—were tested for role-taking ability, real and ideal self-images, and imitativeness. The findings indicated that both groups of nonretarded children had more positive real and ideal self-images than did the retarded individuals. Thus, the retarded not only have a lower opinion but they also expect less from themselves. These findings are consistent with the symbolic-interactionist theory which suggests that self-image may depend on labeled status. It would be interesting to determine if retarded children, who are better than other retarded peers on role taking, are more negatively affected by *mainstreaming*—that is, perhaps cognitive level has ominous implications for the self-image of labeled groups.

Limits of Symbolic Interactionism

Although Mead's theory has had considerable influence on some of our own work (Leahy, 1981; Leahy *et al.*, 1982; Leahy & Huard, 1976), we view this model as limited in developmental scope. Mead describes a "socialized self," one which aims toward convergence of the perspectives of others with the perspectives of the self. It was the ideal of many social behaviorists of Mead's time to describe development in terms of the submersion of the individual in the group, a view which purports to demonstrate the active construction of a citizen within democratic society such that group and individual come to share common goals ("the generalized others") and common definitions of the self. Mead's theory is one of *optimistic functionalism* which carries the child from a point of individual isolation to a developmental milestone of sharing the views of others about the self (Leahy, 1983).

However, empirical facts, alternative theories, and common sense appear to converge on the point that such a functionalist model has serious limitations. Let us take the social self-image (that is, "how I think others see me") as Mead's central aspect of the construction of the self. Perhaps the best known formulation of the relationship between the self-image and the social self-image is embodied in Cooley's (1902) notion of the "looking glass" self. According to this model the self-image reflects "the imagination of our appearance to the other person and the imagination of his judgment of that appearance" (p. 152). Mead would argue that the social self-image and the real self-image become more congruent as role taking develops, since the self comes to apprehend or know more accurately what others think of the self. Consequently, we might expect that the disparity between social self-image and real self-image might decrease with age.

The first problematic assumption of this model involves causal ordering. The causal assumption is that inferences about how the self is perceived by others constitute the primary source of information for self-image formulation. Numerous empirical investigations (see Shrauger & Schoeneman, 1979, for a review) have found moderate to strong relationships between measures of the self-concept and the social self-concept. Needless to say, such correlational evidence is equivocal. The causal path could reasonably be interpreted as flowing in the opposite direction. That is, individuals may form impressions of themselves quite independently from what others think of them and then project these beliefs onto relevant others. Even if one accepts the causal hypothesis of the looking-glass self, another troublesome assumption of this model is that the functional relationship between self and social self-images has been conceptualized agenetically. There are ample theoretical grounds, however, for assuming that this relationship will vary through the course of development.

Given the reflexive character of the cognitive processes implied by the looking-glass model, a threshhold of cognitive development must undoubtedly be reached in order to render such a relationship functional. Certainly, the child embedded in the solitary perspective of egocentrism could hardly be attributed the cognitive facility for constructing a self-image from the imagined perspectives of other persons. Such a model clearly assumes a relatively high level of cognitive differentiation. Interestingly, one might find a close correspondence between the self-image and the social self-image among younger children precisely because of their low level of cognitive differentiation. Katz and Zigler (1967) found significantly less disparity between measures of the real self-image and measures of the social self-image among younger than older children. Without the capacity to distinguish among social perspectives, the inferred perspectives of others could not constitute a source of information about the self. Ironically, with the separation of self and other perspectives, the potential influence of social views of the self is made possible. As Piaget (1930) has pointed out, "After having regarded his own point of view as absolute (the child) comes to discover the possibilities of other points of view and to conceive of reality as constituted no longer by what is immediately given, but by what is common to all points of view taken together" (p. 231). Thus, cognitive differentiation makes possible the construction of a self-image from the integration of perceived social perspectives.

After the child has evolved the ability to apprehend others' perspectives toward the self, the degree to which these social perspectives influence the self-image may vary with development. For example, Elkind (1967) has suggested that the increase in role-taking skills during early adolescence leads to heightened anticipations of the reactions of others to the self. Elkind and Bowen's (1979) research on adolescent self-consciousness indicates that younger adolescents are more concerned with what others think of them than are children or older adolescents. Consequently, early adolescence may represent the period in development when inferences about how the self appears to others exert their greatest influence on the self-image.

There are also grounds for expecting that this influence will decrease at higher developmental levels. For example, the transition from conventional to postconventional moral judgment reflects a change from the other-directed to self-directed forms of reasoning. Rather than orienting to the expectations of significant others or the social group, the postconventional individual orients to standards of conduct that are not contingent on social expectations. One might expect postconventional individuals to construct impressions of themselves that are relatively independent of others' beliefs and expectations about them. Another cognitive developmental factor that may lead to a decrease in the influence of social self-image on the self-image is the continued growth of role-taking ability during later adolescence. Just as the emergence of self-reflective role-taking may intensify the young adolescent's concern about how he or she appears to others, the ability to observe the mutual interplay of self and other perspectives, typical of the role taking of older adolescents, may provide the cognitive basis for reflecting on the social sources of the self. That is, rather than being embedded in the multiplicity of inferred social views of the self, the *relationship* between one's own view of self and others' views of self becomes the object of reflection. As Byrne (1973) suggests, increasingly abstract understandings of reciprocity allows for the separation of the self from its social sources.

There is a limited body of empirical evidence that is consistent with the hypothesis that with increasing development during later adolescence the self-image will become less dependent on how one believes others view the self. Herzberger, Dix, Erlebacher, and Ginsberg (1981) found that older adolescents were more likely to express an awareness of misimpressions of the self formed by parents and peers than were younger adolescents. This pattern is consistent with Katz and Zigler's (1967) findings that disparity between self-ratings from one's own viewpoint versus another's viewpoint (i.e., social self-image) increased during adolescence. Rosenberg (1979) has found that between childhood and later adolescence there is a steady decline in the beliefs that others know the self as well as oneself does. Taken together these findings suggest that during adolescence an image of self, which is relatively independent of how one believes others view the self, begins to emerge. More generally, the foregoing developmental observations suggest that the significance of the social self-image for self-image formation may vary with developmental level.

Recently it has been proposed that interpersonal processes are more closely associated with self-image development for females than males (Adams & Jones, 1983; Gilligan, 1982). Rosenberg and Simmons (1975) have found that adolescent females report greater concern about how others view them than adolescent males. Consequently, the significance of social views of the self for self-image formation could differ for the two genders. In order to investigate the possibility of such a gender difference, Shirk (1983) compared the pattern of relationships between self-evaluations and social self-evaluations among 10-, 13-, and 16-year-old boys and girls. Shirk's (1983) correlational results indicate that with increasing age the relationships between self- and social self-evaluations follow different courses for males and females. Although there is considerable convergence between self and social self-evaluations for males in late childhood, during adolescence there is a marked trend toward greater divergence. In fact, by age 16 years there is a slightly negative relationship between self and social self-evaluations for males. Consistent with the view that development is marked by decreasing reliance on others as the source of one's self-image, Shirk's (1983) results indicate that with increasing age there is decreasing association between self-views and perceived social views of the self.

By contrast, the pattern of development for females was quite different. Rather than reflecting greater divergence between self- and social self-evaluations, there was a slight, though statistically nonsignificant, trend toward increasing convergence. Consequently, by age 16 years, male self-evaluations were relatively independent from their perceptions of how they were evaluated by others but female self-evaluations were somewhat associated with such perceptions. If one interprets the degree of this association as an index of functional dependence of the self-image on perceived social self-images, then adolescent females appear to draw more heavily on beliefs about how they are viewed by others than do adolescent males. While males tend to become *less* "other directed" between ages 10 and 16 years, it appears that females do not. As Rosenberg and Simmons (1975) maintain, the adolescent females' greater orientation toward relationships (compared to males) includes the tendency for these young women to see themselves through the eyes of others. Of course, the foregoing interpretations are based on the causal assumption that the self-image is derived from perceptions of how the self is viewed by others.

Despite the theoretical importance of social self-conceptions there have been few developmental analyses of the relationship between structural changes in these conceptions and cognitive growth. Certainly the most comprehensive study of the structural development of social self-conceptions is the investigation by Herzberger and her colleagues (1981). Drawing upon Werner's (1948) orthogenetic principle, Herzberger *et al.* predicted that social self-conceptions would become structurally more differentiated, specified, and abstract at higher levels of maturity. Consistent with the research on person description, they predicted that with increasing age, social self-conceptions would (1) become more descriptive, that is, conceptions would shift from an emphasis on peripheral qualities (such as physical appearance) to an emphasis on central or dispositional attributes (such as traits); (2) become increasingly more articulated, that is, include more units of information; and (3) exhibit more depth as reflected by greater qualification of impressions and more explanations of why certain impressions were formed. Utilizing a free-description method, parental and peer social self-conceptions were assessed among adolescents between sixth and twelfth grade. As predicted, with age there was an increasing tendency to perceive others' impressions of the self in terms of stable, dispositional characteristics rather than peripheral qualities. The level of articulation increased with age. Older adolescents were also more likely than younger adolescents to qualify social self-conceptions and to explain why others held specific impressions of them. Herzberger *et al.* interpreted these findings as reflecting the development of "abstract, inferential reasoning" characteristic of adolescent and adult cognition. Unfortunately, because the study included no other measures of social cognitive functioning the relationship between the structure of social self-conceptions and cognitive growth remains unspecified. The finding that parental social self-conceptions were more descriptive (were more likely to be given in terms of general interests and patterns of behavior than in terms of surface qualities or isolated actions) than were peer social self-conceptions indicates, as Herzberger *et al.* point out, that the structure of social self-conceptions cannot be completely accounted for by cognitive level. The difference in parent and peer social self-conceptions among children at the same age suggests that the character of the relationship between perceiver and perceived is relevant in the formation of social self-conceptions. This is consistent with Peevers and Secord's (1973) findings that the degree of differentiation and use of dispositions in peer descriptions depended on the affective valence associated with the target person.

As part of their investigation, Herzberger *et al.* compared the structure of social self-conceptions with the structure of self-conceptions of a same-age comparison group. Of particular interest here is the finding that across grade levels, self-conceptions tended to show greater descriptiveness and depth than did social self-conceptions. One explanation offered by the authors for the relative delay in the development of social self-conceptions is that more complex role-taking skills are required to infer how the self appears to others. While this explanation is plausible, it raises serious questions about the functional relationship between self- and social self-conceptions. That self- and social self-conceptions do not share similar structural properties at the same age, compromises the role of the social self-concept as a primary determinant of the self-concept—especially if the social self-concept is *less* descriptive than the self-concept. Of course, a within-subject comparison of the structure of self and social self-conceptions would more directly address this question. Given the purported significance of the social self-concept for self-concept development, studies aimed at clarifying the relationships among the self-concept, social self-concept, and level of social-cognitive functioning are clearly needed.

Finally, less empirically based speculations offered by Chandler (1975) were that adolescents often experience "epistemological loneliness"—that is, a sense that self and others diverge in the manner by which they experience or know both the internal world of the self and the world external to the self. Their role-taking skills help accentuate a recognition that the other's image of the self is based on an inadequate data base and that self and other represent a multiplicity of values, interpretations, needs, and life histories whose variety cannot easily be reduced to a single, veridical, codified perspective (Leahy & Kogan, in press). The loneliness about which Chandler speaks is one of experiencing the separation of subjectivities of self and other and stands starkly in contrast with the ideal exemplified by Mead's children cooperating in groups to reach consensus.

These facts and speculations suggest that, while social-cognitive skills may enhance the ability to engage in dialogues in which self and other may reach agreements, these same social-cognitive skills (of role taking and moral judgment) may make a *lack of consensus* even more apparent to the participants. From these dialogues with peers may emerge, not a "democratic" self which is the repository of the other's values, but rather a *private* self which strives both for independence and protection from being completely public. From the mutuality of group interaction may arise an awareness of the limitations of a "public life" and the beginning of individuating a self which has its own fable, its own projected life history and its own values. To borrow from Mead and to add a different twist: Selves exist both in relation to other selves and in the awareness that self and other *differ*.

STRUCTURAL-DEVELOPMENTAL THEORY OF THE SELF

Cognitive Processes

Piaget (1970) has proposed that one of the consequences of interpersonal interaction is the development of *decentration*. This ability involves two related factors (Feffer, 1970). First, the individual is able to simultaneously focus on two or more dimensions. Second, these dimensions are coordinated through a system of transformations (Feffer, 1970). For example, in the conservation of volume, the child must simultaneously focus on both height and width and relate these two dimensions to one another by recognizing that a decrease in height may be compensated by a decrease in width, thereby conserving volume. Decentering also involves the ability to refocus from perceptually given phenomena to consider either changes in what is perceived (e.g., changes in objects) or to consider "covert" or internal qualities of people (e.g., intentions, traits, or thoughts).

The argument that we proposed is that decentration serves an important function in the elaboration of the self-concept and the manner in which the self–other relationship is understood. An important quality of decentration is the ability to differentiate qualities of the phenomenal field (i.e., focusing on more than one dimension). This is quite similar to the differentiation quality of thought proposed by Zigler's developmental model (see Glick & Zigler, Chapter 1, this volume). However, decentration is a more comprehensive concept which refers to the decrease in perceptual salience and the ability to coordinate or interpret disparate qualities. We return to these issues later.

Decentration is also reflected in the ability to question one's own values. Theories of social development that are based on models of internalization, imitation, or identification (Bandura & Walters, 1963; Freud, 1933/1965) have difficulty explaining why an individual might question or reject the values which she has internalized. For example, if we believe that the strength of a response (or a habit) grows stronger with repeated reinforcement or exposure to models, then we would wonder why some older individuals would question or reject long-learned or established values. The cognitive-developmental model which we advance may be able to address this problem. Specifically, if we consider decentration as a developmental process occurring across the life span, then we might be able to apply this to the development of self during later adolescence or early adulthood. In particular, we propose that the individual may be able to refocus from her values to consider contradictions or limitations of those values.

Moral Judgment and the Self

We propose that Kohlberg's (1969) theory supplements the developmental range covered by Mead's theory. As indicated elsewhere (Leahy, 1983), Mead implies that the self becomes increasingly immersed in the perspectives of others with the implication that the individual, with increasing age, should show greater reliance on the other for self-conception. Mead's stages of the self parallel two developmental stages of Kohlberg's model of moral judgment. The play stage, which refers to a *specific* other for self-definition, parallels Kohlberg's Stage 3—*good boy/good girl* morality by which the child judges action from the perspective of individual peers and conforms to stereotypes and conventions reflected by peer opinion. The game stage in Mead's model represents a coordination of multiple perspectives that are represented in the self as an abstraction of the *generalized* other. This appears to parallel Kohlberg's Stage 4 judgments (*social order maintenance*) in which the views of specific others are abstracted to a more general social or legal convention. At both stages (for both Mead and Kohlberg) the other person serves as the audience and judge to which the self's behavior may be referred.

Because the conventional-level person judges the self and others in terms of social conventions, we may refer to those conceptions as *role dependent* where roles refer to the self's anticipation of the values of others (Leahy & Eiter, 1980). Even though the very young child may acknowledge that these conventions are of an arbitrary nature (Turiel, 1978), older children and young adolescents at the conventional level of moral judgment view conformity to these roles as desirable (Damon, 1977; Kohlberg, 1969, 1976).

An implication of role-dependent conceptions of the self is that individuals ascribing to such conceptions may place considerable emphasis on consensus in determining the value of their behavior: that is, deviance at this level may be defined as the failure to share an interpretation of reality advocated by others. Research on the development of conceptions of deviance does indicate that adolescents are more likely than children to claim that peers who have a distorted perspective on reality or who do not belong to a peer group are emotionally deviant (Coie & Pennington, 1976). It appears that one of the possible consequences of role-taking ability and peer interaction is that thinking and the self become *socialized* in that the individual may defer to others in the interpretation of reality, morals, or the self (Leahy, 1981a, 1983; Leahy & Hunt, 1983).

However, this deference to others is not the endpoint of development in Kohlberg's model. For some adolescents and adults, conventional-level thinking is replaced by postconventional morality. At the postconventional level, the individual believes that conventions may be open to modification either through renegotiated social contracts among participants (Stage 5) or through individual opposition because conventions may conflict with individually chosen values which are seen as universally applicable and, therefore, transcendent of any given conventions. Thus, for the postconventional individual, evaluations of behavior are not entirely based on the consideration of the opinions of others: rather, they refer to values that are experienced as *internal,* that is, values that depend on their validity by considering the self's own moral code or principles. These values for the self may be referred to as *role independent* (Leahy, 1983; Leahy & Eiter, 1980; Leahy & Kogan, in press).

In fact, if one examines the meaning of postconventional judgments in Kohlberg's model, one is impressed with the extent to which the capacity for guilt may be expected to follow from such judgments. For example, the Stage 5B individual may believe that an action is wrong, not because conventions proscribe it, but because she would feel guilt over violating her own moral values. Similarly, Stage 6 judgments also involve concern over violating self-chosen moral principles.

The foregoing extension of cognitive-developmental theory to the study of the self was the basis of two studies on self-conceptions of adolescents and young adults. The first study was concerned with the development of gender-role self-concept (Leahy & Eiter, 1980). Traditionally, conformity to conventionally stereotyped gender-roles was viewed as an indication of emotional adjustment such that males would be expected to be highly masculine whereas females would be expected to be highly feminine. In contrast to this polarization of personality traits on the basis of gender, Bem (1975) proposed that the ability to incorporate *both* masculine and feminine qualities is an index of greater adaptability or "health" in that the androgenous individual is able to effectively respond to a wider variety of situations (e.g., assertiveness or emotional sensitivity and expression). Developmental models of the self that propose that increasing development would be associated with greater internalization of societal norms would predict that higher developmental level would be associated with *greater* gender-typing of self-image (e.g., Freud—identification— or Bandura—imitation). Although Zigler's model predicts greater internalization with development, he does include the orthogenetic principle (differentiation, articulation, and hierarchical structure; see Werner, 1948) and, therefore, may predict that higher developmental level could be associated with coordinating differences within the self (although such a prediction is not easily apparent from that model).

The developmental model advanced here, however, does predict that higher developmental level may be associated with androgynous self-image. According to the structural-developmental model, the attainment of postconventional moral judgment will be related to the tendency to decenter from conventional stereotypes of masculinity and femininity and to consider universal, or more cross-situational, adaptive qualities as desirable in the self-image. Because Kohlberg's theory appears to stress the importance of moral judgment in the construction of an ego ideal, we (Leahy & Eiter, 1980) assessed subjects' real and ideal gender role self-concepts. Subjects were 116 adolescents and young adults forming three age levels—13, 17, and college age subjects. The Bem Sex Role Inventory was administered in both real ("How true of you?") and ideal ("How true you would like the word to be?") self-image formats. In addition, moral judgment stage (MJS) was assessed using Rest's (1975) Defining Issues Test (DIT).

The results offer general support to the structural model predicting increasing incorporation of opposite gender characteristics with increasing developmental level. First, older (17-year-old) males had more feminine and less masculine ideal self-image than younger (13-year-old) males. Second, the only age at which females showed a preference for gender-typed qualities was during college, when they showed a greater preference for masculine compared to feminine qualities (that is, females showed a cross-over in preferring opposite-gender personality qualities). Third, postconventional moral judgment was associated with the incorporation of opposite-gender characteristics for both males and females.

The interpretation of these data was that subjects who emphasize postconventional moral judgment rely less on concern for how others evaluate their behavior and place greater emphasis on integrating qualities that are adaptive across various situations: Thus, postconventional and androgynous subjects are role independent. Those data, as well as Bem's (1974, 1975) observations regarding androgyny, are difficult to reconcile with traditional models of social development which suggest that the ideal self-image is a reflection of the internalization or imitation of the values of others, especially the dominant culture. Moreover, the rationale of this structural model contrasts with Mead's symbolic interactionism which maintains that the development of values and the self are a reflection of the values of others: rather, we have proposed that at higher, postconventional levels these values are not reducible to conventional perspectives.

In a second study, Leahy (1981a) proposed that the development of internal standards of conduct should be distinguished from internalization where "internalization" refers to the introjection or imitation of salient models (e.g., Bandura, 1969; Freud, 1933/1965; Katz & Zigler, 1967). Concern for the opinions of others and reference to conventional stereotype are not reflective of truly internal standards in that they are externally referenced criteria. Strictly speaking we would refer to conventional-level judgments as an internal representation of the values of others. In contrast, as Kohlberg (1969) has maintained, "interiorized" orientations reflect independence from external physical or social sanctions. In Loevinger's (1976) ego-development theory, those values are autonomous.

Since the ideal self-image is understood here as an internal representation of values, it was proposed that subjects who placed greater emphasis on postconventional judgments would have more demanding (or more positive) ideal self-images. Thus, according to this rationale, the ideal self-image is a reflection of cognitive structuring of morality and not an introjection of the values of an individual, such as the ego ideal (Blos, 1962). A second implication of this structural model is that the ideal self-image may serve a self-punitive function in the self-system in that the higher moral-judgment level individual may be more likely to decenter from the ideal to the real self-image, comparing them, and devaluing the real self-image—resulting in higher self-image disparity.

One implication of the structural approach is that the self-image may undergo modification with changes in social-cognitive level. This assumption of isomorphism between social cognition and self-image does not imply, as Mead proposes, that the self is always a construction from the perspective of others. Such a self-concept would necessarily be *public* in that it is shared with others, marking an increasing developmental trend toward real–social self-image congruence. As we have argued, several lines of evidence are suggestive of an increase in real–social self-image disparity as well as increasing recognition of misimpressions and epistemological loneliness. Structural isomorphism, as used here, implies that changes in social cognition will be reflected in the self-concept: some of these social cognitive changes entail a decomposition of a generalized other into a multitude of perspectives and, at the post-conventional level, the emergence of an independently derived set of values that does not hold the peer group or society as the audience for arbitrating just decisions. Thus, the postconventional person may argue values that may conflict with those of others, thereby setting the self in opposition with others.

One advantage of the structural model is that it helps account for the growing distinction during adolescence between a *public* self (that which is known by others and congruent with others' values) and a *private* self. The symbolic-interactionist focus on shared, public, or socialized self leaves little to the individual's sense of an individual perspective or, even, life history. A number of years ago one of us (Leahy) had the privilege of asking the great American philosopher Paul Weiss what he thought of some of the tenets of self-perception theory—for example, the view that self-perception and other-perception are isomorphic. Weiss, in his characteristic Socratic style, responded with the question, "How can I be a me for you?" Even if the self has a public or shared quality, it also has a private quality whereby only the "I" can choose actions, experience pleasure or pain, and know which aspects of the "me" are being made known to the other ("you"): similarly, how can I know what you wish not to disclose to me, or even what it is like to experience your pain or pleasure? The error of a "general process" model of person perception that reduces self- and other-perception to the same model is that it fails to consider the subjective or phenomenal qualities of self-reflection and it fails to take into account the existential separation of self and other.

A similar limitation is reflected in Mead's model that the self is constructed from the point of view of others. This model may be sufficient for describing the younger child's self-concept (Leahy & Huard, 1976), but during adolescence there is an increasing recognition of the separateness of these perspectives. Later in this chapter we describe these changes in terms of the development of a *subjective self*—that is, one that is able to consider differences between self and other in perspectives on the self and one that recognizes the possibility of defending against the self.

Descriptions of Persons

Keller, Ford, and Meacham (1978) investigated the development of self-descriptions in children at 3, 4, and 5 years of age. Of particular interest was whether young children were more likely to describe themselves in terms of body image or activity. Keller *et al.* hypothesized that young children would be more likely to emphasize activity than body image because of the child's early emphasis on action in cognition (Piaget, 1954) and language (Nelson, 1973) among other reasons. Four measures of self-description were employed: open-ended question ("What's the first thing I should put in what I write about you?"); sentence completion ("[child's name] is a boy/girl who____"); I can/I am/I have ("What else can you do/are you/do you have?"); and a forced-choice test of body and action attributes in which the child indicates "The best one to put in what I write about you." The use of such verbal measures with very young children raises questions about the meaningfulness of any findings since verbal fluency may obscure possible competencies. The use of the "I can/I am/I have" measure appears especially biased in that prompts of "can" should elicit actions, whereas prompts of "have" should elicit bodily descriptions. Aside from these methodological shortcomings, Keller et al. combined data from two testing sessions (6 weeks apart) even though the correlation between sessions for different measures varied from −.22 to +.97. Furthermore, they combined responses from the open-ended questions with those from the sentence completion, even though these measures differ and even though no correlations between these tests are reported. No significant age effects were reported for action or body image, although action descriptions appeared to be more frequent than body image descriptions. For "I can, etc." there was greater reference to action than body image only on Test 2. However, given the fact that "I can" appears to demand action responses, whereas "I have" may elicit either references to body image or possessions (which were quite frequent responses), it is difficult to interpret these data. Finally, for body–action choices there were no age effects, but there was significantly greater choice of action statements.

Despite the problems with methodology and analysis in this study, there is a general finding of greater emphasis on action than body image in early self-descriptions. As the authors contended, this would be expected on the basis of a Piagetian approach emphasizing early reliance on activity in the construction of the phenomenal world (including the self-concept). These findings also indicate that other contents of the self-image (e.g., relationships) are used less frequently than the "peripheral" qualities of actions, body image or possessions. However, the absence of significant age trends may be due to the truncated age range (3 to 5 years) employed. The most promising methodology used by Keller et al. (1978) appears to be the forced-choice technique which minimizes problems introduced by verbal limits of the child. Such a technique, with a wider age range and a more varied array of contents from which to choose, would be useful in future research on this topic.

In a study of self-descriptions between childhood and adolescence, Montemayor and Eisen (1977) found a number of age changes consistent with our model. Between childhood and adolescence there were significant decreases in references to physical aspects of the self, body image, and possessions, and increases in references to psychological qualities such as "psychic style," sense of unity, and sense of self-determination. References to interpersonal style also increased during adolescence. Although Montemayor and Eisen discuss their study in terms of Werner's orthogenetic principle (i.e., differentiation, articulation, hierarchy), we concur with Harter (1983) in her claim that the separate content categories have little resemblance to Werner's model. For example, it is unclear how differentiation or articulation are reflected by an understanding of psychological qualities. It is certainly possible to differentiate a variety of physical aspects of the self. The more relevant dimension of difference in these age trends is between the objective and the subjective aspects of the self.

Livesley and Bromley (1973) had children ranging between 7 and 15 years of age write descriptions of themselves. Similar to their research on these children's descriptions of other people, there was a decrease with age in references to observable or external qualities (i.e., *peripheral* responses) and an increase with age in references to inferred or covert qualities (i.e., *central* responses). Peripheral responses which decreased with age included references to appearance, possessions, and family and central responses which increased with age included personality attributes, interests, beliefs, and attitudes toward the self. Livesley and Bromley claimed that older subjects were more likely than younger subjects to evaluate themselves negatively, although no statistical support is provided by them for this assertion.

They note that self-descriptions are longer than descriptions of others for these subjects, but this was primarily due to the lengthier self- versus other-descriptions of the youngest age group (age 7). This finding is consistent with the view that preoperational children are egocentric and may have greater difficulty differentiating the qualities of other people. Further support for the relevance of egocentrism to self–other descriptions is reflected in their finding that the categories used in describing *liked* others were more similar to those used in describing the self than in describing others. This may suggest that the individual differentiates more qualities for affectively valued people (i.e., self and liked others) than for disliked people. A similar finding was obtained by Leahy (1976) who found that descriptions of self and liked peers showed greater differentiation with increasing age compared to descriptions of disliked peers.

Rosenberg (1979) has suggested that individuals have two aspects of self—the overt self and the covert self. The *overt* self refers to those external qualities (e.g., body, possessions, behavior) easily apparent to others. In contrast, the *covert* self refers to what Rosenberg (1979) calls the "psychological interior"—that is, qualities that are more apparent to the self than to the other, such as thoughts, feelings, traits, and motives. In an open-ended interview study Rosenberg (1979) questioned children between 8 and 19 years of age about their locus of self-knowledge (e.g., "Who knows you best? What do they know?"), points of pride and shame, sense of distinctions and commonality with others, and ideal self for the future. Rosenberg's findings are largely consistent with those of Livesley and Bromley. Between childhood and adolescence there was a marked decrease in self-conceptions referring to overt qualities and an increase in references to the psychological interior. (These categories overlap with Livesley and Bromley's peripheral and central categories.)

Rosenberg describes this developmental change in terms of a change from percept to concept or as a change from the child as behaviorist to the child as psychological clinician. The "clinician" quality is not truly reflected in these data in that no evidence is reported regarding the construction of a psychological theory about the self. However, Rosenberg's study does indicate that some fundamental cornerstones of a psychological theory are given by adolescents in their self-conceptions. Adolescents are more likely than children to refer to interpersonal traits which Rosenberg describes as traits referring to being attracted to or attractive to others and interpersonal virtues (e.g., kindness and altruism). Furthermore, the psychological emphasis in these conceptions is also indicated by references to impulse and emotional control.

Rosenberg offers a cognitive-developmental model that draws upon Mead's and Cooley's theories to explain his findings. He argues that the young child is limited in self-reflection and apparently in metacognition (i.e., knowledge of his thought process) by egocentrism. He also suggests that the difficulty in conceptualizing traits is that one may have a variety of behaviors as reflective of a common trait—that is, phenotypic diversity with genotypic commonality. Furthermore, Rosenberg claims that adults teach children to use trait terms. Rosenberg proposes that experiences in communication facilitate understanding the nonegocentric quality of self which allows the child to view the self from the perspectives of others—that is, their evaluations of the self. Although it is true that socializing agents may assist in teaching the child trait terms, it appears somewhat unclear why trait concepts are relatively late in appearance in self-conceptions.

The view that we take is generally consistent with Rosenberg's emphasis on egocentrism and communication opportunities and, in fact, represents an extension of Rosenberg's blend of Piaget and Mead. We propose, like Rosenberg, that a decline in egocentrism follows from communication experiences that require the child to adapt to the perspectives of others. However, we would add that trait conceptions are more difficult than behavioral perceptions because they represent a natural ordering of these categories of person descriptions. In support of this view Barenboim (1981) has provided a valuable theoretical model for understanding the ontogenesis of these psychological conceptions. He proposes that the child develops from comparing behaviors to categorizing behaviors into traits and, finally, to comparing individuals on traits. Although we would propose that a true trait concept necessarily implies comparisons of individuals on traits, Barenboim's model does suggest that the child must first notice behavioral uniformities before an inference of a trait may be made. This, of course, agrees with Kelley's (1967) analysis of variance model of attribution in which the person estimates the variability of behavior across time, situations, and persons before making an inference of person causation. Thus, our argument of priority of behavioral conceptions refers to an information-processing constraint that places behavioral descriptions prior to psychological descriptions.

Furthermore, we would extend Mead's model to consider the relevance of psychological conceptions in the construction of a role. Although many developmentalists refer to role taking in terms of the ability to recognize the perspective of others, there is another excess meaning of role in sociological literature (Sarbin, 1952). Specifically, we refer to the individual's awareness that others have expectations of how the self will behave in a consistent manner given certain situations. For example, students may expect their professor to be serious, intellectual, and uninterested in the "good" life and may express surprise or distaste for the professor who departs from this role definition of the self. Each of these expectations imparts a psychological quality to the professor. In this sense of role expectation, the professor would need to anticipate what the expectations are about his or her personality and values. From this meaning of role, we would expect that the development of role taking would be related to the ability to think of the self in interpersonal terms in which the self's impulses or emotions are submitted to the anticipated scrutiny of the generalized order. Role definitions which refer only to specific behaviors, appearances, or possessions would probably not provide the relevant information to people who desire to cooperate with one another—that is, to take the role of others and to regulate one's behavior by these expectations.

LEVELS OF SELF-CONCEPTION

The model of levels of self-conception that we propose suggests that there are qualitative changes in the dimensions used in describing the self and the relation of the other to the self. This model owes a considerable debt to the work of Kohlberg (1969), Loevinger (1976), and Selman (1980), but, we should add, we hope that whatever shortcomings may exist in our model will not be attributed to their views.

Our review of the research on self-concept or self-descriptions suggests that an important change occurring between childhood and early adulthood is the differentiation of the subjective experiences of self and other. For the young (age 5 years) child the self and other are often seen as having similar interpretations of reality (Chandler & Greenspan, 1972) or as sharing similar activities (Scarlett, Press, & Crockett, 1971). Thus, for the young child the inner life of both self and other is usually not an object of cognition. Emphasis is on the self's physical qualities (e.g., appearance, body image, or sensation) or objects or activities that are simple extensions of the self (e.g., possessions or shared activity). We refer to this as the *objective* self in that the child appears to engage in a simple description of peripheral or external qualities or events. The child at this level may focus on subjective experiences (e.g., labeling the self as "bad"), but has difficulty recognizing other, possibly conflicting, qualities of the self. There is little disparity between real and ideal self-image.

At about age 10 years many children develop a *subjective* self in which their internal or psychological attributes (and those of others) are an object of interest (e.g., traits, feelings, attitudes, motivations). Differences between self and other are now viewed as important sources of information in judging the self's performance (through social comparison) and verifying whether others share the self's views (through role taking). The individual at this level may judge his or her behavior in terms of the expectations of others, attempting to conform to these expectations. This self-conception is role dependent in that the individual may attempt to change the self's behavior to be more acceptable to stereotypes established by others. There is increased self-image disparity and an increase in attempts to hide the self from the other.

The third level of the self is the *subjective-process* level. For some older adolescents, there is a change in self-concept marked by greater qualification in self-descriptions as the self is seen as varying across situations and time. The self's values may become more role independent in that desirable behavior is less determined by consideration of stereotyped roles and more determined by self-chosen principles or values. There is an attempt to integrate, or find acceptable, apparently conflicting qualities in the self (e.g., masculine and feminine traits). Self–other relations are seen, not only from each participant's perspective, but also through the perspective of possible nonparticipating observers (e.g., the "universal person" or an objectifying other). There is an increasing awareness that the other may have inaccurate impressions of the self. For some adolescents there is an increasing sense of isolation or loneliness. This level of the self involves an awareness of how the self is comprised of inner, psychological qualities which throughout adolescence become increasingly differentiated: Thus, the young adolescent may view the self in terms of univalent traits, but with increasing age comes to recognize the variability of the self across time and situations. Furthermore, the older adolescent may recognize how the self is known in different ways by different people—that is, that particular others may have misimpressions of the "true" self, whereas closer friends or intimates know more of the private self.

This third level is probably found among a small percentage of adults, especially those confronting major changes in their lives (e.g., leaving college, starting or losing a job or relationship, becoming a parent). The distinctive quality of the self at this level is the tendency to reflect on the *process of the self's construction or change*. By this we mean the examination of how the self came to be what it is and how the self may come to be something different (or remain the same). The individual at this level may have a *developmental* conception of the self—for example, he may reflect on how the self has changed over the course of the life span. As Butler (1968) and Erikson (1968) suggest, the individual may engage in a "life-review," although we suggest that this review may occur periodically throughout the life span.

SUMMARY

We have attempted to advance a structural-developmental model of the self that elaborates the implications of Piaget and Kohlberg's theories for the cognitive construction of the self-image. Although Mead's symbolic interactionism is a useful model for understanding the development of the child's self-concept, a variety of developmental phenomena suggest that the *socialized self* of Mead's theory eventually gives way to a self-concept that may be role independent, private, unknown by others, and changeable across situations. Rather than view the self as immersed or consistent with the perspectives of others, the older adolescent's nonegocentrism may suggest that the self becomes increasingly separated from others. Later in this volume Leahy (Chapter 8) will describe how these developmental changes in the self may reflect *costs* of development—that is, increasing development in the self-concept may place the adolescent or adult at greater risk for self-critical depression and identity problems.

Our review of the research suggests that there are three general patterns of self-construction that develop between childhood and adolescence. Each level or pattern reflects a change in decentering. The first level—the objective self—is focused on peripheral or observable qualities, such that inner experiences are not well articulated or differentiated from one another. The second level—the subjective self—entails the ability to decenter from the peripheral to recognize the covert, inner or psychological qualities of the self. Decentering is also involved in the role dependence of the subjective self, such that the individual values the perspective or opinion of others. The hallmark of self at this state is the reputation of the individual within a peer group. At the third level there is increasing decentering such that the subjective qualities of the self are seen as variable and developmental in nature. Thus, the young adult may acknowledge changes in his or her behavior, feelings, or thoughts across time and situations and across age. Values are less determined by a particular reference group or one's reputation among peers and more determined by self-chosen principles. This third level is not free from conflict, since opposing qualities of the self are recognized.

REFERENCES

Adams, G., & Jones, R. (1983). Female adolescents identity development: Age comparisons and perceived child-rearing experience. *Developmental Psychology, 19,* 249–256.

Baldwin, J. M. (1897). *Social and ethical interpretations of mental development.* New York: Macmillan.

Bandura, A. (1969). Social learning theory of indentificatory processes. In D. A. Goslin (Ed.), *Handbook of socialization theory and research.* Chicago: Rand McNally.

Bandura, A., & Walters, R. (1963). *Social learning and personality development.* New York: Holt, Rinehart & Winston.

Barenboim, C. (1981). The development of person perception in childhood and adolescence: From behavioral comparisons to psychological constructs to psychological comparisons. *Child Development, 52,* 128–144.

Bem, S. (1974). The measurement of psychological androgyny. *Journal of Consulting and Clinical Psychology, 42,* 155–162.

Bem, S. (1975). Sex role adaptabilty: One consequence of psychological androgyny. *Journal of Personality and Social Psychology, 31,* 634–643.

Blos, P. (1962). *On adolescence: A psychoanalytic interpretation.* New York: Free Press.

Butler, R. (1968). The life review: An interpretation of reminiscence of the aged. In B. Weugarten (Ed.), *Middle age and aging.* Chicago: University of Chicago Press.

Byrne, D. (1973). *The development of role taking in adolescence.* Unpublished doctoral dissertation, Harvard University, Cambridge, MA.

Chandler, M. (1973). Egocentrism and antisocial behavior: The assessment and training of social perspective-taking skills. *Developmental Psychology, 9*, 326–332.

Chandler, M. (1975). Relativism and the problem of epistemological loneliness. *Human Development, 18*, 171–180.

Chandler, M. J., & Greenspan, S. (1972). Ersatz egocentrism: A reply to Borke. *Developmental Psychology, 9*, 326–332.

Coie, J. D., & Pennington, B. F. (1976). Children's perception of deviance and disorder. *Child Development, 47*, 407–413.

Cooley, C. H. (1902). *Human nature and the social order.* New York: Scribner.

Damon, W. (1977). *The social world of the child.* San Francisco: Jossey-Bass.

Dickstein, E. (1977). Self- and self-esteem: Theoretical foundations and their implications for research. *Human Development, 20*, 129–140.

Elkind, D. (1967). Egocentrism in adolescence. *Child Development, 38*, 1025–1034.

Elkind, D., & Bowen, D. (1979). Imaginary audience behavior in children and adolescents. *Developmental Psychology, 15*, 38–44.

Erikson, E. (1968). *Identity: Youth and crisis.* New York: Norton.

Feffer, M. (1970). A Developmental analysis of interpersonal behavior. *Psychological Review, 77*, 197–214.

Flavell, J., Botkin, P., Fry, D., Wright, J., & Jarvis, P. (1968). *The development of role taking and communication skills in children.* New York: Wiley.

Freud, S. (1965). *New introductory lectures in psychoanalysis* (Vol. 22). London: Hobarth Press. (Original work published 1933)

Gilligan, C. (1982). *In a different voice: Psychological theory and women's development.* London: Harvard University Press.

Harter, S. (1983). The development of the self-system. In M. Hetherington (Ed.), *Carmichael's manual of child psychology: Social and personality development.* New York: Wiley.

Herzberger, S., Dix, T., Erlebacher, A., & Ginsberg, M. (1981). A developmental study of social self-conceptions in adolescence: Impressions and misimpressions. *Merrill-Palmer Quarterly, 27*, 15–29.

Katz, P., and Zigler, E. (1967). Self-image disparity: A developmental approach. *Journal of Personality and Social Psychology, 5*, 186–195.

Keller, A., Ford, L., & Meacham, J. (1978). Dimensions of self-concept in preschool children. *Developmental Psychology, 14*, 483–489.

Kelley, H. H. (1967). Attribution theory in social psychology. In D. Levine (Ed.), *Nebraska Symposium on Motivation.* Lincoln: University of Nebraska.

Kohlberg, L. (1966). A cognitive developmental analysis of children's sex role concepts and attitudes. In E. E. Maccoby (Ed.), *The development of sex differences.* Stanford, CA: Stanford Press.

Kohlberg, L. (1969). Stage and sequence: A cognitive development approach to socialization. In D. Goslin (Ed.), *Handbook of socialization theory and research.* Chicago: Rand McNally.

Kohlberg, L. (1976). Moral stages and moralization: The cognitive-developmental approach. In T. Lickona (Ed.), *Moral development and behavior.* New York: Holt, Rinehart and Winston.

Leahy, R. L. (1976). Developmental trends in qualified inferences and descriptions of self and others. *Developmental Psychology, 12*, 546–547.

Leahy, R. L. (1981a). Parental practices and the development of moral judgment and self-image disparity during adolescence. *Developmental Psychology, 18*, 580–594.

Leahy, R. L. (1981b). The development of the conception of economic inequality. I.

Descriptions and comparisons of rich and poor people. *Child Development, 52,* 523–532.

Leahy, R. L. (1983). Development of self and the problems of social cognition: Identity formation and depression. In L. Wheeler and P. Shaver (Eds.), *Review of Personality and Social Psychology, Vol. 4.* Beverly Hills, Sage.

Leahy, R. L., Balla, D., & Zigler, E. (1982). Role taking, self-image and imitativeness of mentally retarded and nonretarded individuals. *American Journal of Mental Deficiency, 86,* 372–379.

Leahy, R. L., & Eiter, M. (1980). Moral judgment and the development of real and ideal androgynous self-image during adolescence and young adulthood. *Developmental Psychology, 16,* 362–370.

Leahy, R. L., & Huard, C. (1976). Role taking and self-image disparity in children. *Developmental Psychology, 12,* 504–508.

Leahy, R. L., & Hunt, T. M. (1983). A cognitive-developmental approach to the development of conceptions of intelligence. In R. L. Leahy (Ed.), *The child's construction of social inequality.* New York: Academic Press.

Leahy, R. L., & Kogan, N. (in press). Social cognition and identity achievement. In S. Messick (Ed.), *Development in young adulthood: Characteristics and competencies in education, work, and social life.* San Francisco: Jossey-Bass.

Livesley, W. J., & Bromley, D. B. (1973). *Person perception in childhood and adolescence.* London: Wiley.

Loevinger, J. (1976). *Ego development: Conceptions and theories.* San Francisco: Jossey-Bass.

Mead, G. H. (1934). *Mind, self, and society.* Chicago: University of Chicago Press.

Montemayor, R., & Eisen, M. (1977). The development of self-conceptions from childhood to adolescence. *Developmental Psychology, 13,* 314–319.

Nelson, K. E. (1973). Structure and strategy in learning to talk. *Monographs of the Society for Research in Child Development, 38*

Peevers, B., & Secord, P. (1973). Developmental changes in attribution of descriptive concepts to persons, *Journal of Personality and Social Psychology, 27,* 120–128.

Piaget, J. (1930). *The child's conception of physical causality.* London: Routledge & Kegan Paul.

Piaget, J. (1932). *The moral judgment of the child.* London: Routledge & Kegan Paul.

Piaget, J. (1954). *The construction of reality in the child.* New York: Basic Books.

Piaget, J. (1970). *Genetic epistemology.* New York: Columbia University Press.

Rest, J. (1975). Longitudinal study of the Defining Issues Test: A strategy for analyzing developmental change. *Developmental Psychology, 10,* 491–501.

Rogers, C., & Dymond, R. (1954). *Psychotherapy and personality change.* Chicago: University of Chicago Press.

Rosenberg, F., & Simmons, R. (1975). Sex differences in the self-concept in adolescence. *Sex Roles, 1,* 147–159.

Rosenberg, M. (1979). *Conceiving the self.* New York: Basic Books.

Ruble, D., Boggiano, A., Feldman, N., and Loebl, J. (1980). Developmental analysis of the role of social comparison in self-evaluation. *Developmental Psychology, 16,* 105–115.

Ruble, D., Feldman, N., & Boggiano, A. (1976). Social comparison between young children in achievement situations. *Developmental Psychology, 12,* 192–197.

Sarbin, T. (1952). A preface to a psychological analysis of the self. *Psychological Review, 59,* 11–22.

Scarlett, H., Press, A., & Crockett, W. (1971). *Children's descriptions of peers: A Wernerian developmental analysis. Child Development, 42,* 439–453.

Selman, R. (1976). Social cognitive understanding. A guide to educational and clinical practice. In T. Lickona (Ed.), *Moral development and behavior*. New York: Holt, Rinehart & Winston.

Selman, R. (1980). *The growth of interpersonal understanding*. New York: Academic Press.

Selman, R., & Byrne, D. (1974). A structural developmental analysis of levels of role taking in middle childhood. *Child Development, 45*, 803–808.

Shantz, C. (1975). The development of social cognition. In E. M. Heterington (Ed.), *Review of child development research*. Chicago: University of Chicago Press.

Shirk, S. R. (1983). Self-evaluation and self-doubt in adolescence: A social cognitive analysis. Unpublished doctoral dissertation, New School for Social Research, New York.

Shrauger, J., & Schoeneman, T. (1979). Symbolic interactionist view of self-concept: Through the looking glass darkly. *Psychological Bulletin, 86*, 549–573.

Smith, M. B. (1978). Perspectives on selfhood. *American Psychologist, 33*, 1053–1063.

Sullivan, H. S. (1953). *The interpersonal theory of psychiatry*. New York: Norton.

Turiel, E. (1978). Social regulations and domains of social concepts. In W. Damon (Ed.), *New directions for child development*. San Francisco: Jossey-Bass.

Werner, H. (1948). *Comparative psychology of mental development*. New York: International Universities Press.

Winnicott, D. W. (1965). *The maturational processes and the facilitating environment*. New York: International Universities Press.

4

Contrasts between Understanding Self and Understanding Others

Daniel Hart
William Damon

INTRODUCTION

Person perception has long interested social and developmental psychologists, for the very good reason that it is a central part of one's social-cognitive repertoire. The way in which one understands people directly influences one's social communications and interactions and changes greatly over the course of the life span. Particularly in the last 10 years, when social-cognitive study has become the vogue in social and developmental psychology, there have been numerous attempts to document varying patterns of person perception within and across individuals.

Each person in the world is of course unique, and there are special problems and challenges in acquiring knowledge of any individual. Further, each individual that one knows stands in a special position relative to oneself. That is, one has different relationships with different individuals: some relationships are intimate, others distant; some domineering, others egalitarian; some competetive, some cooperative; and so on. Certainly the special nature of one's relation with a particular person flavors one's knowledge of that person, just as the special nature of an individual's personal characteristics poses unique demands for one's attempts to acquire knowledge of that individual. A key part of understanding persons lies in recognizing the differences among them both in terms of their relationships to oneself and in terms of their own individual makeups apart from oneself.

Among the universe of persons, there is one class whose position in relation to oneself is totally different from all others, and who therefore presents a radically different type of cognitive task for one's knowledge-acquisition efforts. This class of persons is the self itself. Cognitively, the self is not just another person. When one attempts to know other persons, one is on the outside looking in; when one attempts to know the self, one is on the inside looking both outside and inwards. One has access to the self in a manner impossible with any other person, no matter how intimate the relationship. Further, one has feelings and attitudes about the self unmatched by one's emotions towards others, and these feelings and attitudes may well affect the manner in which one processes information about the self and others. The challenge of "knowing thyself" is unique in the endeavor of person perception.

Despite the many obvious idiosyncrasies of self-perception, psychologists studying person perception have often failed to make a distinction between person perception generally and self-perception in particular. The initial inclination has been to assume that the process of understanding others is similar to the process of understanding the self. Developmental studies have attempted to show that the same general developmental descriptions apply to children's changing conceptions of both self and other over time (Montemayor & Eisen, 1977; Rotenberg, 1982). Such studies have been successful in obtaining empirical evidence in support of this position. However, they have done so by employing developmental descriptions at such a high level of abstraction that they would apply to almost any cognitive-developmental phenomenon. The most common examples of such descriptions are Werner's notion of increasing differentiation and hierarchical integration (Werner, 1957), or Flavell's (1977) notion that development proceeds from "surface" (overt properties) to "depth" (covert properties). Although these characterizations do capture age-related trends in both understanding self and understanding others, much of the unique quality of both developmental tasks eludes them.

The bias in favor of assuming similarities between self- and other-understanding derives from a long tradition within psychology. In fact, some of the most influencial theories of social development are based upon the notion that self- and other-conceptions go hand in hand in the course of development (Baldwin, 1902; Kohlberg, 1969). Baldwin (1902) attributed the existence of social phenomena such as the sense of justice to the identical relationship between the understanding of self and the understanding of others. According to Baldwin, the sense of justice depends on an awareness that others have the same desires as does the self:

> One's interests, the things he wants in life, are the things which, by the same very thought, he allows others, also, the right to want; and if he insists upon the gratification of his own wants at the expense of the legitimate wants of the 'other', then he in so far does violence to his sympathies and to his sense of justice. (p. 21)

Following after Baldwin (1902) and Mead (1934), Kohlberg (1969) assumes an identical relationship between the evolution of an understanding of self and other as a result of the developmental process involved in which an understanding of self is used to inform an understanding of others, and vice versa. The interpenetration of self- and other-understanding yields a social or shared self; since when one thinks of others, the injuries of others are in part experienced as one's own. This empathy arising from the synchronous development of self- and other-understanding, is, according to Kohlberg, the motivation underlying morality.

Whether or not self- and other-understanding develop synchronously and are similar is an empirical question with important ramifications. Should the two types of understanding not develop in a parallel fashion, then the theories of Baldwin and Kohlberg and other authors who explain the social nature of man in terms of a parallel development of self and other would have to be reevaluated.

A more mundane reason for examining the relationship between self- and other-understanding is to evaluate the need to investigate the development of each of the two types of understanding independently. If self- and other-understanding do develop in an exactly parallel fashion, then a researcher would have only to investigate one type of understanding to know the development of the other type. Some authors have, indeed, reached the conclusion that the two types of understanding are essentially similar. For instance, in discussing the results of their study investigating self-understanding, Montemayor and Eisen (1977) described their findings as basically similar to those emerging from the study of the development of an understanding of other people.

However, the value of investigating the development of each type of understanding should not be overlooked simply because there are global similarities between self- and other-understanding. An accurate, faithful portrayal of the development of each type of understanding is important for the study of development. Self-understanding is self-evidently important; the child must be aware of his or her capabilities, personality, and physical qualities in order to survive in our society. The child must also have an understanding of others in order to effectively interact with them even if this knowledge is of the most basic kind. For example, the child must know that the parent is able to give him or her candy before the child asks for it. Because each type of understanding constitutes an important developmental dimension, the delineation of the growth of one ought not be distorted to fit the other. It is precisely this question that concerns us: Is self-understanding development the same as the development of an understanding of others? We shall begin by examining the two theoretical traditions that have considered the issue in greatest detail.

Imitation Theory

The imitation thesis is that the development of an understanding of self parallels the development of an understanding of others. This position has received its clearest exposition in the work of Baldwin. Baldwin (1902) sought to explain the child's socialization and acquisition of competencies necessary to function in society through the process of imitation:

> All were born helpless; all have been educated. Each has been taught; each is to become a teacher. Each learns new things by doing what he sees others do; and each improves on what the other does only by doing what he has already learned. Each teaches simply by doing and rules the others by his example. (p. 80)

For Baldwin, as well as for other imitation theorists (Guillaume, 1926/1971; Kohlberg, 1969; Piaget, 1932/1965), the onset of imitation marks the beginning of selfhood. There are three stages in the process of becoming a self, according to Baldwin.

The first is the *projective stage,* corresponding to the first 6 or 7 months of life. During this period, the child is not aware of a distinction between the self and others. The child's perception of the world is composed of projects, or images, that are assumed to be of personal origin. Projects, or images, of people are particularly interesting to the child for two reasons: first, people are more unpredictable than objects, and second, because there is a growing affective involvement with people.

In the *subjective stage,* which appears late in the first year of life along with the third stage, the child turns his or her attention inwards towards the internal sensations. This happens as a result of imitation. As the child continues to watch other people, he or she becomes aware that the other performs interesting actions. In an effort to renew the interesting perceptions that accompany the actions exhibited by others, the child attempts to recreate or imitate those actions. However, in the course of imitation, the child experiences a significant difference between the actions of the other and those the child recreates. In experiencing his or her own actions, the child is aware of kinesthetic and volitional components which accompany that action. But when observing another perform an action, the child experiences only the visual perceptions associated with a movement. The differing experiential components to the same actions results in self-awareness; the child begins to see that the self and the other are different, and that the self is the locus of subjective experiences such as kinesthetic feedback and volition.

At the third stage in the process of becoming a self, the *ejective stage*, the inner sensations, emotions, and pleasures that were associated only with the self at the previous stage are seen to be applicable to one's understanding of another or are ejected into the other: "Other people's bodies, says the child to himself, have experiences *in them* much as mine has" (Baldwin, 1902, p. 14).

This stage obviously must follow the subjective stage, since the inner experiences accompanying an action are most easily discovered within the self. But once these inner sensations are identified by the child as belonging to certain actions, the child assumes that these same sensations are felt by others when they act. Once this basic correspondence or 'dialectic' is established between the self and other, one's understanding of self and other are basically identical. One comes to think new things about the self by applying thoughts and characteristics of others to the self. Baldwin (1902) offered this example:

> Last year I thought of my friend W as a man who had great skill on the bicycle and who wrote readily on the typewriter. . . . But now, this year, I have learned to do both these things. I have taken the elements formerly recognized in W's personality, and by imitative learning brought them over to myself. I now think of myself as one who rides a "wheel" and writes on a "machine". (p. 16)

Conversely, what one thinks of the self is ejected, "When I have a headache I cannot see a person riding, jumping, etc., without attributing to him the throbbing which such action would produce in my own head." (Baldwin, 1902, p. 18, footnote). Since what one learns about the self is, by the process of ejection, an addition to what one knows about others, and what one knows about others becomes meaningful for understanding of the self, what a person thinks of "another is—not

stands for, or represents, or anything else than is—his thought of himself, until he adds to it a further interpretation; the further interpretation is in turn, first himself, then is—again nothing short of this is—
his thought of the other" (p. 89).

On several points, Baldwin's (1902) theory of the development of
self- and other-understanding falls short of complete adequacy. First,
Baldwin never explains how one comes to have an accurate understanding of another person. Although one can reasonably assume that
the other experiences the same class of inner sensations and emotions
that the self experiences, one cannot easily discern which particular
sensations and emotions the other is currently experiencing. Thus in
the example of ejecting one's headache into another who is riding a
horse, the attribution is likely to be wrong. Indeed, even young children are aware that the self's current sensations and perceptions do not
necessarily correspond to the other's subjective state. The imitation
thesis fails to depict the ontogenesis of accurate ejection or attribution,
or what is more frequently termed role-taking.

Baldwin's assertion that imitation is the mechanism of self- and
other-understanding development has also received criticism in large
part because Baldwin never developed what he meant by imitation.
Dewey (1898) claimed that all Baldwin's theory does is identify a similarity without explaining it, since Baldwin's "imitation" has no specific meaning or mechanism:

> I do not see that we know any more of the psychology of the sense of personality
> and of (the other) society than we did before. . . . Baldwin's method in simply
> sending us from the (other) society to the individual, and from the individual to
> the (other) society, fails as a matter of fact to establish even this interdepen-
> dence. (p. 401)

Of course, Baldwin's failure to detail the psychological mechanisms
involved in imitation does not mean he was wrong. His thesis concerning the interrelationship of self- and other-understanding due to imitation might simply need elaboration, as some of his followers have
attempted to do (e.g., Guillaume, 1926/1971). Furthermore, despite the
problems that we have outlined above, Baldwin's theory has gained the
acceptance of a number of psychologists including Piaget (1932/1965),
Kohlberg (1969), Loevinger (1977), and Lewis and Brooks-Gunn (1979),
which indicates that the imitation thesis is of some explanatory value.

Attribution Theory

Beginning from a social-psychological rather than a developmental
perspective, Jones and Nisbett (1972) have elaborated the basic tenets
of Heider (1958) into a theory relevant to the issue of developmental
similarities and dissimilarities of self- and other-understanding. They

begin with the assumption that the self's and other's actions are the only data from which an understanding of self and other may be inductively constructed, and that these actions are perceived in much the same way that nonsocial objects are perceived. In Jones and Nisbett's theory, the actions of the self and other are interpreted differently for two reasons: There are different data available about the self and other, and there are differences between the way one processes information about the self and other. In regards to the first point, Jones and Nisbett (1972) assert that there is more and better data available for perceiving and interpreting the self's actions than is available for perceiving and interpreting the actions of another. The self knows what experiences accompany the actions of the self, but cannot know with any certainty the experiences accompanying the actions of another because the other's feelings can only be inferred and not known:

> The observer's (self's) knowledge about the actor's (other's) feelings is limited to inferences of two types: attempts to read inner experience from physiognomic and gestural ones, and judgments based on the observer's knowledge of what others and he himself have felt in similar situations . . . . Knowledge of the actor's feeling states is therefore never direct, usually sketchy, and sometimes wrong. (p. 89)

Similarly, one usually knows the intent of one's own actions, while the intentions of another can only be unreliably inferred. A third information difference is that one usually has knowledge of the temporal precursors of one's own acts, whereas in considering the actions of another, one frequently has no idea what circumstances preceded. Thus, when thinking about the self, one tends to think that the self's actions are contingent upon a temporal sequence of events, while regarding the other's actions as simply the result of a disposition. A final difference between the data available to interpret the self's actions and the data available to interpret the actions of another concerns the variability of behavior. "The actor's (self's) knowledge about the variability of his previous conduct—associated, in his mind, with different situational requirements—often preempts the possibility of a dispositional attribution" (p. 85). In interpreting another's action, one frequently has little idea about the variability of the other's behavior and, therefore, a dispositional attribution is not precluded.

Not only are there differing amounts of information available to an individual for interpreting the actions of the self and the other, but even the information that is common both to the knowledge of the self's and other's actions is interpreted differently. Jones and Nisbett (1972) argue that the self perceives its own behavior "To be a response to environmental cues that trigger, guide, and terminate it" (p. 89). In contrast, for the individual observing another's actions "The focal commanding stimulus is the actor's behavior" (p. 6), and the individual is likely to assume that the actor is the cause of the behavior. The individual is likely to view the self's actions as caused by environmental factors, rather than by dispositions, simply because the self literally cannot see itself perform an action very well and, therefore, the self's attention cannot be diverted from environmental contingencies by the perceptual attractiveness of the act. From the attribution theoretical perspective, then, the understanding of self and other will not be similar, nor will they develop synchronously because the two types of understanding are based on different types of information and are oriented towards different features of the action context. Self-understanding is focused on the environmental contingencies that control actions and, therefore, should be constituted of knowledge of these causal contexts; for instance, "I am nice to my mother when she buys me candy and none of my brothers are around to see me act nice." On the other hand, an understanding of other people should be composed of stable dispositions such as "He is always friendly" or "She is always nice."

Criticism of the attribution paradigm has focused on the assumption that the other can be known simply be inferring or attributing dispositions on the basis of the other's behaviors. Hamlyn (1974) has asserted that another person's behavior could not possibly make sense, or be interpreted, unless the self understands what a person is: "In order to construe a facial expression as one, say, of joy, one would have to know first that the expression was one manifested by some thing that could indeed manifest joy—by, that is, a person" (p. 6). This basic knowledge of what constitutes a person cannot be gained in the nonsocial inductive manner postulated by the attributionists. As Peters (1974), Hamlyn (1974), and Damon (1979) among others have pointed out, social knowledge, including an understanding of other people, cannot be gained apart from social interaction. Reciprocity, the give and take of relationships, constitutes the distinguishing characteristic of sociality; it must be experienced by the child in order to understand it. However, once the basic knowledge of personhood is gained, there is no reason that the attribution perspective developed by Jones and Nisbett could not be an accurate description of the process by which self- and other-understanding is accumulated.

EMPIRICAL RESEARCH

Although the theoretical issues involved in the developmental similarities of self- and other-understanding have intrigued psychologists for quite some time, relatively little empirical work has been concerned with this issue; indeed, research on either the development of self- or other-understanding by itself has been relatively scarce. We first discuss the developmental similarities between self- and other-understanding, and then nondevelopmental and developmental differences between the two.

Developmental Similarities between Self- and Other-understanding

Because there is so little research that has directly compared the developmental paths of self- and other-understanding, it is necessary to glean many of the similarities from research that has been concerned with only one of the two types of person understanding. Therefore, we will briefly review self-understanding development and some parallel findings from other-understanding development. After considering research in that literature, we discuss our own study in which developmental parallels between self- and other-understanding were directly assessed.

Self-Understanding Development

Previously, we (Damon & Hart, 1982) reviewed the developmental self-understanding literature, and based upon the review, we proposed a summary model of self-understanding development. Rather than re-review the literature on self-understanding development, we simply present the model. Following after James (1892/1961), we have divided self-understanding into two aspects: the "Me" and the "I."

The *Me* aspect is "the sum total of all a person can call his" (James, 1892/1961, p. 44). The primary elements of the "Me" are what James called the "constituents." These *constituents* are the actual qualities that define the self as known. They include all the material characteristics (body, possessions), all the social characteristics (relations, roles, personality), and all the "spiritual" or psychological characteristics (consciousness, thoughts, psychological mechanisms) that identify the self as a unique individual. In our own model, we have added a fourth constituent: the active qualities of self (capabilities, typical activities).

The *I* is the "self-as-knower," the aspect of self that continually organizes and interprets experience in a purely subjective manner. The individual is aware of the "I" through three types of experiences: *continuity*, *distinctness*, and *volition*. A stable self-identity derives from a sense of the continuity of the self-as-knower. As James (1892/1961)

wrote, "Each of us spontaneously considers that by 'I' he means something always the same" (p. 63). A feeling of individuality, of distinctness from others, also derives from the subjective nature of the
self-as-knower: "Other men's experiences, no matter how much I may
know about them, never bear this vivid, this peculiar brand" (p. 71). A
sense of personal volition is perhaps the quintessential experience of
the self-as-knower. The very notion of subject denotes an active pro-
cessor of experience. Through one's own thoughts and interpretations
of the world, one exerts agency of the most fundamental kind over self.
Finally, implicit in the experience of each of these self-features (continuity, distinctness, and volition) is the additional second-order
awareness of the *self-reflectivity* that knows the nature of self. Although it is impossible to study the "I" directly, Mead (1934) suggested
that one can investigate the "I" through the "Me"; this amounts to
studying an individual's understanding or sense of each of the aspects
of the "I". The changing understanding of these constituents of the
"Me" and the aspects of the "I" from infancy to adolescence is sche-
matized in Figure 4.1.

The logic of the model is as follows. The front face of the cube
represents the self-as-object (James' "Me"), divided into its four basic
constituents (the physical, active, social, and psychological self). At all
ages, children have some knowledge of each of these four constituent
self-schemes, however cursory and primitive this knowledge may be.
In the course of development, knowledge of each self-scheme changes
in character. These changes are represented along the vertical dimensions (the columns of the model's front face). Within the 16 boxes of
the model's front face, we have offered abbreviated descriptions of
these main developmental trends.

In addition to these vertical developmental trends within each of the
four self-schemes, there is another important ontogenetic trend in children's understanding of the self-as-object. This is an age-related shift
that favors, respectively, the physical, active, social, and then psychological aspects of self as the child becomes the adolescent. This movement is represented along the darkly-outlined diagonal boxes of the
model's front face. It is this movement that has been the focus of
previous unidimensional accounts of self-concept development (e.g.,
Montemayor & Eisen, 1977; Selman, 1980). Although we believe that
these previous accounts have erred in their too exclusive focus on this
one ontogenetic movement, we do believe that it is a dominant dimension within a multidimensional developmental progression. For this
reason this movement occupies the central position in our model. The
four boxes along the darkened diagonal represent the prototypical con-

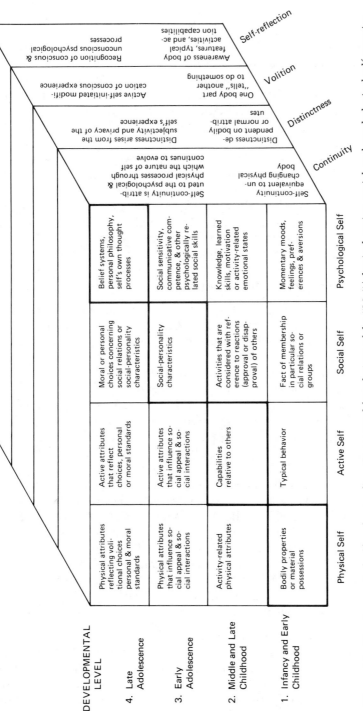

Figure 4.1 Development of self-understanding. Conceptual foundations of the "Me" (physical, active, social, and psychological self-constituents) and the "I" (continuity, distinctness, volition, and self-reflection) at four developmental levels during childhood and adolescence.

ceptions of self at each of the four general self-understanding levels (rows 1, 2, 3, and 4 along the front face).

As for these four self-understanding levels, they are represented by the model's horizontal dimensions (the rows), cutting across each of the four constituent self-schemes. These overall levels consist of general features that the parallel developmental levels of the four self-schemes have in common. In other words, the four aspects of self-knowledge are linked at each developmental level because they share characteristics deriving from the dominant conception of self at that level. This dominant conception at each level is, as noted above, shown in the box along the diagonal. At each new level a new aspect of self assumes dominance and lends its characteristics to parallel-level conceptions of other aspects of self. These characteristics become, in essence, the organizing principles of self-understanding at that level.

Thus, the four general developmental levels of self-understanding with respect to the "Me" are organized as follows:

Level 1: At Level 1, the subject treats self-characteristics taxonomically and physicalistically. There is no synthesis of a variety of characteristics because the subject believes that each characteristic has a definite meaning alone, or simply grouped with very similar characteristics. When asked to explain the importance of a particular characteristic, the subject does not go beyond asserting that its importance resides solely in the name of the characteristic, therefore requiring no elaboration. When describing the physical aspects of the self, this type of response is exemplified by a simple, unelaborated listing of body features or material possessions ("I am big and I have a dog." "WHY IS THAT IMPORTANT?" "I don't know."). References to the active qualities of the self are almost always limited to a simple listing of the self's typical activities ("I play baseball and soccer." "WHY IS THAT IMPORTANT?" "Because that's what I do."). Social qualities are likewise confined to an enumeration of the self's social relationships ("I have a mother." "WHY IS THAT IMPORTANT?" "Just because it is."). References to psychological aspects of the self are most usually preferences and aversions, although occasionally a subject will mention a transient emotion ("I like baseball." "WHY IS THAT IMPORTANT?" "It just is.").

Level 2: Level 2 is different than Level 1 in several ways. First, characteristics of self are more organized. In elaborating the importance of a particular characteristic, the Level 2 subject can draw on several characteristics of the self and at least superficially unite them. Also at Level 2, the subject begins to make relative comparisons between the self and others, particularly about the person's action capabilities. A final difference of the Level 2 response is its usual focus on the person's active qualities, although this focus may manifest itself through a response that is also related to other schemes. Thus, in describing the physical qualities of the self, active qualities are often integrated ("I am big." "WHY IS THAT IMPORTANT?" "Because that makes me a good basketball player."). Active qualities at Level 2 simply refer to a person's active capabilities ("I'm a good basketball player." "WHY IS THAT IMPORTANT?" "Because I'm really good."). In the social scheme, the Level 2 response often refers to another's reactions to the self's actions ("I hit my brother." "WHY IS THAT IMPORTANT?" "Because my mommy gets mad at me when I do that."). Finally, in the psychological scheme, a Level 2 response frequently is concerned with the self's knowledge, either alone or in comparison to other's knowledge; and also frequently with how that knowledge might relate to the active qualities of the self ("I am the smartest person in the class." "WHY IS THAT IMPORTANT?" "Because then I am allowed to stay out for extra recess.").

Level 3: Level 3 continues the trend toward more synthesis among characteristics of the self. Most usually, this synthesis develops among the subject's social relations and interactions. All the schemes at this level are seen to have some bearing on how attractive the self is to others, and how well the self interacts with others. In the physical scheme, this is manifested in a concern with bodily attractiveness ("I have good muscle tone." "WHY IS THAT IMPORTANT?" "Because girls really like that."). Similarly, active components of the self understanding are important insofar as they have bearing on personal attractiveness or social interactions ("I am a really good football player." "WHY IS THAT IMPORTANT?" "Because that makes me really popular."). Level 3 descriptions of social qualities of the self often focus on the person's social personality ("I am friendly and get along well with people."). Psychological qualities such as interpersonal understanding, or communicative competence are frequently mentioned, since these qualities have obvious import for social interactions ("I am really understanding." "WHY IS THAT IMPORTANT?" "Because people really like to have friends that are really understanding.").

Level 4: At Level 4, all qualities of the self are integrated into a personal or moral belief system. Thus, physical qualities are important descriptions of the self only as they reveal that person's personal philosophy ("My name is Kareem." "WHY IS THAT IMPORTANT?" "It shows that I am a Muslim, and that I believe very strongly in Allah.").

Active qualities are likewise important to the extent to which the
self's moral standards or personal philosophy shows through ("I never
cheat when playing cards." "WHY IS THAT IMPORTANT?" "Be-
cause it shows that I really believe in being fair to my friends, and that I
don't like to get ahead at other people's expense."). Social qualities
often refer to moral standards ("I wouldn't have her for a friend, even if
she is really popular." "WHY DOES THAT SAY SOMETHING
ABOUT YOU?" "Well, I wouldn't because she always picks on other
kids and makes fun of them just to make her friends laugh, and I don't
think that is right."). Level 4 references to psychological qualities often
directly mention moral standards or personal belief. ("What is really
important about me is that I run my life according to principles. The
most important one is that I always try to treat people fairly.").

The side face of the model shows the understanding of self-as-subject
(James's "I"), especially with regard to the understanding of continuity, distinctness from others, volition, and self-reflection. Development here is represented as a shift from one pole to the other along
the four respective dimensions, rather than as a progression from level
to level (as is the case with understanding the "Me" aspect of the self).
This is because there is nothing in the self-understanding literature to
indicate that between childhood and adolescence there are a series of
qualitatively distinct levels in the awareness of the "I." Rather, the
literature indicates that during this age range there is a gradual emergence of some new notions in each of these four dimensions.

When asked if the self is the same as it was years before, the child is
likely to respond affirmatively, and defend the assertion by reference to
a physical quality ("I know I am the same as I was 5 years ago because
my hair is still red."). Similarly, a child's claim of distinctness from
others is likely to be based on physical appearance ("No one else looks
like me."). The self's volition is believed to be a matter of one physical
organ communicating to another ("I do what I do because my brain
tells my body what to do."). Since self-understanding is primarily constituted of physical and active qualities, self-reflection results in an
awareness of these attributes.

Unlike the child, the adolescent is likely to integrate psychological
attributes in his or her understanding of the "I." An assertion of continuity of the self through time is based upon the stability of the self's
information processing ("I am the same as I was 5 years ago because I
look at the world the same way."). Because the self's psychological
mechanisms are not available for inspection by others, the self's experience of self is private and distinguishes the self from others ("Nobody
can know about how I feel about things."). The self's volition stems

from its ability to shape and control its own experience ("If I am really mad at someone, I just make myself think good things about them until I'm not mad anymore."). Finally, self-reflection results in the conclusion that nonconscious or unconscious experience affect behavior ("Sometimes I don't know why I do some of the things I do, but I know there's some reason within me."). In addition to its correspondence to the developmental trends in self-understanding outlined in our review of the literature, the model as described has received further verification from preliminary results in our ongoing longitudinal study of self-understanding.

The Development of an Understanding of Others

We believe the same divisions in self-understanding are generally applicable to descriptions of others. In other words, other-understanding components can be ascribed to the "Me" or the "I." When one thinks about the other as an object, the other's physical, active, social, and psychological qualities are considered. One can also consider the other's continuity, distinctness from others, volition, and self-awareness or self-reflectiveness in much the same way as one could consider these same dimensions in the self's "I." Therefore, as a framework for our brief consideration of other-understanding development, we discuss each study in reference to the aspects of the "Me"; unfortunately, to our knowledge there is no research of the development of an understanding of others that pertains to the "I."

In one of the better studies of person-understanding development, Livesly and Bromley (1973) asked children from ages 7–15 years to write descriptions of people they knew. In one analysis of the data, the authors divided the descriptions into peripheral and central statements. Peripheral statements described the other in terms of physical appearance, name, age, activities, possessions, likes and dislikes, social roles, and kinship and social relationships. These types of statements correspond quite closely to Level 1 of the self-understanding model presented previously. Central statements describe the other in terms of personality traits, general habits, motives, needs, values, and attitudes. Data analysis revealed that the proportional usage of central statements increases with age, and the proportional usage of peripheral statements decreases. These results parallel findings summarized in the model of the self-understanding development presented earlier; in particular, the movement away from the characteristics treated in a physicalistic manner (e.g., appearance, name, typical activities) towards a more psychological understanding of personal characteristics.

Barenboim (1981) posited a three-level progression in the development of the understanding of others. At the first level, the child describes other people in terms of behavioral comparisons (e.g., "Jimmy is the fastest runner in the class."). The use of behavioral comparisons leads to the development of psychological constructs in the description of other people, as the child begins to infer stable dispositions that produce the observed behaviors (e.g., "John does well in class because he is smart."). As the child becomes adept at making psychological inferences in the description of other people, he/she begins to make psychological comparisons between people (e.g., "Joan is much friendlier than Fred."). To test this hypothetical sequence in the development of understanding other people, Barenboim interviewed children in the age groups of 6, 8, and 10 years of age, asking each child to describe three people he/she knew well. The same children were reinterviewed 1 year later at which time each was asked to describe three different people. Comparisons between the age groups revealed that there was a significant increase in the usage of behavioral comparisons between the ages of 6 and 8, and a significant decrease in the usage of behavioral comparisons between the ages of 9 and 11. Psychological constructs began to rise in frequency with age with all the older age groups. Finally, psychological comparisons increased in frequency only between the 10- and 11-year-olds. Analysis of the changes occurring within subjects between Time 1 and Time 2 indicated that all but two followed the proposed developmental sequence.

The results do substantiate the developmental sequence hypothesized by Barenboim. However, even though the sequence as depicted may describe a developmental phenomenon, there remains some doubt about how important the sequence is for a description of the development of understanding of others. As Barenboim (1981) himself admitted, the sequence does not characterize all of the subject's actual descriptions: "The non-analyzed residual category contains a large percentage of subject' statements" (p. 137). Perhaps the most valuable aspect of Barenboim's study is that it reveals that behavioral comparisons become an important aspect of understanding of others, just as was found in the case of self-understanding.

In order to directly test whether self-understanding development parallels other-understanding development, we (Damon & Hart, in preparation) asked children in nursery school and in Grades 1, 3, and 5 to describe themselves, their friends, and their parents. These descriptions of self, friends, and parents were then coded using a scoring manual that corresponds to the developmental model of self-understanding found in Figure 4.1. No significant differences among descriptions of the self, friends, and parents, were found for either developmental level or for percentage of statements within each constituent. This suggests that self-understanding is not more developed than person perception, nor less so. Furthermore, the failure to find differences among descriptions of the self, a friend, and a parent for percentage of statements within each constituent may indicate that self-understanding is not more attuned to psychological qualities than is an understanding of others, at least in childhood. Together, these two findings lend some support to the imitation thesis that claims that these two types of understanding develop synchronously. Although this synchrony does not seem to be the usual case in our data, as we shall discuss in a moment, several striking examples of identical structures used in all three descriptions are presented below.

Self Interview:	SO YOU WERE TALKING ABOUT WHAT YOUR BACKGROUND IS AND YOUR PARENTS. And I'm 6 years old. DOES THAT SAY SOMETHING IMPORTANT ABOUT THE KIND OF PERSON YOU ARE? Yes. I am 6 years old. September 12th I will be 7. And when I will be 7 I'm gonna put 17 more dollars in the bank more than I have now. YOUR AGE IS CONNECTED TO HOW MUCH MONEY YOU HAVE IN THE BANK? ANYTHING ELSE? Uh-uh.
Friend Interview:	HOW ABOUT HIS AGE? DOES THAT TELL ABOUT WHAT KIND OF PERSON HE IS? WHY? You know like when you're 6 years old, you're usually big? Like tall. And Kyle's 6, but he's, like, that tall. He's short.
Parent Interview:	DO YOU THINK IT WOULD BE IMPORTANT TO KNOW THAT? (Her age.) HOW COME? Because I want to know how old she is . . . sometimes I compare numbers. I know my father's old. He's 30 something, and my mother's something like 31. (Grade 1)

Self Interview: WHAT ELSE CAN YOU TELL ME ABOUT
                            YOURSELF?
                            I live on 11th and Main Street so in case they
                            want to visit me sometimes.
                            SO THAT'S IMPORTANT.
                            And my phone number so they can call me.

Friend Interview: WHAT ELSE CAN YOU TELL ME ABOUT
                            ANDREW BESIDES THAT HE'S A GOOD
                            WORKER?
                            Well, he just has to jump a fence, and he's right
                            over to my house 'cause he lives on Weston
                            Street, and I live on Main Street. It's a house,
                            and here's a house, and there's a house. And
                            this is my house, and there's a fence. And all's
                            he does is have to jump over it, and he'll be to
                            my house. His address is the same as my ad-
                            dress. His is 11 and mine's 11.

Parent Interview: WHAT SAYS THE MOST A
                            BOUT HIM?
                            The most thing I think is where he lives.
                            YOU THINK THAT SAYS THE MOST
                            ABOUT HIM?
                            WHY?
                            'Cause, like, people have to come to him. And
                            his phone number. I think his phone number
                            too.
                                                                (Grade 1)

In the first example, the child claims that age is a central characteristic of the self, a friend, and her parent; a belief that we would
classify as Level 1 in our developmental model. Similarly, where the
self, the friend, and the parent live is considered very important by the
second child, which again is a Level 1 conception in our scheme.

Although self-understanding is neither more nor less developed than
an understanding of others, this does not mean that either one necessarily develops synchronously with reference to the other one. In our
research we found no significant association between developmental
levels of self- and other-understanding. For instance, in the following
excerpts, the subject describes herself in terms of a Level 2 psychological characteristic (smart), her friend in terms of a Level 3 social characteristic (nice), and her mother in terms of a Level 1 physical characteristic (woman):

Self Interview: WHAT ELSE CAN YOU TELL ME ABOUT YOURSELF?
Well, I like to work, but I only like to work if it's on a computer.
WHY DO YOU ONLY LIKE DOING IT ON A COMPUTER?
Well, 'cause there's different kinds of games and stuff. And it's fun to be small and then be able to know all different things that most of your other friends don't know.

Peer Interview: CAN YOU TELL ME WHAT KIND OF PERSON SHE IS?
She's nice.
WHY IS THAT IMPORTANT TO KNOW ABOUT HER?
If she was mean, then she probably wouldn't like me. And if she did and she was mean, she might cheat a lot and stuff.
WHAT WOULD THAT TELL ABOUT WHAT KIND OF PERSON SHE IS?
She's always angry; she doesn't like people.
WHY WOULD THAT BE AN IMPORTANT THING TO KNOW ABOUT HER?
'Cause if somebody new came and they didn't know it, they would go up to her and she wouldn't like 'em and they would wonder why.

Parent Interview: DOES THAT MAKE A DIFFERENCE, THAT YOUR MOTHER IS A WOMAN?
I Guess.
WHAT DIFFERENCE DOES THAT MAKE?
She wouldn't be a mother; she'd be my father.
(Grade 5)

The failure to find a significant relationship between developmental levels of self- and other-understanding may reflect the inadequacy of our self-understanding measure for uncovering developmental reorganizations in person understanding. Such an interpretation is supported by the very low associations between age and developmental levels of person understanding as measured by the self-understanding scoring manual in our study (age and developmental level of friend descriptions, $r = .32$, $p < .05$; age and developmental level of parent descriptions, $r = .22$, ns). Unfortunately this interpretation ends up confirming what it seeks to avoid, namely that self-understanding and an understanding of others follow different developmental paths. Of course, this anomalous finding could be explained in a number of other ways that preserve the imitation thesis. Furthermore, in general, the studies of the development of person-understanding reviewed above indicate that there are important parallels between the development of self- and other-understanding. Early childhood self- and other-understanding focuses on physical qualities and typical activities, to be replaced by behavioral comparisons in late childhood. Adolescents are primarily concerned with social-personality characteristics and beliefs, whether describing the self or others. These results are concordant with Baldwin's (1902) imitation thesis which predicts self- and other-understanding to be similar.

Dissimilarities between Self- and Other-Understanding

Despite the developmental synchrony and similarities above, there are differences in self- and other-understanding. The most frequently researched dimension distinguishing between the two types of understanding stems from the attribution hypothesis which predicts that the self will be described in terms of environmental conditions eliciting a particular action while the other will be characterized in terms of cross-situational traits. Usually, this research involves an experimental manipulation with adult subjects.

For instance, Nisbett, Caputo, Legant, and Marecek (1973) reported that an adult recounting his or her own actions in a number of experimental situations is more likely to attribute his or her behavior to situational causes and free will, while ascribing the roots of another's behavior in the same situation to personality traits and dispositions. Taylor and Fiske (1975) found that simply the difference in spatial orientation affected the interpretation of a person's behavior. A person sitting *behind* the actor perceived the actor's actions as he or she would perceive the self's (i.e., as elicited by the environment); however, when *facing* the other performing the acts, the causes of the other's acts were more frequently attributed to personality traits and dispositions.Although these two and a host of similar studies have found results consonant with the attribution perspective, implications for the synchrony of self- and other-understanding development stemming from these investigations must be tentative. This is for several reasons. Obviously, neither of the studies cited above was developmentally oriented, and, therefore, can give no direct information about age trends or developmental factors. Second, the experimental manipulations used in these studies were designed to exaggerate differences in self- and other-understanding, and the assessment procedures gave no direct indication of the similarities of self- and other-understanding. Nonetheless, we would argue that the findings of these studies do indicate that there is a significant difference between the understanding of self and other, a difference that has been found in several developmental studies that we will consider now.

Developmental Studies of Dissimilarities in an Understanding of Self and Others

In our own study discussed previously, we did find one obvious difference between descriptions of self and others. Descriptions of friends and parents contained a striking number of self-referent descriptions (e.g., "My mother is nice because she buys *me* candy"). The parallel for the self description would be to describe the self in terms of a specific other person (e.g., "I am nice because I buy *my mother* candy"). Both these types of references were labeled specific-person references and were coded according to whom the specific person was: either the self or a specific other (e.g., a friend, a parent, a sibling).

There were no developmental differences in the number of specific-person references made in the descriptions of self, friends, and parents, but there were significantly more specific person references (self-references) in descriptions of friends and parents. Since self-references are as common in descriptions made by adolescents as those of younger children (Honess, 1980), we do not believe that the self-referencing phenomenon can be explained in terms of egocentrism, as some authors have suggested (Scarlett, Press, & Crockett, 1971; Secord & Peevers, 1974). Rather, we believe that the explanation for the self-referencing phenomenon lies in an egoistic, rather than egocentric, explanation. Simply, at least part of one's understanding of another person is concerned with how that person's qualities directly affect the self. For instance, when children think of their parents as nice, nice in part means what nice things the parents do for the child. In contrast, when one thinks of the self, there is little motive to attach the meaning of a particular characteristic of self to another person. For example, when a child thinks of the self as being nice, it makes little difference to the perceived degree of the self's niceness whether the self is especially nice to friends and not so nice to siblings, or vice versa. We believe this to be an indication of a genuine difference of perspectives between the understanding of self and other.

Other authors have reported differences in the use of psychological categories to describe the self and others. In their development study (described in part previously) Livesly and Bromley (1973) asked children from ages 7 to 15 to write descriptions of themselves and other people they knew. With 7-year-olds, the category of likes and dislikes was by far the most frequently used in self-descriptions, but the same category was rarely used in the description of others. Categories of interests and hobbies, and intellectual aptitudes and abilities, followed the same trend; 7-year-olds used these categories more frequently for self-description than for other-description. Adolescents added still more differences to the schism between conceptions of self and other, using categories of motivation and arousal, and orientation, more frequently when describing the self than in other-description.

In a very similar study, Secord and Peevers (1974) reported that self-descriptions contained more references to preferences, beliefs, and abilities, while descriptions of others mentioned superficial characteristics or role categories. Taken together these last two studies seem to indicate a tendency for children to think of the self in more psychological terms than when thinking about the other, a tendency that becomes more pronounced in adolescence.

This tendency to think of the self in terms of psychological qualities and abilities which becomes especially prominent in adolescence might be explained by the adolescent's meta-cognitive understanding of the process of knowing people. In our own research, (Damon & Hart, in preparation) we have found that adolescents believe that they cannot know the psychological qualities of others. Here is an example from a young adolescent illustrating this point:

> WHO DO YOU KNOW BETTER: YOUR MOM OR YOU?
> Me.
> HOW COME?
> Because I know what I feel, and I know what I think about things more than I know what she does. And I know what I do.
> HOW COME YOU THINK YOU KNOW WHAT YOU THINK AND FEEL ABOUT THINGS MORE THAN YOU KNOW THAT ABOUT HER?
> Because I can't really read her thoughts. You can't read her mind and all that. You can tell what you're thinking 'cause you're you.

The belief that it is difficult to know the thoughts and minds of another probably will inhibit the subject from ascribing as many psychological qualities to that person. Similarly, abilities are perceived to be more *important* for an understanding of the self, because knowledge of one's abilities are necessary to function well in society.

> WHY DO YOU KNOW YOURSELF BETTER?
> Because I have to live with myself. I have to learn about myself, or else I'm not gonna' be able to know what to do.
> WELL, YOU HAVE TO LIVE WITH YOUR MOTHER TOO, SO HOW COME YOU KNOW YOURSELF BETTER?
> Because, like, when I go for a job, I have to know a lot about myself to fill out the forms and things.
> ... WHY DO YOU THINK YOU KNOW YOURSELF BETTER THAN YOU KNOW JACK?
> Because I've been around myself a lot longer, and I've looked at myself more than I've looked at Jack. 'Cause, you know, information about me is to me a lot more important than information about a friend.
> YOU'RE SAYING TWO THINGS REALLY: YOU'RE SAYING YOU KNOW MORE ABOUT YOU BECAUSE—
> Yeah, two reasons really because I've been around myself, and also if you know yourself you can handle lots of things. You know how to handle lots of things, and if it's the best way, how you can improve it. And with a friend, you know, you can't improve his life; he has to do that. You get more out of it if you know yourself.

Again, this subject is unlikely to think of others as frequently in terms of abilities simply because there is less need to do so.

CONCLUSIONS

The literature reviewed above demonstrates that neither the imitation nor attribution paradigm is wholly correct. The imitation thesis cannot account for the empirical developmental and nondevelopmental differences in self- and other-understanding: the tendency to attribute the roots of one's own behavior to the environment and the roots of another's behavior to personality characteristics, the egoistic understanding of other people evidenced in self-referent descriptions, and the presence of more psychological referents in the descriptions of the self than in descriptions of others. The failure of the imitation paradigm to account for significant differences in one's understanding of self as opposed to one's understanding of others is probably due to the orientation of the imitation theorists. Baldwin (1902), and like him, Guillaume (1926/1971) and Kohlberg (1969), was fundamentally concerned with explaining the social nature of man through the structure of the self-concept. Since other people and society actually constitute part of the self, he claimed, social instincts follow quite naturally.

But what Baldwin failed to seriously consider is the possibility that self-understanding has other functions besides connecting the individual to others. As we mentioned before, the "I" aspect of self-understanding, consisting of the sense of self-continuity, the feeling of distinctness from others, and a belief in self-efficacy, have no corresponding research constructs in the other-understanding literature, most certainly because these dimensions are not salient components of one's understanding of others. However, these same dimensions are crucial in one's understanding of the self. A sense of self-continuity, of being the same person and not a succession of facades is a central issue of adolescent self-understanding (Secord & Peevers, 1974). The belief that one is separate from others is crucial to mental health (Laing, 1965). A feeling of self-efficacy is related to depression and negative affect (Joe, 1971). These dimensions of self are emotionally involving and, therefore, surface as salient dimensions of self-understanding. These dimensions are not, however, important components of our thoughts of others, simply because we are not invested in other people's continuity, distinctness, and efficacy. Although we may be able to "eject" or attribute these characteristics to others, we ordinarily do not because there is little affective motivation to do so.

In regards to the empirical differences noted in the review section, we believe them all to be significant. The difference of perspective phenomenon evidenced in adult attribution research is adequately explained by Jones and Nisbett's (1972) theory. Self-references in descriptions of others were explained in terms of egoistic, rather than egocentric features. The tendency in adolescence to describe the self more in terms of psychological qualities may be due to meta-cognitive theories of knowing, which lead the adolescent to believe it is difficult or not as important to know about the psychological qualities of others. These empirical findings point out the need to further investigate the differences between self- and other-understanding.

Although we have argued that the imitation thesis concerning the development of an understanding of self and others fails to consider the unique functions of self-understanding described above, we do believe the imitation thesis to be substantially correct. The substantial degree of developmental synchrony between an understanding of self and an understanding of others described in our own and in others' research indicates that the attribution theory of Jones and Nisbett cannot be accepted as the sole process by which one gains an understanding of self and others. Rather, we view Jones and Nisbett's theory as describing a bias that is only operative sometimes. Everybody has had the experience at one time or another of acting the very way one has criticized others for acting, but explaining the self's action so as to defend it; nonetheless, one does not *always* interpret one's action differently than another's or one would never have the sense of taking the other person's role.

Further empirical investigation into the differences between self- and other-understanding is needed for a number of reasons. As we pointed out in the beginning of this chapter, both an understanding of self and an understanding of others are essential for intelligent social behavior. A depiction of the development of social cognition must therefore include accounts of the development of these two types of understanding. Future research into the differences between self- and other-understanding will serve to encourage theorists to describe the development of each of the two types of understanding independent of the other, which will result in developmental descriptions that are far more meaningful than the simple "surface to depth" truism that in the past has been used to describe self- and other-understanding development.

Research of the differences can also produce findings with implications for developmental paradigms. For instance, the dissimilarities between self-understanding and other-understanding that arise from the attribution bias described by Jones and Nisbett, the egoistic influence explaining the self-referencing phenomenon included in self-references in describing others, the meta-cognitive theories of person knowledge suggested as the cause of more psychological descriptions of self in adolescence, and the fact that a person is affectively bound to his or her sense of the "I" but not to others, can inform social developmental theory. Turning once again to the theories of Baldwin and

Kohlberg, let us examine the consequences of allowing the possibility that self- and other-understanding are not always identical. According to Baldwin and Kohlberg, prosocial action results from a similar understanding of self and other; in those situations in which self and other are not understood similarly, there may be little empathy or helping behavior. For example, since one ordinarily does not think about other people in terms of their volitional capacity, because it is not as emotionally investing as one's understanding of the self's volition, it may be difficult to empathize with someone experiencing a sense of a lack of control and personal efficacy. Conversely, it may be much easier to understand another's sorrow at losing a friend, since social relationships constitute important aspects of an understanding of self and other. As differences between an understanding of self and other are discovered, it may be possible to delineate more clearly those contexts in which prosocial action will result.

As we have suggested at several points in this chapter, we believe that further research into the differences between self- and other-understanding is likely to highlight the importance of a person's sense of the "I" in self-understanding. Research on the development of a person's understanding of the I can be useful for developmental, clinical, and psychometric purposes. In order to achieve ego identity in Erikson's sense, for instance, it may be necessary for an individual to both believe that there is self-continuity despite the flux of experience, and that the self as agent is capable of exerting some influence on the world. Developmental descriptions of the development of the sense of the "I" may then be used to help explain why some individuals achieve ego-identity. Similarly, normative developmental descriptions of the development of the sense of the "I" may help clinicians in their treatment of disturbed children and adolescents. For instance, Broughton (1980) has used his account of the development of the "I" aspect of the self to reinterpret the supposed pathological phenomenology of an adolescent described in Laing (1965) in terms of developmental patterns. On another note, psychometricians could benefit from a description of the development of the sense of the "I." For example, present locus-of-control instruments measuring a sense of personality assume that scale items are equally relevant at all ages; however, if the sense of personal agency or volition undergoes major developmental transformations during childhood and adolescence, all items may not be relevant at all ages. With further research developmentally attuned instruments could be designed that would allow more meaningful comparisons among children of the same age as well as between children of different ages.

In the course of this chapter, we have demonstrated that current research indicates that self- and other-understanding are distinct from one another, despite their many important similarities. Furthermore, we have outlined how a description of these differences can have an impact on many important areas of developmental psychology. What is now needed is further research that will yield accurate faithful accounts of the development of self- and other-understanding that neither disregards the differences nor omits the commonalities between the two types of understanding.

ACKNOWLEDGMENTS

Research presented in this chapter was supported in part by a grant to the second author from the Spencer Foundation.

REFERENCES

Baldwin, J. M. (1902). *Social and ethical interpretations in mental development.* New York: Macmillan.

Barenboim, C. (1981). The development of person perception in childhood and adolescence: From behavioral consequences to psychological contructs to psychological comparisons. *Child Development, 52,* 129–144.

Broughton, J. (1980). The divided self in adolescence. *Human Development, 24,* 13–32.

Damon, W. (1979). Why study social-cognitive development? *Human Development, 22,* 206–211.

Damon, W., & Hart, D. (1982). The development of self-understanding from infancy to adolescence. *Child Development, 53,* 841–864.

Damon, W., & Hart, D. (in preparation). *Self-understanding in childhood and adolescence.*

Dewey, J. (1898). A review of "Social and ethical interpretations in mental development." *Philosophical Review, 7,* 398–409.

Flavell, J. (1977). *Cognitive development.* Englewood Cliffs, NJ: Prentice-Hall.

Guillaume, P. (1971). *Imitation in children.* Chicago: University of Chicago Press. (Original work published 1926)

Hamlyn, D. (1974). Person-perception and our understanding of others. In T. Mischel (Ed.), *Understanding other persons.* Oxford: Basil Blackwell.

Heider, F. (1958). *The psychology of interpersonal relations.* New York: Wiley.

Honess, T. (1980). Self-reference in children's descriptions of peers. *Child Development, 51,* 476–480.

James, W. (1981). *Psychology: The briefer course.* New York: Harper & Row. (Original work published 1892)

Joe, V. C. (1971). Review of the internal–external control construct as a personality variable. *Psychological Reports, 28,* 619–640.

Jones, E. E., Nisbett, R. E. (1972). The actor and observer: Divergent perceptions of the causes of behavior. In E. E. Jones, D. E. Kanouse, H. H. Kelley, R. E. Nisbett, S. Valins, & B. Weiner (Eds.), *Attribution: perceiving the causes of behavior.* Morristown, NJ: General Learning Press.

Kohlberg, L. (1969). Stage and sequence: The cognitive-developmental approach to socialization. In D. A. Goslin (Ed.), *Handbook of socialization theory and research.* Chicago: Rand McNally.

Laing, R. D. (1965). *The divided self.* New York: Penguin Books.

Lewis, M., & Brooks-Gunn, J. (1979). *Social cognition and the acquisition of self.* New York: Plenum.

Livesley, W. J., & Bromley, D. B. (1973). *Person perception in childhood and adolescence.* New York: Wiley.

Loevinger, J. (1977). *Ego development.* San Francisco: Jossey-Bass.

Mead, G. H. (1934). *Mind, self, and society.* Chicago: The University of Chicago Press.

Montemayor, R., & Eisen, M. (1977). The development of self-conceptions from childhood to adolescence. *Developmental Psychology, 13,* 314–319.

Nisbett, R., Caputo, C., Legant, P., & Marecek, J. (1973). Behavior as seen by the actor and as seen by the observer. *Journal of Personality and Social Psychology, 27,* 154–164.

Peevers, B. H., & Secord, P. F. (1973). Developmental changes in attribution of descriptive concepts to persons. *Journal of Personality and Social Psychology, 26,* 120–128.

Peters, R. (1974). Personal understanding and personal relationships. In T. Mischel (Ed.), *Understanding other persons.* Oxford: Basil Blackwell.

Piaget, J. (1965). *The moral judgment of the child.* New York: Free Press. (Original work published 1932)

Rotenberg, K. J. (1982). Development of character constancy of self and other. *Child Development, 53,* 505–515.

Scarlett, H. H., Press, A. W., & Crockett, W. H. (1971). Children's descriptions of peers: A Wernerian developmental analysis. *Child Development, 42,* 439–453.

Secord, P., & Peevers, B. (1974). The development and attribution of person concepts. In T. Mischel (Ed.), *Understanding other persons.* Oxford: Basil Blackwell.

Selman, R. (1980). *The growth of interpersonal understanding.* New York: Academic Press.

Taylor, S., & Fiske, S. (1975). Point of view and perceptions of causality. *Journal of Personality and Social Psychology, 32,* 439–445.

Werner, H. (1957). The concept of development from a comparative and organismic point of view. In D. B. Harris (Ed.), *The concept of development.* Minneapolis: University of Minnesota Press.

5

The Loss of Pete's Dragon: Developments of the Self in the Years Five to Seven

Robert Kegan

AN ANECDOTAL INTRODUCTION

Not long ago I attended a movie with a number of 6-year-old children. The Walt Disney Studio has been lamenting its inability in recent years to attract the 10- to 15-year-old *Star Wars* crew, but it has lost none of its power to recruit the attention of younger children, if my experience is at all representative. What the little ones were watching so intently was a film called *Pete's Dragon*, which seemed, both in its form and in its content, to touch the heart of a 6-year-old's predicament.

To start with, the form of the movie is neither entirely animated nor entirely real life. Instead, an essentially "real" world with natural human characters (Mickey Rooney and Helen Reddy, among them) is interpenetrated by an animated dragon possessed of magical powers and high color. The only link between these two worlds, the only character who can live in both simultaneously, is a young boy, Pete, an orphan, who meets the dragon while escaping from his cruel and exploitative foster parents.

The story is about the adventures of Pete and the dragon, whom only Pete can see, and with whom only Pete can communicate. Through his participation in the dragon's special powers, Pete is able to fly, vanquish foes, and in general operate beyond the constraints of the real world. At the same time, the dragon is a bit of a rascal, impetuous, and occasionally clumsy with his powers, and Pete needs to exercise parent-like disciplines upon the impulsive creature.

The other central relationship in the story is between Pete and a lovely, generous young woman who takes Pete into her home to protect him and care for him. Pete becomes very attached to the woman and eventually learns that she is waiting forlornly for the return of a sea captain whom she had planned to marry. He is many weeks late and she fears he may be lost at sea. In the concluding adventure of the film, the dragon flies out to sea and guides the lost ship to shore; the cruel foster parents are defeated; the lovely woman and handsome sea captain are united, and they ask Pete to live with them and be their son.

Although the story seems to have a happy ending, the children I was with were devastated at the curtain. Despite the invitation to Pete to join the kind woman and brave captain, the children could not recover from an earlier scene in which the dragon takes his leave from his young friend. "What do you mean you have to go?", asks Pete. Indecipherable dragon mumble. "You have to go and help some other child? When will you come back?" Indecipherable gentle dragon mumble. "You mean you're never—ever—*ever*, going to come back?" Whereupon the two, dragon and boy, slowly and sadly say their goodbyes and separate.

Amid inconsolable sobbing to my left and my right, one little girl, shaking her head, says with a voice of weary wisdom, "Why do these movies always have to end *so* sad?" Less than my empathic best, and hustling them up the aisle, I counter, "But why is it so sad? It's too bad the dragon has to go, but Pete gets a mom and dad who are both really wonderful and they will love him and be nice to him and they're going to do lots of fun things together." "No, no, no," the kids say back to me. "You don't understand. Why can't he have both? Why can't he have the dragon *and* the nice parents? Why can't he have both?"

THE SEARCH FOR THE SELF

The movie recalls a number of themes central to the developmental predicament of a child of 6 years of age. Both the Piagetian "pre-operational" world and the Freudian "oedipal" world are depicted in their final days. The film shows the child literally between the worlds of fantasy and reality; between impulse ascendancy and impulse control;

between a fluid, romantic, adhesive relationship to the bigger, protect-
ing persons in a littler person's life, and the more circumscribed role of
a child in relation to parents who set terms on the child's exclusions
and inclusions in the family. It shows the child in the midst of two
simultaneous losses, one dear to cognitive-developmental psychology,
the other to psychoanalytic psychology. With the loss of the dragon,
we literally see the departure of a kind of meaning construction that
can override, intervene in, or disregard the rules of nature; what we
generally call fantasy is losing its last hold on the way the world is
framed. With the loss of sole possession of the lovely woman, the
acknowledgement that she has purposes of her own independent of
mine, the child is giving up the hope for another in the world who is
perfectly attuned to him, body, mind, heart, and soul. That there are
gains to follow for the child on the other side of these losses, that there
are qualitatively new powers and possibilities inherent in these cognitive and affective resolutions, is not yet possible for the child (or the
child audience) to know.

The accounts of transformations, global and particular, in the years 5
to 7 are so numerous and multiform (S. White, 1965, 1970) as to suggest
a major transition in the development of personality analogous to the
better recognized earlier and later transformations of infant individuation (Mahler, 1968; Mahler, Pine, & Bergman, 1975) and adolescence
(Blos, 1967). What is missing in these accounts, since S. White (1965)
first suggested the possibility nearly 20 years ago, is an exploration,
conceptual or empirical, as to possible relationships between these
various transformations. Such an exploration might be unnecessary to
those who consider personality a loose collection of unsystematically
related part-functions (Shweder, 1977). But for those who take seriously
the possibility of an underlying unity to personality—who see the
process of personality development as an activity of organization in
which the "parts" come under the influence of "wholes"—such a
robust array of diverse instances of transformation during a given age
period presents a special opportunity. The opportunity is to address the
basic questions for a psychology of the self: What are the principles of
the self's organization? What are the principles of reorganization in the
self's development?

A robust array of diverse instances of transformation during a discrete age period allows one to explore these questions in two steps, one
conceptual, the other empirical. The first step involves reasoning both
by homology and induction. An homology (as opposed to an analogy) is
a similarity attributable to common origin, a likeness in structure
between different parts of the same organism (an analogy involves

correspondence in function between elements of different structure and origin).

We begin by tentatively assuming that the relationship between the phenomena under exploration *is* homologous, not to beg the question but to test it. In the end we will reflect on whether the assumption seemed warranted. Considering that the phenomena may relate homologously, we ask, "What common structure *could* account for these phenomena existing simultaneously?" If we arrive at a plausible structure, we then move to *induction.* Inductive reasoning proceeds from the part to the whole, particulars to generals, the individual to the universal. From the particular phenomena we hypothesize a general structure that should take account of a whole range of as yet unexamined phenomena. We can see whether any further data would seem to disconfirm or cast doubt on the hypothesized principle of organization. If it still holds promise we are ready to turn to the next step—empirical exploration. While we can never prove that the hypothesized principle of organization is true, to retain confidence in it, outcomes of well-designed experiments inspired by skepticism with our own ideas should fail to disconfirm it. Of course the study of the self's organization is a very young science and no hypothesized principles of organization have yet reached this level of confidence. The present chapter consists entirely of the prior conceptual step and, at that, concerns itself only with a brief period in the history of the self's development. It does, however, by homology and induction, argue for a common principle of organization that seems to relate widely diverse cognitive, affective, behavioral, and, to some extent, even physical phenomena—a principle of organization, or hypothesized "deep structure," in self-development which can be empirically tested.

THE PHENOMENA: REGULAR TRANSFORMATIONS IN THE YEARS FIVE TO SEVEN

We can consider three orders of observation of regular transformation in this age period—simple impression and clinical observations; molar studies of discrete changes; and more global and systematically researched accounts of stage-regular transformation. In this section I attempt to catalog a goodly number of these observations in as descriptive and uninterpretive a fashion as possible. Although in the next section I suggest how these phenomena might be features of a common structure and process, the reader may find the present section of more interest if he or she anticipates this by asking himself or herself if or how the phenomena seem to relate homologously.

Beginning impressionistically and at the level of clinical observation, anyone who has spent time with both a 4- or 5-year-old and an 8- or 9-year-old cannot fail to take account of how different they seem, a difference that feels like more than a child's "getting bigger," or continued psychological growth along the same plane. The older child seems to be functioning on a qualitatively different plane. She or he is not only physically larger, but seems physically more "organized," more "tightly wrapped." The younger child has a hard time sitting still for any length of time, is continuously moving into and out of spaces with little predictability, and has a short attention span for any activity involving accommodations to others; the older child seems capable of adultlike forms of physical patience, "motoric propriety," and perseverance. The difference, most palpable and dramatic on a physical scale, is to be seen over and over again on a score of more subtle dimensions. The younger child uses language as an appendage or companion to her or his means of self-presentation and social intercourse; for the older child, language is the very medium of interaction, central to the social presentation of the self. The younger child's life is filled with fantasy and fantasy about the fantastic (being Spiderman); the older child has taken an interest in things as they are and the fantasy life is about things that actually could be (being a doctor). Younger children will engage their parents in the middle of a conversation that they have already started on their own, as if they have trouble keeping track of which portions of a conversation they have actually had with you and which they have only imagined with you, or as if they take it for granted that their private thinking is as public and monitored as their spoken thinking; older children never do this, and, indeed, in their cultivation of a sense of privacy and self-possession, they seem to have "sealed up" this psychic cavity. The younger children can roam neighborhoods moving in and out of houses with little or no observance of notions of private space or territoriality; older children ring doorbells, become shy, observe politenesses, and, indeed, post signs on their own bedroom doors, "Adults Keep Out." The younger children, asked to describe a movie they have just seen ("What was it about? What happened in the movie?") report discrete, unrelated episodes, discuss what particular characters did, and focus on actions and objects completely unrelated to the story of the film; older children are able to construct a narrative of events, logically and causally linked, representing the movie's story line in a concrete but accurate fashion.

One step up from this level of clinical observation is a variety of molar studies of cognitive, affective, and even physiological transformation that seem to bear little or no similarity to each other (Gardner, 1978; S. White, 1965). For example: (1) in word association tasks the younger children are likely to respond to a word with a word that suggests what might happen next (e.g., "dog" is responded to with "bite"); but children on the other side of the 5–7 shift tend to provide a word that belongs to the same class or set (e.g., "dog" is responded to with "cat") (Ervin, 1961); (2) presented with two patterns and asked which is more like a third, the younger children tend to make the connection based on color; the older children base the connection on form (Brian & Goodenough, 1929); (3) the younger children's drawings are more fanciful and idiosyncratic; the older children are more concerned that their representations look real and their drawings are more stereotyped (Burton, 1981); (4) the children on the earlier side of the 5–7 shift seem to need rewards that are fairly immediate, sensual, and communicating of praise; children on the older side of the shift seem to feel more rewarded by the information that they have been correct (Zigler & Kanzer, 1962); (5) in response to a transgression by a peer, the younger child is more inclined to use physical force in retaliation; the older child is more inclined to use the *threat* of physical force (Selman, Schorin, Stone, & Phelps, 1981); (6) if a blindfolded younger child is touched at two points on her body (e.g., elbow and wrist) and asked to identify where she or he is being touched, the child tends to report only one of the spots; the children on the older side of the shift identify both spots (some children in the midst of the transformation have been known to resolve their conflict with the question by pointing to a spot on their body *between* the two points being touched!) (Fink & Bender, 1953); (7) children who lose a limb or become blind before they are through the shift tend not to have phantom limb responses or memories of sight in later years; children on the other side of the shift usually do have phantom limb responses or memories of sight (Gardner, 1978); (8) the triangularity of vision, coordinating the two eyes on the point of observation, is not completely mastered until around age 7 (Gesell, 1949).

Finally, stage theorists offer global descriptions of transformations in particular domains that tend to occur during the 5 to 7 period. These accounts come from both psychodynamic developmental psychology (e.g., Freud, 1938; Erikson; 1963), where their authority rests on clinical observations and retrospective clinical accounts; and from academic cognitive-, and social-cognitive developmental psychology, where the authority rests on analyses of cross-sectional and longitudinal "laboratory" interviews (e.g., Damon, 1977; Fowler, 1981; Keller, 1981; Kohlberg, 1969; Piaget, 1937/1954; Selman, 1980; & Youniss, 1980).

Piaget describes a shift, commonly occurring between 5 and 7 years, in the organization of the child's "scientific" knowledge about the physical world (Piaget, 1937/1954). Prior to the shift, the child's thought is prelogical, or "magical," in which apparent or imagined events are confused with real events and objects, and perceptual appearances of qualitative and quantitative change are confused with actual change. After the shift, the child's thought is logical, organizing classes, relations, and quantities which maintain logically invariant properties in reference to concrete objects and events (Kohlberg & Gilligan, 1972).

Kohlberg describes a shift, commonly occuring at the same time, in the organization of the child's moral judgment. Prior to the shift children make decisions on the basis of what an outside authority deems to be right and wrong; what is right is to avoid being punished, not to break rules, obey for its own sake, and avoid physical damage to persons and property (with little distinction between their relative worths). After the shift, children make decisions of what is right and wrong on the basis of what is of benefit to themselves or some party's immediate interest; what is right is to meet one's needs, let others do the same, and be fair, where fairness involves simple reciprocity and equal exchange (Lickona, 1976).

Selman (1980) describes shifts in the child's coordination of social perspectives and the child's conception of friendship. Because the younger child "does not clearly distinguish his own perspective from that of another he does not recognize that another may interpret similarly perceived social experiences or courses of action differently from the way he does. Similarly there is still some confusion between the subjective (or psychological) and objective (or physical) aspects of the social world, for example, between feelings and overt acts, or between intentional and unintentional acts" (Selman et al., 1981, p. 46). The older child

> understands that even under similarly perceived social circumstances the self's and another's perspectives may be either the same or different. Similarly, the child realizes that the self and another may view similarly perceived actions as reflections of disparate or distinct individual reasons or motives; the older child is newly concerned with the uniqueness of the covert, psychological life of each person. (Selman et al., 1981, p. 47)

The shift in the child's conception of friendship over this same period is as follows: the younger child's conceptions of friendship

> are based on thinking which focuses upon propinquity and proximity. A close friend is someone who lives close by and with whom the self happens to be playing at the moment. Friendship is more accurately playmateship. Issues such as jealousy or the intrusion of a third party into a play situation are constructed by the younger child as specific fights over specific toys or space rather than as conflicts which involve personal feelings or interpersonal affection. (Selman *et al.*, 1981, p. 46).

Friendship, to the children on the other side of the shift, is described as "one-way," in the sense that "a friend is seen as important because he or she performs specific activities which the self wants done or accomplished. In other words, one person's attitude is unreflectively set up as a standard, and the friend's actions must match the standard" (Selman *et al.*, 1981, p. 47).

Keller studied children's understandings of "moral transgression," failing to keep a promise, for example. She found that younger children

> do not yet clearly understand that the act of promising . . . constitutes obligations of the self that are correlated with reciprocal rights and expectations on the side of the friend. As there is no clear awareness of such an obligation there is no understanding that the action [which breaks the promise] is "morally" inadequate and as such must be explained to the friend; that is, that the actor has to give good and sufficient reasons for an inadequate behavior. The child does not feel any urgent need to give special explanations for his or her action. If asked from the perspective of the friend ("Why didn't you come?"), children answer either by referring to [what they did do] or their own [desires], in neither case showing any hesitation about informing their friend about the inadequate action [which they seem not to see as inadequate]. (Keller, 1981)

On the other side of the shift, children demonstrate an awareness that, for example, going off to a movie instead of keeping a promise to meet a friend is an action that must be explained, is violative in some sense of an agreement, and is likely to have negative consequences for the self in the form of things the other may or may not do. There is also an awareness that there is a choice between telling the truth or disguising the truth in some way.

Keller's work, which in part amounts to a cognitive-developmental approach to the phenomenon of guilt, leads us naturally to the Freudian conception of superego. There are actually two interrelated developmental theories in Freud's conception of childhood, and each suggests a transformation around the time of the transformations the cognitive theories describe: One is a transformation from the oedipal world to the world of latency; the other, from what Freud called "primary process" to "secondary process."

In his description of a move from an oedipal stage to latency, Freud describes a younger child who is intensely involved with both the opposite-sex parent (as a favorite) and the same-sex parent (as a rival for the attentions of the favorite); and an older child who is much less involved in this charged triangular relationship. The preshift child is at the mercy of his or her impulses and requires external controls and constraints on his or her longings; the postshift child has internalized these constraints, has begun to take charge of its own impulses, and in the process has constructed a role for itself as child in relation to parents in a family. The family has changed from a context for romantic rivalry and longing into an institution of authority, hierarchy, and opportunity to demonstrate competent exercises of one's role, built in part on new aspirations to emulate the same-sex parent with whom the child has become identified (Freud, 1938).

In addition to this familiar Freudian developmental theory (oral, anal, oedipal, etc.), Freud actually described the tripartite mind (id, ego, superego) as a concurrent developmental phenomenon which took its full three-part differentiation only after the 5- to 7-age period. In ways strikingly similar to Piaget's description of the infancy shift from the sensorimotor to the preoperational, Freud described a shift from what he called the "reflex id" to "primary process id," the central hallmark of which (like the central hallmark of the preoperational stage) is the capacity to form and retain an image. *Primary process* thinking, according to Freud, is highly intuitive, representational, illogical, fantasy filled, free floating, and associationistic. The essence of primary process thinking is that the wish is taken for the deed and the image is taken as the thing itself. The insufficiency of this form of thought forces the further development of the psyche, according to Freud. Because, for example, the image alone of the mother's nipple is not adequate to relieve hunger, the child is forced actually to go into the world, to take account of reality in the meeting of its needs. Thus the essence of the shift from primary process to *secondary process* (which Freud seems to place concurrently with the previous shift from the oedipal world to the latency world) is the emergence of a "reality principle" which joins, and takes command to some extent over the "pleasure principle."

Erikson also describes a shift concurrent with all the shifts thus far described. He depicts the younger child in an "intrusive mode," intruding "into other bodies by physical attack . . . other people's ears and minds by aggressive talking . . . into space by vigorous locomotion. . . . into the unknown by consuming curiosity" (Erikson, 1963, p. 87). The older child develops a sense of "industry": "He becomes ready to apply himself to given skills and tasks. . . . he learns to win recognition by producing things . . . to bring a productive situation to completion is an aim which gradually supersedes the whims and wishes of play. . . . the child's danger, at this stage, lies in a sense of inadequacy and inferiority" (Erikson, 1963, pp. 259–260).

THE PHENOMENA AS HOMOLOGICAL?
POSITING A DEEP STRUCTURE AND
PROCESS

Despite the surface *heterogeneity* of these various phenomena, the reader may very likely have begun on his or her own to sense a certain common theme or character to these changes and accounts of change. Such sensed similarity, perhaps vague and elusive, might be largely accidental and illusive, a matter of "less here than meets the eye." With full knowledge that this may indeed be the case, I argue that these phenomena may represent windows into a single common enterprise, the development of the self as it ordinarily undergoes a qualitative transformation in the years roughly from 5 to 7. The argument, no matter how persuasive, will prove nothing; if it is successful it may put forth a candidate (for the deep structure and process of self-development) which might then be explored empirically.

I make the argument for homology in the following fashion. First, I state very generally the basic process and structure that I think can take account of these phenomena. Then, I go back to the phenomena and carefully build up a picture of this process and structure. I begin by showing how the deep structure and its process can take account of and integrate the Piagetian observations. Then I try to demonstrate how the observations of the various cognitive-developmental theorists (Kohlberg, Selman, Keller, *et al.*) are themselves related. After integrating the cognitive-developmental observations in the context of the deep structure and process, I show how this same context integrates the cognitive-developmental picture with the psychoanalytic one. Finally, I turn this built-up picture of the deep structure and process on the molar phenomena to suggest how these too are arguably rooted in this common origin.

Among the most striking themes emerging from the specific instances of this childhood transformation is a sense of the young person taking himself or herself in hand, a move toward a kind of cognitive, affective, interior, and behavioral self-sufficiency which was not there before. An evolutionary association that comes to mind is the move from an exoskeletal form to an endoskeletal one. The child's structure seems to "come inside," to be covered over, rather than being constantly open and somehow shared with other objects and persons in the world. Another way of putting it is that the child seems to take over controls in his interior and exterior functioning which had been regulated by people and things other than himself. It is as if he or she now becomes more the exercisor of these controls, and what had "been" him or her becomes the object of the new self's controls. This very general description of a basic process or motion mirrors descriptions of development, evolution, or adaptation in biology or psychology. Psychoanalytic and cognitive-developmental theory, despite the common impression that they agree about very little, actually describe the basic notion in development quite similarly. What modern psychodynamic theory calls *internalization* is quite similar to what Piagetians call *decentration*. Internalization and decentration amount to overcoming, respectively, affective or cognitive egocentricities. When one can internalize processes one was before externalizing, one differentiates others (which had been confused with these processes) from oneself. When one's mental activity decenters, one can take a perspective on that which had been integral to one's perspective (one can *look at* what one had *seen through*). Both internalization and decentration are ways of describing the motion or process to which I refer, a motion Schachtel (1959) referred to as "emergence from embeddedness." Simply put, I propose as a basic motion in development at any age the process of *differentiation* from what had been the basic system of organization, and the *integration* of that system into a more complicated metasystem, a process sometimes described as the whole becoming part of a new whole, or the structure becoming the content of a new structure.

I imagine this description of an underlying process in the self's development is thus far relatively uncontroversial (and so general as to be relatively unilluminating as well). How is this idea of underlying process related to the idea of underlying structure? What I call a *structure* is not radically separable from this process. It is meant to describe a period of relative stability in the process of evolution, a period in which the degree of differentiation and integration is maintaining an economy. A given state of evolution (or *stage* of development) can always be described relative to its degree of differentiation. That which is differentiated (or *object*) had formerly been undifferentiated (or *subject*); that which will one day *be* object is presently undifferentiated (or subject). Put another way, a given economy in the history of individual evolution can be described with respect to the subject–object distinction it creates in the world. If this is true, biology and epistemology are inextricably linked, the idea most central to the vision of Piaget who called himself a "genetic epistemologist." An *underlying structure* is, thus, at once (1) a period of dynamic stability in the process of development, (2) a subject–object distinction which "knows" the world according to the terms of its particular epistemologic, and (3) vulnerable to a transformation (development) in which this structure (and logic) will become object of a new logic.

But what may be the particular structure (subject–object distinction) undergoing transformation in the years 5 to 7? I will begin to propose an answer to this by looking first at the Piagetian observations of the child's construction of the physical world. The typical 4- or 5-year-old has a host of original and to our minds amusingly strange views about nature. The child may believe the moon follows people when they walk; and if you walk off in different directions, the moon can follow both of you with no feeling on the child's part of any contradiction. Or the child may believe it is possible one day to become older than his or her older brother, so that the child can mete out the same kind of oppression the brother is now visiting upon him or herself. Consider Piaget's most famous study. Two identically shaped glasses or beakers are filled with equal amounts of water. The child agrees that each beaker contains the same amount. The contents of one of the beakers are poured into a taller, thinner beaker (resulting in a higher water level than in the remaining beaker), and the child is asked about the relative amounts. The child usually answers that the taller, thinner beaker has more. Now anyone's first response to such an answer is to pour the contents of the taller, thinner beaker back into the original beaker. We imagine that when the levels match once again the child will surely see that the content of the poured beaker are equal to those of the unpoured beaker. "Yes," the typical child may say, "they are equal—*now.*" When the contents are poured once again into a shorter, wider beaker, they become less than the contents of the remaining beaker, and so on.

Now just what is going on here? Piaget's experiments are brilliant (Einstein said they were so simple they could only have been thought of by a genius) because they transform an abstract notion such as structure or subject–object differentiation into something almost palpable. The child's "error" is not something he or she is likely to catch and correct, because according to the terms of the child's present adaptive balance—or evolutionary truce—no error is being made. The deep structure of the truce, simply put, is that the perceptions are on the side of the subject; that is, the child is *subject* to his perceptions in his organization of the physical world. He cannot separate himself from them; he cannot take them as an object of his attention. He is not individuated from them; he is embedded in them. They define the very structure of his attention. For the preoperational child, it is never just one's perceptions that change; rather, the world itself, as a consequence, changes.

Two boys were overheard at the top of the Empire State Building. As their father reported it to me, both took one look down at the sidewalk and exclaimed simultaneously: "Look at the people. They're tiny ants" (the younger boy); "Look at the people. They look like tiny ants" (the older boy). Whether the younger boy really thought the people had become tiny we do not know, but remembering the thousands of children throughout the world who have told researchers how the liquid "gets less" in a wider, flatter glass, we should not be too surprised if he thought exactly that. What we do know is that the older boy could take a perspective on his own perceptions; he said, "They look like tiny ants." His statement is as much about him looking at his perception as it is about the people. The words sound as though they come from someone who is not embedded in his perceptions. Distinguishing between how something appears and how something *is* is just what one cannot do when one is subject to the perceptions. But when this underlying structure, this epistemologic, this evolutionary truce is renegotiated, the perceptions "move over" from subject to object. Now instead of seeing the world through one's perceptions, one is able to see one's perceptions, like the boy who said, "The people *look like* ants." Being able to see one's perceptions leads to their being integrated or coordinated by a new psychologic. A child can coordinate his or her perception of the liquid at Time 1 with the perception at Time 2 and see that the quantity remains the same or the child can coordinate his or her perception of a thinner beaker (therefore less water) with the perception of a taller beaker (therefore more) and see that the changes cancel each other out. As with every rebalancing, what had been subject is recast to the domain of object. I am not my perceptions; rather, I *have* perceptions; my perceptions become the object of my attention, coordinated by what is the new subject of my attention. And what that new subject is, with respect to Piaget's focus, is a conserver of the physical world. Its capacity to move back and forth among its perceptions— what Piaget calls the reversibilities—creates a new logic that constructs "groups" and "classes." The world which before was so labile starts to hold still; it becomes concrete. (At the same time, the 10-year-old child is subject to his own egocentricity, his own embeddedness, but that is a story for another day; see Kegan, 1982).

The structural transformation from being subject to one's perceptions to *having* perceptions as an object seems to integrate an array of Piagetian observations. The fluid, acausal, prelogical, magical way of knowing yields to a recognition, for example, of causality (because the self is now a ground on which different points in time can be figure); a recognition that things have properties of their own, irrespective of my particular view of them, leads to reality becoming more a matter of correspondence to "how things are" rather than simply how I imagine them (which becomes now make-believe).

But does the proposed deep structure also integrate the various so-cial-cognitive observations with each other and with the physical-cog-nitive? It should not be hard to see that the young child's perception-bound psychologic will account for more of his meaning making than merely the construction of the physical world. *Social* objects (that is, people) will be known in the same egocentric way. A child who thinks there can be more popcorn in a box just by shaking it also happens to have one brother. If we asked him if he has a brother he would say yes. If we asked him if his brother has a brother he would say no. He is unable to get outside of himself, to look at things from his brother's point of view and see that, indeed, his brother does have a brother, and it is he. The meaning-constructive activity which we colloquially refer to as "getting outside of oneself" is analogous to what I have meant by moving from subject to object, or "disembedding" or "differentiating."

Piaget's preoperational children give strange answers to conserva-tion tasks because they cannot take the role of their perceptions while still being themselves, someone other than their perceptions. Kohl-berg's (1969) first moral stage is the *social correlate,* the inability to distinguish between the other and my perception of the other, the inability to get behind my perceptions and see the other as her- or himself having to do with her or his properties. Piaget's own research in moral development (1948) anticipated the distinction Kohlberg makes. Piaget told preoperational and concrete operational children the following story (1948): One little boy was told by his mother not to touch some fragile cups, but he purposely picked one up and smashed it to bits on the floor. Another little boy was not told anything about not touching the cups: to help his mother, he tried to carry a tray of 12 cups to where she needed them. He accidentally dropped all of them onto the floor, and they were smashed to bits. "Are these children equally at fault (*la même chose vilain*)?" Piaget asked. If not, "Which of the two children is the naughtier, and why?" Some children think the first child is naughtier, and some think the second, but not at all randomly. The children who do not see that there is the same amount of liquid in the beakers, or who in other ways appear preoperational, tend to feel that the child who broke the 12 cups is the naughtier; the concrete-operational children think the first boy is naughtier. The perception-bound children are orienting to the results because they are embedded in the social "surface"; the children who have renegotiated this subject–object relation, I am suggesting, can pierce this surface, can move beyond result to *intention*. Just as their disembeddedness permits them to see that the liquid has properties of its own and that they are not determiners of its properties, so they can see that they are not the determiners of another's properties. The other person is allowed a measure of self-creation which in the earlier subject–object balance he is not. It is not until a child moves to this new subject–object balance that he or she stops seeing the parents as "mean" whenever their behaviors deprive him or her whether or not the parents intend to be depriving.

It is this evolutionary renegotiation (in which we differentiate ourselves from the perception as the psychologic which defines us) that brings into being the kinds of simply reciprocity we see in the social-cognitive descriptions (Selman, Keller, *et al.*). Simple *reciprocity* is homologous with the concrete operational *reversibility*. The ability to take the role of other persons, to see that their behaviors are the consequence of something that generates their behaviors, a "something" distinct from my perception is homologous with the concrete-operational ability to transcend the shadows of Plato's cave to see that there is something that projects those shadows, to get behind the perceptual surface. We could even compare the *kinds* of reciprocity evident in the social descriptions we saw earlier with the *kinds* of reversibility Piaget observes (see Figure 5.1). Piaget talked of the ability to hold two points in time (inverse) and two points in space (reciprocal). We can consider the capacity to coordinate two social perceptions in social time and social space. For example, the capacity to take the role of another is related to the ability to create the notion of a continuing social order which retains its properties from one social perception to the next. This is like Piaget's inverse and brings into being the social equivalent of the class or group, which in simpler terms is the *social self*, a social object conserved through time. Similarly, the kind of tit-for-tat reciprocity is homologous to the compensating form of reversibility Piaget called the reciprocal; a kind of social "space" is conserved by the way retribution evens out the initial assault (simple fairness).

Describing the underlying structural transformation as a shift from perception-as-subject to perception-as-object has served well enough to argue for the homological relationship of a wide array of social-cognitive phenomena. It is not the fullest description of the subject–object

	The coordination of two points in time (the logic of "class")	The coordination of two points in space (the logic of "relations")
The physical-cognitive sphere (Piaget's concrete operations; two kinds of reversibility [1937/1954])	**Inverse** (holding two perceptions together across time)	**Reciprocal** (holding two perceptions together in a common space)
The social-cognitive sphere (Kohlberg's moral instrumentalism [1969]; Selman's one-way social perspective-taking [1976])	**Taking the role of the other** (holding two social perceptions together across time)	**Simple reciprocity or tit-for-tat compensation** (holding two social perceptions together in a common space)
The intrapersonal-affective sphere (Loevinger's "Delta" or opportunist [1976]; Kegan's imperial self [1982])	**Needs** (as distinct from labile, moment-to-moment wishes), or **Enduring dispositions** (holding two impulses together across time)	**Ambivalence** (holding two impulses together in a common space)

Figure 5.1 Homological relations among three different spheres of personality development in the school-age child.

distinction, however. If what I am calling *the perception* makes up the subject of the younger child's evolutionary state and the object of the older child's, the question might be asked, "What is the object of the younger child's state? What is it which 'perceptions' organize or coordinate?" Or: "What is the simpler evolutionary state beyond which the younger child's perception embeddedness is itself a metaleap?" Such a question directs us to infancy when, by all accounts, the child is embedded in its sensing and moving, its reflex inheritances; it is completely undifferentiated; nothing is "on the side of the object." When the child's self-development undergoes its first qualitative evolution (Piaget's "sensorimotor" to "preoperational"; Freud's "reflex id" to "primary process id") sensation, movement, and reflex are all "made object," or reflected upon. For example, the young child can now control its reflexes to eliminate (internalize them, decenter from them, or take them as an object) and becomes toilet-trained. When the cognitivists and social-cognitivists look at the young child they direct themselves to those organizations of sensing and moving that have to do with relations between the self and its organization of others and other things (*exodermic* meanings, meanings beyond the skin). The coordination of sensing and moving with respect to the self's constitution of its relations to others and things I have called the perceptions. But it is also possible to look at the same subject–object distinction with respect to those coordinations of sensing and moving that have to do with experiences I now see as arising "in me", i.e., internal perceptions. This coordination of the same object is what people generally call *impulse*. Hence a fuller description of the structure or subject–object distinction of children before the 5 to 7 shift is that they are embedded not only in their *perceptions* (the more cognitive and interpersonal focus) but in their (structurally equivalent) *impulses* (the more affective and intrapsychic focus) as well.

Thus the younger child is said to lack impulse control, but it would be as true to say that it lacks perception control, where *control* refers to the ability to "have" the impulses and perceptions as objects of a new system. Embeddedness in the impulses leads to as labile an intrapsychic and affective life as embeddedness in the perceptions does cognitively. Thus phenomena otherwise as apparently diverse as the older child's abilities to both conserve liquid and experience ambivalence may be homological by virtue of their common origin in the new capacity to take the former structure as object, integrating two points (be they two perceptions or two impulses) in space. The same child who cannot reason causally by holding two perceptions outside itself (i.e., make itself the ground upon which the perceptions can be figure) cannot hold two contradictory impulses inside itself (i.e., make itself the ground upon which the impulses can be figure), and so the self temporarily "breaks down," the most common expression of which is a tantrum. When the older child can hold two impulses in space, it becomes possible for the self to experience, and even declare, "Gee, I want to go to the store with you, but I also kinda want to stay home and watch *Happy Days*."

If holding two impulses in "space" brings about the intrapsychic or affective equivalent of the *logic of relations* (ambivalence), what are the consequences of the tandem ability to hold two impulses across time (see Figure 5.1)? Where the younger child's feelings, wants, thoughts about itself had been so highly changeable and self-contradictory, the structural transformation that makes the impulse an object brings into being the enduring disposition, a "way I tend to feel." Needs as expressions of a self's purposes over time get created. Inner life, in other words, becomes itself conserved. One of the most fundamental achievements of the 5 to 7 shift, many theorists and researchers have noticed, is the emergence of a *self-concept*, a certain stable self-reference, or inner and outer conservation of that most important "thing," the self (Sarnoff, 1976; Sullivan, 1953; R. W. White, 1976).

With the capacity to take command of one's impulses (to have them, rather than be them) can come a new sense of freedom, power, independence—agency, above all. Things no longer just happen in the world; with the capacity to see behind the shadows, "to come in with" the data of experience, the self now has something to do with what happens. The end of Kohlberg's first moral stage, where authority is all-powerful and right by virtue of its being authority, is probably brought on by this construction of one's own authority. As is the case with every new development, the new liberation carries new risks and vulnerabilities. If I now have something to do with what happens in the world, then whether things go badly or well for me is a question of what I myself can do. Looming over a system whose hallmark is newly won stability, control, and freedom is the threat of the old lability, loss of control, and what now appears as the old subjugation from without. How much of the control and manipulation we experience when we are the object of this meaning-making balance is a matter of a person's efforts to save herself from an old world's threat of ungovernable and overwhelming impulse life?

Does the proposed deep structure and its transformation bring together cognitive-developmental and psychoanalytic depictions of the 5 to 7 period? Certainly both depictions of this shift center on an acquisition of *role*, although they seem to be speaking of two quite different phenomena. Cognitive-developmentalists point to the emerging capacity to take the role of another, to see that others have a perspective of their own. Psychoanalytically oriented theorists point to the processes of oedipal resolution and identification by which the child gives up its impossible hopes for the opposite-sex adult and takes on the social role of a child—a child who will grow up to be an adult, a child in relation to parents. Both of these reconstructions of the self may be the consequence of a single motion in the self's development. Central to this evolution, as to all, is a specific loss. At the same time we say the child's transformation involves the creating of a self-sufficiency, we must also say it involves the discovery of the "other-sufficiency" of the world. The physical object that before had so much to do with me that my changing perception of it occasioned *its* very change is now seen to have an existence of its own. Human beings who before had so much to do with me that I imagined their vantage point on the world was the same as mine are now seen to have a perspective of their own. Viewed from the outside, the child is moving from a fantasy orientation to a reality orientation; the child is growing. But the evolution of meaning is also *experienced* by the evolving person, and the same process involves the loss of a very special involvement with the objects and others which the child himself discovered only a few years ago as a result of the earlier great upheaval in his evolution of meaning.

What we describe from the "outside" as the process of differentiation may involve for the child inside a growing disappointment and disillusionment with an object world that the child comes to see does *not* have so much to do with him or her that its very poses and purposes are a function of his or her own. An infant discovers that there is a world separate from him or her; but not until years later does the child discover that this separate world is not subject *to* him or her. In bringing impulses and perceptions under his or her own regulation, the child creates a self that is distinct and in business for itself; in its fullest flush of confidence this is the bike-riding, money-managing, card-trading, wristwatch-wearing, pack-running, code-cracking, coin-collecting, self-waking, puzzle-solving 9- or 10-year-old known to us all. But in its first fragile moments on the scene, this is as likely to be a 6-year-old who is more struck by the reciprocal reality—that other people, too, are in business for themselves, have enduring dispositions of *their* own, and, however much they love him or seem to, are not regulated by, indeed are not even perfectly attuned to, his longing for satisfaction, comfort, relief, embrace. ("Why do these movies always have to end *so* sad?") The cognitivist's "learning to take the role of the other" and the analyst's "giving up the oedipal wishes" both find a reading in this same evolutionary transformation.

Finally, let us consider whether the molar observations, apparently so unrelated, do not seem to share a logical unity when viewed in the context of the development of the subject–object distinction. Consider three phenomena each of which seems to bear no relation to the other two: (1) the younger children are more likely to respond to peer transgression with physical force; the older, with the threat of force; (2) the younger children seem to need rewards from teachers which are immediate, sensual, and communicating of praise; the older children seem to feel more rewarded by the information that they have been correct; (3) children who lose a limb or become blind before the shift tend not to have phantom limb responses or memories of sight in later years; children who sustain these losses after the shift, say beyond 7 or 8 years of age, almost always do have visual memories and often have phantom limb responses (sensation located in space, beyond the body, where the limb would be).

Of course the child who uses force rather than threat can be said, in a glib, descriptive way, to be more impulsive, but I have tried to give a specific structural meaning to *impulse* which separates it from more developed nonimpulsiveness along lines that are not merely about emotional or energic self-control. How might threat rather than force be a function of a more evolved subject–object evolution? The structural properties of threat reveal the impulse coordinated across both time and space. Threat requires a self that links two points in time; it expresses an if-then proposition. Threat also expresses a self that "contains" given actions or possible actions as among its properties; it names a psychological self-organization that stands behind, or is the expressor of, particular behaviors, rather than being the behaviors or actions themselves. Taken together, the ability to threaten bespeaks a psychological organization that at the least conserves a social self.

What is experienced as support at any time in one's life is surely a function of just what self it is that is being supported. Support must in some way communicate that *the way the self runs* is confirmable, valuable, approvable. How might the difference between support that is immediate, sensual, and praising, and that which provides the information one is correct be a function of the now-familiar underlying subject–object distinctions? When the self is still confused with its perceptions and impulses it has no distinct point of view on itself or anything else, no distinct point of view whose similarity or lack of similarity to another's view it might wonder about. It has no independent standard. Praise needs to be immediate and sensual because the self is embedded in the immediate and sensual; joining the younger self means being a participant in its impulse life and its egocentricity. Joining a self that takes perception and impulse as object means joining a self whose essential function is to take charge of its inner and outer experience. The self has become (1) a contained system with executive responsibilities, (2) creative of its own point of view or standard, and (3) able to recognize that there are different points of view people can take on a thing, including the self. As the self has become regulative of its own impulses, its confirmation or support is not a matter of finding others to gratify its impulses, but finding others who might praise the way the executive system is itself gratifying or dealing with the demand for gratification of its own impulses. As the self has become disembedded from its own perceptions it is interested in "reality," the correspondence of its own productions to how things "actually are," and it may see in the other's distinctness a source of this information.

The observations regarding visual memories among the blind or phantom limb responses among those who lose a limb are actually a part of the bigger subject of memory itself and its qualitative alterations during the same age period under examination here (Schachtel, 1959; S. White, 1970). Most people have a difficult time recalling much at all before the age of 5 years or so, and what they do recall is usually an image or "still shot," rather than a narrative or sequence of events that can be placed in a context. In addition to considering these molar phenomena we might ask, more generally, "Why should it be that the nature of people's memories of their first 5 years (roughly) are so different from memories after this period?" Freud-the-clinician was, of course, especially interested in this question, and Freud-the-theorist attributed amnesia in the early childhood years to *repression*, a purposeful form of forgetting due to the painful experiences surrounding oedipal hopes and disappointments. It is difficult to credit this interpretation in the face of the generality and extensiveness of the non-recall; that is, why should *all* aspects of experiencing in these early years be hard to recall, rather than just those concerning parent–child relations? But the real difference between Freud's interpretation and the one that emerges here is directed at the metaphor of *amnesia* or *forgetting*. These words suggest that the events of the early years may have been experienced by the child in a form more like that of later life, involving at the least a series of impressions sequentially related in the child's mind (inner narrative), or a context in which the events are placed (theme). The impression from Freud's account is that early experience is constructed at this level of differentiation, and then the inability to recall it is due to other processes that act on our relation to these complexly constructed experiences. The account that emerges in the present chapter questions whether (1) the early experiences were *ever* constructed in a form that would make them accessible to recall in the complex form of later experience and (2) the early childhood self having the experiences was complex enough to store experience in forms similar to the storing of later life.

Both the lack of narrative memory and the capacity for still-shot memory of the earlier years is accounted for in the argument for homology. If the early childhood self cannot take perception or impulse as object, it does not construct a self that conserves a spatial or temporal context; unable to hold the two points in space or time, the self can neither contextualize nor narratize, respectively, that is, the limits in our recall of early childhood experience may be due to the limits in the way those experiences were *originally* constructed and stored. If the early childhood self cannot store perception and impulse (i.e., take them as object), what it *can* store is sensation and movement (the sensorimotor world made object) which permits the recall of occasional single decontextualized perceptions and impulses. If there is a point in development before which there will be neither visual memory among the blind nor phantom limb responses among those who lose a limb, it may be due to the lack of a self that can store, respectively, perception and impulse, such that a seeing eye or a feeling arm lives on in some way in the history of the self.

CONCLUSION: PURSUING
THE HOMOLOGICAL HYPOTHESIS

Analogical phenomena share a common function but have different structures and origins. Homological phenomena share a common structure and origin despite the dissimilarity of their functions. In this essay I have proposed that a very wide array of affective, cognitive, behavioral, and body-based transformations, occuring usually between the ages of about 5 and 7 years, share a common origin and structure located in the unitary process of psychological development. Development, I have argued, is intrinsically about constructions and reconstructions of the subject–object distinction in nature. Specifically, the regular phenomena composing a 5 to 7 shift may be the consequence of a single transformation from a subject–object distinction in which impulse and perception are the subject of knowing (organizing sensation and motion as object) to a subject–object distinction in which impulse and perception are taken as objects of knowing.

Is the assumption of homology warranted? That, of course, is a question that cannot yet be answered. If this essay has been successful, however, then at the least one might be willing to concede that the assumption cannot yet be called untenable; or more than that, that the specific suggestion as to the basis for the homology is worthy of further investigation. This suggestion—that transformations in the subject–object relation form an underlying process and structure in developments of the self—extends beyond considerations of early childhood. Indeed, one way to examine further the plausibility of the present argument would be to consider whether its implications for a common origin between regular cognitive and affective transformations before and after early childhood also seem tenable. For example, the earlier subject–object transformation involves a move from complete subjectivity to the differentiation that brings into being any object world. Might this underlying process serve as the single source of the two universally regular cognitive and affective transformations of this period: the development of object permanence, and the development of separation anxiety—both of which, as it happens, begin around 6 to 9 months of age and run their course by 21 to 24 months? Elsewhere my colleagues and I have explored, in different ways and at greater length, the possibility that transformations in the subject–object distinction form the underlying process in personality development (Kegan, 1982; Noam & Kegan, 1981; Kegan, Noam, & Rogers, 1982; Kegan, Rogers, & Quinlan, 1981).

But the specific argument of the present chapter can and should be pursued empirically. While there are studies relating various cognitive and social-cognitive measures, there have not been studies that seek, for example, assessments on all the following dimensions with children between, say, 4 and 8 years old: (1) Piagetian physical–cognitive conservation; (2) Selman-type social perspective; (3) Kohlberg-type moral judgment; (4) reality-oriented or fantasy-oriented fantasy, play, drawing; (5) ability to narratize in the retelling of a heard story or seen film; (6) ability to "conserve the self" in a "Describe Yourself" interview; (7) class-oriented or action-oriented word association; color-oriented or form-oriented three-way comparisons; (8) impulsivity versus impulse control; (9) involvement with parents versus involvement with own projects; (10) open- or closed-boundary orientation in the home.

The null hypothesis of such an investigation would be that relations on the different measures within subjects would not differ from random. The predicted outcome is that one cluster of indicators (nonconservation; Kohlberg Stage 1; egocentrism; fantasy-oriented play, fantasy, and drawing; inability to narratize; inability to conserve the self; action-oriented word association and color-oriented comparison; impulsivity; involvement with parents; and open-boundary orientation) would tend to occur within a single subject, and in general, younger subjects; and the opposite cluster would tend to occur within another set of subjects, generally the older children.

It is an open question as to *how* uniform these results should be within subjects in order to conclude that the homology hypothesis has gained further credibility, but I am reminded of Mendeleev's experience before the Academy of Science in the nineteenth century. Mendeleev proposed that the then-known elements might have a logical relation to each other as a function of the number of electrons in each element's outer orbit. He presented the academy with a Table of Elements that consisted of more holes than entries. His colleagues were less than kind in response and suggested derisively it would be better to group the elements alphabetically since that plan had as much scientific merit and was easier to understand. And yet, as future elements were discovered, they took their places in Mendeleev's table, and his sense of the order of nature's elements is now somewhat more widely shared. It remains for us to learn whether the academy's response might not be more fitting for the present proposal, or whether the Walt Disney Studio captured a fundamental truth in its recognition that the loss of Pete's dragon and the gain of a circumscribed role as child-within-a-family tend indeed to be simultaneous processes.

ACKNOWLEDGMENTS

The author wishes to thank the Max Planck Institute's International Conference on Social-Cognitive Development, Schloss Ringberg, Federal Republic of Germany, for which an earlier version of this chapter was prepared, and Wolfgang Edelstein for helpful comments on several drafts of this chapter.

REFERENCES

Blos, P. (1967). *The second individuation process of adolescence.* New York: International Universities Press.

Brian, C. R., & Goodenough, F. L. (1929). The relative potency of color and form perception at various ages. *Journal of Experimental Psychology, 12,* 197–213.

Burton, J. (1981). *Lines, space and the organization of meaning in human figure drawings made by children eight to fifteen years.* Unpublished doctoral thesis, Harvard University, Cambridge, MA.

Damon, W. (1977). *The social world of the child.* San Francisco: Jossey-Bass.

Erikson, E. (1963). *Childhood and society.* New York: Norton.

Ervin, S. M. (1961). Changes with age in the verbal determinants of word-association. *American Journal of Psychology, 74,* 361–372.

Fink, M., & Bender, M. B. (1953). Perception of simultaneous tactile stimuli in normal children. *Neurology, 3,* 27–34.

Fowler, J. (1981). *Stages in faith.* New York: Harper & Row.

Freud, S. (1938). *The basic writings of Sigmund Freud* (A. A. Brill, Ed. & Trans.). New York: Modern Library.

Gardner, H. (1978). *Developmental psychology.* Boston: Little, Brown.

Gesell, A. (1949). *Vision: Its development in infant and child.* New York: Paul B. Hoeber.

Kegan, R. (1982). *The evolving self: Problem and process in human development* Cambridge, MA: Harvard University Press.

Kegan, R., Noam, G., & Rogers, L. (1982). The psychologic of emotion. In D. Chichetti & P. Hesse (Eds.), *Emotional development.* San Francisco: Jossey-Bass.

Kegan, R., Rogers, L., & Quinlan, D. (1981). *Constructive-developmental organizations of depression.* Paper presented at APA Symposium on New Approaches to the Study of Depression, Los Angeles.

Keller, M. (1981). Children's explanations of moral transgressions: Competence and performance aspects. Paper presented to International Conference on Social-Cognitive Development, Schloss Ringberg, West Germany.

Kohlberg, L. (1969). Stage and sequence: The cognitive developmental approach to socialization. In D. Goslin (Ed.), *Handbook of socialization: Theory and research.* New York: Academic Press.

Kohlberg, L., & Gilligan, C. (1972). The adolescent as a philosopher. In J. Kagan & R. Coles (Eds.), *Twelve to sixteen: Early adolescence.* New York: Norton.

Lickona, T. (1976). *Moral development and behavior.* New York: Holt, Rinehart & Winston.

Mahler, M. (1968). *On human symbiosis and the vicissitudes of individuation: Vol. I. Infantile psychosis.* New York: International Universities Press.

Mahler, M., Pine, F., & Bergman, A. (1975). *The psychological birth of the human infant.* New York: Basic Books.

Noam, G., & Kegan, R. (1981). Social cognition and psychodynamics. In W. Edelstein & M. Keller (Eds.), *Social cognition.* Frankfurt: Zuhrkamp.

Piaget, J. (1948). *The moral judgment of the child.* Glencoe: Free Press.

Piaget, J. (1954). *The construction of reality in the child.* New York: Basic Books. (Original work published 1937)

Sarnoff, C. (1976). *Latency.* New York: Jason Aronson.

Schachtel, E. (1959). *Metamorphosis.* New York: Basic Books.

Schweder, R. (1977). Likeness and likelihood in everyday thought: Magical thinking in judgments about personality. *Current Anthropology, 18,* 637–658.

Selman, R. (1980). *The growth of interpersonal understanding: Developmental and clinical analyses.* New York: Academic Press.

Selman, R., Schorin, M. Z., Stone, C. R., & Phelps, E. (1981). *A naturalistic study of children's social understanding as expressed in reflective interviews, group discussions and group activities.* Paper presented to International Conference on Social-Cognitive Development, Schloss Ringberg, West Germany.

Sullivan, H. S. (1953). *The interpersonal theory of psychiatry.* New York: Norton.

White, R. W. (1976). Thoughts on developments in middle childhood. Paper delivered to First Year Seminar, Massachusetts School of Professional Psychology, Newton, MA.

White, S. (1965). Evidence for a hierarchical arrangement of learning processes. In L. P. Lipsitt & C. C. Spiker (Eds.), *Advances in child development and behavior* (Vol. 2, pp. 195–210). New York: Academic Press.

White, S. (1970). Some general outlines of the matrix of developmental changes between five and seven years. *Bulletin of the Orton Society, 20,* 41–57.

Youniss, J. (1980). *Parents and peers in social development.* Chicago: University of Chicago Press.

Zigler, E., & Kanzer, P. (1962). The effectiveness of the two classes of verbal reinforcers in the performance of middle- and lower-class children. *Journal of Personality, 30,* 157–163.

6

Self-Concept and Psychological
Well-Being in Adolescence*

Morris Rosenberg

INTRODUCTION

As interest in the self-concept has grown both in professional and lay circles, it is not uncommon to hear people speaking of "good" or "positive" self-concepts and "bad" or "negative" ones. An examination of the context of such statements usually reveals that what the writer or speaker has in mind is high or low self-esteem. Self-esteem, however, is only one of the many dimensions of the self-concept. The purpose of this chapter is to direct attention to certain self-concept dimensions (including self-esteem) that deserve consideration in characterizing an adolescent self-concept as healthy or unhealthy.

Unfortunately, it is not clear what criteria should be used to assess psychological health and illness. In this chapter, we consider only one possible criterion—the criterion that Parloff, Kelman, and Frank (1954) once described as "psychological comfort"; one might also speak of it

*The research reported in this article was funded by a grant from the National Institute of Mental Health (MH27747). The data utilized in this paper were made available in part by The Inter-University Consortium for Political and Social Research. The data were originally collected by Jerald G. Bachman. Neither the original source or collectors of the data nor the Consortium bear any responsibility for the analyses or interpretations presented here.

as "psychological well-being" or "euphoria–dysphoria." From this perspective, a *bad* or *unhealthy self-concept* is one that is associated with feelings of depression, anxiety, life dissatisfaction, and so forth. A good self-concept is the reverse. We do not suggest that "feeling good" is the sole criterion of mental health but we do consider it to be an important one.

The aim of this chapter is to describe certain self-concept dimensions associated with psychological well-being. We argue that, in these terms, a *good self-concept* is characterized by the following: (1) high self-esteem, (2) high feelings of "mattering," (3) high self-concept certitude, (4) low vulnerability, (5) high feelings of personal control, (6) low public anxiety, and (7) harmonious plane coordination. Since these concepts are not entirely clear, nor are the terms always used consistently in the literature, one of the main aims of this chapter is to describe the central features of each dimension.

Although the self-concept is important at all life stages, it is probably most *problematic* during adolescence. Whether or not it is appropriate to speak of adolescence as a "crisis" is a matter of debate (cf. Offer, Ostrov, & Howard, 1981; Simmons, Rosenberg & Rosenberg, 1973). Nevertheless, it is noteworthy that when people at various life stages were asked about the *worst* age in life, more than two-fifths said that adolescence was the worst—a proportion even exceeding old age (selected by one-third) (Lowenthal, Thurner, & Chiriboga, 1975, p. 133). Self-criticism and other negative self-feelings were also most severe at this period of life. We believe that self-concept problems are serious and widespread during adolescence. In the course of this chapter, we consider which self-concept dimensions are particularly problematic at this life stage, whether these problems are more apt to arise in early or late adolescence, and whether they more seriously afflict boys or girls.

DATA

In examining the relationship between self-concept dimensions and psychological well-being, we have looked at three large-scale studies of adolescents. The first is Bachman's Youth in Transition (YIT) study (Bachman, Kahn, Mednick, Davidson, & Johnston, 1967), a nationwide sample of 2213 tenth-grade boys in 87 high schools throughout the nation. The second is a study of 1678 juniors and seniors conducted in 10 high schools throughout New York State (NYS) (Rosenberg, 1965).

The third is the adolescent portion of a sample of 1988 pupils in Baltimore City (BALT), that is, 1155 pupils 12 years or older (Rosenberg & Simmons, 1972).

Each of these three studies contains measures of several, but not all, of the self-concept dimensions mentioned above as well as measures of psychological discomfort or well-being. Whenever possible, we have explored the relationship between each self-concept measure and each psychological comfort measure across all three studies in order to learn whether consistent findings appeared in these spatially and temporally separated samples. Unfortunately, not all measures are adequately represented in all three studies, but we shall present whatever data are available.

These data have both strengths and limitations. On the positive side, all three studies are large probability samples of adolescents, and it is possible to generalize to their respective populations with confidence. At the same time, each study has a different set of independent and dependent variables. Under these conditions, it would not be meaningful to compare the results of separate regression analyses across studies. It is thus necessary to forego more rigorous analysis at this point and to see whether the results of the various studies are consistent at the zero order level. As a result, the data are essentially descriptive, and the results suggestive.

The self-concept measures to be considered in this chapter are self-esteem, mattering, certitude (stability), vulnerability, personal control, two measures of self-consciousness, false self-presentation, and tendency to fantasize. The measures of psychological comfort (or euphoria–dysphoria) are varied, and fall under three broad categories.

The first are those centering on psychological depression or depressive affect. All three studies contain measures of depressive affect (e.g., feelings of being cheerful, in good spirits, enjoying life, on the one hand, or being discouraged, blue, or sad, on the other). The YIT study also contained two related measures. One is a "happiness" measure, reflecting the individual's tendency to describe the self in terms of degree of happiness. The second is a 40-item "negative affective states" measure reflecting a variety of dysphoric experiences but containing a strong depressive component.

The second set of measures center on feelings of anxiety. Two of these (BALT and YIT) reflect general anxiety (e.g., nervousness, fearfulness, and related states). Two other measures (NYS and YIT) focus more on psychophysiological or somatic indicators of anxiety (e.g., palmar perspiration, heart beating hard, hand trembling, insomnia, and other somatic experiences). Finally, YIT included a measure of "anx-

TABLE 6.1
Coefficients Alpha for New York State and Baltimore
Measures

	Coefficients alpha	
Self-concept dimensions	New York State	Baltimore
Self-Esteem	.7745	.6984
Mattering	—	.5519
Certitude (stability)	.7164	.6769
Vulnerability	.7642	.6871
Control over destiny	—	.5284
Preoccupation with self	.6358	.7375
Public anxiety	—	.6029
False front	.6866	—
Daydream	—	.5692
Depression	.7953	.6815
Anxiety (somatic)	.7638	—
Anxiety (general)	—	.4517

iety-tension," reflecting such experiences as feeling nervous, jumpy, relaxed, and so forth.

It is not easy to characterize the third set of euphoric–dysphoric measures, although they plainly bear some kinship to depressive affect. This includes measures of irritability, resentment, overt aggression, impulse to aggression and anomie. Because hostility, embitterment, and disenchantment are the dominant features of these measures, we refer to these as HED (hostility–embitterment–disenchantment) variables; these mostly appear in YIT.

Internal reliabilities as assessed by coefficient alpha (Cronbach, 1951) for all NYS and BALT measures used in this paper appear in Table 6.1. Because scale scores were already entered on the YIT tape and were analyzed in that form, no reliability data are available for those measures. In general, the internal reliabilities of the NYS measures are higher than those in the BALT measures. Whether these results reflect differences in the quality of the measures or of the samples is uncertain.

This chapter has both a conceptual and a descriptive purpose. On the conceptual level, it attempts to clarify and spell out the essential features of selected self-concept dimensions. On the descriptive level, it attempts to examine the relationship between these dimensions and certain measures of psychological well-being. To demonstrate that people with certain self-concepts are more psychologically comfortable, of course, does not prove that they are comfortable *because* of the self-concepts. At this early stage it suffices simply to ascertain the existence of such relationships.

SELF-ESTEEM

To assert that self-esteem is a powerful human motive is scarcely a novel insight. According to Hobbes, "the greatest joy of the human soul" is to have a high opinion of oneself (quoted in Allport, 1968, p. 16). Even Adam Smith, who insisted that making money was the most powerful motive of mankind, acknowledged that this desire usually reflected an underlying wish to command the good opinion of others (Lane, 1981, p. 1). Many prominent theorists of our own time share this view. Allport (1961) observed that "if we are to hold to the theory of multiple drives at all, we must at least admit that the ego-drive (or pride or desire for approval, call it what you will) takes precedence over all other drives" (p. 155–156). In developing his elaborate system of "sentiments," McDougall (1932) identified *self-regard* as the "master sentiment," the sentiment to which all others were subordinated. Maslow (1954) identified *self-esteem* as one of the "prepotent" human needs. Furthermore, the fact that self-concept researchers have focused so heavily on self-esteem to the comparative neglect of most other features of the self-concept (see McGuire & Padawer-Singer, 1976; Wylie, 1979) testifies to the widespread recognition of its importance.[1]

But to assert that self-esteem is important is a good deal easier than specifying what it is. One useful way to begin is to suggest what, in our view, high self-esteem is *not*. First, high self-esteem does not mean feelings of superiority. Although the person with low self-esteem is indeed likely to have feelings of inferiority (Ansbacher & Rowena, 1956), the person with high self-esteem does not characteristically view himself or herself as better than other people. On the contrary, high self-esteem people tend to be free of arrogance or contempt for others or to manifest other behavior that we associate with the idea of superiority.

Second, high self-esteem does not involve feelings of perfection. On

---

[1]In fact, according to Offer *et al.:* "A positive self-image was described as among the more important aspects of mental health by the vast majority of psychotherapists surveyed in a national sample (Goldman & Mendelsohn, 1969) and unacceptable feelings about oneself have been assigned a critical role in emotional disturbance in virtually every major theory of psychopathology" (1981, p. 114).

the contrary, the high self-esteem adolescent recognizes his or her limitations and hopes and strives to overcome these deficiencies. He is not one to gaze in awe, admiration, and wonder at himself; he knows that there are things wrong with him, and hopes and expects to improve in this regard.

Third, high self-esteem does not necessarily reflect high feelings of competence or efficacy. Efficacy, we shall see, is an extremely important dimension of the healthy self-concept; although it contributes to self-esteem, the two are not identical. Self-esteem refers to the feeling of being satisfied with oneself, believing that one is a person of worth. Although it may also reflect confidence that one can work one's will upon a recalcitrant world, that is not necessarily the case.

What, then, are the features of *high* self-esteem? The first is self-acceptance. Although recognizing his or her shortcomings, the high self-esteem individual is basically satisfied to be the type of person he or she is. The individual is aware of his or her faults but accepts these as inevitable expressions of human frailty. He recognizes that it is part of the human condition to make occasional errors in judgment, to be disliked by one or another person, to lose one's self-control on occasion, and so on. The high self-esteem person, then, is characterized by a high level of self-tolerance.

Second, the high self-esteem person likes him- or herself. Admittedly, this formulation may sound strange. Can one like oneself in the same sense that one likes another human being? To accept this idea requires us to be sensitive to the process of self-objectification. This process is best expressed in Mead's (1934) distinction between the "me" and the "I." The "me" is that feature of the personality that reflects on, judges, and responds to the self; it is the self as object. The other feature of the personality is the self as subject—the "I." This is the spontaneous, unpredictable, impulsive self. Consider the following strange phenomenon: that people laugh at their own jokes. A funny idea pops into our heads; that is the "I"—the unpredictable, unanticipated feature of personality. The other part of the personality is the "me"—the part that finds the joke funny, laughs at it, relishes it. It is the "I" that discovers the brilliant move in chess, that engrosses the listener with a fascinating story, that feels impulses of sympathy, kindness, or generosity; it is the "me" that takes satisfaction in what is observed and experienced. It is the "me" that likes the self. We suggest that self-liking is a meaningful concept and that it characterizes people with high self-esteem.

Finally, persons with high self-esteem have proper *respect* for themselves and their worth as a person. Such respect may be of two sorts:

TABLE 6.2

Correlations of Global Self-Esteem and Psychological Well-Being among Adolescents[a]

Relationship of self-esteem to	New York State	Baltimore	Youth in transition
Depressive measures			
General depressive affect	−.4988	−.3272	−.5089
Happiness			.5606
Negative affective states			−.4847
Anxiety measures			
General anxiety		−.2782	−.2478
Psychophysiological measures	−.2361		−.3325
Anxiety-tension			−.3614
HED measures[b]			
Impulse to aggression			−.3252
Overt aggression			−.3182
Irritability			−.4233
Resentment			−.3852
Anomie			−.4579
Gender	−.0969	−.1111	

[a]All correlations are significantly different from zero at the .001 level.

[b]HED (hostility–embitterment–disenchantment).

unconditional or conditional (Rosenberg, 1965). It is unconditional in the sense that the individual respects him- or herself as a human being, independent of qualities or accomplishments. The individual believes that he or she is entitled to respectful treatment from others without having to prove his or her worth. But there is also a conditional type of self-respect, one that rests on meeting one's own standards of competence, morality, or any other criteria of worth or excellence. The high self-esteem person feels such self-respect, the low self-esteem person lacks it.

A measure of self-esteem that incorporates all these dimensions has yet to be devised. Currently, most self-esteem measures primarily reflect self-acceptance. Bearing in mind this limitation, the question is: Is there any evidence to indicate that high self-esteem, so conceived, is empirically associated with psychological well-being? Table 6.2 provides convincing evidence that global self-esteem is related to diverse measures of euphoria–dysphoria. *Low* self-esteem people are clearly more depressed (the correlations between self-esteem and depression in all three adolescent studies range between −.3272 and −.5089). They also rank lower on a measure of "happiness" (.5606) and higher on a measure of "negative affective states" (−.4847).

Low self-esteem people are also more likely to be anxious. In two of the adolescent studies, the correlations of self-esteem and general anxiety are $-.2782$ and $-.2478$; the correlations of self-esteem and psycho-physiological (or somatic) measures of anxiety are $-.2361$ and $.3325$; and the correlation with the anxiety-tension measure is $-.3614$.

Finally, global self-esteem is related to a range of HED measures: impulse to aggression $(-.3252)$; overt aggression $(-.3282)$; irritability $(-.4233)$; resentment $(-.3852)$; and anomie $(-.4579)$. All relationships are significant at the .001 level.

Is the association between low self-esteem and dysphoric dispositions confined to adolescents? By no means. Adult studies expand the range of dysphoric traits associated with low self-esteem. Pearlin's (1975) large-scale survey of Chicago metropolitan area adults found a relationship of $r = -.49$ between depressive affect and global self-esteem, as well as a strong correlation between self-esteem and anxiety. Kaplan and Pokorny (1969) also reported significant relationships between low self-esteem and both high depressive affect and many psychophysiological symptoms among a sample of 500 adults.

In addition, according to Carmines (1978): "Recent research has indicated that persons with low self-esteem manifest a variety of adverse personality traits" (p. 169). For example, they tend to be "guilt-ridden, cautious, morbidly afraid of a failure, chronically anxious, and psychologically vulnerable." Conversely, persons with high self-esteem "feel a sense of command over themselves and their immediate environment: they are well-integrated, candid, and willing to take risks" (p. 169).

Finally, there is evidence to indicate that self-esteem is closely connected to feelings of life satisfaction. Andrews and Withey (1976) found that a three-item index of self-esteem proved to be the best predictor of global life satisfaction. Furthermore, Campbell (1981) reported that "dissatisfaction with self had a more damaging effect on general feeling of well-being than dissatisfaction with any of the other domains of life" (p. 217). Crandall (1973) also found self-esteem to be central to life satisfaction.

These studies all treat self-esteem as a general trait or tendency. But self-esteem may also be situationally variable; it may be high at one moment, low at another. Interestingly, such momentary self-esteem states are also characteristically accompanied by momentary euphoric or dysphoric feelings. Epstein (1981), for example, studied people's emotional responses to events that raised or lowered self-esteem. He noted: "When self-esteem was raised, high levels were reported for happiness, security, affection, energy availability, alertness, calmness, clear-mindedness, singleness of purpose, lack of restraint, and spontaneity. When self-esteem was lowered, high levels were reported for unhappiness, anger, feelings of threat, weariness, withdrawal, nervousness, disorganization, conflict, feelings of restraint and self-consciousness" (p. 21).

The systematic quantitative data reported here accord strikingly with clinical reports. According to Beck (1967), fully 81% of severely depressed patients but only 38% of nondepressed people showed low self-evaluation. In addition, 80% of the former but 43% of the latter were high in self-blame and self-criticism.

It would exceed the scope of the present discussion to detail the many other ways in which high and low self-esteem people differ. But it is clear from this evidence that the high self-esteem person is both a happier and a more effective human being (Gecas, 1982; Rosenberg, 1965; Sniderman, 1975). Although self-esteem studies are legion, we have yet to discover any showing low self-esteem to be associated with more favorable feelings of psychological well-being.

The Adolescent Stage

Is self-esteem particularly disturbed during adolescence? O'Malley and Bachman (1983) have presented rather persuasive evidence that, between the ages of 13–23, there is a regular and consistent improvement in global self-esteem. In other words, the earlier the adolescent stage, the greater the self-esteem disturbance. The question is: Is this development a continuation from earlier years, that is, can one extrapolate backwards to infer that the younger the individual, the lower the self-esteem? Our data suggest that one cannot. Table 6.3 shows that between the ages of 8–11, the proportion with low self-esteem appears to be average (25% low). Between 12–14 years of age, low self-esteem rises somewhat (30% low), declining again in the later adolescent years, that is, 14 years or older (22% low). Although the differences are modest, they suggest that early adolescence is somewhat more apt to be a period of self-esteem disturbance.

A number of writers have suggested that women in American society occupy a lower status than men and have inferred that the self-esteem of girls would therefore be lower than that of boys. In general, the empirical literature has produced inconsistent findings (Maccoby & Jacklin, 1974; Wylie, 1979). Since YIT is a male sample, this issue could not be explored in that study. In NYS and BALT, girls are slightly (but significantly) more likely than boys to have low self-esteem (NYS: $r = -.0969$; BALT: $r = -.1111$). These data are consistent with a recent extension of the YIT study (Monitoring the Future) which showed self-

TABLE 6.3
Age and Self-Concept Dimensions among Boys and Girls in Baltimore Study

Self-concept dimensions		Age			Significance
		8–11	12–13	14–18	
Self-esteem (% low)	Total	25%	30%	22%	*
	Boys	23%	26%	20%	n.s.
	Girls	27%	34%***	24%	**
Mattering (% low)	Total	26%	29%	26%	n.s.
	Boys	30%	29%	29%	n.s.
	Girls	22%	30%	21%	n.s.
Certitude (% low)	Total	19%	32%	27%	***
	Boys	15%	26%	22%	n.s.
	Girls	23%	38%**	31%*	***
Control over destiny (% low)	Total	23%	23%	10%	***
	Boys	25%	23%	12%	***
	Girls	22%	23%	9%	***
Vulnerability (% high)	Total	28%	27%	23%	*
	Boys	19%	17%	14%	n.s.
	Girls	37%***	37%***	32%***	n.s.
Public anxiety (% high)	Total	17%	30%	30%	***
	Boys	16%	25%	19%	*
	Girls	19%	36%**	42%***	***
Preoccupation (% high)	Total	22%	23%	31%	***
	Boys	19%	22%	27%	n.s.
	Girls	24%	24%	36%	**
Fantasy (% high)	Total	27%	28%	23%	*
	Boys	28%	33%	20%	**
	Girls	25%	24%	25%	n.s.

$^*p < .05$; $^{**}p < .01$; $^{***}p < .001$. Significance levels across age categories presented in right-hand column. Significance of difference between boys and girls within age categories presented in higher percentage categories.

esteem to be slightly (though significantly) lower among girls during adolescence (O'Malley & Bachman, 1979). The BALT data suggest that the gender difference in self-esteem may be stronger in adolescence ($r = -.1111$) than in childhood ($ = -.0506$), but that, even during adolescence, the gender differences are fairly minor. Whatever gender differences exist are most perceptible in early adolescence.

MATTERING

Whereas an immense amount of attention has been given to the dimension of self-esteem, almost no attention has been given to the concept of mattering. *Mattering* refers to the individual's feeling that he or she counts, makes a difference, "signifies." In developing this concept, it is useful to differentiate two types of mattering: societal and interpersonal. *Societal* mattering refers to the feeling of making a difference in the broader scheme of sociopolitical events—of feeling that one's thoughts and actions have an impact, create ripples, are felt. Fromm (1941) vividly described the societal conditions that foster a feeling of insignificance in people. Living in a world dominated by large businesses, unions, media, governments; swept along by impersonal social, economic and political forces; controlled by immense and distant sources of power affecting the course of events—these conditions were said to induce in the average person the feeling that he or she is irrelevant to the society in general, that these forces operate independently of anything he does.

A very different type of mattering is the feeling that one makes a difference to specific-other people. We call this *interpersonal* mattering (Rosenberg & McCullough, 1981; Whiting, 1982). It is this type of mattering, we believe, that is particularly important to psychological well-being.

Mattering, of course, does not refer to the objective significance of an individual to another person but to his subjective interpretation of it. It may be expressed in a number of ways. The most elementary form of mattering is feeling oneself to be the object of another person's attention or notice. The person low on mattering experiences himself as invisible, as making no impression on another's mind. As James (1890) described it: "If no one turned around when we entered, answered when we spoke, or minded what we did . . . a kind of rage and impotent despair would ere long well up in us, from which the cruellest bodily tortures would be a relief" (p. 293–294).

Being the object of another person's interest, notice, or attention is thus important to the individual. This may even be true of negative attention. For example, a sample of high school students was asked how their parents typically reacted when they brought home poor report cards from school. Not surprisingly, those who said that their parents helped and encouraged them had the highest self-esteem. What is especially noteworthy in the present regard is the fact that the adolescents who said their parents punished them had *higher* self-esteem than those who said their parents paid no attention to their report cards (Rosenberg, 1963; see also Lefcourt, 1976, p. 103). One possible explanation is that the punished students felt that they mattered enough for their parents to be concerned with their progress.

A classic example of the importance of mattering is the famous "Hawthorne effect" (Roethlisberger & Dickson, 1939). The investigators were interested in learning how physical conditions affected output. They found that when they improved the lighting, output increased, but when they decreased the lighting, output increased further. In fact, even the control group, who were subjected to no changes in physical environment, improved productivity. One possible reason was that outsiders were *paying attention* to the workers. The feeling that they mattered—were of special interest rather than being anonymous and unrecognized workers—evidently spurred productivity.A second sense of mattering is the feeling of being missed. If we wish others to be aware of our presence, we also wish them to be aware of our absence. If we are not there, we want to leave a gaping hole. For example, if a mother must turn over the care of a child to someone else for a time—say, because of hospitalization—is there a dim twinge of disappointment when she returns to find the child completely happy and well? When the executive is obliged to be separated from his or her office, is he or she entirely pleased to discover that the division has operated smoothly and without a hitch during his or her absence? The person who believes his or her absence will not be missed is one who has low feelings of mattering.

The third sense of interpersonal mattering is the feeling that we are important to the other person or are objects of his concern. To believe that the other person cares about what we want, think, and do, or is concerned with our fate, is to matter. Whether the adolescent goes on to college or becomes hooked on drugs may deeply concern his or her parents, whereas they would have no corresponding feelings regarding the fate of the boy or girl down the street. This fact may help us to understand certain empirical puzzles that have appeared in our research. In our study of New York State adolescents (Rosenberg, 1965), we encountered the following finding: children of divorced mothers whose mothers remarried had *lower* self-esteem than those whose mothers did not remarry. These results are surprising since, by and large, one would assume that a surrogate parent is better than no parent at all and that the restoration of an approximation to a normal family life would be better than the abnormality of having but a single parent. A father—even if he is not the biological father—can give the child someone to lean on, to turn to for advice and support, and can ease the family's economic burdens. One would certainly expect the child's self-esteem to respond favorably to these circumstances.

But consider the matter from another viewpoint. When the father is removed from the family, either through divorce or death, what happens to the mother and child? It is a common observation that when people are faced by a common problem, they tend to draw more closely together. They "huddle together for warmth." Both mother and child must share the responsibilities that would ordinarily be assumed by the husband. The broken family is thus likely to make mother and child more dependent upon one another. The mother's life comes to focus more centrally on the child; the child may be a burden, but he or she is of supreme importance to her.

But what happens when the mother remarries? The child may still retain the affection of his mother, but he is no longer the exclusive center of her universe. She becomes less dependent upon him or her for emotional and physical support, less involved in his or her needs. The child is now one among several in whom she is interested. A decline in mattering may explain why such children appear to be characterized by reduced self-esteem.

A fourth expression of interpersonal mattering is the feeling that we are someone's ego extension (Cialdini et al., 1976; Rosenberg, 1979)—that we reflect on or constitute a part of him or her. Adolescents who know their parents will swell with pride at their achievements feel themselves to be the parents' ego extension. The adolescent's triumph is the parents' success, his or her defeat their failure. When we feel that the other person's sense of self extends beyond his or her own skin to encompass us—that he or she takes personally what happens to us—then we feel that we matter to that person.

Finally, mattering is apt to be strong when we believe that the other person depends on us. That our behavior should be influenced by our dependence on other people is easily understood, since most of our needs are satisfied by other human beings. What is much more mysterious is why our actions are equally governed by *their* dependence on *us*. The mother who rushes to put dinner on the table is impelled by the pressure of the fact that others are dependent on her to appease their hunger. The husband who feels his family is dependent on his earnings is under a tremendous burden of obligation. The mother's feeling that she matters to her baby may be the quintessential expression of this feeling because her baby is totally dependent on her.

Although the three adolescent studies available to us included questions reflecting one or another of these aspects of interpersonal mattering, no study included them all. In addition, the data to be presented are limited to mattering to parents; we do not explore the importance of mattering to other people. Most of the indicators reflected the adolescents' feelings that their parents were interested in them or cared about them. Despite this limitation, mattering proved to be consistently related to diverse measures of dysphoria.

First, Table 6.4 shows that parental mattering is inversely related to

TABLE 6.4

Correlations of Parental Mattering to Psychological Well-Being and Self-Esteem among
Adolescents[a]

Relationships of mattering to	Baltimore	Youth in Transition
Self-concept measures		
Global self-esteem	.2353	.3315
Depressive measures		
General depressive affect	−.2729	−.3537
Happiness		.3245
Negative affective states		−.3649
Anxiety measures		
General anxiety	−.1543	−.1619
Psychophysiological		.3235
Anxiety-tension		−.2078
Hostility-Embitterment-Disenchantment measures		
Impulse to aggression		−.2640
Overt aggression		−.2463
Irritability		−.2860
Resentment		−.3646
Anomie		−.3927
Gender	.0504*	

[a]All correlations are significantly different from zero at the .001 level with the exception of those marked with an asterisk.
*Nonsignificant correlation.

global self-esteem; in all three studies, the relationship of mattering to self-esteem was −.2798, −.2353, and −.3315. Low feelings of mattering among adolescents are also clearly associated with other indicators of psychological disturbance. Youngsters who feel that they matter little to their parents are substantially more likely to be high on depression, unhappiness, and negative affective states. They are also more likely to show general anxiety and tension, although these relationships are perceptibly weaker. The low-mattering adolescent is also strikingly more likely to express feelings of hostility, embitterment, and disenchantment; the relationships to feelings of resentment and of anomie are particularly high. (All relationships are significant at the .001 level.) Low parental mattering is a strikingly dysphoric disposition; sourness, resentment, embitterment, and depression follow in its wake.

These relationships, it should be noted, are not explained by the higher self-esteem of the high-mattering adolescents, for even when self-esteem is controlled, they remain virtually unchanged. Mattering is thus strongly related to psychological well-being independent of its bearing on self-esteem.

Why mattering matters is still uncertain, but its association with psychological well-being appears to be beyond dispute. The person low on mattering feels irrelevant, unimportant, or peripheral in the minds of others. He is the invisible man who passes through unnoticed, whose presence evokes no emotional response—either positive or negative—and whose absence is unremarked. It would appear that mattering is important to the human being, and that the adolescent high on parental mattering lives a richer, fuller, more satisfying life. Among adolescent boys, mattering to parents apparently has a stronger impact on psychological well-being than mattering to any other category of others (Whiting, 1982).

The Adolescent Stage

Mattering, of course, is a feature of the perceived self—a judgment of one's position in a significant other's value system. There is ample evidence to indicate that such perceptions are frequently inaccurate. Although in many cases the adolescent's judgment of the parent's values is correct, it is probably also true that erroneous inferences are not unusual. If the error is a positive one—the adolescent inferring that he or she matters greatly to his or her parent even though this is not the case—the outcome of this error is benign. In other cases, however, the parent has somehow failed to convey to the adolescent that he or she matters greatly, and the dysphoric consequences are far from trivial.

Although we are unable to test our speculations with data, we would expect mattering to be low during adolescence.[2] The adolescent is something of a sociological superfluity, an irrelevance. In less-advanced societies, mattering presumably would be high because the adolescent would already have established his or her own family. In America half a century ago, the adolescents' families would have depended on their earnings or their work on the farm. It may be that one reason why the adolescent clings so tenaciously to his or her peers is that to them, at least, he or she matters. If it is true that the feeling of being socially irrelevant is widespread among adolescents, this fact may underly some of the problems of contemporary youth.

For obvious reasons it would not be meaningful to compare *parental* mattering of adults and adolescents, even were such data available. The Baltimore study shows no relationship of age to mattering among boys but does indicate that girls in early adolescence are somewhat

---

[2]There is also reason to think that mattering may be low in old age. As Murphy (1947) remarks: "Few societies protect those in the declining years of life from the loss of importance in the group that is their usual lot" (p. 566).

more likely than girls at other ages to be low in feelings of mattering. Because good measures of mattering are not yet available, however, these conclusions are by no means firmly established.

CERTITUDE OR STABILITY

Compared to the voluminous literature on self-esteem, research on self-concept certitude or stability has been extremely modest (Carlson, 1965; Engel, 1959; Franzoi & Reddish, 1980). Yet there is theoretical reason to think that the individual may be as concerned with whether his self-concept is certain or unsure as with whether it is favorable or unfavorable. Why is it so important to know for sure what one is like? The reason is that the individual's self-concept is his most fundamental frame of reference; without a firm and clear picture of what one is like, the individual is virtually immobilized. According to Lecky (1945):

> We conceive of the mind or personality as an organization of ideas which are felt to be consistent with one another. The nucleus of the system, around which the rest of the system revolves, is the individual's idea or conception of himself. Any idea entering the system which is inconsistent with the individual's conception of himself cannot be assimilated . . . the individual's conception of himself is the basic axiom of his whole life theory. (p. 263–265)

Other writers, using different terminology, have reached essentially the same conclusion. It is a major aspect of what Erikson (1959) terms "identity diffusion" or "identity confusion" (although Erikson includes not only the current self-picture but also the individual's commitment to a future self). Proshansky and Newton (1968), speaking of the identity problems of blacks, describe the black's uncertainty about who he is, what he is, what he wants to become.

Furthermore, as Mead (1934) pointed out, the self-concept is essential for rational human action. One of the considerations that enter into any human decision is one's assumptions about the self. People are aware that it is important to have a sure sense of what they are like; without such certainty, the individual is afflicted with torments of doubt, hesitation, and indecision.

In general, then, people prefer to have clear and definite ideas of what they are like; although there are exceptions (cf. Dipboye, 1977; Jones, 1973), information that raises doubts about these ideas are apt to be experienced as distressing. According to Rogers (1951): "Any experience which is inconsistent with the organization or structure of self may be perceived as a threat" (p. 515). If the self cannot defend itself against deep threats, the result is a catastrophic psychological break-down and disintegration.

Anecdotal support for this view appears in a study by Backman, Secord, and Pierce (1963). In this investigation, subjects ranked their needs and then were given a personality assessment that disagreed with some of their self-assessments. The authors report: "The success of the experimental manipulation was . . . apparent from the loud sighs of relief that arose when the subjects learned that they had been deceived with respect to the assessment" (p. 107). These subjects were genuinely distressed to learn that the objective test conflicted with their views of what they were like, whether or not these disagreements were favorable or unfavorable.

There is thus reason to think that a shifting, volatile, uncertain self-concept is dysphoric. Certitude and stability, unfortunately, are not readily separable. This is readily understandable. The person whose self-attitude changes from moment to moment can scarcely develop a firm assurance about what he or she is like. Conversely, the person uncertain about a self-concept element is apt to find it varying in different situations. Certitude and stability thus affect one another. The measures appearing in the three studies do not distinguish certitude from stability, and we shall here treat these concepts inter-changeably.Table 6.5 shows generally strong relationships between self-concept incertitude and dysphoria. Adolescents with uncertain self-concepts, we see, are decidedly more likely to have low self-esteem (although this relationship is weaker in YIT). In addition, all three studies show certitude to be inversely related to general measures of depressive affect, and YIT shows it to be positively related to happiness and inversely related to negative affective states. Adolescents high in incertitude are also strikingly more likely to be anxious, whether this anxiety is reflected in general measures, in somatic symptoms, or in a specific anxiety-tension measure. Finally, adolescents unsure of what they are like manifest dysphoria on all five HED measures—impulse to aggression, overt aggression, irritability, resentment, and anomie. All relationships are significant beyond the .001 level.

We do not suggest, of course, that all these dysphoric states are consequences of incertitude; that is certainly not the case. We expect, for example, that incertitude is more likely to contribute to anxiety than to depression. But as a simple descriptive fact, self-concept incertitude is associated with psychological discomfort. This association, furthermore, is not entirely attributable to low self-esteem. Even when self-esteem is controlled, self-concept incertitude continues to be associated with psychological discomfort, though at a reduced level.

In showing that an uncertain or volatile self-concept tends to be

TABLE 6.5

Correlations of Certitude (Stability) and Psychological Well-Being among Adolescents[a]

Relationship of certitude to	New York State	Baltimore	Youth in Transition
Self-concept measures			
Global self-esteem	.4043	.4252	.2318
Depressive measures			
General depressive affect	−.2774	−.1871	−.3320
Happiness			.1624
Negative affective states			−.4332
Anxiety measures			
General anxiety		−.2942	−.4277
Psychophysiological measures	−.1917		.2544
Anxiety-tension			−.3128
Hostility-Embitterment-Disenchantment measures			
Impulse to aggression			−.2524
Overt aggression			−.1752
Irritability			−.3490
Resentment			−.3369
Anomie			−.3110
Gender	−.1169	−.1546	

[a]All correlations are significantly different from zero at the .001 level.

dysphoric, we do not mean to imply that the mentally healthy person never has doubts about what she is like or is completely resistant to self-concept change. A healthy self-concept, we believe, is sure and stable in its essential and central features but may be changeable regarding its peripheral elements. In addition, features of the self are held as working assumptions, subject to revision in the light of new evidence. Finally, in a number of cases people seek to change in the direction of a more desirable self.

Overall, however, the person who feels sure that she knows what she is like tends to be high on psychological well-being; the person whose self-attitudes shift from moment to moment, who lacks firmness or certainty about what she is like, is likely to be distressed. But maximal certitude is not optimal certitude. Some change or uncertainty about the self is consistent with mental health; general confusion or uncertainty is not.

The Adolescent Stage

One of the major tasks of growing into adulthood is to settle finally on some picture of what the self is like and to stick to it. Adolescence is probably the stage of life when uncertainty about the self-concept is at its peak; we believe that this is a large component of what some writers mean by an adolescent identity crisis (Erikson, 1959). Table 6.3 shows that during childhood (age 8–11), the self-concept is moderately sure and stable (19% low), but at the age of 12–13 years there is a sharp drop in certitude (32% low). After age 14, certitude shows some improvement (27% low) though it does not reach the childhood level.

If there is any *distinctive* self-concept problem in early adolescence, we believe, it would probably be that of self-concept incertitude. This is not surprising. Adolescence is a stage of life when attention shifts from a nearly exclusive preoccupation with features of external experience to an intense probing, scrutiny, and evaluation of the self (Rosenberg, 1979). What was hitherto taken for granted about the self now becomes problematic. Doubts and uncertainties are introduced. Particularly in early adolescence, new, even dramatic, physical changes are taking place; new potentialities are emerging but, yet untested, remain in doubt; change in other people's behavior toward the self introduces further uncertainty about what one is like; physiological changes also challenge the taken-for-granted self. It is therefore not surprising to find that the adolescent is apt to experience a sharp rise in confusion and uncertainty about the self.

At all age levels, but particularly in early adolescence, girls are more likely than boys to be uncertain of what they are like (Table 6.3). Although it is not possible to enter into detail at this point, the greater instability of female self-concepts is attributable in part of their greater interpersonal sensitivity (Rosenberg & Simmons, 1975) and their more intense awareness of their changing physical appearance. During the school years, then, early adolescence is the period of the greatest uncertainty about the self, and this uncertainty is particularly likely to afflict girls.

LOCUS OF CONTROL

The self-concept has been characterized in many ways: as a set of working assumptions (Shibutani, 1961), a group of guiding attitudes, a system of self-expectations (Rosenberg, 1984); a "theory" (Epstein, 1973), and a "schema" (Markus, 1977).

Through the experience of the "me" observing the "I," the individual develops expectations concerning his or her interests, aptitudes, preferences, and so forth. These expectations are, to some extent, self-fulfilling prophecies. Lecky (1945) provides a number of examples. The child who defines himself as a poor speller will unconsciously persist in making spelling mistakes, despite adequate ability and careful instruction. The boy who has been defined in the family as the "slow one," in contrast to his brother who is the "fast one," will unconsciously evolve a variety of techniques for killing time. To say that people act in accordance with their self-concepts is largely equivalent to the statement that they act in accordance with a system of self-expectations.

One important feature of the individual's system of self-expectations is his internal or external *locus of control*. When Rotter (1966) introduced this concept into the literature, he defined it as "generalized expectancies" concerning the outcomes of one's actions. People characterized by an internal locus of control felt that what happened to them in life was essentially a consequence of their own actions. Those with an external locus of control orientation tended to feel that what happened to them was a consequence of events governed by external forces.

Since that time a number of terms have entered the literature which, though not identical, bear a decided kinship to Rotter's concept. Bandura (1977) speaks of "self-efficacy," Smith (1968) and White (1959) of "competence," Franks and Marolla (1976) of "inner and outer self-esteem," Brim (1974) and Gurin, Gurin, Lao, & Beattie (1969) of "personal control," Abramson, Seligman, and Teasdale (1978) of "learned helplessness," deCharms (1968) of "personal causation," Coleman *et al.* (1966) of "control over destiny," and Pearlin and Radabaugh (1976) of "mastery." Although these terms reflect somewhat different nuances of meaning, their common core is aptly expressed in Brim's (1974) definition of personal control as a "belief system about causality: whether outcomes are a consequence of one's own behavior, or tend to occur independently of one's own behavior" (p. 3).

The possible attitudinal and behavioral consequences of internal and external locus of control appear endless. In 1974, Brim was able to report that "scores on measures of internal versus external attribution have been shown to be related to smoking, to alcoholism, to seat belt nonuse, to reporting the experience of romantic love, to voting behavior, to participation in the women's movement, to belief in the Protestant ethic, to improved school performance, to ability to control heart rate by thinking, to lower amounts of cheating in school, and to higher levels of performance by male bridge experts" (p. 4). In addition, Macdonald (1973) reports that locus of control has been related to achievement behavior, birth control practices, reaction to disability, reaction to influence attempts, psychopathology, and more.

In BALT, locus of control was measured by Coleman *et al.*'s (1966) 3-item "control over destiny" measure. YIT included a 12-item measure of internal–external locus of control called total control. (This measure represented a merger of two other measures, called "first person" and "third person" control, to be discussed later.)

Table 6.6 shows that internal–external locus of control is significantly associated with global self-esteem, depressive affect, anxiety, and various hostility–embitterment–disenchantment measures. "Internals" are characterized by higher levels of psychological well-being. All of the relationships are significant at the .001 level. Although some of these relationships are not as strong as those observed in discussing other self-concept measures, the relationship of locus of control to psychological well-being is clear.

Studies of adults yield similar findings. Consider Pearlin and Radabaugh's (1976) concept of *mastery*, defined by them as "the extent to which people see themselves, at one extreme, as being in control of the important circumstances of their lives or, at the other extreme, as having to submit fatalistically to external forces" (p. 658). In their sample of adults, the correlation between mastery and global self-esteem is .54 and the correlation between mastery and depression is

TABLE 6.6

Correlations of Locus of Control and Psychological Well-Being among Adolescents[a]

Relationships of locus of control to	Baltimore	Youth in transition		
		First person	Third person	Total control
Self-concept measures				
Global self-esteem	.2153	.2197	.1881	.2470
Depressive measures				
General depressive affect	−.1742	−.1877	−.1754	−.2205
Happiness		.1449	.1533	.1838
Negative affective states		−.2302	−.2205	−.2738
Anxiety measures				
General anxiety	−.2111	−.1387	−.0954	−.1388
Psychophysiological		.2132	.2744	.3032
Anxiety tension		−.1247	−.0986	−.1330
HED measures[b]				
Impulse to aggression		−.1868	−.2282	−.2561
Overt aggression		−.1700	−.2092	−.2344
Irritability		−.1759	−.1801	−.2187
Resentment		−.2388	−.2581	−.3033
Anomie		−.2437	−.2608	−.3090
Gender	−.0333*			

[a]All correlations are significantly different from zero at the .001 level except those marked with an asterisk.
[b]HED (hostility–embitterment–disenchantment).
*Nonsignificant correlation.

−.43. Pearlin and Radabaugh also show that those scoring high on the mastery scale are much more likely than those scoring low to rank low on a score of 12 common psychophysiological indicators of anxiety.

Among adults, feelings of control are also associated with life satisfaction. In their landmark study of quality of life, Campbell, Converse, and Rodgers (1976, p. 59) showed a positive and significant association between sense of personal competence and overall well-being ($r = .35$). According to Campbell (1981): "People who see the control of their lives within themselves are far more likely to describe their life experience positively than those who see themselves controlled by outside forces. They are happier; more likely to report affectively positive experiences; less likely to report negative experiences, worries, and strain; more satisfied with life and the domains of life; and more ready to say that they have had their share or more than their share of happiness in life" (p. 215). Even controlling for income, health, attractiveness, and apparent intelligence, the relationship between personal control and feelings of well-being remains virtually undiminished.

Research attempting to build on Rotter's pioneer work has suggested that the locus of control measure is multidimensional (Gurin et al., 1969). Two factors appear to emerge fairly consistently in the literature. The first, called Personal Control, refers to people's beliefs that they are generally in charge of their fates. The other, called Control Ideology, refers to people's views of the internal or external causes of outcomes in the broader society. It has been found (Brim, 1974) that the sense of personal control is associated with achievement and performance whereas control ideology is not. The question is: Does the same hold true for psychological well-being?

Youth in Transition (YIT) study included two measures that reflected these concepts. The first was a five-item measure in which the statements were expressed primarily in first-person terms (e.g., "Sometimes I feel that I don't have enough control over the direction my life is taking"). These items correspond to what we think of as Personal Control. The second measure consisted of a seven-item index expressed primarily in third-person terms (e.g., "Capable people who fail to become leaders have not taken advantage of their opportunities"). These reflect the concept of Control Ideology. (The Total Control measure, discussed above, combines the items from both indexes.)

The relationship of these measures to psychological well-being appear in Table 6.6. Although the relationship between these two measures is only .34, thus suggesting the presence of decidedly distinct psychological dimensions, each relates to all of the well-being measures almost identically. Both low feelings of personal control and

negative feelings concerning control ideology are associated with dysphoric states.

The Adolescent Stage

Locus of control is not a problem distinctive to adolescents. Not
surprisingly, it has been found that adolescents are less likely than
adults but more likely than children to feel that they are in control of
their lives. According to Brim (1974): "Good studies [Milgram, 1971;
Beebe, 1971] show increases in the sense of personal control from first
to tenth grade, and from fourth to tenth grade, and my own national
survey of attitudes toward intelligence demonstrates increases of a
substantial nature in the sense of personal control from tenth to
twelfth grades" (p. 13). The BALT data (Table 6.3) are generally consistent with these findings: 23% of the 8–11 year olds, 23% of the 12–
13 year olds, and 10% of the 14–18-year-olds were low on the "control
over destiny" measure. In general, boys and girls differ little in this
regard, a finding consistent with most others in the literature.

VULNERABILITY

In the present context we shall use the term *vulnerability* to refer to
the individual's sensitivity to negative responses from other people.
The vulnerable person is hypersensitive, touchy, easily hurt; the
slightest hint of criticism is apt to produce acute pain or profound
depression. The hypersensitive person might be described as one with
a "psychological sunburn"; the most delicate touch generates the most
acute anguish.

If an individual never encountered negative information about the
self, of course, then hypersensitivity would make no difference. But
that is impossible. One important feature of daily living is that self-
esteem is always under threat. As Allport noted:

> Every day we experience grave threats to our self-esteem: we feel inferior,
> guilty, insecure, unloved. Not only big things but little things put us in the
> wrong; we trip up in an examination, we make a social boner, we dress inap-
> propriately for an occasion. The ego sweats. We suffer discomfort, perhaps anx-
> iety, and we hasten to repair the narcissistic wound. (1961, p. 155–161)

Broadly speaking, threats to self-esteem may emanate from two
sources; the first is other people, the second, ourselves. Threats from
other people can be expressed in a near infinity of ways: they may

TABLE 6.7

Correlations of Vulnerability to Psychological Well-Being and Self-Esteem among Adolescents[a]

Relationships of vulnerability to	New York State	Baltimore
Global Self-Esteem	−.2504	−.2757
General depressive affect	.3137	.1113
General anxiety		.2888
Psychophysiological	.2943	
Gender	.2331	.2753

[a]All correlations are significantly different from zero at the .001 level.

criticize us, attack us, derogate us, scorn us, belittle us, snub us, laugh at us, ignore us, point up our faults, flaws, and deficiencies, and so forth. Other people represent an omnipresent peril to our self-esteem.

But no less dangerous to our self-esteem are ourselves. In Meadian terminology, the "I" poses a constant threat to the "me." We make errors in judgment, forget what we should remember, express ourselves awkwardly, break our most sacred promises to ourselves, lose our self-control, behave childishly—in short, act in ways that we regret or deplore. As a consequence, we suffer chagrin, shame, remorse, guilt, regret, self-contempt, and so forth.

None of us is immune to such threats to our worth. What is critically important, then, is people's sensitivity or responsiveness to these threats. An event that plunges one person into a state of profound depression has little effect on another.

Although YIT lacked a satisfactory vulnerability measure, BALT and NYS contained reasonably reliable measures, mostly focusing on sensitivity to criticism. Respondents were asked whether they were "deeply disturbed" at some fault or inadequacy in the self; whether they agreed that "criticism or scolding hurts me terribly"; how "bothered" they were if another person held a poor opinion of them; how "disturbed" they felt if someone laughed at them or blamed them for doing something wrong; and so forth. In general, these measures were heavily weighted toward interpersonal sensitivity.

As Table 6.7 indicates, vulnerability is inversely related to global self-esteem; the low self-esteem person is more deeply hurt and disturbed when criticized by others, and so forth. The vulnerable person also tends to be depressed; although the relationship is rather weak in BALT, it is fairly strong in NYS. Finally, Table 6.7 shows that more vulnerable people tend to be more anxious, whether this anxiety is expressed in general fears or in psychophysiological indicators of anxiety. These associations are all significant at the .001 level.

The relationship bewteen vulnerability and low self-esteem has also been demonstrated in other research. A study of normal controls in a research hospital showed that subjects with low self-esteem were more likely than those with high self-esteem to be described by observers as "touchy and easily hurt," and "easily embarrassed" (Rosenberg, 1965). Combs and Soper (1959) argue that "there is a reciprocal relationship between self-adequacy and perceived threat on the part of the individual. . . . To speak of a nonthreatened person, then, is another way of referring to one who is self-acceptant and who perceives himself as a basically adequate person" (p. 44). Vulnerability may be said to amplify and intensify the painful experiences of low self-esteem.

In suggesting that the healthy self-concept tends to be characterized by lower vulnerability, we do not mean that the individual has developed artificial strategems, such as cultivating a "tough hide," "thick skin," or "hard shell"; such strategems are defensive and have other damaging consequences. But the person who is not greatly disturbed at evidence of personal faults (the individual described by Combs and Soper as the "nonthreatened personality"), who can accept with equanimity the fact that his plans go awry at times, and who can shrug off criticism or laughter with little difficulty—this person is less anxious and probably less depressed.

We do not intend to imply that the healthy individual is totally indifferent to, or unaffected by, the reactions of other people or of the self to her own behavior, dispositions, or other qualities. The person who never condemns the self for immoral behavior, or who is totally indifferent to others' responses, is known as a psychopath. Healthy people, however, are probably so secure in their feeling of worth, and have such a fundamentally positive attitude toward the self, that they can usually accept negative evidence about the self, whether coming from others or from the self, with little anguish. Constructive criticism may even be welcomed.

The Adolescent Stage

Most writers on adolescence seem to agree that this is a very sensitive period of life. Although absolute immunity to self-esteem threat is never to be found, adults probably do develop some imperviousness to the incessant threats to self-esteem. With the passing years, people come to accept the fact that mistakes are inevitable, flaws trivial, interpersonal attacks groundless, and so forth. Hence, on the average, the adult is probably less apt to be disturbed by such evidence regarding the self.

The BALT data show few differences in vulnerability among the several age groups, although more of the older adolescents (14 years or more) scored low on the vulnerability scale than others. Gender differences, by contrast, are very large. At every age, girls are about twice as likely as boys to score high on hypersensitivity. The correlation between gender and vulnerability in NYS is .2331, and in BALT it is .2753—the strongest relationships of gender to any self-concept dimension.

Vulnerability thus appears to heighten and accentuate the dysphoric consequences of low self-esteem. The person low in vulnerability, unlike the threatened personality, appears to have sufficient self-tolerance to accept the fact that he or she will occasionally fall short of his or her standards or be criticized by others; this person can take it in stride or slough it off.

SELF-CONSCIOUSNESS

The concept of *self-consciousness* refers to the individual's state of consciousness at a given moment in time. What is salient to the individual, in the forefront of attention, at any particular moment? Broadly speaking, one of two things may be salient: oneself or something else. Such a formulation is, of course, artificial, because both the self and other things are simultaneously present in awareness. We almost never totally lose self-awareness, for the self is an omnipresent and inescapable part of our conscious existence; but so, too, are our environments. The issue, then, is one of figure and ground. Either the self stands out in the forefront of attention, sharp and clear, with other things in the background of awareness, or the reverse.

The distinction is easily recognized in our experience. If we are preparing for a job interview, going out on a date for the first time, or making a public speech, we are likely to be highly self-conscious; we pay close attention to our actions, appearance, manner, and so forth. But when we are rooting for the home team, reading an absorbing novel, or engaged in a challenging task, the self is in the background of awareness.

Duval and Wicklund (1972) bear the major responsibility for directing attention to this feature of the self-concept. They distinguish between "objective self-awareness," in which attention is focused on the self to the relative exclusion of other parts of the environment, and "subjective self-awareness," which is the reverse. Such self-consciousness has been shown to be easily manipulable in experimental settings. Duval and Wicklund are able to make their subjects self-conscious by placing them in a room with a mirror, having them listen to their own tape-recorded voices, or placing them in the presence of a television camera; they reduce self-consciousness by having their subjects do anagrams or by assigning them some manual task that requires careful concentration for proper performance.

The question is: Is high self-consciousness healthy or unhealthy? Buss (1980) attributes a number of desirable outcomes to high self-awareness, which he associates with superior and more accurate knowledge of the self. Similarly, Parloff *et al.* (1954) cite self-awareness as a criterion of mental health, although they appear to have in mind accurate knowledge of underlying cognitive and affective elements.

On the other hand, certain theorists suggest that the healthy person shows *low* self-consciousness. According to Barron (quoted in Jahoda, 1958): "We pay no attention to ourself when we are in the best of health. It is when we are sick that the self comes to our notice. A person just being himself is not self-conscious. Self-consciousness arises from malfunction" (p. 26). Consistent with this view is Bertrand Russell's assertion that the secret of attaining happiness and avoiding unhappiness is not to think about yourself. In this view, the healthy person is one whose attention, like that of the child, is directed outward to the world of action and events, not focused inward on the self.

One reason it is difficult to draw any generalizations regarding the mental health implications of self-consciousness is that the term has different meanings. The Random House Dictionary (1966) distinguishes two recognized meanings of the term self-conscious: "1. excessively conscious of oneself as an object of observation to others. 2. conscious of one's own thoughts, well-being, etc." (p. 1293).

These definitions refer to distinctly different concepts. The first definition describes the person who pays too much attention to the impression he or she is making on others, is excessively concerned with how other people are responding to him or her. One might describe this type of self-consciousness as expressive of *public anxiety*. The second definition refers to the degree to which the individual directs attention to the self relative to other features of the environment; we will refer to this dimension as *preoccupation with the self*. Both concepts will be treated as dispositions.[3]

Both NYS and BALT included measures of preoccupation with the self but only BALT included questions dealing with public anxiety. YIT lacked measures of either concept.

[3]Our data do not permit us to deal with the self-consciousness dimensions yielded by the factor analysis conducted by Fenigstein, Scheier, and Buss (1975).

TABLE 6.8

Correlations of Preoccupation with Self and Public Anxiety to Self-Esteem and Psychological
Well-Being among Adolescents[a]

	New York State	Baltimore	
	Preoccupation	Preoccupation	Public anxiety
Global self-esteem	−.0089**	−.0718*	−.2796
General depressive affect	.1500	−.0136**	.1025
General anxiety		.1203	.3243
Psychophysiological	.0998		
Gender	.1253	.1225	.2581

[a]All correlations are significantly different from zero at the .001 level except those
marked with an asterisk.
*$p < .05$; **n.s.

The items included in the "preoccupation with the self" measures
focused chiefly on the question of whether or not one spent a great deal
of time thinking about what one was like. For reasons noted above, we
would expect those scoring high on the preoccupation with the self
scale to show greater evidence of psychological dysphoria. Table 6.8
offers little support for this reasoning. The relationship of preoccupation with the self to self-esteem and anxiety are low, and the relationship to depression is null in one study and modest in the other.
Whether the adolescent spends a great deal of time or little time reflecting on the self appears to have little bearing on psychological well-
being.

The public anxiety data yield very different results. In BALT, public
anxiety was measured by such questions as whether the adolescent is
nervous when someone watches her work or would feel uncomfortable
talking before the class. This measure showed a clear inverse relationship to self-esteem, a fairly strong positive association with anxiety, and a modest relation to depressive affect. A high level of concern
with how one is viewed by others is evidently associated with
dysphoria.

The Adolescent Stage

In the view of a number of writers, preoccupation with the self is
particularly characteristic of adolescence. According to Stone and
Church (1957):

> Writers on the subject of adolescence . . . have been struck by the adolescent's
> agonies of self-consciousness, his preoccupation with who he is and where he

belongs. . . . The central theme of adolescence is finding one's self. The adolescent must learn to know a whole new body and its potentials for feelings and behavior, and fit it into his picture of himself. . . . This means an intensified self-awareness—largely manifested as self-consciousness. (pp. 268–270)

Although we are unable to compare adolescent preoccupation with the self with adult preoccupation, we can make such comparisons with children. The data support the contention of Stone and Church that preoccupation is indeed higher in adolescence. Interestingly, however, this increased concern appears only in *later* adolescence; early adolescents (age 12–13) do not differ from children in this regard (Table 6.3).

With regard to public anxiety, adolescents again are higher than children. In contrast to preoccupation, however, it is *early* adolescence (age 12–13) that witnesses such a striking rise in concern with the impression they make on others, and this high level persists into later adolescence (Table 6.3). Whether such acute awareness of others' reactions abates in adulthood is unknown, although that would certainly be our expectation.

Girls show higher levels of both types of self-consciousness, but the relationship is stronger for public anxiety (.2581) than for self-preoccupation (.1253 and .1225). It is, then, the more dysphoric type of self-consciousness that is particularly likely to afflict girls, particularly during adolescence. Girls are evidently socialized to attach greater importance to interpersonal harmony and success, and to be more anxious about the outcome of their efforts in this regard.

PLANE COORDINATION

One factor enormously complicating the search for a healthy self-concept is the fact that the human mind operates on different *planes* (Piaget, 1951)—a plane of reality, a plane of possibility, a plane of fantasy, a plane of self-presentation, and so forth. The self-concept, viewed as the totality of the individual's thoughts and feelings with reference to her- or himself as an object, includes all these planes. When we deal with the plane of reality, we are concerned with the individual's view of what he or she is actually like—the extant self-concept. When we turn to the plane of wish or desire, we are concerned with the self that we would like to be. This plane may be deadly serious (a committed image) or simply pleasurable fantasy (an idealized image) (Horney, 1950); we call this the desired self-concept. Finally, there is the dramaturgical, self-presentational, or impression-management plane (Goffman, 1956). The individual presents a certain self for the purpose of effecting a certain impression on the minds of others.

All these planes coexist in the mind as important aspects of the self-concept. The relevance of this fact is that, from the viewpoint of psychological well-being, it may be less important what the concrete content of these self-concept planes are than whether there exists a coordination or harmony among them.

Three problems of coordination stand out. The first is the failure to keep these planes clearly distinct in one's mind. For most people, the ability to keep these planes separate is not difficult. The 4-year-old soldier who interrupts his ecstatic destruction of the enemy to have his milk and cookie is well aware that the self as imagined is not the self that exists. It is when the planes are confused, for example, when the self as desired is believed to be the self that exists, that problems emerge (Horney, 1950). When the individual who, contrary to fact, dreams of himself as dazzlingly brilliant and on these grounds demands a corresponding respect from others, interpersonal difficulties inevitably arise.

Equally important is the need to keep the impression-management plane distinct from the extant plane. Maslow (1954) observes that the self-actualizing personality characteristically observes the norms of politeness or other social superficialties without necessarily believing that this behavior reflects genuine feelings. This person is able to recognize a clear distinction between his or her presenting self and extant self. Although some might view this behavior as hypocrisy, self-actualizing people are able to maintain the integrity of the self while behaving in accordance with norms of social behavior. What is important for mental health is not to be taken in by one's own act—to believe that the self one presents to others is necessarily the self one believes in.

Contemporary attribution theory would suggest that it is difficult to keep the dramaturgical and extant planes separate. In the behaviorist version of attribution theory advanced by Bem (1967), the individual draws conclusions about his inner states by observing and interpreting his own overt behavior. In part, certainly, that is correct, as is apparent from cognitive dissonance research (Bem, 1967). Nevertheless people are aware of inner states or cognitions, and they are able to choose which of these they wish to express behaviorally and which they elect to conceal. Every normal person, then, is aware that part of his behavior is an act and part is believed to be genuine. A healthy personality possesses the ability to recognize a clear distinction between a self-presentational level and a level in which one believes.

A second question relates to the level on which the mind predominantly exists. According to the phenomenologist (Snygg & Combs, 1949), behavior is always governed by the individual's phenomenal field at the instant of action. The self-concept, however, is an extremely complex structure, containing numerous elements, dimensions, or planes (Rosenberg & Kaplan, 1982). Not all of these can be in the forefront of attention simultaneously. We therefore must know not only what the self-concept is but which planes dominate one's conscious awareness—the extant, desired, or presenting self?

For the healthy person, we believe, the chief focus of attention and interest is on the extant self. The self-concept that dwells predominantly on one of the other planes is unhealthy. The adolescent whose mind is incessantly occupied with the particular model of perfection that represents his or her desired self finds real life to be pallid, bare, and uninteresting by comparison; he or she is apt to lose interest in real life and the real self. Similarly, the person who focuses exclusively on the presenting self, bending his mind and energies to the task of creating a certain public self, becomes a pure facade, with no solid structure behind it. The primary focus of interest in the healthy adolescent is on the extant self.

Third, in the healthy self-concept, the planes, though recognizably distinct, are nevertheless in essential harmony. The person who presents one self to the world while fundamentally believing in another finds her- or himself under constant strain. The spontaneous organism constantly threatens to betray him, thereby destroying the impression he is trying to make, stripping the mask away. The individual may also feel like a hypocrite or a fraud; this feeling, in many cases, accentuates self-hatred. Life is much easier if we are able to believe in our performances.

In the healthy self-concept, there is also a continuity or harmony between what one is, actually or potentially, and what one desires to be. The individual whose thoughts are permanently occupied with being a great athlete or an alluring beauty when nature has failed to provide these endowments is doomed to disappointment and frustration. In the unhealthy personality, there is a fundamental split between a world of desire and a world of reality. In the healthy self-concept, the desired self is smoothly connected with the individual's inclinations and possibilities.

In sum, the healthy self-concept has the following characteristics: (1) the individual is able to see the different self-concept planes as distinct, to keep them segregated in her mind, rather than allowing them to blur and shade into one another; (2) the focus of major interest is on the self that exists—the extant self; and (3) the planes articulate or are in harmony with one another.

TABLE 6.9
Correlations of "False Front" and "Fantasy" to Psychological Well-Being and
Self-Esteem among Adolescents[a]

	New York State	Baltimore
Relationship of false front and fantasy to	False front	Fantasy
Global self-esteem	−.1938	−.1092
General depressive affect	.2408	.0115*
General anxiety		.2063
Psychophysiological	.1279	
Gender	−.1495	−.0184*

[a]All correlations are significantly different from zero at the .001 level except
those marked with an asterisk.
*Nonsignificant correlation.

The data available to us in these three studies are clearly inade-
quately to test these speculations. Two measures do, however, bear
somewhat tangentially on our speculations. The first is what might be
called a "false front" or "facade" measure. What this measure reflects
is the adolescent's sense of a fundamental discrepancy between the self
that is set forth to others (the *presenting self*) and the self that actually
exists (the *extant self*). NYS contained a brief measure of this concept.

A second measure refers to a tendency to retreat into a world of
fantasy. Most of the items included in this measure refer to daydreaming. Such daydreaming, it is reasonable to assume, centers inordinately
on a desired self and neglects the extant self. This measure appeared
only in BALT.

Table 6.9 shows that in NYS the tendency to present a false front or
facade is inversely related to self-esteem and directly related to anxiety. These relationships, though significant, are decidedly weaker
than those we have been examining to this point. There appears to be
an effect, though not a major one.

Fantasy, or the tendency to daydream, shows a modest relationship
to anxiety, a still weaker relationship to self-esteem, and no relationship to depression in the BALT study. In adolescence, at any rate,
the tendency to daydream is a weak predictor of dysphoria.

The data available thus offer some support for our speculations concerning the relationship between plane coordination and psychological
well-being, but this support is modest at best. Because these measures
are questionable, however, the data should be considered as no more
than suggestive.

There is, to be sure, an abundant empirical literature dealing with
the psychological consequences of a discordance between the extant

and desired selves. These are called self-ideal discrepancy studies (Butler & Haigh, 1954). But these have proved to be unsatisfactory in certain ways. First, discrepancy scores are unrevealing in the sense that the same scores may reflect different attitudes (Wylie, 1974). Second, research shows that the "ideal self" shows little variability (i.e., ideally everyone would like to be all good things), so that the chief differences among people are their descriptions of their extant selves.

Although self-ideal discrepancy scores do not satisfactorily achieve their objective, the idea they seek to reflect is undoubtedly sound. People do indeed suffer if they believe they fall short of the standards they have set for themselves, that is, if the extant and desired planes are discrepant.

The Adolescent Stage

There is ample theoretical reason to expect the tendency to present a false front to rise in early adolescence. As Allport (1961) observes: "The search for identity is revealed in the way an adolescent tries on different masks. He first develops one line of chatter, then another, one style of hairdress and then another (always within the range permitted by the peer-group). He imitates one hero and then another. He is still searching for a garb that will fit" (pp. 125–126).

Especially during early adolescence, the planes are apt to lack distinctness, to be discontinuous, and to center on the desired and presenting selves. The result is apt to be serious confusion concerning what one is. It is not surprising that adolescence has been viewed as a time of identity crisis. In NYS, girls are appreciably more likely than boys to experience feelings of false self-presentation; they are more likely to feel that they present a front or facade. Since this variable did not appear in BALT, it was not possible to explore its relationship with age.

In BALT, the tendency to live in a world of fantasy shows little relationship with age, although those 14 years or older appear somewhat less likely than children or adolescents to manifest this tendency. Boys and girls appear equally likely to engage in such behavior.

VERIDICALITY

In discussing the relevance of various self-concept dimensions, we have carefully sidestepped what might appear to be the central issue, namely, the issue of correctness (Jahoda, 1958). That substantial inaccuracy in the self-concept is unhealthy is apparent. The psychotic who believes him- or herself to be Alexander the Great obviously cannot function in society. Although gross self-concept inaccuracy is assuredly pathological, we suggest that precise self-concept accuracy is not possible, and, in fact, is not always even desirable.

The chief reason why we cannot know whether the individual's self-concept is correct is that, with regard to most characteristics, there is no way to obtain precise and objective evidence about the person. And, in the absence of such evidence, there is no way to judge whether the self-concept is true or false.

For example, assume that we wished to measure objectively and precisely how kind, generous, brave, loyal, or well-intentioned a person is. What valid, standardized measures are currently available for assessing these traits? Where are the scholastic aptitude tests for kindness, the college examination board tests for courage? For much of this century psychologists by the hundreds have studied intelligence, yet the debate concerning IQ tests goes on. How then can one accurately and precisely measure the multitude of traits for which no measures are available? All we can do at present is to use certain coarse indicators of these concepts or to rely on the judgments of external observers. But coarse indicators cannot provide precise measurement, and the judgments of external observers, even if reliable, do not constitute validity. Hence, only in rather gross cases of distortion can we establish the inaccuracy of a self-concept component.

The second point is that even in those situations in which it is possible objectively to establish accuracy, such accuracy does not necessarily promote psychological comfort. For example, in a pattern of consistent relationships that amount almost to a law, people are far more likely to judge themselves to be above than below average. Heiss and Owens (1972) found that when adults were asked to judge themselves as above average, average, or below average, only a tiny proportion judged themselves as below average on any of the 10 characteristics studied. By definition, some of these ratings are inaccurate; yet they appear to do no psychological harm.

Research also shows that people hold misconceptions about what others think of them. But these inaccuracies are of a characteristic sort. A study by Reeder, Donohue, & Biblarz (1960) is illustrative. Groups of soldiers were asked to rate themselves and one another on leadership qualities and to judge how other soldiers would rate them. It is thus possible to show objectively how accurate or inaccurate the individual's perceived self is. The nature of the inaccuracy is noteworthy.

Of the 52 soldiers studied, 21 believed that other people rated them more highly than these others actually did whereas only 3 underestimated the level of regard in which they were held by the group as leaders.

Consistent results are reported in the investigation of Sherwood (1965, 1967), who studied a number of human relations training groups. Among the items of information obtained were (1) what each person thought of every other and (2) what each believed every other thought of him. Sherwood referred to the summation of the attitudes toward her- or himself that the individual attributed to others as "subjective public esteem" and the summation of others' actual attitudes toward the individual as "objective public esteem." Again, the results not only showed a substantial relationship between the two, but also showed that subjective public esteem was higher than objective public esteem, that is, that overall the respondents believed others viewed them more favorably than was actually the case (see also Shrauger & Schoeneman, 1979). We believe that no particular harm, and probably substantial good, issues from these misconceptions.

Furthermore, Lewinsohn and Mischel (1980) reported that clinically depressed patients were *more* realistic in their self-perceptions than others. Specifically, when self-assessments of competencies were compared to the external ratings of observers, the match was closer among depressives than among normal people. Finally, Brim (1974) found in his study of adolescents that those high on "personal control"—universally interpreted as a desirable disposition—were more likely to *overestimate* their intelligence.

Completely accurate self-knowledge is thus not possible, nor is it a requirement of psychological well-being. In many cases these misconceptions about the self are harmless illusions that do no damage to social adjustment but do support feelings of self-worth.

None of this, of course, is intended to suggest that veridicality is unimportant or undesirable. Effective living is dependent largely on correct perceptions of reality, including the reality of the self; in the long run, substantially false perceptions will interfere with effective living. Unfortunately, our data do not enable us to assess factual accuracy; hence, there is no way to judge whether children or adolescents, or males and females, differ in these respects.

DISCUSSION

This effort to describe the nature of a healthy self-concept is, of course, little more than preliminary. For one thing, there is a good deal more to positive mental health than the dimensions of psychological well-being discussed in this chapter. Indeed, in her classic statement of the nature of positive mental health, Jahoda (1958) accorded little place to such emotional states. Second, there are many other dimensions of the self-concept that must be considered before we can hope to gain an adequate understanding of the subject matter.

The three adolescent studies available to us lacked measures of a number of other important self-concept dimensions, such as consistency (Gergen & Morse, 1967), individuation (Zimbardo, 1969), ego identity (Erikson, 1956), and self-monitoring (Snyder, 1979). Although these features of the self-concept may be associated with psychological euphoria–dysphoria, we were unable to explore such associations. Finally, our discussion has remained largely on the descriptive level. Although description is a useful first step in attempting to learn something about a problem, in no sense can it serve as a substitute for causal analysis. In this chapter we have not attempted to untangle the causal thicket; the reciprocal or cumulative effects are too complex at this point to straighten out theoretically, let alone empirically. In most, but not all, cases, we have been able to offer some empirical evidence, based on three studies of adolescents, that certain dimensions are indeed associated with signs of psychological well-being or disturbance. But the causal links among these variables remain to be discovered.

We believe that adolescence is a period of considerable self-concept turmoil but not all writers agree. Offer *et al.* (1981) find little evidence of such disturbance. There are at least two reasons why it is currently impossible to resolve this issue. The first is that so long as we lack agreement on the nature of a healthy self-concept, we are unable to ascertain whether it is disturbed. The second is that research on the self-concept across the life span, taking account of its multiple dimensions, remains to be undertaken. Until we are able to compare adolescents with people at other age stages in terms of a range of self-concept dimensions—self-esteem, mattering, incertitude, locus of control, vulnerability, and so forth—it will not be possible to say whether the self-concept is inordinately disturbed in adolescence. At this point we can only point to the following: for those self-concept dimensions for which data are in fact available, problems do appear to be particularly severe during adolescence; and for those dimensions for which little or no data are available, there are reasonable theoretical grounds for expecting self-concept problems to be inordinately severe at this age.

According to our data—and here we have had to depend on a single study—self-concept disturbance appears to be most acute during *early* adolescence, around the ages of 12–13. This is not true of all self-concept dimensions but it does appear to be true of most of them. The psychologically comfortable self-concepts of childhood are replaced by the acute disturbance of early adolescence, often (but not always) followed by some improvement in later adolescence.

This chapter has also explored the question of self-concept disturbance among girls. Many writers have contended that society treats women as inferior and incompetent and that women internalize these social definitions of their worth and develop feelings of inferiority. Careful reviews of the literature (Maccoby & Jacklin, 1974; Wylie, 1979), as well as current research (O'Malley & Bachman, 1979), however, suggest that the self-esteem differences of boys and girls are fairly minor. Such findings, however, do not support the conclusion that girls do not confront more serious self-concept problems than boys. During adolescence, girls' self-concepts are characterized by lesser certitude or stability, greater vulnerability, higher public anxiety, and a somewhat greater tendency to present a facade. These self-concept dimensions, furthermore, show decided associations with dysphoria. Girls thus do experience greater self-concept disturbance during adolescence but the problem is not one of self-esteem.

REFERENCES

Abramson, L. Y., Seligman, M. E. P., & Teasdale, J. D. (1978). Learned helplessness in humans: Critique and reformulation. *Journal of Abnormal Psychology, 87,* 49–74.

Allport, G. W. (1961). *Pattern and growth in personality.* New York: Holt, Rinehart & Winston.

Allport, G. W. (1968). The historical background of modern social psychology. In G. Lindzey & E. Aronson (Eds.), *The handbook of social psychology* (Vol. 1, 2nd ed., pp. 1–80). Reading, MA: Addison-Wesley.

Andrews, F. M., & Withey, S. B. (1976). *Social indicators of well-being.* New York: Plenum Press.

Ansbacher, H. L., & Rowena, R. (Eds.). (1956). *The individual psychology of Alfred Adler.* New York: Basic Books.

Backman, C. W., Secord, P. F., & Pierce, J. R. (1963). Resistance to change in the self-concept as a function of consensus among significant others. *Sociometry, 26,* 102–111.

Bachman, J. G., Kahn, R. L., Mednick, M. T., Davidson, T. N., & Johnston, L. D. (1967). *Youth in transition: Vol. I. Blueprint for a longitudial study of adolescent boys.* Ann Arbor, MI: Institute for Social Research.

Bandura, A. (1977). Self-efficacy: Toward a unifying theory of behavioral change. *Psychological Review, 84,* 191–215.

Beck, A. T. (1967). *Depression: Clinical, experimental and theoretical aspects.* New York: Hoeber Medical Division, Harper & Row.

Beebe, J. S. (1971). Self-concept and internal–external control in children and adolescents. *Dissertation and Abstracts International, 31,* 4966–4967.

Bem, D. J. (1967). Self-perception: An alternative interpretation of cognitive dissonance phenomena. *Psychological Review, 74,* 183–200.

Brim, O. G. (1974, September). *The sense of personal control over one's life.* Invited address to Divisions 7 and 8 of the American Psychological Association, New Orleans, LA.

Buss, A. H. (1980). *Self-consciousness and social anxiety.* San Francisco: W. H. Freeman.

Butler, J. M., & Haigh, G. V. (1954). Changes in the relation between self-concepts and ideal concepts consequent upon client-centered counseling. In C. R. Rogers & R. F. Dymond (Eds.), *Psychotherapy and personality change.* Chicago: University of Chicago Press.

Campbell, A. (1981). *The sense of well-being in America.* New York: McGraw-Hill.

Campbell, A., Converse, P. E., & Rodgers, W. L. (1976). *The quality of American life.* New York: Russell Sage.

Carlson, R. (1965). Stability and change in the adolescent's self-image. *Child Psychology, 36,* 659–666.

Carmines, E. G. (1978). Psychological origins of adolescent political attitudes: Self-esteem, political salience, and political involvement." *American Politics Quarterly, 6,* 167–186.

Cialdini, B., Borden, R. J., Thorne, A., Walker, M. R., Freeman, S., & Sloan, L. R. (1976). Basking in reflected glory: Three (football) field studies. *Journal of Personality and Social Psychology, 34,* 366–375.

Coleman, J. S., Campbell, E. Q., Hobson, C. J., McPartland, J., Mood, A. M., Weinfeld, F. D., & York, R. L. (1966). *Equality of educational opportunity.* Office of Education, U.S. Department of Health, Education, and Welfare. Washington, DC: U.S. Government Printing Office.

Combs, A. W., & Soper, D. W. (1959). The self, its derivate terms, and research. In A. E. Kuenzli (Ed.), *The phenomenological problem* (pp. 31–48). New York: Harper.

Crandall, R. (1973). The measurement of self-esteem and related constructs. In J. P. Robinson & P. R. Shaver (Eds.), *Measures of social psychological attitudes* (rev. ed., pp. 45–168). Ann Arbor, MI: Institute for Social Research.

Cronbach, L. J. (1951). Coefficient alpha and the internal structure of tests. *Psychometrika, 16,* 297–334.

de Charms, R. (1968). *Personal causation.* New York: Academic Press.

Dipboye, R. L. (1977). A critical review of Korman's self-consistency theory of work motivation and occupational choice. *Organizational Behavior and Human Performance, 18,* 108–126.

Duval, S., & Wicklund, R. A. (1972). *A theory of objective self-awareness.* New York: Academic Press.

Engel, M. (1959). The stability of the self-concept in adolescence. *Journal of Abnormal and Social Psychology, 58,* 211–215.

Epstein, S. (1973). The self-concept revisited: Or a theory of a theory. *American Psychologist, 28,* 404–416.

Epstein, S. (1981). The ecological study of emotions in humans. In P. Pliner, K. R. Blankstein, & I. Spigel (Eds.), *Advances in the study of communication and affect: Vol. 5. Perceptions of Emotions in Self and Others.* New York: Plenum Press.

Erikson, E. H. (1959). Identity and the life cycle: Selected papers. *Psychological Issues, 1,* 1–171.

Fenigstein, A., Scheier, M., & Buss, A. (1975). Public and private self-consciousness: Assessment and theory. *Journal of Counseling and Clinical Psychology, 43,* 522–527.

Franks, D. D., & Marolla, J. (1976). Efficacious action and social approval as interacting dimensions of self-esteem: Formulation through construct validation. *Sociometry*, *39*, 324–341.

Franzoi, S. L., & Reddish, B. J. (1980). Factor analysis of the stability of self scale. *Psychological Reports*, *47*, 1160–1162.

Fromm, E. (1941). *Escape from freedom*. New York: Rinehart.

Gecas, V. (1982). The self-concept. *Annual Review of Sociology*, *8*, 1–33.

Gergen, K. J., & Morse, S. J. (1967). Self-consistency: Measurement and validation. *Proceedings of the 75th Annual Convention of the American Psychological Association*, *2*, 207–208.

Goffman, E. (1956). *The presentation of self in everyday life*. Edinburgh: University of Edinburgh.

Goldman, R. K., & Mendelsohn, F. A. (1969). Psychotherapeutic change and social adjustment. *Journal of Abnormal Psychology*, *74*, 164–172.

Gurin, P., Gurin, G., Lao, R. C., & Beattie, M. (1969). Internal–external control in the motivational dynamics of Negro youth. *Journal of Social Issues*, *25*, 29–53.

Heiss, J., & Owens, S. (1972). Self-evaluations of blacks and whites. *American Journal of Sociology*, *78*, 360–370.

Horney, K. (1950). *Neurosis and human growth*. New York: Norton.

Jahoda, M. (1958). *Current concepts of positive mental health*. New York: Basic Books.

James. W. (1890). *The principles of psychology*. New York: Holt.

Jones, S. C. (1973). Self and interpersonal evaluations: Esteem theories versus consistency theories. *Psychological Bulletin*, *79*, 185–199.

Kaplan, H. B., & Pokorny, A. D. (1969). Self-derogation and psycho-social adjustment. *Journal of Nervous and Mental Disease*, *149*, 421–434.

Lane, R. (1981, June). *Government and self-esteem*. Paper presented at the Institute of the USA and Canada, Academy of Sciences, Moscow.

Lecky, P. (1945). *Self-consistency: A theory of personality*. New York: Island Press.

Lefcourt, H. M. (1976). *Locus of control: Current trends in theory and research*. Hillsdale. NJ: Erlbaum.

Lewinsohn, P. M., & Mischel, W. (1980). Social competence and depression: The role of illusory self-perceptions. *Journal of Abnormal Psychology*, *89*, 203–212.

Lowenthal, M. F., Thurner, M., & Chiriboga, D. (1975). *Four stages of life*. San Francisco: Jossey-Bass.

Maccoby, E. E., & Jacklin, C. N. (1974). *The psychology of sex differences*. Stanford, CA: Stanford University Press.

Macdonald, A. P. (1973). Internal–external locus of control. In J. P. Robinson & P. R. Shaver (Eds.), *Measures of social psychological attitudes* (Ch. 4). Ann Arbor, MI: Institute for Social Research.

Markus, H. (1977). Self-schemata and processing information about the self. *Journal of Personality and Social Psychology*, *35*, 63–78.

Maslow, A. H. (1954). *Motivation and personality*. New York: Harper.

McDougall, W. (1932). *The energies of men*. London: Methuen.

McGuire, W. J., & Padawer-Singer, A. (1976). Trait salience in the spontaneous self-concept. *Journal of Personality and Social Psychology*, *33*, 743–754.

Mead, G. H. (1934). *Mind, self and society*. Chicago: University of Chicago Press.

Milgram, N. A. (1971). Locus of control in Negro and white children at four age levels. *Psychological Reports*, *29*, 459–465.

Murphy, G. (1947). *Personality*. New York: Harper.

Offer, D., Ostrov, E., & Howard, K. I. (1981). *The Adolescent: A psychological self-portrait*. New York: Basic Books.

O'Malley, P. M., & Bachman, J. G. (1979). Self-esteem and education: Sex and cohort comparisons among high school seniors. *Journal of Personality and Social Psychology, 37*, 1153–1159.

O'Malley, P. M., & Bachman, J. G. (1983). Self-esteem: Change and stability between ages 13 and 23. *Developmental Psychology, 19*, 257–268.

Parloff, M. B., Kelman, H. C., & Frank, J. D. (1954). Comfort, effectiveness, and self-awareness as criteria of improvement in psychotherapy. *American Journal of Psychiatry, 3*, 343–352.

Pearlin, L. I. (1975). Sex roles and depression. In *Life-span developmental psychology: Normative life crises* (191–207). New York: Academic Press.

Pearlin, L. I., & Radabaugh, C. (1976). Economic strains and the coping functions of alcohol. *American Journal of Sociology, 82*, 652–663.

Piaget, J. (1951). *The child's conception of the world.* London: Routledge and Kegan Paul.

Proshansky, H., & Newton, P. (1968). The nature and meaning of Negro self-identity. In M. Deutsch, I. Katz, & A. R. Jensen (Eds.), *Social class, race, and psychological development* (178–218). New York: Holt, Rinehart & Winston.

Random House dictionary of the English language. Unabridged edition (1966). New York: Random House.

Reeder, L. G., Donohue, G. A., & Biblarz, A. (1960). Conceptions of self and others. *American Journal of Sociology, 66*, 153–159.

Roethlisberger, F. J., & Dickson, W. J. (1939). *Management and the worker.* Cambridge, MA: Harvard University Press.

Rogers, C. R. (1951). *Client-centered therapy: Its current practice, implications, and theory.* Boston: Houghton Mifflin.

Rosenberg, F., & Simmons, R. G. (1975). Sex differences in the self-concept in adolescence. *Sex Roles: A Journal of Research 1*, 147–159.

Rosenberg, M. (1963). Parental interest and children's self-conceptions. *Sociometry, 16*, 35–49.

Rosenberg, M. (1965). *Society and the adolescent self-image.* Princeton: Princeton University Press.

Rosenberg, M. (1979). *Conceiving the self.* New York: Basic Books.

Rosenberg, M. (1984, July). Depersonalization: The loss of identity in adolescence. Paper presented at Self and Identity Conference, Cardiff, Wales.

Rosenberg, M., & Kaplan, H. B. (Eds.). (1982). *Social psychology of the self-concept.* Arlington Heights, Il.: Harlan Davidson.

Rosenberg, M., & McCullough, B. C. (1981). Mattering: Inferred significance and mental health among adolescents. *Research in Community and Mental Health, 2*, 163–182.

Rosenberg, M., & Simmons, R. G. (1972). *Black and white self-esteem: The urban school child* (Monograph: Arnold and Caroline Rose Series.) Washington, DC: American Sociological Association.

Rotter, J. B. (1966). Generalized expectancies for internal versus external control of reinforcement. *Psychological Monographs 80* (1, Whole No. 609).

Sherwood, J. J. (1965). Self identity and referent others. *Sociometry, 28*, 66–81.

Sherwood, J. J. (1967). Increased self-evaluation as a function of ambiguous evaluations by referent others. *Sociometry, 30*, 404–409.

Shibutani, T. (1961). *Society and personality.* Englewood Cliffs, NJ: Prentice-Hall.

Shrauger, J. S., & Schoeneman, T. J. (1979). Symbolic interactionist view of self concept: Through the looking glass darkly. *Psychological Bulletin, 86*, 549–573.

Simmons, R. G., Rosenberg, F., & Rosenberg, M. (1973). Disturbance in the self-image at adolescence. *American Sociological Review, 38*, 553–568.

Smith, M. B. (1968). Competence and socialization. In J. Clausen (Ed.), *Socialization and society.* Boston: Little, Brown.

Sniderman, P. M. (1975). *Personality and democratic politics.* Berkeley: University of California Press.

Snyder, M. (1979). Self-monitoring processes. In L. Berkowitz (Ed.), *Advances in experimental social psychology* (Vol. 12). New York: Academic Press.

Snygg, D., & Combs, A. W. (1949). *Individual behavior: A new frame of reference for psychology.* New York: Harper.

Stone, L. J., & Church, J. (1957). *Childhood and adolescence.* New York: Random House.

White, R. W. (1959). Motivation reconsidered: The concept of competence. *Psychological Review, 66,* 297–333.

Whiting, B. E. (1982). *Determinants and consequences of mattering in the adolescents' social world.* Unpublished doctoral dissertation, University of Maryland College Park.

Wylie, R. (1974). *The self-concept: Revised Edition Vol. 1. A review of methodological considerations and measuring instruments.* Lincoln, NE: University of Nebraska Press.

Wylie, R. (1979). *The Self-Concept: Revised Edition. Vol. 2. Theory and research on selected topics.* Lincoln, NE: University of Nebraska Press.

Zimbardo, P. G. (1969). The human choice: Individuation, reason, and order versus deindividuation, impulse, and chaos. In W. J. Arnold & D. Levine (Eds.), *Nebraska Symposium on Motivation, 17.* Lincoln, NE: University of Nebraska Press.

7

Adolescent Self-Concept Development*

Jacqueline Smollar
James Youniss

INTRODUCTION

Several investigations of adolescent self-concept development have
addressed the issue of developmental continuity versus discontinuity
(Carlson, 1965; Constantinople, 1969; Dusek and Flaherty, 1981; Long,
Ziller, & Henderson, 1968; Monge, 1973). Discontinuity in development is defined as a qualitative change in the structure of the self-
concept, with quantitative changes over time signifying a continuous
developmental process (Dusek & Flaherty, 1981). One purpose of these
investigations was to assess the validity of the theoretical proposition
that adolescence represents a time of dramatic change in an individual's conception of self (McCandless, 1970). Such a change could be
the result of corresponding biological or social–psychological changes
which occur in adolescence marking it as a period of storm and stress
(Hall, 1904) or identity crisis (Erikson, 1968).

Although research results have been inconclusive with regard to this
question, two of the most comprehensive studies (Dusek & Flaherty,
1981; Monge, 1973) have demonstrated a continuity in the structure of
the self-concept throughout the adolescent period. Age differences that

* This study was supported by a research grant from the W. T. Grant Foundation, New
York, NY.

247

were found were slight and appeared to represent a slow continuous development rather than a dramatic shift. These findings lead Dusek & Flaherty (1981) to conclude that the adolescent self-concept does not reflect a period of storm and stress or identity crisis and further that ". . . the person who enters adolescence is basically the same as that who exits it" (p. 39).

The research discussed above has provided valuable information about self-conceptions in adolescence. In particular, their findings have shown that the self-concept consists of several aspects and cannot be conceptualized as a unitary phenomenon (Wylie, 1974). In addition, the investigators were able to organize various aspects of the self-concept into a factor structure thus facilitating the investigation of age changes in structural properties. Despite these contributions, however, the findings of Dusek & Flaherty (1981) and Monge (1973) do not necessarily warrant the conclusion that there are no qualitative changes in the self-concept during adolescence or that the individual who enters adolescence is basically the same as that who exits it. The difficulty with accepting such a conclusion from these research results is a function of both methodological and theoretical considerations.

The method of data collection utilized by Dusek & Flaherty (1981) and Monge (1973) was a 21-item semantic differential scale describing "my most characterisic self." This type of data collection presents a problem in the assessment of self-concept development in that the preselection of self-descriptions by an investigator does not allow for the possibility that new aspects of the self may emerge in adolescent self-conceptions that are not reflected in the items presented on the scale. Discontinuity in self-concept development may be a function of the incorporation of aspects into the concept of self that were not part of the self-concept at an earlier age, rather than a function of a shift in self-assessment with regard to particular characteristics of self (e.g., how "refreshed" or "tired" I am; how "friendly" or "unfriendly" I am). In fact, studies of younger children that allow free responding about the self have found developmental differences in the types of self-descriptions generated at different age levels (Guardo & Bohan, 1971; Montemayer & Eisen, 1977). Thus, it would appear that self-concept development in general as well as the issue of developmental continuity or discontinuity of the self-concept, cannot be fully assessed without allowing some opportunity for free responding among subjects.

From a theoretical perspective, the various conclusions regarding adolescent self-concept development (Carlson, 1965; Engel, 1959; Dusek & Flaherty, 1981; Long *et al.*, 1968; Monge, 1973; Montemayer & Eisen, 1977) are based on the assumption that the self-concept is a set of constructs about the way the self *is* which remains constant across changes in situational variables. It is assumed that there is such a thing as a "most characteristic self" and that an individual can describe "Who I am" or the "Way I am" without any external referent. Evidence from several studies of personality (Mischel, 1968) and from attribution-theory research (Jones *et al.*, 1972) suggest that such an assumption about the self-concept may not be entirely valid. If an individual's behavior and his or her attribution of characteristics to the self and other have been shown to vary significantly with changes in situational variables, it would seem entirely possible to propose that his or her self-concept may show similar situationally related variations. In fact, there is some evidence to support this proposition. One of the situational variables that has been found to affect the self-concept is the type of interpersonal relation in which the self is referenced. Scores on a self-esteem scale were found to vary significantly when subjects were given the external referents of father, mother, friend, and teacher (Gecas, 1972). In addition, assessments of self with regard to sensitivity to others and independence were significantly higher when the external referent was a friend than when it was a parent (Volpe, 1981).

The possibility that conceptions about the self may differ depending on the interpersonal context has important implications for assessing self-concept development. For one, developmental differences in the self-concept may be apparent in one relational context but not in another. Correspondingly, discontinuities in the development of the self-concept may be a function of the discrepancy in the conception of self between or among various relational contexts, rather than of the structure of the self-concept within any single relational context. This perspective is particularly plausible with respect to adolescent self-concept development since this period is generally seen as a time of restructuring interpersonal relations (McCandless, 1970).

A theoretical basis for the proposition that conceptions about the self may depend, at least in part, on the interpersonal context is found in Youniss's (1980) discussion of the developmental perspectives of Sullivan (1953) and Piaget (1932/1965). Through a synthesis of these theoretical perspectives into the Sullivan–Piaget thesis, Youniss proposes a view of social-cognitive development in which social understanding is viewed as developing through the individual's participation in interpersonal relations, and the cognitive organization of the interactions that take place within these relations into forms of interacting which characterize particular relations. The result of this cognitive process is that relations come to be known with respect to the types of interacting that characterize them, and that the *self* and *other* come to be known as a function of the relation and its characterisic form of interacting. Thus conceptions about the self in one type of relational context may be quite different from self-conceptions in another type of relation.

One purpose of this chapter, then, is to examine whether or not there are variations in conceptions about the self across relations and, if so, to determine the nature of the variations and assess the developmental properties of the self-concept within a given relational context. The relations chosen for investigation are those of parent–child and close-friend. These relations were selected for two reasons. First, theoretically, parent–child and close-friend relations are viewed as characterized by distinctly different forms of interacting (Hinde, 1978; Piaget, 1932/1965; Sullivan, 1953; Youniss, 1980). Interactions within parent–child relations are seen as primarily unilateral in form with the parent providing directives or information with regard to behavior and the child either complying or rejecting depending on possible outcomes. In contrast, friend interactions are viewed as mutual in form with both participants free to offer their conceptions to one another in an atmosphere of cooperation and mutual respect.

The second reason for the selection of these relations is based on some empirical evidence with regard to cognitions about these relations. Some studies have shown that parent–child and friend relations are conceptualized quite differently by children and adolescents (Volpe, 1980; Youniss, 1980) and that conceptions of these relations change with increasing age (Bigelow, 1977; La Gaipa, 1979; Reisman & Shorr, 1978; Volpe, 1980; Youniss, 1980). It is suggested here that if conceptions about the self are an aspect of conceptions about a given relational context, then these self-conceptions should demonstrate developmental changes corresponding to those found for relational conceptions.

An additional goal of this chapter is to address the issue of discontinuity versus continuity in self-concept development. More specifically to determine whether or not there is a qualitative change in the self-concept during adolescence. This question is assessed with respect to both the incorporation of aspects into the self-concept during adolescence that were not part of the self-concepts of younger children and the degree of discrepancy between the self-concept in parent–child and close-friend relations during adolescence.

METHOD AND ANALYSIS

This study involved individual interviews with 80 subjects, 20 at each of age levels: 10–11 years (preadolescents), 14–15 years (mid-adolescents), 18–19 years (late adolescents), and 22–23 years (young adults). Males and females were equally represented at each age level. All subjects were from middle to upper-middle class "intact" suburban families. The late adolescents and young adults lived away from their parents and were either in college or employed full time. All had several contacts with their parents during the course of the year prior to the interview.

Subjects were individually interviewed and asked to give three responses to the stem: "When I am with my close-friend of the same sex (mother, father) I am_____." They were also asked to state whether they felt they had changed in their relations with their close friend, mother and father, over the past 4–5 years and, if so, how they have changed. Several other questions, not pertaining to this chapter, were also asked of the subjects at this time.

Responses to the self-description task (i.e., "When I am with my mother, I am_____) were classified on the basis of content similarity into eight categories regardless of relational context. Interrater agreement on assignment of responses to categories was .94. The eight categories and the self-descriptions included are

1. *Content:* happy, relaxed, comfortable, secure, joyful
2. *Extroverted:* outgoing, talkative, playful, rowdy, joking
3. *Sociable/cooperative:* nice, friendly, helpful, obedient, polite
4. *Intimate/sensitive:* open, caring, loving, emotional
5. *Spontaneous:* free, myself, not worried about what the other will say
6. *Capable/serious:* intellectual, creative, intelligent, smart
7. *Hostile/withdrawn:* angry, defensive, cold, aloof, disgusted, rude
8. *Anxious:* confused, upset, feel worthless, tense, discouraged, frustrated

Subjects' responses to how they felt they had changed were also categorized on the basis of content similarity into the following categories:

1. *More sociable/cooperative:* "I am friendlier now." "I don't argue as much." "I cooperate more, I used to just fight."
2. *More intimate/sensitive:* "I am more concerned with their

needs now than before." "I am more sensitive to their feelings now." "I am more open. Not afraid to tell them anything."

3. *More capable/serious:* "I have my own ideas now and I express them." "I am more responsible now." "I'm more independent now, take charge of my own life."

4. *More hostile/anxious:* "I'm afraid of him now, afraid to say what I think." "I've become more hostile, fight more." "I'm more defensive now."

The frequency distributions of categories for age, gender, and relations were tabulated for both category sets and the distribution of perceived changes in self were analyzed by chi-square tests for independence for age and gender within each relational context.

Differences in self-conceptions between relations were assessed by establishing a similarity score. The three responses for each subject in one relation were compared with the responses for each of the other relations with regard to similarity of category. That is, if a subject gave a response categorized as intimate/sensitive in both relations under comparison, but none of the other categories were the same, he was given a score of 1. The possible range of similarity scores was 0 (no similarity) to 3 (identical). These scores were analyzed by a three-factor (Age × Sex × Relations) analysis of variance (ANOVA) with repeated measures across relations.

Self-Conceptions in Close-Friend Relations

The distribution of the self-description categories in the close-friend relation for age and gender are presented in Table 7.1. From a developmental perspective, there are two categories appearing frequently in the self-descriptions of adolescents and young adults that are not represented in the self-descriptions of preadolescents. These are intimate/sensitive (Category 4) and spontaneous (Category 5). Descriptions of self as extroverted (Category 2) and as sociable/cooperative (Category 3) appear more frequently in the responses of preadolescents than at other age levels. Slight gender differences in self-conceptions are apparent with regard to the categories intimate/sensitive (22% of female responses; 11% of male responses) and sociable/cooperative (4% of female responses; 15% of male responses).

The subjects' reports of their own changes within the context of close-friend relations were classified into the two categories shown in Table 7.2. The distribution of these categories was found to be dependent on the age (but not gender) of the subjects ($\chi^2[3] = 26.67$; p

TABLE 7.1
Descriptions of Self in Close-Friend Relations

Aspects of self	Age levels				Gender	
	10–11	14–15	18–19	22–23	F	M
1. Content	17	16	17	11	36	25
2. Extroverted	22	16	8	9	25	30
3. Sociable/cooperative	11	2	6	4	5	18
4. Intimate/sensitive	2	7	13	17	26	13
5. Spontaneous	0	13	13	16	21	21
6. Capable/serious	2	3	2	2	1	8
7. Hostile/withdrawn	4	2	0	0	2	4
8. Anxious	2	1	1	1	4	1

$< .001$). Preadolescents reported changes in self with regard to increases in sociability and cooperation while late adolescents and young adults indicated increases in intimacy and sensitivity. Midadolescents were evenly divided between the two categories.

The data presented above suggest that preadolescents (age 10–11) tend to see themselves in close-friend relations as content, extroverted, sociable, and cooperative and to describe their own development in terms of increasing sociability and cooperation. They are simply "better friends" than they were at age 5 or 6 years, nicer and more aware of the need to cooperate—to take the other person's perspective into account. In contrast, at late adolescence, subjects describe themselves as primarily content, intimate, sensitive, and spontaneous and tend to define their own self-development as an increase in their intimacy and sensitivity to the other. By this age, then, adolescents are not only aware of the need to cooperate in a friendship, but they also feel free

TABLE 7.2
Perceived Changes in Self over 4–5 Years in Close-Friend Relations[a]

Changes in self	Age levels			
	10–11	14–15	18–19	22–24
Increase in sociability/cooperation	14	10	3	1
Increase in intimacy/sensitivity	3	10	17	14
$n =$	17[b]	20	20	15[b]

[a]$\chi^2(3) = 26.67$.
[b]Missing n due to subjects who reported they had not changed.

enough to share their personal feelings and thoughts with one another and to be aware of the feelings and thoughts of the other.

These findings suggest that within the context of close-friend relations, conceptions of self undergo a qualitative change from preadolescence to adolescence. The self-concept of the adolescent incorporates a view of self as an intimate, sensitive, and spontaneous being. Such aspects of the self do not appear to be part of the self-concept of the preadolescent. While these qualitative changes do not imply a time of "storm and stress" or identity crisis, they do suggest that the individual who enters adolescence is qualitatively different from that who exits it, at least with regard to the close-friend relational context.

Self-Conceptions in Parent–Child Relations

The distribution of self-description categories across age and sex for parent–child relations are presented in Table 7.3. In the mother–child relational context, developmental changes are apparent with regard to descriptions of self as intimate/sensitive and as hostile/withdrawn. In both cases, these categories appear more frequently in the responses of adolescents and young adults than in those of preadolescents. Description of self as hostile/withdrawn appear most frequently in the self-descriptions of midadolescents. While there are no overall gender differences in responding, the categories of hostile/withdrawn and anxious did produce an Age × Gender interaction. That is, of the 18 responses falling into these two categories at age 14–15 years, 13 were provided by males, while of the 13 responses in these categories give at the 18–19 level, 11 were generated by females.

With respect to the father–child relational context, no clear developmental changes are apparent. There is, however, a dramatic increase in descriptions of self as hostile/withdrawn at the midadolescent level which is almost entirely accounted for by the descriptions of females at this age (11 out of the 13 responses were given by females). In the context of this relation, females were more likely than males to describe themselves as hostile, withdrawn, anxious, intimate, and sensitive.

In order to further examine the relationship between descriptions of self as hostile or anxious and the subject's age, sex, and type of parent–child relation, the three responses given by each subject for each parent–child relation were coded with either a "1," if they represented a response in Category 7 or 8, or a "0" if they did not. Each subject was then assigned a hostile/anxious score for each parent–child relation

TABLE 7.3
Descriptions of Self in Parent–Child Relations

Aspects of self	Age				Sex	
	10–11	14–15	18–19	22–24	Female	Male
	Mother–child relation					
1. Content	18	10	15	13	32	24
2. Extroverted	8	10	8	7	17	16
3. Sociable/cooperative	17	10	10	10	17	30
4. Intimate/sensitive	2	8	9	10	17	12
5. Spontaneous	0	2	3	2	5	2
6. Capable/serious	3	2	2	2	3	6
7. Hostile/withdrawn	3	12	8	8	16	15
8. Anxious	5	6	5	8	10	14
Miscellaneous	4	0	0	0	3	1
	Father-child relation					
1. Content	17	9	11	8	25	20
2. Extroverted	10	4	6	6	12	14
3. Sociable/cooperative	8	9	10	9	14	22
4. Intimate/sensitive	1	2	4	5	10	2
5. Spontaneous	1	0	4	1	1	5
6. Capable/serious	8	10	8	13	14	25
7. Hostile/withdrawn	2	13	4	6	16	9
8. Anxious	8	13	12	12	25	20
Miscellaneous	5	0	1	0	3	3

ranging from "0" to "3," determined by summing the scores for each of the three responses. These scores were then analyzed by an Age × Gender × Relation ANOVA with repeated measures across relations. The results of this analysis were a significant finding for age (F [3,72] = 3.62; $p < .05$) and a significant Relation × Gender interaction (F [1,72] = 5.71; $p < .05$). The significant finding for age was further analyzed using Duncan's multiple range test (alpha .05). Preadolescents were found to have lower hostile/anxious scores than any of the other age groups, and midadolescents were found to have higher hostile–anxious scores than late adolescents. The significant Gender × Relation interaction was further analyzed by an F test for simple effects. It was found that females had significantly higher hostile/anxious scores in the father–child relation than in the mother–child relation ($F = 3.97$; $p < .05$) while males did not differentiate.

Subjects' descriptions of how they had changed over the past 4 or 5

TABLE 7.4

Perceived Changes in Self in the Context of Mother–Child and Father–Child Relations

How self has changed	Age in years				Sex	
	10–11	14–15	18–19	22–23	Female	Male
Mother–child relation[a]						
Increase in cooperation/sociability	6	3	4	2	10	5
Increase in capability/seriousness	9	9	6	7	6	25
Increase in intimacy/sensitivity	0	7	10	10	22	5
	15[b]	20	20	19[b]	38	35
Father–child relation						
Increase in cooperation/sociability	2	2	6	0	3	7
Increase in capability/seriousness	2	3	1	9	3	12
Increase in intimacy/sensitivity	0	5	7	7	14	5
Increase in hostility/anxiety	2	5	3	0	9	1
	6[b]	15[b]	17[b]	16[b]	29	25

[a]$\chi^2(3)$ [with Categories 1 & 2 combined] = 12.25; $p < .05$. Gender differences: $\chi^2(2)$ = 23.93; $p < .001$.
[b]Missing n due to subjects reporting no change in self.

years in the context of parent–child relations were classified into the categories presented in Table 7.4. For the mother–child relation, description of change was found to be dependent on the gender $(\chi^2[3] = 23.93)$ and age of subjects $(\chi^2[3] = 12.25; p < .05;$ with Categories 1 and 2 combined). Females and adolescents were more likely than males and preadolescents to describe change in terms of an increase in intimacy and sensitivity, while males were more likely to describe themselves as more capable or serious. Increases in intimacy/sensitivity were given almost exclusively by adolescents and young adults. The distribution for the father-child relation could not be analyzed because of the large number of subjects reporting no change in self in the context of the father-child relation. It is important to note, however, that the five subjects reporting increases in hostility and anxiety at the midadolescent level were all females.

The data presented above depict a more complex picture of self-concept development than the results for the close-friend relational context. As in the close-friend relation, however, there does appear to be a qualitative shift in conceptions of self from preadolescence to adolescence with regard to the inclusion of descriptions of self as intimate/sensitive into the self-concept, particularly in the context of the mother–child relation. There also appears to be a shift from preadolescence to adolescence in the frequency of descriptions of self as hostile, withdrawn, and anxious although the frequency of these descriptions is highest at midadolescence and depends upon the gender of both the subject and the parent. In general, it appears that at some time during adolescence, there is an awareness of self as hostile and/or anxious in the context of parent–child relations that is not apparent at the preadolescent level. This aspect of self may be included in the self-concept with regard to one parent-child relation but not the other, or it may be an aspect of self in the context of both relational perspectives.

Variations in Self-Conceptions across Relational Contexts

The distribution of the eight categories of self-descriptions across the three relations are presented in Table 7.5. The close-friend relation is clearly differentiated from parent–child relations by the relatively high frequency of descriptions of self as intimate/sensitive and spontaneous and the relatively low frequency of descriptions of self as capable/serious, hostile/withdrawn, and anxious. The father–child relational context differs from the others in the frequency of descriptions

TABLE 7.5
Self-Descriptions in Three Relational Contexts

	Relations		
Descriptions	Close–friend	Mother–child	Father–child
1. Content	61	56	45
2. Extroverted	55	33	26
3. Sociable/cooperative	23	47	36
4. Intimate/sensitive	39	29	12
5. Spontaneous	42	7	6
6. Capable/serious	9	9	39
7. Hostile/withdrawn	6	31	25
8. Anxious	5	24	45
Miscellaneous	0	4	6

of self as capable/serious and as anxious and the low frequency of descriptions of self as intimate, sensitive, or spontaneous.

In general, the self-concept in the close-friend relational context is dominated by the aspects of contentment, extroversion, spontaneity, and intimacy. Within the mother–child relational context, the dominant features of the self-concept are contentment, sociability, extroversion, and hostility, while in the father–child context they are contentment, anxiety, capability, and sociability.

These data demonstrate that self-conceptions vary considerably across relational contexts, particularly with regard to parent–child and close-friend relations. In order to analyze the effect of age and gender in this difference, the similarity scores established for the mother–father, mother–friend, and father–friend relations were analyzed as described in the methods section.

Similarity scores were found to decrease significantly with increasing age $(F\ [3,72] = 5.72;\ p < .01)$. Applications of Duncan's Multiple Range Test (alpha .05) resulted in significant differences between preadolescents and all other age groups. Preadolescents had more similar self conceptions across relations than did midadolescents and young adults. Similarity scores were also found to vary as a function of the relations being compared $(F\ [2,160] = 5.44;\ p < .001)$. That is, the father–friend comparison was found to be significantly more different than the mother–friend or the mother–father comparisons.

These results suggest that self-conceptions do vary across relational contexts and that the degree of variation is itself a function of development. That is, conceptions of self became more disparate across relational contexts from preadolescence to adolescence. This age difference suggests another type of qualitative change in the structure of the self-concept.

Self-Concept Development

According to the findings presented above, the dominant features of the self-concept in close-friend relations at preadolescence are contentment, extroversion, sociability, and cooperation (83% of all self-descriptions). Changes in the self are described primarily in terms of increasing sociability or willingness to cooperate. Thus close-friend relations during preadolescence appear to provide a context for the expression of prosocial aspects of the self. Friends are people with whom one is happy and playful and friendship is conceptualized as a relation requiring helpfulness, consideration, and cooperation. These features of the self are also prevalent in the preadolescent's view of self in the context of the mother–child relation, although not to the same extent (72%). In this relation, however, preadolescents were less likely to describe themselves as extroverted and more likely to focus on the aspects of sociability and cooperation. At this age level most of the "cooperative" self-descriptions in the parent–child relations involve compliance (e.g., "good," "obedient," "trying to please"). For preadolescents, then, the mother–child relation also provides a context for the expression of prosocial aspects of the self, with the particular nature of this sociability and cooperation involving a compliance with the behavioral expectations of the mother.

The major variation in self-concept at the preadolescent level occurs in the father–child relational context where contentment, extroversion and sociability still appear frequently as aspects of self (58%), but different features such as capable, serious, and anxious also emerge with relatively high frequency (27%). For preadolescents, the father–child relation is one in which feelings of contentment and anxiety coexist and the self is seen as capable and serious as well as extroverted and sociable. This joint appearance of the features of capable/serious and anxious as aspects of the self-concept in the father–child relation may be related. If the father–child relation is viewed as one requiring an expression of self as having various capabilities and serious attitudes, this very requirement may be causative of the anxious feelings also attributed to the self in this relational context. Some support for this proposition may be found in the fact that in the father–child relation, where descriptions of self as capable/serious account for 16% of all self-descriptions, anxiety accounts for 19% of self-descriptions.

In contrast, in the mother–child relations where the aspect capable/serious was given by only 4% of the subjects, descriptions of self as anxious account for only 10% of all self-descriptions.

By midadolescence, the dominant features of the self-concept in close-friend relations are contentment, extroversion, and spontaneity (75%). As for preadolescents, the self is seen as happy and playful in close-friend relations, but the relation itself is now seen as one allowing the self to *be* the self, that is, spontaneous. This emergence of spontaneity as a major feature of the self-concept in close-friend relations suggests that by midadolescence individuals are aware that there *can* be a difference between a "real self" and a "self as actor" and that a real self can only be expressed in a relation where actions and feelings are received by the other in an atmosphere that is accepting and nonjudgmental. This point is underscored by the very low frequency of descriptions of self as spontaneous in either of the parent–child relations, coupled with the high frequency of descriptions of self as hostile/withdrawn at this age level. The emergence of a view of self as angry, defensive, and withdrawn at midadolescence may be a function of the awareness that one cannot be a real self in parent–child relations because the consequences may be highly negative to the self.

In comparison to preadolescents, the self-concept of midadolescents is more differentiated across relational contexts and incorporates an awareness of a distinction between the "way I am" and the "way I act." The major change that occurs at late adolescence simply involves an incorporation of the aspects of intimacy and sensitivity into the self-concept, primarily in the context of close-friend relations. At the two older age levels, contentment, intimacy, sensitivity, and spontaneity account for 72% of all self-descriptions. This finding suggests that once there is a cognitive awareness of the separation of real self and self as actor, the self can begin to express more personal aspects, when the relational context is appropriate, and to be aware of the personal feelings and aspects of another.

DISCUSSION

The data reported here have several important implications for understanding self-concept development in adolescence. First, it is clear that the self-concept not only consists of several aspects or features, but that many of these features are a part of the self-concept in one relational context but not another. A view of self as capable or serious, for example, occurred almost exclusively in the context of the father–child relations, while a perception of self as spontaneous or free was found only in the close-friend relational contexts. In addition, the incorporation of the features of hostility and anxiety into a concept of self occurred in the parent–child relational contexts but not the close-friend context.

These relational discrepancies in the self-concept appear to reflect the nature of the relation itself. Friendship relations have been found to be conceptualized by subjects of similar ages to those studied here in terms of mutual respect, cooperation, and intimacy (Bigelow, 1977; Bigelow & LaGaipa, 1975; Kon & Losenkov, 1978; Reisham & Shorr, 1978; Smollar & Youniss, 1984; Youniss, 1980; Youniss & Volpe, 1978) thus allowing for a view of self as spontaneous, open, and sensitive to other. Similarly, parent–child relations seem to be conceptualized in terms of authority, dominance and unilateral respect (Volpe, 1980; Youniss, 1980) corresponding to a perception of self as hostile or anxious vis-à-vis the parent. In addition, a finding that father–child relations are characterized principally by instrumental interactions involving parental instruction or assistance (Breznitz & Kugelmass, 1965; Dahlem, 1970; Osofsky & O'Connell, 1972; Volpe, 1980) corresponds to the emergence of a self-view as capable or serious in this relational context.

In summary, concepts about the self were found to vary across relational contexts and these variables are reflected in conceptions about the relations themselves. This finding suggests that the nature or structure of the self-concept cannot be fully understood without a consideration of the various types of relations individuals are involved in and how they conceptualize these relations. Such an approach would appear to be particularly useful when studying the development of the self-concept since from early childhood to old age individuals are continually involved in new types of relations or in a restructuring of old relations that would have implications for a changing view of self.

With respect to development of the self-concept, this study found that adolescents conceptualized the self in ways that were quite different from the self-conceptions of preadolescents. In fact, variation in the self-concept across relations was itself developmentally related in that adolescents and young adults tended to differentiate the self across relations to a significantly higher degree than did preadolescents. This increase in differentiation suggests a qualitative difference in the structure of the self-concept of adolescents and preadolescence. While some researchers may view increased differentiation as indicative of a "storm and stress" period or an identity crisis, such a conclusion is not necessarily justified. Instead, it is possible that the differentiation of self across relational contexts is a productive developmental process that begins in adolescence and continues throughout the life span. Rather than an identity crisis, such a differentiation may reflect an identity development in which the self comes to be understood as constituting different features in different types of relations just as in social development relations themselves come to be further differentiated with respect to the types of interactions that characterize them. While this last point is highly speculative at this time, it is included here only to underscore the possibility that qualitative changes or developmental discontinuity in the structure of the self-concept at adolescence may not indicate a disorganization or disorientation of the self in reaction to biological or social psychological events, but rather a cognitive reorganization of conceptions of self perhaps in response to corresponding changes in biological, cognitive, and interpersonal processes.

In addition to the emergence of a higher differentiation of self across relations during adolescence, self-concepts in adolescence were also found to incorporate features not present in the self-concept of preadolescents. In the context of close-friend relations, aspects of self such as intimacy, sensitivity and spontaneity do not emerge with any frequency until adolescence, but by late adolescence they are dominant features of the self-concept. This age change with respect to concepts of self within close-friend relations corresponds to age changes found in conceptions of this relation itself. Several studies have found that concepts of friend relations begin to include notions of intimacy and sensitivity during adolescence (Bigelow, 1977; Kon & Losenkov, 1978; LaGaipa, 1979; Smollar & Youniss, 1984; Youniss & Volpe, 1978). It has also been found that during adolescence, friendship comes to be conceptualized as a relation of mutual acceptance (Smollar & Youniss, 1984) thus allowing for the emergence of a view of self as spontaneous or free.

The new aspects of self which emerge during adolescence in the context of parent–child relations are those of hostility and anxiety. These feature of the self are particularly dominant at age 14–15. This finding suggests that at some time during midadolescence, the self within the context of one or both parent–child relations is reconstructed to incorporate reactions or feelings about the authority role or unilateral control of the parent. This finding regarding self-concept in parent–child relations corresponds to conceptions about parent–child relations themselves. Volpe (1980) found that mid- and late-adolescents tended to conceptualize parent–child relations as more unilateral in form than did preadolescents or young adults. In addition, the "Gender × Relation" interaction found with respect to the self-concept was reiterated in that females described the father–child relation as more unilateral than the mother–child relation, while males did not differentiate to the same extent.

In conclusion, the results of this study support the proposition that self-concept development in adolescence is discontinuous. That is, the self-concepts of adolescents are qualitatively different from those of preadolescents in several ways. Yet it is clear that these qualitative differences would not have been uncovered without utilization of a relational perspective and a method of free responding. At the same time, such a method also presents problems for analysis since it does not allow for more sophisticated forms of analysis and perhaps allows for too much "experimenter bias." Thus it appears that future work on self-concept development requires a corresponding methodological development once the relevant variables have been identified. In addition, as Dusek & Flaherty (1981) point out, some longitudinal work is necessary in order to validate these developmental trends, although the age span required for differences to appear (i.e., sometimes 4 to 5 years) make this a difficult undertaking. Finally, the relationship found here of self-concept development to the development of concepts about interpersonal relations supports the theoretical perspective on cognitive-social development provided by the Sullivan–Piaget thesis (Youniss, 1980). That is, the development of social understanding proceeds as a function of participation in interperonal relations and individual interactions and events can have meaning for the self only as an aspect of the relation in which they occur. This means that different types of relations would have different implications for development both of a concept of self and a concept of the social world. Clearly the role that self-concept development plays in the development of more general social understanding would be a productive concern for future research.

REFERENCES

Bigelow, B. J. (1977). Children's friendship expectations: A cognitive developmental study. *Child Development, 48,* 246–253.

Bigelow, B. J., & LaGaipa, J. J. (1975). Children's written descriptions of friendship: A multi-dimensional analysis. *Developmental Psychology, 11,* 857–888.

Breznitz, S., & Kugelmass, S. (1965). The perception of parents by adolescents: Consideration of the instrumentality-expressivity difference. *Human Relations, 18,* 103–113.

Carlson, R. (1965). Stability and change in the adolescent's self-image. *Child Development, 36,* 659–666.

Constantinople, A. (1969). An Eriksonian measure of personality development in college students. *Developmental Psychology, 1,* 357–372.

Dahlem, N. W. (1970). Young Americans' reported perceptions of their parents. *Journal of Psychology, 74,* 187–194.

Dusek, J. B., & Flaherty, J. F. (1981). *The development of self-concept during the adolescent years. Monographs of the Society for Research in Child Development, 46.*

Engel, M. (1959). The stability of the self-concept in adolescence. *Journal of Abnormal and Social Psychology, 58,* 211–215.

Erikson, E. H. (1968). *Identity, youth, and crisis.* New York: Norton.

Gecas, V. (1972). Parental behavior and contextual variations in adolescent self-esteem. *Sociometry, 35,* 332–345.

Guardo, E. J., & Bohan, J. B. (1971). Development of a sense of self-identity in children. *Child Development, 42,* 1909–1921.

Hall, E. S. (1904). *Adolescence* (2 Vols.). New York: Appleton.

Hinde, R. A. (1978). Interpersonal relations: In quest of a science. *Psychological Medicine, 8,* 373–386.

Jones, E. E., Kanouse, D. E., Kelley, H. H., Nisbett, R. E., Valins, S., & Weiner, B. (Eds.). (1972). *Attribution: Perceiving the cause of behavior.* Morristown, NJ: General Learning Press.

Kon, I. S., & Losenkov, V. A. (1978). Friendship in adolescence: Values and behavior. *Journal of Marriage and the Family, 40,* 143–155.

LaGaipa, J. J. (1979). A developmental study of the meaning of friendship in adolescence. *Journal of Adolescence, 2,* 201–213.

Long, B. H., Ziller, R. C., & Henderson, E. H. (1968). Developmental changes in the self-concept during adolescence. *School Review, 76,* 210–230.

McCandless, B. R. (1970). *Adolescents: Behavior and development.* Hindsdale, IL: Dryden.

Mischel, W. (1968). *Personality and assessment.* New York: Wiley,

Monge, R. H. (1973). Developmental trends in factors of adolescent self-concept. *Developmental Psychology, 8,* 382–393.

Montemayor, R., & Eisen, M. (1977). The development of self-conceptions from childhood to adolescence. *Developmental Psychology, 13,* 314–319.

Osofsky, J. D., & O'Connell, E. J. (1972). Parent–child interaction. *Developmental Psychology, 7,* 157–168.

Piaget, J. (1965). *The moral judgment of the child* (M. Gabain, Trans.). New York: New York Free Press. (Original work published 1932)

Reishman, J. M., & Shorr, S. I. (1978). Friendship claims and expectations among children and adults. *Child Development, 49,* 913–916.

Smollar, J., & Youniss, J. (1984). Social development through friendship. In K. Rubin & H. Ross (Eds.), *Peer relationships and social skills in childhood.* New York: Springer Verlag.

Sullivan, H. S. (1953). *The interpersonal theory of psychiatry.* New York: Norton.

Volpe, J. (1980). *The development of concepts of parent-child and friend relations and of self within these relations.* Unpublished doctoral dissertation, The Catholic University of America, Washington, DC.

Volpe, J. (1981). The development of concepts of self: An interpersonal perspective. In J. A. Meacham & N. R. Santilli (Eds.), *Social development in youth: Structure & content.* Basel, Switzerland: S. Karger.

Wylie, R. C. (1974). *The self-concept.* Lincoln: University of Nebraska Press.
Youniss, J., & Volpe, J. (1978). A relational analysis of children's friendship. In W. Damon (Ed.), *Social cognition* (pp. 1–22). San Francisco: Jossey-Bass.
Youniss, J. (1980). *Parents and peers in social development.* Chicago: University of Chicago Press.

8

The Costs of Development:
Clinical Implications

Robert L. Leahy

THE COSTS OF DEVELOPMENT

Evolutionary theory and the idea of progress have had a pervasive influence on developmental theorists from G. Stanley Hall to Jean Piaget. The development of the child is identified as the structural companion of the acquisition of knowledge, values, skills, flexibility, and adaptation. It is an optimistic business, tracing the growth of the individual from a state of dependency to an adult functioning independently within a complex society. We speak of internalizing the values of ego ideals, parents, and models as if the child were to become increasingly similar to and immersed in the perspectives of the wider groups to which he belongs. In this chapter I play the devil's advocate to this optimistic developmentalism. Rather than stress the advantages of development, I argue that development carries costs. It is an argument which, to borrow from Freud (1962), weighs the "discontents" of development along with its achievements. It is not a proposal that fixation or repression at earlier stages is desirable: Rather, I shall propose that with the development of social cognition and the self-image there are negative as well as positive consequences which we should not ignore.

The rationale guiding this speculation is that certain forms of psy-

chopathology, or certain interpersonal problems, are partly a consequence of *higher* developmental level. The major focus is on the development of depression, especially self-critical depression, which may
depend, for some individuals, on increased cognitive capacity. Thus,
the view advanced here is that development marks changes in the style
of psychopathology rather than the alleviation of difficulties.

I argue that our understanding of psychopathology may be partly
enhanced by a brief excursion into this more pessimistic view that
development carries "costs." At the same time, I recognize that the
benefits of higher developmental functioning are revealed by its association with generally more favorable prognosis. However, this is an
exercise in examining a side of development that often is left
unexamined.

Development as Adaptation

A general assumption guiding developmental theories is that the
course of individual development is marked by *adaptation* to the environment or to individual conflicts. Piaget's (1970) theory of intellectual development stresses the balance (equilibration) of assimilation
and accommodation which attempts to "adapt" knowing to the structure of cognitive schemes or the structure of the environment. Thus,
knowledge of the world may not be direct apprehension of external
reality, but this knowledge is nonetheless determined by experience in
the world or reflection on this experience. Increasing development,
then, results in intelligence which is increasingly more "adapted" in
that it is more flexible, independent of immediate experience, or more
abstract. Thus, the developmental process is described in the optimistic perspective of stages which unfold in a universal sequence and
which resolve the cognitive limitations or conflicts of earlier levels of
thought.

Werner's (1948) theory of cognitive development is also based on the
optimistic view of the orthogenetic principle: Increasing age or intelligence is associated with thinking that is more differentiated or hierarchical. Research during the past decade on social cognition—for example, role taking or moral judgment—similarly stresses the advantages in social functioning associated with advanced social cognition.
This research compares the superior social cognitive level of individuals who are "normal" with those who are delinquent (Chandler,
1973) or emotionally disturbed (Chandler, Greenspan, & Barenboim,
1974; Sampson, 1981).

Notwithstanding the significant contribution of these cognitive-developmental approaches, the purpose of the present chapter is to advance the view that cognitive development may result in negative consequences of development: Rather than emphasize adaptation, I stress the *costs* of development.

The plan of this chapter is to present a basic outline of the cognitive theory of depression. Second, a developmental analysis of depression is described; this analysis attempts to integrate Beck's cognitive theory with Bowlby's description of the effects of early loss on subsequent depression. Specifically, Guidanno and Liotti's view that early object relations set the stage for schematic processing of self–other relations is the basis of this developmental analysis. Third, the fundamental principles of a structural-developmental model of the development of the self, which are described in Chapter 3 (Leahy & Shirk) of this volume, are reviewed. In this section the possible negative consequences of the development of social cognition are examined. The final section describes developmental transformations of self-schemes by case history of developmental cognitive therapy for a chronically depressed adult patient.

Throughout this chapter my emphasis is on a specific kind of depression—*self-critical depression*. The primary symptomatology of self-critical depression is hatred of the self, belief that the past is filled with failures, suicidal ideation, and hopelessness. It is this which I refer to when I speak of a *cost* of development.

COGNITIVE THEORY

The last decade has been marked by a surge of interest in the cognitive components of a variety of emotional disorders. Although the roots of such a revolution in models of psychopathology may be found in earlier writings (Ellis, 1962; Horney, 1945; Kelley, 1955), Beck and his colleagues have attempted to identify the specific cognitions associated with the major affective disorders (Beck, 1976; Beck, Rush, Shaw, & Emery, 1979).

General Principles

A central tenet of cognitive theory is that each of the emotional disorders may be characterized by a distinctive set of thoughts. For example, the depressive believes in the "negative triad"—that is, a negative view of self, experience, and the future (Beck, 1976). The anxious patient believes that something "awful" is likely to happen (Beck & Emery, 1979), and the agoraphobic patient believes that he will lose control of either his mind or his physical being and, consequently, become insane or die (Beck, 1983, personal communication).

Although a common misunderstanding among critics of cognitive theory is that cognitive theory proposes that thinking creates feelings, this is not the assumption advanced by Beck (see Riskind, 1983). Affect and cognition may be viewed as contributing mutually to one another such that mood-induced sadness (affect) may produce depressive cognitions (Clark & Teasdale, 1982) and depressive cognitions may produce sadness (Beck et al, 1979). However, given the emphasis on hydraulic energies in psychoanalysis, lack of rewards in the behavioral models, and biochemical influences in the physiological models of depression and anxiety, it certainly appears to be an important contribution of cognitive theory to recognize the influence of thought on emotion.

The three constructs used in cognitive theory to describe these thought processes are *automatic thoughts, maladaptive assumptions,* and *early schemes.* Automatic thoughts are ideas which are plausible, spontaneous, and associated with negative feelings. These automatic thoughts often entail cognitive distortions such as dichotomous thinking ("I am totally worthless"), overgeneralization ("Everyone will reject me"), personalizing ("He said that because he thinks I'm worthless"), and selective focus on the negative ("That mistake proves I'm worthless"). Maladapative assumptions refer to the general values that a person has, such as "I must be perfect," "Bad things happen to bad people," "If people don't love me, then I am worthless."

Recently, Guidano and Liotti (1983) have expanded on Beck's (1976) and Beck, Rush, Shaw, and Emery's (1979) reference to early schemes to describe a *developmental analysis* which attempts to assist the patient in uncovering the origins and nature of early ideas of self–other relations. Early schemes are those ideas about the self that determine the manner by which the individual searches for information to confirm the validity of early self-labels. Examples of early schemes are "I am a bad person," "Others will reject me," "Others are my salvation," "Abandonment means I am nothing," "I may die soon," "My self is chaotic." Seldom does the patient early in therapy ennunciate these early schemes: More commonly the patient will be able to identify the automatic thoughts associated with anger or depression.

Schematic Processing

According to cognitive theory the individual's conception of self and other is determined by "schemes" which determine the kinds of information which the individual will consider as relevant to himself. *Schemes* are the habitual patterns of thought that determine the way in which the individual focuses attention on information or remembers events. According to the schematic-processing model, information that is consistent with a scheme is more likely to be either stored in or retrieved from memory. For example, the individual with a scheme, "I am a loser," is more likely to retain and retrieve details about past failures. Furthermore, schemes may alter memory retrieval such that the individual may falsely recognize or construct information that is consistent with the scheme. An example of this would be the depressive's tendency to exaggerate the degree of his "failure" in a situation.

An interesting point advanced by Guidano and Liotti (1983) is that schemes determine the manner by which individuals *inquire* about self and others. In this sense, schemes are like the "patterns of discovery" which Hanson (1965) suggested are "theory-driven"—that is, inquiries or experiments usually are determined by a theory—they are not haphazard. Thus, if the depressive believes that he is a failure, his "inquiries" or experiments will be designed to confirm that hypothesis—not out of masochism, but rather out of schematic processing. As a consequence, the depressive may not attempt novel behaviors that could dispel him from his theory of failure. The depressive would not be inclined to approach new people at a party because he believes he will be rejected, even though he might obtain information to the contrary. Similarly, the paranoid may assume others are hostile and respond in kind, thereby provoking others and confirming his hypothesis that others are hostile. The irony of the schematic-processing model is that it suggests that man is a poor scientist, to paraphrase Kelly (1955). It is as if the person begins with the conclusion ("I am a loser") and then seeks out confirmatory evidence without attempting to find evidence to the contrary.

Formation and Persistence of Schemas

According to the cognitive theory of emotional disorders (Beck, 1976; Beck *et al.*, 1979), the individual may form *schemas* or models of the self and the environment during early childhood. These models or schemas remain dormant until they are activated by a stressful life experience. Once activated, the schema becomes self-perpetuating. For example, the depressive may have a schema reflecting the "negative triad" (Beck, 1976) by which the self, experience, and the future are viewed in a negative fashion. This negative triad is activated by a stressor, such as a loss of a love object or a job. We may view the negative triad as an *expanding prototype* in that it begins to seek confirmation of its negative premises by testing reality in a biased fashion. Thus, the depressive who experiences the breakup of a relationship begins to view the breakup as indicative of his lack of worth as a person, not only in relationships, but in his work or private life as well. Further, the effect of the stressor may be to lead to selective recall of many other past failures that confirm his negative view of himself.

The cognitive components of depression entail a number of cognitive errors which may be found among many nondepressed individuals in a less pronounced and less self-defeating manner. For example, the depressive will *overgeneralize* from a single instance to believe that this is indicative of all future experiences (Beck *et al.*, 1979). Thus, the depressive who suffers a loss at work may begin to see his or her personal relationships as failures and predict continued failure in similar and different experiences in the future. This overgeneralization is reminiscent of a "spreading activation" effect in memory (in this case, both retrospective memory and prospective anticipation): The negative prototype spreads to trigger off recollections of other losses which help confirm the belief that the future will be just as bleak. What might have been perceived as minor setbacks in the past when they occurred, now during the depressive phase are viewed as major failures in a pattern of downward spirals of catastrophe.

A similar cognitive error is reflected in what Beck (1976) refers to as *dichotomous thinking*—that is, the belief that experiences can only be placed at the extremes of a bipolar dimension ("I am a *total* failure," "My job is *totally* boring"). This kind of thinking is similar to the rigid classifications of the young preoperational child (Inhelder & Piaget, 1964). It is also similar to what Werner (1948) describes as undifferentiated thought in that the world or the self is viewed in global terms, rather than along a continuum of degrees. For example, we have found that young children are able to sort personality traits into categories of masculine and feminine (i.e., girls and boys) (Leahy & Shirk, 1984). However, when asked whether there are boys who manifest feminine behavior or girls who manifest masculine behavior, the younger child, lacking multiple classification skill, denies the possibility of these instances. Similarly, in the description of the self, the younger adolescent is less likely than the older adolescent to refer to middle points along the continuum of personality traits in describing the self, that is, he or she is less likely to qualify self-descriptions (Leahy, 1976).

The inability to view experience or the self along a continuum may reflect the depressive's inability to apply seriation skills to the self-concept. In *seriation*, the individual is able to compare degrees or magnitudes of differences such that transitivity relationships are recognized. For example, we may view height in terms of the transitivity of measurement of inches: If Susan is taller than Bill and Bill is taller than Mike, is Susan taller than Mike? This ability to perform seriation on symbolic content (i.e., names of individuals) requires formal operational thought. Most adults are capable of recognizing degrees of existence of personality traits—for example, we generally recognize that some people are more intelligent than others, but that there are different degrees of intelligence. The depressive may claim that he is *completely* stupid because he makes one mistake, whereas others are intelligent because they did not make that mistake.

Because many of these depressive self-schemes are formed during early childhood, they carry with them many of the qualities of preoperational thought. They follow what Piaget has described as *egocentric logic*—they are based on intuition rather than empirical facts, they often are experienced as images rather than direct logical inferences, they are dichotomous rather than continuous, and they entail early qualities of moral realism. When the individual is free from depression, his thinking about the self may be developmentally advanced. However, the occurrence of a stressor that precipitates a depressive episode activates these earlier schemes about the self, including their preoperational quality. In this sense, depressive schemes appear to be *regressive*.

EARLY SCHEMES OF VULNERABILITY

According to Guidano and Liotti (1983) the depressive may begin early in life with a set of assumptions about self–world–other relations which lead him to select information that confirms his idea that he is helpless. What are these early ideas that the depressive holds that are activated later in life when there is a loss of love, prestige, or rewards?

Bowlby (1969) has indicated that many depressives have experienced either the death or separation of a parent early in life. Since the very young child is ill-equipped to provide for himself with the absence of a parent, this may establish the fear that the other parent may leave, thereby rendering the child completely helpless (Wallerstein & Kelly, 1980). Thus, the depressive's early self-scheme for object loss is that the self may be depleted by forces beyond one's control (that is, the death or separation of a parent), establishing the foundation for later helplessness: "No matter what I do, it can all be taken away." This early loss may establish a *perspective of vulnerability* such that actual or potential subsequent losses activate more infantile schemes of threats to psychobiological integrity.

Schematic Processing of Vulnerability

The formation of this early scheme may constrain the information search of the depression-prone child to selectively recall or recognize information confirming the idea that the self is rejected. Thus, the child may be exquisitely tuned to the lack of nurturance of the remaining parent or to the teasing of peers. With the emergence of role-taking skills in later childhood and adolescence, the individual may anticipate that others have negative views of the self—even if these views are only imagined. Later in adolescence or adulthood, the termination of relations or the loss of the security of home as the young person moves away to college may activate the early scheme that the self cannot cope without the supportive love object. Because the processing is schematic rather than objective, the depressive may fail to store or retrieve information about his or her achievements which, ironically, would help dispel the early schemes of vulnerability. Further, because the depressive is so concerned about the disruptive nature of social rejection, he may withdraw from peers during adolescence thereby depriving himself of social rewards. Moreover, since the adolescent is likely to judge the value of a person in terms of the ability to be liked by others (Kohlberg, 1969; Leahy & Hunt, 1983), his judgment of his social withdrawal will add to his self-criticism. Thus, the schematic processing leads to selective focus on the negative, filtering out the positive, and behavioral deficits which contribute to the development of further depression.

Adaptations to Vulnerability

Two common assumptions of the depressive are "I must be loved" and "I must be perfect" with the negative corollaries, "I am unlovable and I am flawed." The belief that one must be loved by everyone may result in attempts to please others and to establish dependent relationships with powerful or competent people (Horney, 1945). Consequently, some depressives may be prone to indiscriminately attach themselves to unrewarding people simply because they fear the anticipated vulnerability of being alone. Since their choices are made on the basis of preventing loneliness, their friendships or intimate relationships are less likely to involve assertion which might assure some reward or mutuality in their relationships. Consequently, they are often disappointed in their relationships and may use this as evidence that they are unlovable or flawed.

For example, one patient whose father left her family when she was 5 years old recalled that the history of her relationships with her mother, boys, and men was characterized by consistent attempts to please them, deny her own interests, and tolerate abuse. The nonassertive contract that she used was that if she gave up her rights, then others would take care of her. Her depressive episodes were precipitated by separations from home or lovers, thereby replaying early themes of abandonment and vulnerability ("I can't take care of myself").

The assumption that one cannot cope without a protector places the individual within new vulnerabilities: the new protector also can leave—a condition beyond the control of the individual in the dependent role. Agoraphobic patients who fear that they may become insane if they become too anxious or who fear that they may become physically ill often develop dependent relationships with a spouse. This dependency then adds to a sense of vulnerability because the spouse may decide to leave. For many depressives, new relationships, which are highly sought after, represent new vulnerabilities.

Finally, another attempt to cope with the vulnerability of rejection by others is to separate a *public* from a *private self*. Usually, first seen during adolescence, the individual who believes that she is unlovable will "play the role" of being a pleasant, adaptive person. Unfortunately, any rewards she receives for her public performances are easily discounted because the depressive may say that the public performance was only an attempt to cope, not the "real" me.

Agoraphobia and Vulnerability

Agoraphobia, which is often misdiagnosed as multiple or simple phobias, has traditionally been viewed as a fear of the open market place, or fear of being outdoors. However, many agoraphobics have a common transsituational fear—the fear of going insane or of suffering physical incapacity (Mathews, Gelder, & Johnston, 1981). Bowlby (1969) and Guidano and Liotti (1983) have found that many agoraphobics have early histories of either brief separations or threats of suicide or separation by a parent. It is quite common for agoraphobics to show a marked reduction in their fear if their spouse is present.

One adult female agoraphobic illustrates the persistance of the early scheme of vulnerability. As an infant she suffered from an undiagnosed medical condition which produced intermittent pain and resulted in her hospitalization as an infant. This aroused pervasive fears of abandoment and fears that she might die in later life. Apparently, the early scheme was, "I might die at any moment" or "I might be abandoned at any time." Subsequently, as an adult, any symptoms of anxiety were interpreted by her that she might die, resulting in her fear of bridges, subways, and airplanes. The protection against abandonment began during early adulthood when she joined a convent. Her agoraphobia, with panic attacks, began when she left the convent and exposed herself to her fears of physical vulnerability in living on her own in a strange city.

STRUCTURAL-DEVELOPMENTAL THEORY

The major points of a structural-developmental theory have been discussed elsewhere (Leahy, 1983a; Leahy & Shirk, see Chpater 3, this volume). According to the structural-developmental theory of the self, conceptions of the self are determined by the cognitive level of the individual, especially, social-cognitive level. The view that I advance here argues two complementary perspectives on dysfunction of self-development. First, I suggest that early self-schemes are formed at the preoperational level and, consequently, may entail many of the limitations of thinking at that level. Because these self-schemes of the depressive or agoraphobic are negative, they are not commonly shared with others, and therefore, they are difficult to disconfirm. Further, the preoperational thinking associated with early schemes assists the individual in continually *confirming* the negative quality of the scheme. For example, the early scheme—"I am bad"—is confirmed by the individual's concentration (a preoperational quality) on negative behaviors with a failure to refocus on positive qualities of the self (i.e., centration). Consequestly, preoperational thinking may lead to the failure to assimilate positive experiences in one's self-esteem. This, of course, qualifies the reinforcement models of depression in that the failure to process reinforcements in the self-schemas results in the failure to accumulate self-confidence.

A second principle of the structural-developmental model is that there are *costs* of development in that early self-schemas are further transformed by increasing cognitive skills (Leahy, 1984a; Leahy & Kogan, in press). Specifically, changes in conceptions of personality (Leahy & Shirk, 1984a), role taking, and moral judgment add further to the self-critical quality of depression as the individual reaches adolescence. Similarly, the ability to recognize that the self may be an object of the thoughts of others results in a sense of *self-transparency* in anxiety disorders such that the individual is concerned that others may see his anxiety and reject him.

Let us consider the influence of preoperational thought on the child's self-image following loss or rejection. Egocentric thinking will be indicated by the following self-statements: "I have caused the loss (egocentric causality); "He is rejecting me" (personalism); "I am the only one who experiences this" (lack of consensus); "I feel bad, therefore the world or I am bad" (egocentric logic); and "This one thing makes me bad" (centration). Moral realism will be reflected by the belief in imminent justice ("Since something bad has happened to me, that means I did something bad") and by the belief in the infallibility of parental evaluations ("They must be right—they are my parents"). Dichotomous thinking leads to the conclusion that "I am either all good or all bad." Finally, the depressive's magical thinking is indicated by the idea that desires or thoughts may be bad because they are seen as causing negative consequences for others.

Guidano and Liotti have proposed that the child forms an early schema about the self which they refer to as the "metaphysical hardcore" in that it represents the self-representation that the individual employs to direct his inquiry about the self and others. According to this model, the early self-schema engages information search through schematic processing, such that the child will selectively attend to schema-consistent information (i.e., failures or rejections) and discount or fail to recall schema-inconsistent information (i.e., successes or acceptances).

I would add a point to this model of schematic processing: the self-schema will remain intact to the degree to which the individual lacks opportunities to disconfirm the schema. Later, in this chapter, I shall illustrate this lack by a case example of a patient whose self-schema was formed in a pseudomutual family that created the conditions for isolation from peers which, in turn, led the patient during adolescence to draw a distinction between a *public* and a *private* self.

THE COSTS OF ROLE TAKING
AND MORAL DEVELOPMENT

A fundamental assumption of Mead's (1934) symbolic interactionism is that role taking is an essential component of social development. A variety of developmentalists also contend that the development of role-taking skill is associated with higher moral development (Kohlberg, 1969; Selman, 1980) and with "adjusted" as opposed to delinquent or emotionally disturbed behavior (Chandler, 1973; Chandler, Greenspan, & Barenboim, 1974). However, there are a number of ways in which role taking may have a negative influence on personality development.

First, with an increasing awareness that the self may be an object of others' thoughts, the adolescent becomes more self-conscious and attempts to prevent others from knowing the "true" self (Elkind, 1973). Elkind refers to this as *imaginary audience behavior* in that the adolescent may exaggerate the importance he or she plays in the perspective of others, attempting to conceal the self from others. In the case histories of patients—especially avoidant personalities—we may often see the emergence of a distinction between a *public self* (one which is known by others) and a *private self* (one which is known only by the self) during early adolescence when recursive role-taking ability has developed. Thus, the avoidant personality may desire friendship, but he is unwilling to allow anyone the opportunity to see the true self. An interesting consequence of this is that performances by the public self that are socially rewarded are not viewed by the individual as reflective of the private self. As one avoidant patient recalled, "They only saw what I wanted to show them. So, if they liked me, they only liked that—*not really me.*" In this sense, one can say that part of the self has become externalized which implies that attributions for success are seldom internal—that is, seldom does the avoidant person take credit for success. If the private self is negative in content, the individual who is prone to depression may claim that any negative public performance is an indication of the true self. As a consequence, only negative experiences are assimilated into the true self, with positive experiences attributed to the role conformity.

Consistent with this distinction between public and private self is the increasing sense of loneliness during adolescence. Chandler (1975) gives the exquisite description of "epistemological loneliness" to describe the phenomenon of believing that self and other have different interpretations of realty—each unknowable to the other. I would make this less intellectual and refer to it as *existential loneliness* in that the adolescent may sense that self and other have different lives, perspectives, needs, and futures and that each must seek out his own goals and values. The loneliness is a result of the adolescent's desire for companionship, but is frustrated by his fear of disclosing the private self.

Another consequence of role-taking ability is the capacity to reflect on the self—especially on how the self does not measure up to the values established by others. Thus, the young adolescent may decenter from his behavior to ask how it appears to his peers.

This structural-developmental model serves to complement Zigler's cognitive-developmental model (Leahy, 1983a; Glick & Zigler, see Chapter 1, this volume). According to Zigler, higher developmental level is associated with greater internalization and differentiation of the self-image resulting in greater demands on the self and greater disparity between real and ideal self-image. As Glick and Zigler note in this volume, there is substantial evidence supporting this view: higher IQ, mental or chronological age, and higher premorbid social competence are associated with a greater disparity between the real and ideal self-image. The specific complementary view offered by the structural model is to suggest that social cognitive skills—such as role taking or moral judgment—are related to self-image disparity. Thus, the adolescent who is adept at role taking is more likely to judge himself negatively from the perspective of others. Furthermore, the emergence of postconventional moral judgment is also associated with greater disparity between real and ideal self-image due to higher demands on the self and lower self-esteem (Leahy, 1981, 1983a).

According to the structural-developmental model advanced here, the development of internalized symptoms should be related to the development of social-cognitive skills. Specifically, symptoms characterizing moving against the self (e.g., guilt) or symptoms that rely on thought (or internal representations) rather than actions would be expected to be related to higher role-taking or moral judgment level.

In an attempt to test this model, Posner (1983) tested children who were in psychotherapy for a variety of problems. Subjects comprised two age groups (6 and 10) and were categorized as having thought or action symptoms. *Thought symptoms* were generally consistent with internalized symptoms—for example, crying, sadness, or guilt, whereas *action symptoms* were largely externalizing symptoms (tantrums and other behavioral problems). Subjects were tested on role-taking, moral judgment, IQ, and conservation level.

Posner's (1983) findings confirmed the structural-developmental approach. Consistent with Zigler's model, higher chronological and mental age and higher IQ were associated with greater emphasis on thought symptoms and less emphasis on action symptoms. However, a path analysis revealed that the best predictor of thought symptoms was role-taking ability. Moral judgment level was positively associated with thought symptoms as expected, but did not retain its significant relationship with symptom type when the path analysis was conducted. The foregoing discussion suggests that the development of role taking and moral judgment may enhance the development of self-critical depression. We shall turn now to a developmental analysis of other attributional qualities related to self-critical depression and attempt to illustrate these phenomena with a case history.

COSTS OF DEVELOPMENT

We may begin with the question, "What cognitive skills are required to become depressed?" This may sound like an odd question, because we generally view psychopathology as a failure in the application of skills. However, the perspective that I advance is that there are qualitative shifts in the nature of depression between early childhood and adolescence that may be related to the development of social-cognitive skills.

Although there is some disagreement as to whether young children experience depression, most accounts of depression in young children refer to changes in behavior related to loss of love objects (Blatt, 1974; Bowlby, 1969; 1981; Spitz, 1949). Some psychoanalytic writers have proposed that young children do experience depression of a self-critical nature, but that they "mask" this with other symptoms, usually related to either excesses or deficits in behavior. However, a review of childhood depressive symptoms reveals that symptoms of self-hatred, seeing the self as a failure, hopelessness, and suicidal ideation are generally uncommon in young children. This has led some writers to distinguish dependency from self-critical depression, with the latter occurring in later development (Blatt, 1974; Blatt et al., 1981).

Original psychoanalytic formulations of depression argued that *melancholia* (sadness and excessive self-reproach) is a consequence of the loss of a love object that is accompanied by two conflicting feelings— sadness and anger (Freud, 1950). However, because the superego cannot admit the anger to consciousness, the individual turns this anger against the self in the form of melancholia (Freud, 1950). Since the superego is not well formed until later childhood or early adolescence, the young child is viewed as lacking the internalized values that produce this "introjective" depression (Blatt, 1974; Blatt, Quinlan, Chevron, McDonald, & Zuroff, 1982).

The structural-developmental model that I advance may be consistent with these psychoanalytic predictions. Specifically, both models predict that self-critical depression is preceded by dependency depression in development. Both models also predict that the development of moral judgment will enhance the likelihood of self-critical depression. However, the structural model places greater emphasis on a wider range of social-cognitive skills, does not posit any retroflected energies to explain self-criticism, and does not propose that repression of anger is the heart of the depressive's dynamic.

I illustrate aspects of this model by considering the developmental implications of Abramson, Seligman, and Teasdale's (1978) attribution model of depression. Abramson et al. (1978) realized that Seligman's (1976) earlier model of learned helplessness could not adequately account for the self-criticism that follows from the perception that behavior is unrelated to outcomes. Consequently, they turned to the attribution cube to determine what explanations an individual gives for why he is helpless. The consequence of this question for the depressive is to claim that others would succeed where the self has failed (personal versus universal helplessness), that the self is at fault rather than the environment (internal versus external), that the self will continue to fail at the task (stable versus unstable), and that this failure will generalize to other situations (general versus specific).

I have argued elsewhere (Leahy, 1983a) that the older child or adolescent is at greater risk for self-critical attributions because of higher social-cognitive skill. First, the idea that others would succeed depends on social comparison processes: The tendency to evaluate the self's performance by comparing it with others increases after the age of 10 years (Ruble, Feldman, & Boggiano, 1976), resulting in the belief that the self is inferior. Second, stable internal attributions are more likely to be found among older children who are considerably more likely than young children to describe self and other in terms of stable personality traits rather than behavior or appearances (Livesley & Bromley, 1973). Consequently, it would appear that younger children are less likely to use the global trait attributions which lead to their belief in stable and generalizable helplessness. For example, the older child would be more likely to say, "I failed here because *I* am *stupid* and I will continue to fail because I am stupid."

Third, self-critical depression is more likely for people who believe that their goals are unattainable. Research indicates that increasing age is associated with higher ideal self-images and greater emphasis on competence (Leahy & Hunt, 1983; Glick & Zigler, Chapter 1, this volume): These greater demands for competence for the self add to the perfectionistic quality of the depressive's unattainable goals, contributing to helplessness. Finally, the question of "Why am I helpless?" may result in comparing the real and the ideal self-images. Again, this ability to reflect on the self's performances and compare it with the ideal increases with age.

Development and Maladaptive Assumption

According to Beck's (1976; Beck *et al.*, 1979) cognitive theory of depression, the depressed individual has a set of assumptions which are maladaptive in that they result in impossible demands on the self or others. These assumptions often comprise the content of moral judgments about the self in the depressed individual. I propose that several of these assumptions reflect concerns which are more likely to arise in later childhood (Age 8) than in early childhood (Age 4).

The first set of assumptions are those that pertain to the individual's construction of interpersonal events. We shall refer to these as *sociality* assumptions (Beck, 1983). Three such assumptions are (1) "Everyone must love me or I am unlovable and worthless"; (2) "If I do well, people will like me"; (3) "Someone else must make me happy." These assumptions are dysfunctional in that they are untrue (e.g., even successful people are disliked), they demand the impossible (e.g., "Everyone must love me"), and they produce negative affect (depression, anxiety, and anger).

The first two assumptions reflect concern for how one's social competence or self will be judged by others. Although even very young children are aware of rejection, older children are more sensitive or concerned with social rejection because of their advanced role-taking skills and because they often place a high premium on social competence (Cole & Pennington, 1976; Leahy & Hunt, 1983). For example, the younger child who is egocentric would be unlikely to ask the question of whether everyone loves him or whether people approve of his performance in activities. This may be why tangible reinforcers, rather than social reinforcers, have a greater effect on very young children.

I would suggest, however, that the assumption that "someone else must make me happy" is a primitive dependency assumption which may be traced to infant attachment and separation conflicts (Blatt,

1974; Bowlby, 1981). Other assumptions—"Everyone must love me or I am unlovable and worthless" and "If I do well, others will like me"— also involve these earlier dependency concepts. However, the distinction between being liked and being taken care of is that the latter assumption implies a pervasive helplessness when one is left to his own abilities. Thus, it may be true that others do not like you, but that need not imply that without their affection you will fail to exist. Concern about being liked is more developmentally advanced than concern about being taken care of.

A second set of assumptions is related to *competent achievement* which is relatively autonomous of others' approach: (1) "I must be perfect at what I do or I am a failure" and (2) "I must be able to solve my own prolbems or I am weak and a failure." Again, these assumptions imply self-criticism rather than helplessness. Although even infants are motivated by competence concerns (White, 1959), research on the development of concern for achievement where there are standards of excellence indicates an increasing emphasis on competence as the child grows older (Harter, see Chapter 2, this volume).

Hopelessness and Development

It may appear to be ironic or self-contradictory to propose that the belief in hopelessness is a consequence of higher developmental level. I argue that the belief in hopelessness is a selective sampling of past failures. These past failures are then assimilated to the individual's psychological theory of the stability of his personality and events in the environment—all of which are developmental attainments.

Hopelessness is indicated by the belief that events will not change for the better and that the self faces unremitting negative experiences. First, a fundamental tenet of hopelessness is *future time perspective*— that is, the ability to anticipate the nature of the future. Presumably, if one seldom anticipates or plans the future, then hopelessness is a less likely experience. Future time perspective is more commonly found among adolescents or adults, allowing them to anticipate long-range future experiences for oneself, thereby contributing to their hopelessness.

A second factor affecting hopelessness is the belief that one has a *stable personality deficit*. For example, the depressive believes that his inability to obtain rewards is based on a deficit in his character or ability—"I am lazy" or "I am stupid." The self-critical component of this kind of depression relies on the depressive's inference that failure in a few situations represents a collection of personality deficits, that is, the depressive believes in a set of flaws. As suggested earlier, references to stable personality traits increases during later childhood, placing the older child at greater risk for future setbacks.

Not only are depressives prone to claim that they will continue to be unable to obtain rewards, but they also believe that their negative mood will continue in the future. This is also related to the depressive's belief in a stable personality deficit in the self—that is, not only does the individual believe that his personal deficits that gave rise to the depressive episode will continue to plague him, but he also believes that his present dysphoria will not lessen. This expectation of unremitting unhappiness is generally based on the individual's assumption that his personal deficits will continue.

Third, it may appear too obvious to say, but most children believe that they will grow up and, in so doing, outgrow the frustrating circumstances that give rise to their unhappiness. They may not be able to articulate too clearly what they will be like when they are adults, but they can easily say, with a touch of optimism in their anticipated escape, that others should "wait until I grow up" or "when I'm bigger I won't have to listen to this" or "I'll run away." As casual and unplanned as these hopes are, they reflect the child's understanding of the culture's view that "growing up" is equivalent to progress which, it would seem, implies relief from suffering. Thus, the belief that one may outgrow the problem counteracts feelings of hopelessness.

DEVELOPMENTAL TRANSFORMATIONS OF SELF-SCHEMES

In this section I review the rationale and method of examining the developmental nature of early self-schemes. In analyzing the individual's self-scheme it is essential to determine the cognitive level of the individual at the formation of the scheme. Further, the nature of the self-scheme may be transformed as higher social-cognitive level is attained, for example, the acquisition of role taking or conventional moral judgment may alter the nature of the self-scheme so that the individual believes that he is incompetent in the eyes of others and, consequently, must attempt to hide this from peers.

Early Limitations

According to the structural-developmental model, conceptions of the self or of others will depend on the social-cognitive level of the child at the formation of the scheme. Because many schemes are formed at the preoperational stage, they will reflect the qualities of preoperational thought. Thus, they will be dichotomous ("I never can do things for myself"), egocentric ("I cause bad things to happen"), and unilateral ("Others can take care of me"). Since these schemes are formed early, the child lacks the ability to decenter from these conceptions and challenge them. These early schemes of incompetence, vulnerability, and dependency are later transformed by the acquisition of higher social-cognitive functioning. This transformation may represent a *cost* of development as the child begins to describe his clumsy behavior by referring to personality traits—for example, "I am an idiot."

Increasing cognitive level is associated with new views of competence and incompetence. Thus, for the 6-year-old who is physically awkward, competence is defined by being unable to run as fast as the next child. At age 14, competence is defined in terms of sharing perspectives, values, or fitting into a peer group (Leahy & Hunt, 1983). With the acquisition of conventional level moral judgment (e.g., Stage 3: "You are good if others like you"), the young adolescent may begin to criticize himself for his unpopularity and find a personality theory to explain it: "I'm a loser and I'm unlovable."

Developmental Cognitive Therapy

Beck's (1976; Beck *et al.*, 1979) cognitive therapy for depression has been shown to be an effective treatment for major depression. The focus of cognitive therapy is on the current dysfunctional behavior and thoughts of the patient that are associated with low moods. The therapist plays an active, directive but Socratic role in helping the patient dispute his negative view of the self, experience, and the future. Cognitive therapists help the patient identify dichotomizing, jumping to conclusions, discounting the positive—and replace this with a more empirical approach to life problems. This form of therapy is quite effective in reversing major depressive episodes in 15 to 20 sessions.

Recently, Guidano and Liotti (1983) have introduced an additional phase in cognitive therapy—*developmental analysis*. They argue that lasting and pervasive changes in the patient's identity are best achieved by a long-term treatment following traditional cognitive therapy. In the developmental analysis the patient's underlying assumptions and dysfunctional patterns are identified from early childhood through adulthood, indicating to the patient how they have selectively pursued confirmation of their maladaptive assumptions.

I outline some basic principles of developmental-cognitive therapy which I have derived from Guidano and Liotti's approach as well as from my own applications of cognitive therapy from a structural-developmental perspective. I believe there are several advantages of the developmental analysis in therapy. First, regardless of the rewards of symptom relief, patients seek an *understanding* of how they got that way, that is, they seek to understand the past and present to establish their identity (Leahy & Kogan, in press). Second, by illustrating how their schemes "made sense" at an earlier developmental level (because they were preoperational) and how they engaged in schematic processing to confirm these schemes, they can understand why they remain so compelling in the present. Third, by tracing previous episodes of depression, the patient recognizes his or her individual patterns of behavioral and cognitive symptoms which may help the patient conduct an early "self-diagnosis" of the onset of future depressive episodes and utilize his cognitive-behavioral techniques to turn the depression around. This provides the patient with an *inoculation plan.* Fourth, by understanding the developmental course of depression, the patient may feel freed from the responsibility of having "made" himself depressed: Thus, if he sees that his depression was not "chosen" by himself but was caused by child-rearing experiences, which were beyond his control, he may understand that the cause of his depressive thinking was out of his control and out of his responsibility. However, by knowing that his earlier cognitive level precluded his dispute of these early schemes—but that his new advances in cognitive therapy allow him to see the irrationality of these schemes—the patient may recognize that what was once beyond his control is now under rational control as an adult.

Phases of Developmental Cognitive Therapy

Phase I. Traditional Cognitive Therapy

Following Guidano and Liotti's suggestions, the first phase utilizes Beck's cognitive and behavioral strategies for reducing depressive symptoms and identifying maladaptive automatic thoughts and underlying assumptions. This phase includes activity scheduling, graded task assignment, monitoring automatic thoughts and disputing them, and abstracting common themes of dysfunctional thinking (see Beck et al., 1979).

Phase II. Identification of Major Depressive Episodes

The patient describes in detail the particular events that precipitated depressive episodes in the past. These may include breakups in relationships, initiating contact with new groups of people, or incurring new work responsibilities. Particular attention is given to the patient's specific behavioral and cognitive symptoms: for example, decreased independent or social activities, belief that the self is a total failure because of a single current setback (overgeneralizing), or the belief that new relationships will never be possible.

The *inoculation phase* begins with this initial identification of previous depressive episodes. Since the patient has already acquired many of the self-help skills in the initial phase of therapy, he may begin to develop his own therapeutic responses to previous depressive episodes. The patient is asked to list the behavioral and cognitive symptoms of each depressive episode and to describe a specific plan of action for each of these symptoms. This accomplishes several goals: the patient may see that his depressive episodes were not inevitable and thereby learn that alternatives to depression exist; further, the patient is primed for early onset of depression for future episodes and is given a sense of self-efficacy to handle these problems on his own in the future. Thus, any hopelessness about future depression is diminished. The reason to include this inoculation phase at this point is that the patient may not be motivated to continue to an earlier developmental analysis and the therapist is ethically bound to provide a foundation for the maintenance of therapeutic gains.

Phase III. Earlier Developmental Analysis

The patient is asked to restate the maladaptive assumptions and self-labels that have been at the center of his depression. This information is available from the patient's written homework assignments from the earlier phases of cognitive therapy. These cognitions then become the targets for what must be understood developmentally. The patient then is asked about when he began to believe these ideas and how his parents or peers reinforced or modeled these beliefs. This provides the patient with a social-learning framework for recognizing that his self-schemes were acquired directly from others' tuition. For example, the patient who believes that he is evil is asked if anyone every made him believe that when he was a child. One patient, who as an adult failed to assert herself and therefore felt trapped and angry, had been told when she was 5 years of age by her mother that anger made you a bad person.

The patient is then given a quick overview of cognitive-developmental theory, specifically, the major points of how egocentric thinking may have precluded him from disputing his dysfunctional thinking when he was younger. This allows the patient to recognize that, now that he is an adult, he may dispute what was once taken for granted. This fosters a belief that change in what was apparently constant may be achieved.

The fundamental nature of schematic processing is also explained to the patient. The underlying assumptions are then examined as determinants of much of the behavior of the patient throughout childhood and early adolescence resulting in the patient recognizing how he continually sought confirmation for his self-schemes. For example, the patient who assumed that she is unlovable may see that she avoided friendships when she was an adolescent and thereby prevented herself from acquiring information that others could like her. A further goal of this analysis is to indicate how the development of role-taking skills during adolescence may have produced new problems, such as dividing the self into a public and private self, thereby allowing discounting of positive rewards from others.

Phase IV. Reconstructive Cognitive Therapy

As the patient comes to recognize that child-rearing experiences produced the depressive self-schemes and assumptions, the patient is asked to imagine her- or himself as a child, knowing what she or he knows now about cognitive therapy, answering the parent or peer who contributed to the dysfunctional thinking. The patient may write out point–counterpoint dialogues between self and other, disputing the other (or the self) who gives these dysfunctional thoughts. For example, if the patient was made to believe that she was unlovable, she may use information from her current positive relationships to argue that others do like her. Patients who have early schemes of vulnerability ("I cannot take care of myself" or "I will be abandoned") are urged to use evidence in the present and the past that dispute these thoughts.

There are several consequences to be expected from this developmental analysis. First, the patient may feel freed from the responsibility of his depression and blame her- or himself less for having been depressed. Second, the patient may begin to experience anger toward parents or peers for the socialization to depression. Third, by understanding the etiology of the depression, the patient generally has less belief in the underlying schemes and assumptions: They may see how these thoughts "made sense" to a preoperational child, but that they do not make sense to an adult. Fourth, by tracing some of the family dynamics, or self–other relationships, the patient may be less prone to future depressive influences.

The clinician should use caution in employing the developmental analysis. Patients who do not have chronic depressions or patients whose personality is highly disorganized (e.g., borderlines) may not be suitable for this review of the past.

Case Illustration

The patient was a young woman who presented complaints of depression and anxiety accompanied by panic attacks. Her negative self-schemes were "I am unlovable" and "I don't make sense to others." Her major underlying assumption was, "If I'm perfect, my parents will accept me." There was no apparent precipitating factor for her recent 3-year history of depression. Following the recommendations of Beck *et al.* (1979) and Guidano and Liotti (1983), the initial targets of therapy were the reduction of her depression and anxiety and the identification of her assumptions and self-schemes through cognitive therapy. Once symptomatic relief was obtained (in 18 sessions), it was possible to examine the development of her self-scheme and assumptions.

The patient claimed that she suffered no serious conflicts with her family before the age of 8 years, but had a general belief that she was physically awkward and shy. The patient's family emphasized perfectionism, represented others as rejecting, did not acknowledge her feelings of dissatisfaction, and claimed that the family was the source of all that was good. Given her unilateral respect for her family—which was assured by her lack of peer relations—she attempted to live up to the perfectionism of her parents with the inevitable consequence of failure. Consequently, she labeled herself as awkward, and given the belief that others would be rejecting, she avoided peers, thereby depriving her of alternative reinforcements or evidence that she could be accepted. Since she was avoidant as a young adolescent, she was able to obtain little evidence that others were accepting: In fact, her avoidance only added provocation to her peers' rejection of her.

She attempted to adapt to her perception of rejection by others. First, during adolescence, she began to act the part of the genteel young "lady" while simultaneously assuming that her "real" self was unknown by others and that if others knew her they would reject her. This division of herself into a *public* and *private self* reflected the emergence of imaginary audience behavior described by Elkind (1968).

For her, the self that was obscured was derogated by her. With this division of public and private self, any positive reinforcements which she obtained from peers would be discounted as irrelevant to her real self. If she received criticism from her peers, this indicated to her that her real self was showing through, thereby confirming her self-derogation. The consequence was to avoid friendships and, as a result, reduce her opportunities to disconfirm her self-scheme through self-disclosure.

A second attempt to cope followed from her apprehension of and selective focus on social rejection: she retreated into her family. Convinced by her parents and by her experience that others would be rejecting, she assumed that if she achieved then her parents would accept her. However, her parents would vacillate between praise and harsh criticism, resulting in her belief that (1) "there is something that I *can* do to get praise," (2) "there is something wrong with me," and, most importantly, (3) "no matter where I turn I am rejected." Imagery induction revealed that she described herself as trapped within a cold icy wall with no way out. Her experience of social rejection with peers resulted in her increased reliance on a family that also rejected her. She had no place to which to turn.

This case history illustrates a number of developmental effects on depression. First, she experienced little depressive symptomatology before 8 years of age. Second, her self-critical depression was first evident when the demands of peer conformity led her to experience rejection after 10 years of age. Third, at this age she began to use personality labels to derogate herself. Fourth, her imaginary audience behavior resulted in her splitting of two selves—a public and a private self. This resulted in her maintenance of the belief that rewards for public performance were irrelevant to the private self, thereby frustrating the reinforcements which might have counteracted the unfolding of the depression. Finally, she used role-taking skills and conventional level moral judgment to evaluate herself from the perspective of others. Since she "played" to the audience of her rejecting family, she concluded from this, "If others don't accept me, then I am not worthwhile."

Therapy with this patient proved quite successful. During the year of treatment, her depression was eliminated and her panic attacks disappeared after 2 months. She developed a group of friends, one of whom she took special delight in because she also came from a pseudomutual family ("my pseudomutual friend"). This was an especially important friend, since it helped her realize that others came from similar families—that she was not all alone. Her recognition of her parents' values resulted in an increase in her anger toward her parents, followed by a growing indifference toward them. Toward the end of therapy, a man whom she had grown to love proposed to her. Quite creative at imagery, she described herself as "no longer a rat in a maze. I feel like I'm a rat with very long legs staring over the walls of the maze."

Differences between Developmental Analysis and Psychoanalysis

Since developmental analysis in cognitive therapy focuses on the origins of self-schemas, there is the inevitable comparison with psychoanalytic technique and theory. There are several similarities between these approaches. Both models recognize the importance of early child-rearing experiences and primitive thinking in depression, and both models represent the depressive as one whose socialization has resulted in severely high standards applied against the self. Further, because of the emphasis that I have placed on early object relations in the emergence of schemes of vulnerability, psychoanalytic parallels may be found with the implication that early relations result in general representations of future relations.

However, there are numerous important differences between this developmental analysis and psychoanalytic technique and theory. First, there is no emphasis on the hydraulic model, with its direction and redirection of energies. Second, the emphasis on the unconscious is replaced by the emphasis on thoughts which are not repressed, but are within the consciousness of the patient (i.e., automatic thoughts and maladaptive assumptions). Third, although current transference issues may be important in helping the patient recognize his assumptions about self and other, the transference is not a major focus of therapy. Fourth, "regression" in developmental analysis does not entail a regression of the patient to earlier modes of functioning; rather, the patient collaborates with the therapist to specifically identify earlier patterns *and* to find solutions to those experiences. Finally, there are many other procedural and stylistic differences between developmental analysis and psychoanalysis, with the cognitive therapist using a developmental analysis emphasizing specific targets of treatment, homework assignments, empirical verification of the patient's hypotheses, and an explicit plan of therapy which is shared with the patient. Psychoanalytic therapists may wish to include many of the strategies of cognitive therapy and developmental analysis, while maintaining their theoretical model of the emotional disorders.

CONCLUSION

To summarize, it has been proposed that early schemes may persist because of their self-fulfilling quality. The individual selectively collects information confirming the scheme, discounts information inconsistent with the scheme and develops a pattern of behavior that maintains a view that he is unique and inferior. With the acquisition of social comparison, role taking, and conventional moral judgment, there is an increasing risk of self-critical depression.

In some cases, it is useful to educate the patient regarding the quality of primitive thinking at the formation of the scheme and then employ cognitive therapy to reexamine whether the scheme merited formation in the first place. It should be noted that simply identifying the scheme without reconstructing it may only strengthen the patient's belief that his personality is permanently established. The structured phases of cognitive therapy and developmental analysis provide the patient with active coping strategies, inoculation against future depression, and an understanding of how earlier schemes persisted through schematic processing. By following this developmental analysis to its conclusion, the patient is assisted in a reconstruction of the self.

ACKNOWLEDGMENTS

I would like to thank the following people who have contributed to my thinking but who should not be held responsible for those parts of this chapter with which they disagree: Aaron Beck, Edward Zigler, Jeffrey Young, and Stephen Shirk.

REFERENCES

Abramson, L. Y., Seligman, M. E. P., & Teasdale, J. D. (1978). Learned helplessness in humans: Critique and reformulation. *Journal of Abnormal Psychology, 87,* 49–74.

Beck, A. T. (1976). *Cognitive therapy and the emotional disorders.* New York: International Universities Press.

Beck, A. T. (1983). Cognitive therapy of depression: New perspectives. In P. Clayton (Ed.), *Depression.* New York: Raven Press.

Beck, A. T., & Emery, G. (1979). *Cognitive therapy of anxiety and phobic disorders.* Philadelphia: Center for Cognitive Therapy.

Beck, A. T., Rush, A. J., Shaw, B. F., & Emery, G. (1979). *Cognitive therapy of depression: A treatment manual.* New York: Guilford Press.

Blatt, S. J. (1974). Levels of object representation in anaclitic and introjective depression. *Psychoanalytic Study of the Child, 29,* 107–157.

Blatt, S. J., Quinlan, D. M., Chevron, E. S., McDonald, C., & Zuroff, D. (1982). Dependency and self-criticism: Psychological dimensions of depression. *Journal of Consulting and Clinical Psychology, 50*, 113–124.

Bowlby, J. (1969). *Attachment.* New York: Basic Books.

Bowlby, J. (1981). *Loss.* New York: Basic Books.

Chandler, M. J. (1973). Egocentrism and antisocial behavior: The assessment and training of social perspective-taking skills. *Developmental Psychology, 9*, 326–332.

Chandler, M. J. (1975). Relativism and the problem of epistemological loneliness. *Human Development, 18*, 171–180.

Chandler, M. J., Greenspan, S., & Barenboim, C. (1974). Assessment and training of role-taking and referential communication skills in institutionalized emotionally disturbed children. *Developmental Psychology, 60*, 546–553.

Clark, D., & Teasdale, J. (1982). Diurnal variation in clinical depression and accessibility of memories of positive and negative experiences. *Journal of Abnormal Psychology, 91*, 87–95.

Coie, J. D., & Pennington, B. F. (1976). Children's perception of deviance and disorder. *Child Development, 47*, 407–413.

Elkind, D. (1967). Egocentrism in adolescence. *Child Development, 38*, 1025–1034.

Ellis, A. (1962). *Reason and emotion in psychotherapy.* New York: Lyle Stuart.

Freud, S. (1950). Mourning and melancholia. In *Collected papers.* (Vol. 4). London: Hogart Press.

Freud, S. (1962). *Civilization and its discontents.* New York: Norton.

Guidano, V., & Liotti, G. (1983). *Cognitive processes and the emotional disorders.* New York: Guilford Press.

Hanson, N. R. (1965). *Patterns of discovery.* Cambridge: Cambridge Univ. Press.

Horney, K. (1945). *Our inner conflicts.* New York: Norton.

Inhelder, B., & Piaget, J. (1964). *The early growth of logic in the child.* London: Routledge & Kegan Paul.

Kelly, G. A. (1955). *The psychology of personal constructs.* New York: Norton.

Kohlberg, L. (1969). Stage and sequence: The cognitive developmental approach to socialization. In D. Goslin (Ed.), *Handbook of socialization: Theory and research.* New York: Rand McNally.

Leahy, R. L. (1976). Developmental trends in qualified inferences and descriptions of self and others. *Developmental Psychology, 12*, 546–547.

Leahy, R. L. (1981). Parental practices and the development of moral judgment and self-image disparity during adolescence. *Developmental Psychology, 17*, 580–594.

Leahy, R. L. (1983). Development of self and the problems of social cognition: Identity formation and depression. In L. Wheeler & P. Shaver (Eds.), *Review of personality and social psychology.* Beverly Hills, CA: Sage.

Leahy, R. L., & Hunt, T. (1983). A cognitive developmental approach to the development of conceptions of intelligence. In R. L. Leahy (Ed.), *The child's construction of social inequality.* New York: Academic Press.

Leahy, R. L., & Kogan, N. (in press). Social cognition and identity achievement. In S. Messick (Ed.), *Development in young adulthood:* San Francisco: Jossey-Bass.

Leahy, R. L., & Shirk, S. (1984a). The development of social cognition: Conceptions of personality. In G. J. Whitehurst (Ed.), *Annals of Child Development, Vol. I.* Greenwich, CT: JAI Press.

Leahy, R. L., & Shirk, S. (1984b). The development of classificatory skills and sex-trait stereotypes in children. *Sex Roles. 10*, 281–292.

Livesley, W. J., & Bromley, D. B. (1973). *Person perception in childhood and adolescence.* New York: Wiley.

Mathews, A. M., Gelder, M., & Johnston, D. (1981). *Agoraphobia: Nature and treatment.* New York: Guilford.

Mead, G. H. (1934). *Mind, Self and Society.* Chicago: University of Chicago Press.

Piaget, J. (1970). Piaget's theory. In P. Mussen (Ed.), *Carmichael's manual of child psychology* (Vol. 1, 3rd ed.). New York: Wiley.

Posner, J. (1983). *Symptom formation in children from a cognitive developmental point of view.* Unpublished doctoral dissertation, Graduate Faculty, New School for Social Research, New York.

Riskind, J. H. (1983, August). *Misconceptions of the cognitive model.* Paper presented at meetings of the American Psychological Association, Anaheim, CA.

Ruble, D. N., Feldman, N. S., & Boggiano, A. K. (1976). Social comparison between young children in achievement situations. *Developmental Psychology, 12,* 192–197.

Sampson, E. E. (1981). Cognitive psychology as ideology. *American Psychologist, 36,* 730–743.

Seligman, M. E. P. (1976). *Helplessness: On depression, development and death.* San Francisco: Freeman.

Selman, R. L. (1980). *The growth of interpersonal understanding.* New York: Academic Press.

Spitz, R. (1946). Anaclitic depression. *Psychoanalytic Study of the Child, 2,* 313–342.

Wallerstein, J., & Kelly, J. (1980). *Surviving the breakup.* New York: Basic Books.

Werner, H. (1948). *The comparative psychology of mental development.* New York: International Universities Press.

White, R. (1959). Motivation reconsidered: The concept of competence. *Psychological Review, 66,* 297–333.

9

The Development of the Self: Conclusions

Robert L. Leahy

DEVELOPMENT

The contributions to this volume suggest a variety of dimensions and processes of change in the self-concept. The simple proposal that links together this work is that the child *constructs* the self through *qualitative* changes in content and process in self-definition. This *developmental* perspective stands in contrast to social-learning models which view development as the acquisition of skills or information. The developmental model argues that the content of self-concept differs at different ages and the processes whereby the self is known may change at different levels of development. I trace some parallels of content for different developmental models later in this chapter.

The emphasis that I stress on *construction* may not be equally shared by all contributors. But the *self* is one concept that the individual almost necessarily constructs or makes on his own. Because it is constructed by the individual, it will reflect the cognitive level that the child brings to bear on this domain. Thus, much of what has been said in this volume clearly indicates that the child does not simply imitate what others think.

In this final chapter I review the relevance of these contributions to three issues: First, how does the content of self-description change with age? Second, how does self-evaluation develop? And, third, what are the clinical implications of these findings?

CONTENT AND CONFLICT

Several authors have proposed substantial transformations of the content of self-concept with increasing development. Perhaps Hart and Damon's model is the most differentiated, including a variety of axes of change. But what is notable is the considerable overlap of these proposed models. The younger child is more focused on external or behavioral qualities or simple skills, whereas the adolescent focuses on intrapsychic and interpersonal qualities.

Each change in content may involve transformations in the *audience* which evaluates the self, the areas of most relevant *conflict*, and the degree to which competence may be *verified*. First, as different areas of self-definition change, the individual may rely on different people to judge the self. For example, Kegan describes the impulsive self of childhood, one which finds itself in conflict with parental and adult regulations: The relevant audience is the adult whose immediate presence may be necessary to control the impulse. In contrast, the older adolescent or young adult who, in Kegan's terms, establishes an interpersonal self may judge the self from the perspective of peers. Perhaps at this level being known is more relevant than being controlled. Similar changes in audience may be described for other stage models of self. Thus, Mead's (1934) proposal that the self is known through role taking requires us to ask, "Whose role?" or "Which other?"

Second, the emergence of different areas of self-definition reflect changes in potential conflict areas. Kegan's descriptions of acquisition and loss of different selves is an interesting model for understanding relevant conflicts. Harter's description of changes in competence across age indicates that emphasis on behavioral achievement and concrete rewards is replaced by subjective and interpersonal achievements and abstract or social rewards. Thus, one might expect that each age level involves a different set of potential conflicts. However, it is unclear if these developmental changes imply that conflicts are left behind or continue to affect later conflicts, as one might suppose from a psychodynamic perspective. The foregoing supports the view that, as earlier conflicts are resolved, conflicts at higher levels become possible (Leahy, 1983).

Perhaps because the developmental and cognitive models are so strongly stressed in this volume, the reader is left with the unanswered question of how transitions are produced or resolved. Developmentalism often seems to carry an implicit *imminence* with it, as if the child's nature were unfolding like so many Platonic ideals. This inability of developmentalists to *specify* experiences that may produce change has handicapped them in explaining individual differences or suggesting therapeutic interventions. The work of Kegan assists our understanding of transitional mechanisms, resolutions or causes of change and may help direct clinicians and researchers to pragmatic questions and answers.

A third change in self-concept content pertains to the *verifiability* of the self: "How do I know if my self-concept is accurate?" I do not pretend that adolescents become skeptical logical positivists; but the change in content may make some self-definitions more uncertain than others. Let us take the behavioral self-descriptions which a number of our contributors have found most common among young children. "Who am I? I am 5, I have brown hair, and I wear a cowboy outfit." The certitude of these statements is established by two factors—I can point to a calendar, my hair, and my outfit and I do not ask if anyone else disagrees (I make little distinction between public and private definitions at age 5). But at 16 years of age, the content of my self-definition focuses on my personality and my interpersonal skills. Not only do I have an ephemeral object of my thinking, but I wonder continually about the universality of that definition. Thus, my self-definition becomes less verifiable, more uncertain, more unstable. I believe that this accounts for a link between the change in content (Harter, Kegan, Damon, & Leahy) and stability and certainty of self-concept (Rosenberg).

The developmental perspectives described in this volume lead one to ask questions about the stage-like quality of self-concept. Are these levels of self-conception organized wholes arranged in a universal invariant sequential hierarchy? The contributors to this volume do not offer such a bold claim: rather, they suggest *order* where chaos may more likely characterize much of the development of the self-concept. The Piaget–Kohlberg tradition proposes that sequences of thought are organized in a hierarchy because of a natural ordering of concepts. This appears to be the case for conceptions of physical reality, but is there a natural order to self-conception? For example, are descriptions of one's personality necessarily more complex than descriptions of one's behavior?

I think so. Barenboim (1981) has offered a convincing model of the development of personal constructs (about others) which may be applied to the self. One begins with observations of behavior, then moves to comparisons of behavior, and finally ends up with concepts of personality and explanations of personality. The same appears to hold for self-descriptions as indicated by Hart and Damon, Rosenberg, and Leahy and Shirk. Personality constructs are generalizations about specific actions which the perceiver believes distinguish one individual from the average. You cannot have personality constructs without the classification and comparison of behavior.

Hierarchy does not mean "better." Research on the *existence* of stable personality differences has left the field in a quandary of uncertainty (Mischel, 1968). Reality may be better described by the minimalism of behaviorism that describes contingencies rather than individual predispositions. But the "higher" levels of personality theorizing that children and adolescents engage in involves something quite different from behaviorism: Perhaps this is one cost of their development.

Are these stages *organized wholes?* Little evidence is presented in this volume for so bold a claim. And, certainly, nothing gives credibility to any claims of *universal sequence.* There is a considerable need for cross-cultural research to test the idea of universal sequence. If these are truly developmental or structurally ordered, then should the sequence be universal? Again, speculation may lead one to conclude, with Gilligan (1982), that there may be different directions that one might follow after the initial levels have been achieved. Inasmuch as the *self* is as social as it is cognitive we might imagine different sequences for different societies. Such a finding would support the view that the construction of the self is mutual—the participants being the child and society.

Finally, the orderly trends for mostly "normal" subjects in these contributions lead us to wonder if the sequences must be so invariantly progressive. Even cognitive theory (Beck, Rush, Shaw, and Emery, 1979) recognizes the possibility of activation of primitive schemes during stress—another way of talking about regression. Personally, I have seen too many examples of psychopathology that demonstrate that the progressive developments we find in nonsocial cognition are not always matched when we consider the affectively charged quality of self-concept. Research on clinical populations or normal individuals exposed to important developmental transitions may reveal temporary disequilibrium in self-concept similar to the disequilibrium noticed in transitions in moral development.

SELF-EVALUATION

How does self-evaluation change with age? The two relevant developmental questions are concerned with the *process* and the *content* of self-evaluation. The cognitive and structural models described in this volume propose that processes of self-evaluation undergo modification between early and later childhood. Glick and Zigler demonstrate that there is an increasing differentiation of real from ideal self-image (i.e., increased self-image disparity) associated with increasing age, IQ, or developmental level. Zigler's work draws upon Werner's (1948) orthogenetic principle which proposes that development is marked by increasing differentiation, articulation, and hierarchization. This model has been a very useful guide to generating research on symptom roles and self-image disparity. It's heuristic potential may be carried further if one fully adapts this orthogenetic principle. One might expect that increasing age would be associated with an increasing capacity to differentiate and articulate a variety of domains of self-evaluation, thereby resulting either in a greater variety of contents to value or devalue in the self. Further, this model would suggest that hierarchization would result in the tendency to view certain qualities of self as *central* or more important than others. These central qualities may then become more strongly emphasized in self-evaluation. Finally, hierarchization implies that other specific self-concepts may be subsumed under more general self-concepts—for example, talking and cooperating with others may be subsumed by the category "socially competent" in self-evaluation.

The structural–symbolic interactionist views taken by Leahy and Shirk and Hart and Damon emphasize taking the perspective of others in self-evaluation. The process of self-evaluation according to these models stresses continuing inputs of social interaction and the ability of the individual to decenter and anticipate the perspective of others.

Because the older individual evaluates the self from the perspective of others, the content of self-evaluation will change with age. Thus, using Kohlberg's (1969) moral judgment model, the egocentric child may rely on physical punishments and rewards to tell him he is competent, whereas the older child may rely on his peers. Since it may not always be so clear how peers evaluate the self, the adolescent's self-image may undergo some vacillation in certainty of self-description (Rosenberg). Further, the process of decentering also suggests that the content of self-evaluation will also shift toward social competence as the young adolescent emphasizes acceptance by peers (Harter; Hart & Damon; Leahy & Shirk).

What are the contents of self-evaluation at different ages? Rather than view self-evaluation simply in global self-esteem terms, it is helpful to know which qualities of self the individual stresses: "I may know that I am rather mediocre in tennis, but it may matter much more to me that I am reasonably competent as a teacher." The contributions to this volume indicate that there are substantial changes in content of self-evaluation associated with age. The general distinction between *objective* and *subjective* selves (Leahy & Shirk) suggests that the younger child may be more concerned with inadequacies in behavior, whereas the young adolescent may be more concerned with inadequacies in personality. Because of this shift in the use of personality or trait concepts, I have suggested that there are cognitive-developmental parallels to the emergence of self-critical depression during adolescence (Leahy, 1983).

Just as each level of self-concept may reflect a new attainment, it also holds open the possibility of new vulnerabilities. For example, in Hart and Damon's model, the adolescent is more likely to have doubts or conflicts related to social competence or his beliefs. Similarly, the work of Smollar and Youniss suggests that younger children are less likely to feel inferior because they are unable to adapt to the demands of peers. These developmental models offer a basis for researchers to determine what besides global self-esteem is important in self-evaluation at different ages.

CLINICAL IMPLICATIONS

The concept of *self* is central to a variety of theoretical systems that have had relevance to the treatment of patients. Freud (1964), Sullivan (1953), Adler (1964), Horney (1950), Rogers (1951), and Beck (1976; Beck et al., 1979) proposed that the individual's view of the self is a significant source of anxiety, depression, and maladaptive functioning. A variety of therapeutic applications have stressed the importance of uncovering repressed qualities of the self, "accepting" the real self, recognizing conflicting neurotic desires in the self, understanding how one's current behavior is an attempt to compensate for a concept of an inferior self, or recognizing how one's self-labels and values may be distorted or extreme. Unfortunately, none of these major theoretical positions have provided a clear framework for understanding how the self-concept may change with age.

Why is this endeavor important? It is important because *diagnosis* must begin with an understanding of two things: first, it must reflect an understanding of *normal functioning* (that is, average expectable or age-appropriate functioning); second, it must consider what is the natural *process of change* in functioning. Simply speaking, we must know what is normal to know what is abnormal and we must know what is the natural process of development before we can ask what is the process of intervention. Further, in knowing what the natural process of development might be, we might also learn what might be likely to occur next in the *sequence* of change. I believe that these points apply to both the understanding of the child's development and of the adult's development.

First, let us consider the question of what normal development may tell us about understanding psychopathology. Zigler's work indicates that self-image disparity is not a function of psychopathology per se, but rather reflects the individual's developmental level: the higher the developmental level, the higher the disparity. Similarly, a child's ego-centric view of self and reliance on external sanctions or rewards to guide one's behavior may be more a function of lower developmental level than antisocial character. Because developmental diagnosis provides a framework for reinterpreting maladaptive functioning as within the boundaries of developmental levels, it may avoid the iatrogenic consequences of attributing pathology to children who simply experience the disequilibrium of development.

Second, the understanding of development allows us to foresee the direction and process of change. It gives us something to aim for: If we are trying to enhance normal growth, it seems essential that we know what qualities we wish to establish. This is the problem inherent in the behavioral tradition where the age of subjects is often irrelevant. For example, behaviorists might help a child become more motivated to perform a task by associating contingent rewards (e.g., tokens) with performance. Unfortunately, normal development, as Harter shows, involves the development of intrinsic motivation—viewing the self as efficacious. In fact, contingent positive rewards might undermine the individual's motivation in the absence of rewards.

Another implication of developmental changes in the self is that there are different "selves" for different domains at different developmental levels (Hart & Damon). Failing to focus on the relevant areas in treatment may result in only making progress on topics of little concern to the child. The dialogue of treatment means that child and therapist are talking about the same topics with the same priorities. Developmental focus should enhance that mutuality.

In recent years there has been a substantial contribution by object-relations theorists in enriching our understanding of how adolescent or adult functioning may reflect unresolved primary object conflicts (Kernberg, 1975; Mahler, 1975; Masterson, 1976). Unfortunately, these provocative claims are largely unsubstantiated by empirical data. The value of that work is in its heuristics: it assists us in perceiving trends (e.g., individuation and rapprochement as fundamental conflicts for borderlines in relationships in and out of treatment). Similarly, the work reported in this volume allows us reasonably to expect to find that 6-year-olds will have a set of problems somewhat distinct from those of 16-year-olds. Furthermore, the younger child's unilateral respect for authority will contrast with the adolescent's insistence on reciprocity in the therapeutic relationship. Thus, the collaborative approach, stressing mutual responsibility, will be more acceptable to the adolescent than the more authoritarian style inherent in *some* forms of behavior modification.

Clinical work may be enhanced by understanding the *process* of change in effecting modifications of distressing self-concepts. The specific change mechanisms for self-concept include stable affective bonds (Bowlby, 1969), cognitive challenge (Beck, 1976), and role-taking opportunities (Kohlberg, 1969). These are obviously related to one another. In attempting to modify the individual's self-concept one might begin with the assumption that negative self-concepts are often established by parental histories in which there is a failure to establish positive, primary attachments, failure to reflect on and challenge one's values or self-concept, and failure to accurately understand the role of others. The therapeutic alliance begins with the formation of an empathic, predictable, supportive relationship. This facilitates the collaboration necessary to challenge the distorted thoughts or assumptions about the self and replace them with information processing more consistent with the nature of reality. Further, the individual may enhance social skills, obtain social rewards, and develop a more objective (less self-centered) view of the self through role-taking opportunitites and social interaction: The profound isolation which is common for depressed children or children facing incipient schizophrenia may be offset by developing social skills and interactions that provide both more positive content for the self-concept and a more objective referent in others. This emphasis on positive social interaction is consistent with Mead's (1934) proposal that the self is constructed from the point of view of others. The *other* for the child prone to social isolation is an imaginary and often harsh audience.

The contributions to this volume may be helpful to research in developmental psychopathology. Rather than simply divide subjects into normal and maladjusted groups, the developmental trends reported in this volume may be of use in identifying the specific conflicts that are the basis of psychopathology at different age levels. For example, the egocentric nature of the self during early childhood would suggest that oppositional or noncompliant behavioral problems would be most characteristic of this age group. Similarly, the emphasis on social comparison and skills at age 10 years would suggest that feelings of inferiority might become accentuated at this age. Finally, the development of social competence as a value in the self and the increased recursive thinking of the adolescent implies that the desire for close relationships may come in conflict with the belief that one is scrutinized and evaluated. The implication of the foregoing is that each developmental level carries its own set of conflicts and crises.

Although most of the research reported here involves cross-sectional designs, it would be of interest to determine if problems at earlier levels influence the development of problems at later levels. This, of course, was the central tenet of Erikson's (1963) stages of psychosocial development: for example, unresolved problems of trust during infancy might appear at the adolescent stage of identity formation—"Can I trust my ideology, my choices?" Longitudinal designs which trace developmental continuities of issues such as these may help answer questions of the relevance of early experience or personality for later development. Again, given the too prevalent enthusiasm of clinicians to treat deviation from the norm as pathological, it may be of considerable value to learn whether these deviations have any predictive value of later pathology.

SUMMARY

This volume brings together the research and theory of a number of major contributors on the study of the development of the self. There appears to be some agreement that as the child or adolescent develops there is a change in the content of self-concept. These changes in content may, themselves, precipitate new vulnerabilities, as much of the research on adolescent development illustrates. Further, the development of the self is not marked by unmitigated adaptation, but rather may result in greater and more abstract demands for competence and success in social interactions. If the "other" is a major source of the self-construct, it is also the case that the other is not always viewed as an ally whose perspective is immediately apprehended. Thus, for some adolescents, the increased socialization of the self-concept may result in attempts to hide the self from others (Elkind, 1974). Finally, a number of clinical implications have been examined which may help in directing our attention to developmental diagnosis and treatment of developmental changes in the self.

REFERENCES

Adler, A. (1964). *Social Interest.* New York: Capricorn.
Barenboim, C. (1981). The development of person perception in childhood and adolescence. *Child Development, 52,* 129–144.
Beck, A. T. (1976). *Cognitive therapy and the emotional disorders.* New York: International Universities Press.
Beck, A. T., Rush, A. J., Shaw, B. F., & Emery, G. (1979). *Cognitive therapy of depression.* New York: Guilford.
Bowlby, J. (1969). *Attachment.* New York: Basic Books.
Elkind, D. (1974). *Children and adolescents.* New York: Oxford University Press.
Erikson, E. H. (1963). *Childhood and society.* New York: Norton.
Freud, S. (1964). *New introductory lectures on psychoanalysis.* London: Hogarth Press.
Gilligan, C. (1982). *In a different voice.* Cambridge, MA: Harvard University Press.
Horney, K. (1950). *Neurosis and human growth.* New York: Norton.
Kernberg, O. (1975). *Borderline conditions and pathological narcissism.* New York: Aronson.
Kohlberg, L. (1969). Stage and sequence: The cognitive-developmental approach to socialization. In D. Goslin (Ed.), *Handbook of socialization: Theory and research.* New York: Rand McNally.
Leahy, R. L. (1983). Development of self and the problems of social cognition. In L. Wheeler & P. Shaver (Eds.), *Review of personality and social psychology.* Beverly Hills, CA: Sage.
Mahler, M. (1975). *The psychological birth of the human infant.* New York: Basic Books.
Masterson, J. F. (1976). *Psychotherapy of the borderline adult: A developmental approach.* New York: Brunner-Mazel.
Mead, G. H. (1934). *Mind, self and society.* Chicago: University of Chicago Press.
Mischel, W. (1968). *Personality and assessment.* New York: Wiley.
Rogers, C. (1951). *Client-centered therapy.* Boston: Houghton Mifflin.
Sullivan, H. S.(1953). *The interpersonal theory of psychiatry.* New York: Norton.
Werner, H. (1948). *The comparative psychology of mental development.* New York: International Universities Press.

Author Index

Numbers in italics show the pages on which the complete reference is cited.

A

Abelson, W., 26, *52, 53*
Abramson, L. Y., 225, *242,* 281, *292*
Achenbach, T., 2, 3, 7, 8, 10, 14, 16, 18, 22, 32, 35, 37, 38, 39, 42, 43, *47,* 69, *117*
Adams, G., 131, *147*
Adler, A., 86, *117,* 300, *304*
Agnew, J., 96, *117*
Alexander, S., 42, *48*
Allport, G. W., 1, 15, 44, 45, *47,* 81, *117,* 209, 228, 238, *242*
Altrocchi, J., 7, 16, 37, 38, 42, *47*
Anderson, S., 26, 27, *47*
Andrews, F. M., 212, *242*
Ansbacher, H. L., 209, *242*
Axelrod, H. S., 42, *48*

B

Bachman, J. G., 206, 213, *242, 245*
Backman, C. W., 221, *242*
Baer, M., 43, *53*
Baldwin, J. M., 15, 45, *47,* 123, *147,* 153, 154, 155, 156, 170, 174, *177*
Balla, D., 8, 12, 15, 18, 19, 20, 21, 22, 23, 30, 32, 33, 34, 36, 39, 40, 41, *49, 50, 52, 53,* 69, *121,* 128, 129, *149*

Bandura, A., 87, 95, 96, *117,* 135, 138, *147,* 224, *242*
Bankes, J., 43, *49*
Bannister, D., 96, *117*
Barenboim, C., 144, *147,* 166, *177,* 268, 278, *293, 297, 304*
Bauer, S. R., 42, *47*
Beattie, M., 225, 227, *244*
Beck, A. T., 213, *242,* 269, 270, 271, 272, 282, 285, 286, 289, *292,* 298, 300, *302, 304*
Beebe, J. S., 228, *242*
Beigel, D., 88, 97, *117*
Bem, D. J., 235, *243*
Bem, S., 137, 138, *147*
Bender, M. B., 184, *202*
Benesh-Weiner, M., 90, *120*
Berger, E. M., 42, *47*
Bergman, A., 181, *203*
Biblarz, A., 239, *245*
Bierer, B., 71, 97, *117*
Bigelow, B. J., 250, 261, 262, *263*
Bills, R. E., 42, *47*
Blatt, S. J., 280, 281, *292, 293*
Block, J., 42, *47*
Blos, P., 139, *147,* 181, *202*
Boggiano, A. K., 127, *149,* 281, *294*
Bohan, J. B., 248, *264*

305

Subject Index

A

Academic; competence, scholastic
  physical, 94, 96; *see also* Competence,
    athletic
  scholastic, 59, 71, 104; *see also*
    Competence, academic; Compe-
    tence, cognitive
  social, 3–6, 16, 26, 37–42, 94, 96, 282,
    299–300
Academic competence, *see* Competence
Active self, 159–162, 164
Actual competence, 71–74, 85, 104–105;
  see also Competence
Adaptation, 268
Adaptive self, 61
Affect, 56, 85–97, 115–116
Agoraphobia, 275–276
Amnesia, 199
Athletic competence, *see* Competence
Attribution theory, 156–158, 173–175
Automatic thoughts, 270, 286, 291

B

Beneffectance, 57, 95–113
  in children, 97–113

C

CA, *see* Chronological age
Chronological age, 8–9, 13, 16–17, 32–
  34, 279–280

Close friend relations, 252–254, 257–263
Cognitive competence, *see* Competence
Competence, 55–61, 67–80, 84–97, 103–
  104, 113–114, 210, 225–227, 285,
  296; *see also* Actual competence,
  Perceived competence
  academic, 104, 115; *see also*
    Competence, cognitive; Compe-
    tence, scholastic
  athletic, 59, 97; *see also* Competence,
    physical
  cognitive, 59, 70, 85, 88–89, 92, 94,
    96–97, 103, *see also* Competence
Competence affect, *see* Affect
Competence evaluation, 88
Content dimensions
  in self-evaluation, 74–76, 80
Continuity, 159
Control ideology, 227–228
Core personal constructs, 59
Covert self, 142, 147

D

Decentration, 134–135, 147, 189
Defensive style, *see* Self-image disparity
Dichotomous thinking, 272, 277, 285
Differentiation, 2, 4–6, 10, 18, 22–23, 27,
  29–31, 34–35, 38, 44–45, 56–59, 76–
  79, 130, 132–133, 135, 137, 142,
  189–190, 197, 199–200, 261–263,
  268, 296, 299
Distinctness, 159

TIFFANY MARTINI FIELD, SUSAN GOLDBERG, DANIEL STERN, and ANITA MILLER SOSTEK. (Editors). *High-Risk Infants and Children: Adult and Peer Interactions*

GILBERTE PIERAUT-LE BONNIEC. *The Development of Model Reasoning: Genesis of Necessity and Possibility Notions*

JONAS LANGER. *The Origins of Logic: Six to Twelve Months*

LYNN S. LIBEN. *Deaf Children: Developmental Perspectives*